GRAMMAR EXPRESS

For Self-Study and Classroom Use

Marjorie Fuchs

Margaret Bonner

Longman

To my Aunt Gerry, who loved words.—MF

To Aline and Luke.—MB

Grammar *Express*

Pearson Education, 10 Bank Street, White Plains, NY 10606

Vice president, director of publishing: Allen Ascher
Editorial director: Louisa Hellegers
Senior development manager: Penny Laporte
Senior development editor: Françoise Leffler
Vice president, director of design and production: Rhea Banker
Executive managing editor: Linda Moser
Production manager: Alana Zdinak
Senior production editor: Christine Lauricella
Senior manufacturing manager: Patrice Fraccio
Manufacturing supervisor: Edie Pullman
Photo research: Stacey Hunter
Cover design: Patricia Wosczyk
Text design: Patricia Wosczyk
Text composition: Preface, Inc.
Text art: Preface, Inc.
Photo credits: see p. xiii
Illustrators: see p. xiii
Cover image: © David Barnes, ICL 2000

Parts of *Grammar Express* are adapted from the intermediate
and high-intermediate levels of *Focus on Grammar,*
Second Edition © 2000.

ISBN: 0-13-032743-3

11 12 13—CRK—12 11 10

Contents

v

Appendices

About the Authors

Marjorie Fuchs has taught ESL at New York City Technical College and LaGuardia Community College of the City University of New York and EFL at the Sprach Studio Lingua Nova in Munich, Germany. She holds a Master's Degree in Applied English Linguistics and a Certificate in TESOL from the University of Wisconsin–Madison. She has authored or co-authored many widely used ESL textbooks, notably *On Your Way: Building Basic Skills in English, Crossroads, Top Twenty ESL Word Games: Beginning Vocabulary Development, Around the World: Pictures for Practice, Families: Ten Card Games for Language Learners, Focus on Grammar: An Intermediate Course for Reference and Practice, Focus on Grammar: A High-Intermediate Course for Reference and Practice,* and the workbooks to the *Longman Dictionary of American English,* the *Longman Photo Dictionary, The Oxford Picture Dictionary,* and *Focus on Grammar: Intermediate* and *High-Intermediate.*

Margaret Bonner has taught ESL at Hunter College and the Borough of Manhattan Community College of the City University of New York, at Taiwan National University in Taipei, and at Virginia Commonwealth University in Richmond. She holds a Master's Degree in Library Science from Columbia University, and she has done work towards a Ph.D. in English Literature at the Graduate Center of the City University of New York. She has contributed to a number of ESL and EFL projects, including *Making Connections, On Your Way,* and the Curriculum Renewal Project in Oman, where she wrote textbooks, workbooks, and teachers manuals for the national school system. She authored *Step into Writing: A Basic Writing Text,* and co-authored *Focus on Grammar: An Intermediate Course for Reference and Practice, Focus on Grammar: A High-Intermediate Course for Reference and Practice, Focus on Grammar: High-Intermediate Workbook,* and *The Oxford Picture Dictionary Intermediate Workbook.*

About the Book

Welcome to *Grammar Express*—the fast way to study and learn English grammar.

Grammar Express features

- Short, easy-to-use **four-page units**
- **Grammar points** presented and **contextualized** through cartoons, photos, and other illustrations
- Clear **Grammar Charts** showing the forms of the grammar point
- **Chart Checks** to help you use the grammar charts
- Clear **Grammar Explanations** and **Examples**
- **Usage Notes** telling you how English speakers use the grammar point
- **Be careful! Notes** showing typical mistakes students make
- **Pronunciation Notes** to help you pronounce words correctly
- A **variety of exercise types** to practice the grammar points
- **SelfTests** to check your progress
- **Appendices** with helpful lists and information
- An **Index** to help you quickly find grammar points
- An **Answer Key** so you can check your answers
- A **CD-ROM** with additional editing exercises

UNITS

Grammar Express has 76 units. Each unit has four pages—two pages of grammar presentation and two pages of practice. Here's how a typical unit looks:

Presentation

The grammar point is presented in three steps.

1. Illustration

Each unit begins with an **illustration**—a cartoon, comic strip, photo with speech bubbles, newspaper headline—which introduces the grammar point in a real-life, real-language context. It also introduces the topic of the unit. *(For example, in Unit 8 the cartoon introduces the grammar point* used to, *and the unit topic, fashion.)*

A **Check Point** helps you think about the meaning of the grammar point in the illustration.

2. Charts

Grammar Charts show the forms of the grammar point. *(In Unit 8 you can see* used to *in statements, questions, and short answers.)*

Chart Checks ask questions about the grammar charts. They help you notice important information about the forms and uses of the grammar point you are studying.

An **Express Check** follows the Grammar Charts. This is a quick and easy way for you to try out the forms in the charts.

3. Notes

Grammar Notes present **Grammar Explanations** on the left and **Examples** on the right. Timelines show the meaning of verb forms. *(For example, in Unit 8 the timeline for* used to *shows that you can use it only for the past.)*

Usage Notes tell you how English speakers use the grammar point. *(In Unit 8 the Usage Note for* used to *explains that this form is more common in affirmative statements than in negative statements or questions.)*

Be careful! Notes point out typical mistakes that English students make. *(One of the Be careful! Notes in Unit 8 tells you not to confuse* used to *with* be used to *or* get used to.*)*

Pronunciation Notes tell you how to correctly pronounce the grammar point in everyday speech. These notes use easy pronunciation spellings.

Check it out! tells you where to look in the book (appendices or other units) to find more information about the grammar point.

Practice

Two pages of exercises give you practice in understanding and using the grammar point. A typical unit has four exercises.

Exercise 1

The first exercise is always a "**for recognition only**" exercise. This means that you will have to find or understand the grammar point, but you will not have to use it yet. *(For example, in Unit 8 you will read a short magazine article about fashion, and find and underline all the examples of* used to *which refer to past habits.)*

Exercises 2 and 3

In these exercises you actively practice the grammar point. There are a **variety of exercise types**, including multiple choice, fill-in-the-blanks, describing pictures, sentence combining, and asking and answering questions. The exercises always show the grammar point in a context that is related to the unit topic. *(In Unit 8, Exercise 2, you will complete sentences about fashion in the past while you describe pictures. In Exercise 3, you will use an old advertisement to ask and answer questions about sneakers.)*

Exercise 4

This is always an **editing** exercise. In this exercise, you will have to find and correct typical mistakes that students make when they use the grammar point.

TESTS

The 76 units of *Grammar Express* are divided into 15 parts. After each part you will find a **SelfTest**. These tests will help you review and see how well you have learned the material in the part. The **SelfTests** have multiple-choice questions similar to questions found on the TOEFL®, a test that is widely used for foreign students who want to attend college in the United States.

APPENDICES

In the back of the book, you will find 28 **Appendices** with useful information, such as lists of common irregular verbs, verbs followed by the gerund, verbs followed by the infinitive, and spelling and pronunciation rules.

ANSWER KEY

The **Answer Key** provides answers to the Check Points, Charts Checks, Express Checks, all the practice exercises, and the SelfTests.

CD-ROM

A **CD-ROM** is included with the book. On it you will find additional editing exercises.

Grammar Express can be used for self-study or in the classroom. Start with Unit 1 and work through the entire book, or choose the units you want to focus on. *Grammar Express* can help you reach your language goals quickly.

Your journey through English grammar can be an adventure of discovery. We hope you will enjoy traveling with *Grammar Express*.

All Aboard!!! . . .

Credits

Photographs

Grateful acknowledgment is given to the following for providing photographs.
p. 18 Stephen Danelian/Exposure New York; **p. 26** *(top)* © Asian Art & Archeology, Inc./CORBIS; **p. 26** *(bottom)* © CORBIS; **p. 28** © Bettmann/CORBIS; **p. 48** © S. Carmona/CORBIS; **p. 62** Jeff Sciortino Photography; **p. 66** PhotoDisc, Inc.; **p. 70** AP/Wide World Photos; **p. 76** AP/Wide World Photos; **p. 88** © Jennie Woodcock, Reflections Photolibrary/CORBIS; **p. 110** Copyright 2000 by Bob Sacha; **p. 124** © The New Yorker Collection 1988 Charles Addams from cartoonbank.com. All Rights Reserved.; **p. 132** HI-AYH Photo by Joe Hochner; **p. 142** Courtesy of the New York State Governor's Traffic Safety Committee; **p. 162** © Gala/SuperStock, Inc.; **p. 166** © Peter Guttman/CORBIS; **p. 169** © Kevin Schafer/CORBIS; **p. 175** Courtesy of Beth Boyd; **p. 176** RubberBall Productions; **p. 192** AP/Wide World Photos; **p. 195** © Kevin R. Morris/CORBIS; **p. 202** © SuperStock, Inc.; **p. 206** RubberBall Productions; **p. 210** © TSM/Greg Davis; **p. 214** © The New Yorker Collection 1989 Tom Cheney from cartoonbank.com. All Rights Reserved.; **p. 226** AP/Wide World Photos; **p. 235** Liaison Agency, Inc.; **p. 238** Library of Congress; **p. 244** PhotoDisc, Inc.; **p. 256** © Michael Dwyer/Stock Boston, Inc.; **p. 258** © The New Yorker Collection 1964 Frank Modell from cartoonbank.com. All Rights Reserved.; **pp. 264, 266** Reprinted with permission from *Reader's Digest.* Copyright © The Reader's Digest Association, Inc.; **p. 268** AP/Wide World Photos; **p. 286** PEANUTS © UFS; **p. 290** © John Springer Collection/CORBIS; **p. 304** © Hulton-Deutsch Collection/CORBIS; **p. 306** *(top)* photo by Dutton Signet, a division of Penguin Books USA, Inc.; **p. 306** *(bottom)* RubberBall Productions; **p. 324** Tony Freeman/PhotoEdit.

Illustrators

Ronald Chironna: pp. 27, 34, 35, 65, 160, 190, 191; **Brian Hughes:** pp. 20, 188; **Jock MacRae:** pp. 53, 180; **Paul McCusker:** pp. 38, 98, 294; **Andy Myer:** pp. 10, 24, 32, 46, 54, 80, 82, 88, 102, 112, 116, 158, 172, 192, 222, 232, 246, 254, 272, 282, 300, 314, 322, 326; **Dusan Petricic:** pp. 2, 6, 8, 14, 16, 17, 18, 21, 36, 40, 50, 58, 60, 66, 74, 84, 92, 96, 106, 120, 128, 146, 150, 184, 198, 236, 250, 278, 308, 318, 330

p. 136 *Source:* Roper Reports Worldwide 1998 Global Consumer Study

Acknowledgments

Writing *Grammar Express* has been an exhilarating ride for us, the authors. The company of the following editors and colleagues has made the journey even more enjoyable. We are grateful to:

Françoise Leffler, our wonderful editor, for her dedication, her impeccable attention to detail, and, above all, for her sense of style and humor, which infuse the book. She's a pleasure to work with. *Mille mercis, Françoise!*

Louisa Hellegers, for her expert coordination of the many aspects of this project and for her readiness to go the extra mile. Despite an incredibly busy schedule that has her flying all over the world, she always had time for us.

Chris Lauricella, for expertly conducting the book through its various stages of production, and for keeping everything on track.

Rhea Banker and **Pat Wosczyk**, for an outstanding design: clear, user-friendly, and beautiful to look at.

Robyn Roth of Preface, Inc., for her intelligent and creative work in bringing together text and design.

Stacey Hunter and **Iris Bodre-Baez**, for their diligent work on several aspects of the project, notably photo research and obtaining permissions.

Diana Nott, for coming up with the perfect title.

We would also like to acknowledge the following reviewers for their careful reading of the manuscript and their thoughtful suggestions, many of which we incorporated into the book:

■ **Haydée Alvarado Santos**, University of Puerto Rico College of General Studies, Río Piedras Campus, Puerto Rico ■ **Frankie Dovel**, VESOL Coordinator, Orange County Public Schools, Orlando, Florida ■ **Marcia Edwards Hijaab**, Center for International Programs, Virginia Commonwealth University, Richmond, Virginia ■ **Steve Horowitz**, UESL Program, Central Washington University, Ellensberg, Washington ■ **Susan Jamieson**, International Programs, Bellevue Community College, Bellevue, Washington ■ **Martha McGaughey**, Language Training Institute, Englewood Cliffs, New Jersey, and New School ELSC, New York ■ **Angelita Moreno**, Instituto Cultural Brasil-Estados Unidos, Belo Horizonte MG, Brazil ■ **Gabriella Morvay**, CUNY Language Immersion Program, Bronx Community College, Bronx, New York ■ **Michaela Safadi**, South Gate Community Adult School, California ■ **Barbara Smith-Palinkas**, Assistant Director for Curriculum and Instruction, English Language Institute, University of South Florida, Tampa ■ **Cleide Silva**, Open House, Santos SP, Brazil ■ **Sávio Siqueira**, ACBEU, Salvador BA, Brazil ■ **Berrin Yildiz**, Dogus University Prep Program, Turkey.

Thanks to the following teachers for pointing us in the right direction with their valuable feedback during the developmental stages of this project:

■ **Belgún Akgeúk**, Private ATA High School, Turkey ■ **Marlene Almeida**, Wordshop, Belo Horizonte MG, Brazil ■ **Fatima Badry**, American University of Sharjah, Dubai, United Arab Emirates ■ **Ellen Balleisen**, CUNY Language Immersion Program, Bronx Community College, Bronx, New York ■ **Sheila Barbosa Fialho**, EPI, São José dos Campos SP, Brazil ■ **Matthew Bellman**, TCLC Language Academy, Nagoya, Japan ■ **Patricia Brenner**, University of Washington, Seattle, Washington ■ **Heloísa Burrowes Raposo**, Raposo English Center, Campos dos Goytacazes RJ, Brazil ■ **Fábio Delano Carneiro**, DEC, Fortaleza CE, Brazil ■ **Elton Carvalho**, Fundação Educacional do Distrito Federal, Brasília DF, Brazil ■ **Sergio J. Chiri**, Universidad Del Pacifico, Lima, Peru ■ **Judy A. Cleek**, Intensive English Program, Martin, Tennessee ■ **Jill Cook**, Zayed University, Dubai, United Arab Emirates ■ **Jason H. Davis**, CUNY Language Immersion Program, Bronx Community College, Bronx, New York ■ **Ricardo Delgado**, CCBEU, Belém PA, Brazil ■ **Beatriz B. Diaz**, Robert Morgan Voc. Tech., Miami, Florida ■ **Luiz Alberto Ferrari**, Colégio Barão de Mauá, Mauá SP, Brazil ■ **Patty Heiser**, University of Washington, Seattle, Washington ■ **Jung-Sinn Hyon**, Hunter College, New York, New York ■ **Amy Lewis**, Keio University, Tokyo, Japan ■ **Chao-Hung Lin**, Hunter College, New York, New York ■ **Maria Esther Linares de Pedemonte**, International Exams, Lima, Peru ■ **Joan McAuley**, CUNY Language Immersion Program, Bronx Community College, Bronx, New York ■ **Angelita Moreno**, Instituto Cultural Brasil-Estados Unidos, Belo Horizonte MG, Brazil ■ **Sandra Moreno Walter**, Masters, Sorocaba SP, Brazil ■ **Gabriella Morvay**, CUNY Language Immersion Program, Bronx Community College, Bronx, New York ■ **Marisa Nickle**, University of Washington, Seattle, Washington ■ **Martha Oval**, Orel Bilim Koleg, Ankara, Turkey ■ **Hyangmi Pae**, Hannam University, Segu Daegon, Korea ■ **Rosemary Palmer**, Bloomfield College, Bloomfield, New Jersey ■ **Stephen Russell**, Tokyo University of Foreign Studies, Tokyo, Japan ■ **John Ryder**, Kyoto Gakuen High School, Kyoto, Japan ■ **Maria Benedita Santos**, Casa Thomas Jefferson, Brasília DF, Brazil ■ **Cleide Silva**, Open House, Santos SP, Brazil ■ **Sávio Siqueira**, ACBEU, Salvador BA, Brazil ■ **Ricardo Augusto de Souza**, Wordshop, Belo Horizonte MG, Brazil ■ **Lee Spencer**, CUNY Language Immersion Program, Bronx Community College, Bronx, New York ■ **Ann Streeter**, Seattle Central Institute of English, Seattle, Washington ■ **Cláudia Suzano de Almeida**, Casa Thomas Jefferson, Brasília DF, Brazil ■ **Gerald Talandis, Jr.**, Toyama College of Foreign Languages, Toyama, Japan ■ **Lorena Trejo**, AU. Los Samanes, I. E. Henry Clay, Caracas, Venezuela ■ **Diane Triester**, University of Washington, Seattle, Washington ■ **Elkin Urrea**, Hunter College, New York, New York ■ ■ **Dr. Wilma B. Wilcox**, Southern Illinois University at Carbondale in Niigata, Japan ■ **Belkis Yanes**, AU. Los Samanes, I.E. Henry Clay, Caracas, Venezuela ■ **Shari Zisman**, CUNY Language Immersion Program, Bronx Community College, Bronx, New York

In addition we are grateful to the following institutions for helping us organize Focus Groups for teachers and students:

■ **Bronx Community College**, Bronx, New York
■ **Hunter College**, New York, New York
■ **University of Washington**, Seattle, Washington

Finally, we would like to thank **Rick Smith** and **Luke Frances**, as always, for their help and support along the way. They made the journey and the stops, few and far between as they were, a lot more fun.

MF and MB

UNIT 1

Present Progressive

Hundreds of fans **are waiting** for The Airheads to arrive.

Wow! The Airheads **are dropping** from the sky!

CHECK POINT

Check the best advertisement for this TV news show.

☐ It's happening now!

☐ It happens every day!

CHART CHECK 1 →

Check the correct answer.

The present progressive is made up of two parts:

☐ *be* + base form of verb

☐ *be* + base form of verb + *-ing*

Which part changes with different subjects?

☐ *be*

☐ base form of verb + *-ing*

AFFIRMATIVE STATEMENTS

SUBJECT	BE	BASE FORM OF VERB + -ING
I	am 'm	
He/She/It	is 's	waiting.
We/You*/They	are 're	

NEGATIVE STATEMENTS

SUBJECT	BE	NOT	BASE FORM OF VERB + -ING
I	am 'm		
He/She/It	is 's	not	waiting.
We/You/They	are 're		

You is both singular and plural.

2

	YES/NO QUESTIONS		
	BE	**SUBJECT**	**BASE FORM + -ING**
	Am	I	
	Is	she	**standing**?
	Are	you	

CHART CHECK 2

Circle T (True) or F (False).

T F In questions, **be** comes after the subject.

SHORT ANSWERS						
	AFFIRMATIVE			**NEGATIVE**		
Yes,		you	**are.**	**No,**	you	**aren't.**
		she	**is.**		she	**isn't.**
		I	**am.**		I	**'m not.**

WH- QUESTIONS			
WH- WORD	**BE**	**SUBJECT**	**BASE FORM + -ING**
Why	**am**	I	
	is	she	**standing**?
Where	**are**	you	

EXPRESS CHECK

Complete these sentences with the present progressive form of the verbs in parentheses.

Why _____ you _____? They _____ still _____.
                        (leave)   (perform)

Grammar Explanations

Examples

1. Use the **present progressive** to describe something that is happening <u>right now</u>.

- I**'m standing** outside the King Theater *right now*.

- As I**'m talking** to you, the fans **are gathering** in front of the theater.

2. Use the **present progressive** to describe something that is happening <u>these days</u>, even if it's not happening right now.

Now
Past ·········· ‿‿‿‿‿ ▸ Future
I'm studying guitar

- The Airheads **are playing** at the King Theater *this week*.

- I**'m studying** guitar *this semester*.

3. USAGE NOTE: The **contracted form** is usually used in <u>speech</u> and in informal writing.

A: Bye, Jana, we**'re leaving** now.
B: Wait! I**'m coming** with you.

Check it out!

For different forms of negative contractions with *be,* see Appendix 24 on page 345.

For spelling rules for the present progressive, see Appendix 19 on page 343.

1 **IDENTIFY** • *Read this letter. Underline the present progressive verbs that describe something happening right now. Circle the present progressive verbs that describe things that are happening these days (but not necessarily right now).*

Dear Yev,

I'm working very hard these days, but I have some good news. Right now,

I'm sitting at a desk in the Entertainment Section of the *Tribune*! Of course I'm

still taking journalism classes at night as well. The job is temporary—Joe Sims,

the regular reporter, is taking this month off to write a book. This week we're

preparing to interview your favorite group, the Airheads. In fact, at this very

moment they're flying into town by helicopter. They're performing at the King

Theater all week. How are you doing? Are you still writing music? Oops! The

crew is calling me. They're leaving for the theater now. Write soon!

Steph

2 **COMPLETE** • *Read this conversation. Complete it with the present progressive form of the verbs in parentheses. Use contractions whenever possible.*

BEV: Bye, Joe, I ____'m leaving____ now.
                        1. (leave)

JOE: Where _____ you _____?
                                        2. (go)

BEV: Running. Ann _____ downstairs.
                            3. (wait)

JOE: Great! Why don't you take the dog out with you?

BEV: Why don't *you* take him? It's your turn.

JOE: I can't. I _____ on my book.
                    4. (work)

BEV: But you _____ anything right now. You _____ just
                      5. (not do)

_____ there.
        6. (sit)

JOE: That's not true. I _____ here, but I _____ also
                            7. (sit)

_____ about my work. Can't the dog run with you?
        8. (think)

BEV: No, because afterwards we want to go to the Plaza. The Airheads

_____ there this week, and Ann wants to get their autographs.
        9. (stay)

You know she's a big fan of theirs.

3

ASK & ANSWER • *Steph is interviewing the lead singer of the Airheads, Paul. Write questions using the words in parentheses. Give short answers.*

STEPH: Paul, <u>are you introducing any new songs on this tour?</u>
1. (introduce / any new songs on this tour?)

PAUL: <u>Yes, we are</u> . We're introducing some songs from our
2.

new album, *In the Air.*

STEPH: Your fans are so excited to see you after such a long time.

_____
3. (Why / tour / again?)

PAUL: We want to play for live audiences. We need that.

STEPH: _____
4. (What / work on / these days?)

PAUL: Some exciting new material. But we're not talking about it yet.

STEPH: _____
5. (Who / sing / with you now?)

She has a nice voice.

PAUL: Sylvia Sylva is singing some of the songs from the album.

STEPH: _____
6. (she / replace / Toti?)

PAUL: _____ . Toti has a new baby, but she'll be back in
7.

a few months.

 4

EDIT • *Read this letter. Find and correct six mistakes in the use of the present progressive. The first mistake is already corrected.*

Dear Toti,
     'm writing
    I ~~write~~ to you from my hotel room. Everyone else is sleep, but I sitting here and watching

the ocean. We're staying at the Plaza in Atlantic Beach, and the view is beautiful. The tour is

goes well. The audience is crazy about the new songs, but the fans is always asking for you.

How is the baby? She has a great voice. Do you teaching her to sing yet? Maybe both of you

will come along for the next tour!

                                    Sylvia

Simple Present Tense

Hank **is** always in a hurry and he **does** everything at once.

He **works** all the time—he never **relaxes**.

CHECK *POINT*

Check the best title for the cartoons.

❏ Hank at Work This Week

❏ Hank's Working Habits

CHART CHECK ⟶

Circle T (True) or F (False).

T F The form for *he/she/it* ends with *-s.*

T F Negative statements have *do not* or *does not* before the base form.

T F Questions have *do* or *does* after the subject.

AFFIRMATIVE STATEMENTS	
SUBJECT	**VERB**
I/We/You*/They	**work**.
He/She/It	**works**.

NEGATIVE STATEMENTS		
SUBJECT	**DO NOT**	**BASE FORM**
I/We/You/They	**do not**	**work**.
He/She/It	**does not**	

You is both singular and plural.

YES/NO QUESTIONS		
DO	**SUBJECT**	**BASE FORM**
Do	you	**work**?
Does	he	

SHORT ANSWERS					
AFFIRMATIVE			**NEGATIVE**		
Yes,	I	**do**.	**No,**	I	**don't**.
	he	**does**.		he	**doesn't**.

WH- QUESTIONS			
WH- WORD	**DO**	**SUBJECT**	**BASE FORM**
Where When	**do**	you	**work**?
	does	he	

EXPRESS CHECK

Unscramble these words to complete the question.

rush • Why • he • does _____ all the time?

Grammar Explanations

Examples

1. Use the **simple present tense** to talk about what <u>regularly happens</u>.

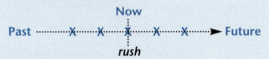

- Some people **rush** through life.
- They **don't relax**.
- Other people **are** calm.
- They **don't feel** tense.

2. Use **adverbs of frequency** with the simple present tense to express <u>how often something happens</u>.

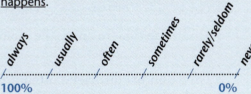

- She *never relaxes*.
- You *usually* take life easier.
- We *sometimes* sleep late.
- They *seldom* take a vacation.

▶ **BE CAREFUL!** Adverbs of frequency usually come before the main verb, but they go after the verb *be*.

- We *usually* rush around too much.
- We*'re often* stressed out.

3. Use the **simple present tense** to talk about <u>scientific facts</u>.

- Stress **causes** high blood pressure.
- Water **freezes** at 32°F.

Check it out!

For spelling rules for the third person singular *(he/she/it)* of the simple present tense, see Appendix 20 on page 343.

For pronunciation rules for the third person singular *(he/she/it)* of the simple present tense, see Appendix 27 on page 348.

1 **IDENTIFY** • *Read this part of a book review. Underline the simple present tense verbs. Circle the adverbs of frequency.*

Books Section 10

CALM DOWN! By Dr. Sara Roads

In today's fast-paced world, we (never) escape stress. Stress always affects us psychologically, but according to Dr. Roads, author of the new bestseller, *Calm Down!*, it also affects us physically. For example, stress causes high blood pressure. Doctors often prescribe medication for stress-related illnesses. Medicine usually lowers a patient's blood pressure. But, Dr. Roads claims, "You don't always need pills. Relaxation exercises are sometimes as effective as pills. For example, breathing exercises both relax you and lower your blood pressure. It only takes a few minutes!"

---

2 **COMPLETE** • *Megan and Greg have completely different types of personality (A and B). Read about one, write about the other.*

Type A: Megan

1. Megan **doesn't relax** easily.

2. She _____doesn't take_____ time to enjoy the moment.

3. Megan and her boyfriend never **take** vacations.

4. She _____ through the day.

5. She **is** nervous.

6. She **is** always in a hurry.

7. She **finishes** other people's sentences for them.

8. She _____ a lot.

9. She _____ enough time to finish things.

10. Megan **has** high blood pressure due to stress.

Type B: Greg

• Greg _____relaxes_____ easily.

• He **takes** time to enjoy the moment.

• Greg and his girlfriend often _____ vacations.

• He **doesn't rush** through the day.

• He _____ nervous.

• He _____ never in a hurry.

• He _____ other people's sentences for them.

• He **doesn't worry** a lot.

• He **has** enough time to finish things.

• Greg _____ high blood pressure due to stress.

3 **ASK & ANSWER •** *Todd is an accountant. Look at his schedule. Write questions and answers about his day.*

MONDAY NOVEMBER **18**			
6:00–7:00	get up, exercise	**12:00–12:30**	lunch
8:00–9:00	work on reports	**12:30–5:00**	return phone calls
9:00–12:00	see clients	**5:30–7:00**	attend night school

1. When / get up?

　　When does he get up?　　　　　　　　　　He gets up at 6:00.

2. exercise in the morning?

　　Does he exercise in the morning?　　　　Yes, he does.

3. work on reports in the afternoon?

4. When / see clients?

5. take a lunch break?

6. What / do / from 12:30 to 5:00?

7. Where / go / at 5:30?

4 **EDIT •** *Read Todd's journal entry. Find and correct ten mistakes in the use of the simple present tense. The first mistake is already corrected.*

> 　　　　　　　　never have
> I'm so tired. I ~~have never~~ time to relax. I work all day and studies all night. My boss tell
> me that I need a vacation. I agree, but I afraid to take one. Does my boss thinks that
> the office can function without me? I dont want them to think I'm not necessary.
> But my wife is unhappy too. She complain that she never sees me anymore. My
> schedule are crazy. I don't think I can keep this up much longer. I don't wants to quit
> night school, though. I think often that there has to be a better way.

Non-Action Verbs

How **is** it?

It **tastes** like chicken.

Check the correct answer.

According to the fish, the worm

☐ has the flavor of chicken.

☐ acts like a chicken.

CHART CHECK

Circle T (True) or F (False).

T F Some verbs have both a non-action and an action meaning.

T F A verb used with a non-action meaning is not used in the progressive.

VERBS WITH NON-ACTION MEANINGS
I **want** to go fishing.
He **owns** a big boat.
The weather **seems** fine.
They **hate** fish.

VERBS WITH BOTH NON-ACTION AND ACTION MEANINGS	
NON-ACTION	**ACTION**
The fish **weighs** five pounds.	He**'s weighing** the fish now.
We **think** it's a good day for fishing.	We**'re thinking** about going.
This fish **tastes** delicious.	I**'m tasting** the fish now.
This food **smells** good.	The cook **is smelling** the food.

EXPRESS CHECK

Complete these sentences with the correct form of the verb **taste**.

I _____ the soup right now. It _____ salty.

Grammar Explanations	Examples

1. Many verbs <u>describe states or situations</u> instead of actions. These verbs are called **non-action verbs** (or stative verbs).

Most non-action verbs are <u>not</u> usually <u>used in the present progressive</u> even when they describe a situation that is happening right now.

- John **has** a boat.
  *(The verb **has** describes John's situation, not something he is doing.)*

- He **wants** fish for dinner.
  NOT ~~He is wanting fish for dinner.~~

2. Non-action verbs are usually verbs that:

a. describe a **state of being**
(be, feel)

- Jane **is** tired but happy.
- She **feels** good.

b. express **emotions**
(hate, like, love)

A: Do you **like** my new dress?
B: I **love** it!

c. describe **mental states**
(know, remember, believe, think [= believe], suppose, understand)

- I **know** a lot of good recipes.
- Ari **remembers** your number.
- I **think** you're right.

d. show **possession**
(have, own, possess, belong)

- Cesar **has** a headache.
- Some students **own** microwaves.

e. describe **perceptions** and **senses**
(hear, see, smell, taste, feel, notice, seem, look [= seem], appear, sound)

- I **hear** the telephone.
- Dina **seems** tired.

f. describe **needs** and **preferences**
(need, want, prefer)

- I **need** a pen.

g. describe **measurements**
(weigh, cost, contain)

- How much **does** it **cost**?

3. **BE CAREFUL!** Some verbs can have non-action and action meanings *(taste, smell, feel, look, think, have, weigh)*.

NON-ACTION
- I **taste** garlic. Did you put some in here?
  (I notice garlic.)
- The soup **tastes** good. Try some.
  (The soup is good.)

ACTION
- I'm **tasting** the soup to see if it needs more salt.
  (I'm trying the soup.)

Check it out!
For a list of common non-action verbs, see Appendix 2 on page 337.

IDENTIFY • *Read this conversation. Underline all non-action verbs that describe a situation that is in progress. Circle all non-action verbs that describe a situation that is generally true.*

ALINE: This steak <u>tastes</u> delicious. Your salmon looks good too.

BEN: Here, I'm putting some on your plate. I think you'll like it.

ALINE: Mmm. I like it. Funny, I usually (don't like) fish.

BEN: Red has that effect on people.

ALINE: I have no idea what you're talking about. What do you mean?

BEN: Well, colors can change the way we feel. For example, people often feel hungrier in a red room. I notice that you're looking right at the red wallpaper.

ALINE: And I certainly feel hungry right now. I'm eating half your salmon.

BEN: That's OK. I'm tasting your steak.

CHOOSE • *Complete this magazine article with the correct form of the verbs in parentheses.*

Lenny Kramer is in a sports store. He ____smells____ flowers, but he isn't
____1. (smells / is smelling)
really paying attention to the aroma very much because he _____ at a
____2. (looks / is looking)
pair of running shoes. They _____ a lot more than he usually pays, but
____3. (cost / are costing)
Lenny really, really _____ those shoes. He's the victim of "smart scents,"
____4. (wants / is wanting)
aromas that stores use to make customers buy more.

Across town, Lenny's daughter Myra is taking a history test in a classroom
that was recently painted yellow. Although Myra _____ history, she
____5. (hates / is hating)
_____ to be doing well on this test. She _____ the new
____6. (seems / is seeming)   ____7. (likes / is liking)
color of her classroom. She _____ that it's helping her on the test,
____8. (doesn't suspect / isn't suspecting)
but it is. Scientists have shown that yellow improves both memory and concentration.

We now _____ that odors, colors, and sounds affect our moods and
____9. (know / are knowing)
even our health. In fact, right now Lenny's wife, Cindy, _____ about
____10. (thinks / is thinking)
Lenny and Myra. She's sure that Lenny is spending too much on shoes and that
Myra is failing another history test. Cindy suffers from migraine headaches, but
she _____ a headache today. She's in the garden, and she
____11. (doesn't have / isn't having)
_____ birds and insect sounds. They always calm her down.
____12. (hears / is hearing)

3 **COMPLETE** • *Read this conversation. Complete it with the correct form of the verbs in parentheses. Use the present progressive or the simple present tense.*

A: Hi, Ana. Mmm. Something _____smells_____ good! What's cooking?
1. (smell)

B: Fish soup. I _____ it to see if it _____ more garlic.
2. (taste) **3. (need)**

_____ you _____ to try it?
4. (want)

A: Mmmm. It _____ good, but I _____ it needs salt.
5. (taste) **6. (think)**

B: OK. I _____ about adding canned tomatoes too, even though it
7. (think)

_____ in the recipe.
8. (not be)

A: That _____ like a good idea. But wait a minute. I _____
9. (sound) **10. (look)**

at the recipe, and it says you can add milk. How about that?

B: I _____ if the milk _____ fresh.
11. (not know) **12. (be)**

A: I'll check. Hmm. I _____ it, but I _____ sure. Let's add
13. (smell) **14. (not be)**

the tomatoes instead.

B: OK. I _____ cooking! The whole house _____ great
15. (love) **16. (smell)**

when you cook. And it always puts me in a good mood.

A: I _____ what you _____ . I _____ the
17. (know) **18. (mean)** **19. (feel)**

same way.

4 **EDIT** • *Read this journal entry. There are eight mistakes in the use of action and non-action verbs. Find and correct them. The first mistake is already corrected.*

March 16

Not a good day! I feel kind of depressed and I'm having a headache. I'm needing to do

have (written above "I'm having")

something right away to change my mood and get rid of this pain. Last week, I read an article

about how smells can affect mood and even health, so right now I smell an orange (for the

depression) and a green apple (for the headache). They smell nice, but I'm not thinking that

I notice a difference in how I feel! I think I'm preferring to eat something when I feel down.

But I worry that I'm weighing too much. So, at the moment I have a cup of peppermint tea with

lemon. The article says that the peppermint smell helps you eat less. Well, I don't know about

that! A chocolate ice cream sundae sounds pretty good right about now! It's seeming that

there are no easy solutions.

Present Progressive and Simple Present Tense

Cross-Cultural Confusion

Friends from different cultures often **have** different ideas about time.

Sometimes they **don't agree** about social distance, either.

CHECK *POINT*

Circle T (True) or F (False).

T F Karl is arriving late tonight.

T F In Sami's culture, people rarely stand close to each other.

CHART CHECK

Check the correct answers.

The present progressive has:

☐ one part

☐ two parts

The simple present tense has:

☐ one form

☐ two forms

PRESENT PROGRESSIVE			
SUBJECT	**BE**	**BASE FORM + -ING**	
I	am		
We/You*/They	are	arriving	now.
He/She/It	is		

You is both singular and plural.

SIMPLE PRESENT TENSE		
SUBJECT		**VERB**
I/We/You/They	never always	arrive	on time.
He/She/It		arrives

14

EXPRESS CHECK

Complete the following charts with the verb **buy**.

PRESENT PROGRESSIVE			
SUBJECT	*BE*	**BASE FORM + -ING**	
I			
You			flowers now.
He			

SIMPLE PRESENT TENSE			
SUBJECT		**VERB**	
I			
You	usually		chocolates.
He			

Grammar Explanations

Examples

1. Use the **present progressive** for things happening <u>right now</u>.

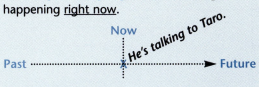

Use the **simple present tense** to describe what <u>regularly</u> happens.

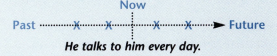

He talks to him every day.

- ■ Sami **is talking** to Taro.
- ■ At the moment, Taro **is speaking** English.

- ■ Sami **talks** to Taro every day.
- ■ Taro **speaks** Japanese at home.

2. Use the **present progressive** for things happening <u>these days</u>.

- ■ We**'re studying** in the U.S. *this month*.
- ■ Laura**'s studying** in France *this year*.
- ■ **Are** you **studying** hard *these days*?

3. REMEMBER! Most **non-action verbs** are <u>not usually used in the present progressive</u> even when they describe a situation that exists at the moment of speaking.

- ■ Jane **wants** to go home right now.
  NOT ~~Jane is wanting to go home right now.~~

4. Use the **simple present tense** to talk about <u>scientific facts</u> and <u>physical laws</u>.

- ■ Stress **causes** high blood pressure.
- ■ Water **boils** at 100°C.

Check it out!

For a list of common non-action verbs, see Appendix 2 on page 337.

1 **IDENTIFY** • *Read these journal entries by Brian, a Canadian summer exchange student studying in Argentina. Circle all the verbs that describe what is happening now. Underline the verbs that describe what generally happens.*

June 28: I'm sitting in a seat 30,000 feet above the earth en route to Argentina! I usually have dinner at this time, but right now I have a headache from the excitement. My seatmate is eating my food. She looks happy.

June 30: It's 7:30. My host parents are still working. Carlos, my father, works at home. My little brother Ricardo is cute. He looks (and acts) a lot like Bobby. Right now, he's looking over my shoulder and trying to read my journal.

July 4: The weather is cold now. I usually spend the first weekend of July at the beach. Today I'm walking around in a heavy sweater.

August 6: I feel so tired tonight. Everyone else feels great in the evening because they take long naps in the afternoon.

2 **COMPLETE** • *Students are talking outside a classroom. Complete their conversations with the present progressive or the simple present tense of the verbs in parentheses.*

1. **LI-WU:** Hi, Paulo. What _____*are*_____ you _____*doing*_____?
    a. (do)

    PAULO: Oh, I _____ for class to begin.
    b. (wait)

    LI-WU: How are you? You _____ tired.
    c. (look)

    PAULO: I *am* a little tired. I _____ evenings this semester. Hey, is that
    d. (work)
    your teacher over there?

    LI-WU: Yes. She _____ to one of my
    e. (talk)
    classmates.

    PAULO: I wonder what's wrong. He _____ at
    f. (not look)
    her. He _____ embarrassed.
    g. (look)

    LI-WU: Oh. That _____ anything. In Taiwan
    h. (not mean)
    it's not respectful to look directly at your teacher.

2. **MORIKO:** Look, there's Miguel. He _____ to Luisa.
    a. (talk)

    NINA: Yes. They _____ a class together this semester.
    b. (take)

MORIKO: They _____ very close to each other. _____ you
c. (stand)

_____ they _____?
d. (think)   e. (date)

NINA: No. I _____ it _____
f. (not think)   g. (mean)

anything special. I _____ from Costa Rica,
h. (come)

and people there normally _____ that
i. (stand)

close to each other.

3. RASHA: There's Hans. Why _____ he

_____ so fast? Class _____
a. (walk)   b. (start)

at 9:00. He still _____ ten minutes!
c. (have)

CLAUDE: He always _____ fast. People from
d. (walk)

Switzerland often _____ to be in a hurry.
e. (appear)

4. YOKO: Isn't that Sergio and Luis? Why _____ they
a. (shake)

hands? They _____ each other.
b. (know)

JING: In Brazil, men _____ hands every
c. (shake)

time they _____.
d. (meet)

3 **EDIT** • *Read this student's journal. Find and correct eleven mistakes in the use of the present progressive or simple present tense. The first mistake is already corrected.*

>   **I'm sitting**
> It's 12:30 and ~~I sit~~ in the library right now. My classmates are eating lunch together,
>
> but I'm not hungry yet. At home, we eat never this early. Today our journal topic is
>
> culture shock. It's a good topic for me right now because I'm being pretty homesick.
>
> I miss my old routine. At home we always are eating a big meal at 2:00 in the
>
> afternoon. Then we rest. But here in Toronto I'm having a 3:00 conversation class.
>
> Every day, I almost fall asleep in class, and my teacher ask me, "Are you bored?" Of
>
> course I'm not bored. I just need my afternoon nap! This class always is fun. This
>
> semester, we work on a project with video cameras. My team is filming groups of
>
> people in different cultures. We are analyze "social distance." That means how close to
>
> each other these people stand. According to my new watch, it's 12:55, so I leave now
>
> for my 1:00 class. Teachers here really aren't liking when you come late!

Imperative

> To do the Jab:
> **Bend** your knees and
> **place** your right foot in front,
> like this. **Punch** with your
> right fist.

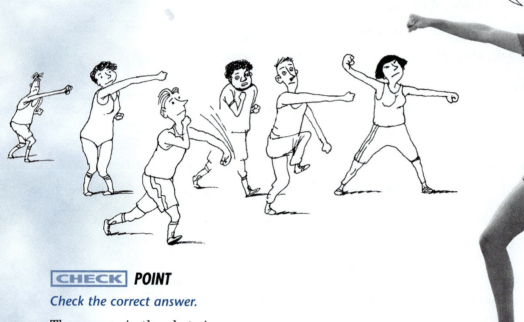

CHECK POINT

Check the correct answer.

The woman in the photo is

☐ inviting someone to learn the Jab.

☐ giving instructions on how to do the Jab.

☐ ordering someone to do the Jab.

CHART CHECK

Check the correct answer.

Imperative sentences

☐ include a subject.

☐ don't include a subject.

AFFIRMATIVE	
BASE FORM OF VERB	
Bend	your knees.
Punch	with your fists.

NEGATIVE		
DON'T	**BASE FORM OF VERB**	
Don't	**bend**	your knees.
	punch	with your fist.

EXPRESS CHECK

Use these verbs to complete the charts.

touch   listen   stand

AFFIRMATIVE	
BASE FORM OF VERB	
	to the music.
	your toes.
	straight.

NEGATIVE		
DON'T	**BASE FORM OF VERB**	
		to the music.
		your toes.
		straight.

Grammar Explanations

Examples

1. The **imperative** form of the verb is always the <u>base form</u>. It is the same whether it is directed to one or several people.

■ Marla, please **get** ready.
■ **Get** ready, guys!

2. The **subject** of an imperative statement is **you**. However, we <u>do not say or write *you*</u> in imperative sentences.

■ **Stand up** straight.
   NOT ~~You stand up straight.~~

3. The imperative form has a number of **uses**.
   Use the imperative to:

   a. give **directions** and **instructions**

   ■ **Turn** left at the traffic light.

   b. give **orders** or **commands**

   ■ **Don't move!**

   c. make **requests** (Use *please* in addition to the imperative form.)

   ■ *Please* **read** this article.
   ■ **Read** this article, *please*.

   d. give **advice** or make **suggestions**

   ■ **Don't exercise** when you're sick.

   e. give **warnings**.

   ■ **Be** careful! **Don't trip!**

   f. **invite** someone

   ■ **Work out** with us tomorrow.

MATCH • *Each imperative goes with a situation. Match the imperative with the correct situation.*

Imperative

    _g_   **1.** Don't touch that!

_____ **2.** Look both ways.

_____ **3.** Dress warmly!

_____ **4.** Don't bend your knees.

_____ **5.** Mark each answer true or false.

_____ **6.** Come in. Make yourself at home.

_____ **7.** Try a little more pepper.

Situation

a. Someone is visiting a friend.

b. Someone is going out into the cold.

c. Someone is crossing a street.

d. Someone is taking an exam.

e. Someone is exercising.

f. Someone is tasting some food.

g. Something is hot.

MATCH • *You're going to give instructions for making a banana-strawberry smoothie. Match a verb from column A with a phrase from column B.*

Column A	**Column B**
Add	the ingredients until smooth.
Slice	six strawberries.
Wash	a banana.
Cut	orange juice into the blender.
Blend	the strawberries in half.
Pour	the fruit to the orange juice.

LABEL • *Now write the sentences in order under the correct pictures.*

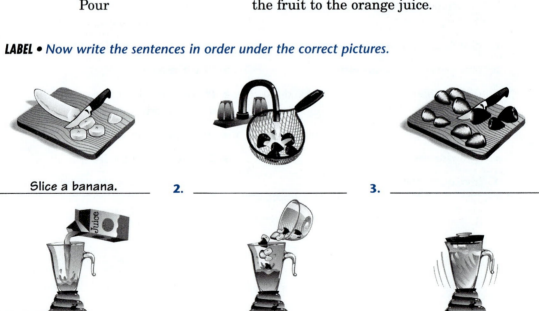

1. ___Slice a banana.___   **2.** _____   **3.** _____

4. _____   **5.** _____   **6.** _____

3

CHOOSE & COMPLETE • *Read this advertisement for a martial arts school. Complete it using the affirmative or negative imperative form of the verbs in the box.*

become	choose	decrease	increase	learn
miss	register	take	~~think~~	wait

MARTIAL ARTS ACADEMY

___*Don't think*___ that martial arts is only about physical training. A good
_____1.
martial arts program offers many other benefits as well. _____
_____2.
self-defense and more at the Martial Arts Academy:

◆ _____ stress. Martial arts training helps you relax.
_____3.

◆ _____ concentration. Martial arts students focus better.
_____4.

◆ _____ fit. Strength and flexibility improve as you learn.
_____5.

We are offering an introductory trial membership. _____ this
_____6.
special opportunity. _____ classes with Master Lorenzo Gibbons,
_____7.
a ninth-level Black Belt Master. _____
_____8.
classes from our convenient schedule.

_____! _____ now
_____9.   _____10.
for a two-week trial.

ONLY $20. ◆ **UNIFORM INCLUDED.**

4

EDIT • *Read part of a martial arts student's essay. Find and correct five mistakes in the use of the imperative. The first mistake is already corrected.*

For the Black Belt essay, Master Gibbons gave us this assignment:
   Write
~~You write~~ about something important to you. My topic is *The Right
Way*, the rules of life for the martial arts. First, respects
other people—treat them the way you want them to treat you.
Second, helped people in need. In other words, use your strength
for others, not to use it just for your own good. Third, no lie
or steal. These are the most important rules to me.

SelfTest

Circle the letter of the correct answer to complete each sentence.

> **EXAMPLE:**
> Jennifer never _____ coffee.   A Ⓑ C D
> (A) drink   (C) is drinking
> (B) drinks   (D) was drinking

1. _____ ready for school? It's already 7:00.   A B C D
   (A) Do you get   (C) You get
   (B) Are you getting   (D) You are getting

2. Nick _____ to Greece every year to visit his family.   A B C D
   (A) is going   (C) go
   (B) he goes   (D) goes

3. Why _____? Class isn't over yet.   A B C D
   (A) are you leaving   (C) do you leave
   (B) you are leaving   (D) you leaving

4. Something _____ good. Is that fresh bread in the oven?   A B C D
   (A) smells   (C) smell
   (B) is smelling   (D) smelling

5. Which class _____ best?   A B C D
   (A) are you liking   (C) you like
   (B) you are liking   (D) do you like

6. _____ loose clothes to exercise. You'll be more comfortable.   A B C D
   (A) Wear   (C) Wears
   (B) Wearing   (D) You wear

7. Please _____ to class on time. We start at exactly 9:00.   A B C D
   (A) we come   (C) you're coming
   (B) come   (D) comes

8. I _____ something outside. Are the doors locked?   A B C D
   (A) 'm hearing   (C) hearing
   (B) hear   (D) hears

9. Walk! _____ run!   A B C D
   (A) Not   (C) Don't
   (B) No   (D) You don't

10. —Do you like fish?   A B C D
    —Yes, I _____.
    (A) am   (C) don't
    (B) do   (D) like

22

11. Harry works all the time. He _____.   **A B C D**
   (A) never relaxes   (C) often relaxes
   (B) relaxes never   (D) relaxes sometimes

12. What _____ these days?   **A B C D**
   (A) are you doing   (C) you are doing
   (B) do you do   (D) you do

13. The baby's so big! How much _____ now?   **A B C D**
   (A) weigh   (C) is she weighing
   (B) she weighs   (D) does she weigh

14. —Are you taking an English class this semester?   **A B C D**
   —Yes, I _____.
   (A) take   (C) do
   (B) am taking   (D) am

15. Water _____ at 212°F.   **A B C D**
   (A) boil   (C) boiled
   (B) boils   (D) is boiling

SECTION TWO

Each sentence has four underlined words or phrases. The four underlined parts of the sentence are marked A, B, C, and D. Circle the letter of the one underlined word or phrase that is NOT CORRECT.

> **EXAMPLE:**
> Mike <u>usually</u> <u>drives</u> to school, but <u>today</u> he <u>walks</u>.   **A B C Ⓓ**
>   A   B   C   D

16. Fran usually <u>is swimming</u> before <u>work</u>, but this morning <u>she's</u> <u>jogging</u>.   **A B C D**
                 A   B   C D

17. The wind is <u>blowing</u>, <u>it</u> <u>rains</u>, and the sky <u>looks</u> gray.   **A B C D**
                 A   B C   D

18. <u>Where</u> <u>you are</u> <u>working</u> these days <u>after school</u>?   **A B C D**
      A   B   C   D

19. The floor <u>is</u> wet, so <u>walk</u> slowly and <u>no</u> <u>fall down</u>!   **A B C D**
           A   B   C D

20. <u>Something</u> <u>is seeming</u> different—<u>are</u> you <u>wearing</u> a new perfume?   **A B C D**
      A   B   C   D

21. We <u>always</u> <u>eat out</u> because we <u>hates</u> to <u>cook</u>.   **A B C D**
        A   B   C   D

22. Luis <u>arrives usually</u> early, <u>but</u> <u>today</u> he<u>'s</u> late.   **A B C D**
          A   B C D

23. I <u>need</u> my CD player if you <u>don't</u> <u>using</u> it <u>at the moment</u>.   **A B C D**
      A   B C   D

24. I <u>never</u> <u>have</u> anything to write with <u>because</u> <u>I'm always lose</u> my pens.   **A B C D**
       A   B   C   D

25. <u>Turn</u> left at the light, and <u>you</u> <u>don't</u> <u>forget</u> to signal!   **A B C D**
      A   B C D

Simple Past Tense:
Affirmative Statements

Oh, Albert! You **were** a good man but a lousy poet!

I was a poet.
I **traveled** far and wide.
I **lived** until 80,
and then I **died**.
ALBERT RIMES
1910-1990

RIP

CHECK *POINT*

Check the year these sentences appeared in a newspaper.

"Poet Albert Rimes lives in Belgium."

☐ 1989   ☐ 1999

"Poet Albert Rimes lived in Belgium most of his life."

☐ 1989   ☐ 1999

CHART CHECK

Check the correct answer.

How many forms does the past tense of **be** have?

☐ one   ☐ two

What do you add to the base form of regular verbs to form the past tense?

☐ -*d* or -*ed*   ☐ -*t*

THE SIMPLE PAST TENSE: *BE*

Subject	*Be*	
I/He/She/It	**was**	young in 1930.
We/You*/They	**were**	

You is both singular and plural.

THE SIMPLE PAST TENSE: REGULAR VERBS

Subject	Verb	
I/He/She/It/We/You/They	**moved**	fifty years ago.
	worked	

THE SIMPLE PAST TENSE: IRREGULAR VERBS

Subject	Verb	
I/He/She/It/We/You/They	**wrote**	poetry.
	became	famous.
	built	a monument.

24

EXPRESS CHECK

Complete the chart.

BASE FORM OF VERB	SIMPLE PAST TENSE
be	_____ and _____
come	_____
save	_____

Grammar Explanations

Examples

1. Use the **simple past tense** to talk about things that are now <u>finished</u>.

                   Now

Past ·············X··············┊············► Future
   He was a poet.

- Albert Rimes **lived** in the twentieth century.
- He **was** a poet.
- He **wrote** poetry.

2. You can use the **simple past tense** with **time expressions** that refer to the past *(last week, by 1980, in the twentieth century, fifty years ago).*

- *By 1930*, he **was** famous.
- He **died** more than *ten years ago*.

3. The **simple past tense** of **regular verbs** is formed by adding **-d** or **-ed**.

▶ **BE CAREFUL!** There are often <u>spelling changes</u> when you add **-ed** to the verb.

Many common verbs are **irregular**. Their past tense is not formed by adding **-d** or **–ed**.

BASE FORM		SIMPLE PAST
live	→	live**d**
join	→	join**ed**
play	→	play**ed**
study	→	stud**ied**
hop	→	hop**ped**
be	→	**was/were**
have	→	**had**
get	→	**got**
go	→	**went**

Check it out!

For spelling rules for the simple past tense of regular verbs, see Appendix 21 on page 344.

For pronunciation rules for the simple past tense of regular verbs, see Appendix 28 on page 348.

For a list of irregular verbs, see Appendix 1 on pages 336–337.

1 **IDENTIFY •** *Read about Japanese poet Matsuo Basho. Underline all the regular past tense verbs. Circle all the irregular past tense verbs.*

Matsuo Basho (wrote) more than 1,000 three-line poems, or "haiku." He chose topics from nature, daily life, and human emotions. He became one of Japan's most famous poets, and his work established haiku as an important art form.

Matsuo Basho was born near Kyoto in 1644. His father wanted him to become a samurai (warrior). Instead, Matsuo moved to Edo (present-day Tokyo) and studied poetry. By 1681, he had many students and admirers.

Basho's home burned down in 1682. Then, in 1683, his mother died. After these events, Basho felt restless. Starting in 1684, he traveled on foot and on horseback all over Japan. Sometimes his friends joined him, and they wrote poetry together. Travel was difficult in the seventeenth century, and Basho often got sick. He died in 1694, during a journey to Osaka. At that time he had 2,000 students.

2 **CHOOSE & COMPLETE •** *Read this biography of another poet, Emily Dickinson. Complete it using the simple past tense form of the verbs in the boxes.*

be	become	lead	leave	~~live~~	see	wear	write

Emily Dickinson, one of the most popular American poets,

_____lived_____ from 1830 to 1886. She _____
    1.   **2.**

about love, nature, and time. These _____ her
                          3.

favorite themes. Dickinson _____ an unusual life.
                          4.

After just one year of college, she _____ a recluse—
                          5.

she almost never _____ her house in Amherst,
               6.

Massachusetts. At home, she _____ no one except her
                  7.

family, and she only _____ white.
           8.

address	appear	happen	write

In addition to her poetry, Dickinson _____ many letters. Other
9.
people always _____ the envelopes for her. During her lifetime only
10.
seven of her 1,700 poems _____ in print—and this _____
11.   12.
without her knowledge or permission.

Now complete these lines from a poem by Emily Dickinson.

bite	~~come~~	drink	eat	hop	see

A bird _____came_____ down the walk:
13.
He did not know I _____;
14.
He _____ an angle-worm in halves
15.
And _____the fellow raw.
16.
And then he _____ a dew
17.
From a convenient grass,

And then _____ sidewise to the wall
18.
To let a beetle pass.

3 **EDIT** • *Read part of a student's journal. Find and correct eight mistakes in the use of the
simple past tense. The first mistake is already corrected.*

>   *enjoyed*
> Today in class we read a poem by Robert Frost. I really ~~enjoy~~ it. It was about a
> person who choosed between two roads in a forest. Before he made his decision, he
> spents a lot of time trying to decide which road to follow. Many people thought the
> person were Frost. In the end, he take the road that was less traveled on. He decided
> to be a poet. That decision change his life a lot.
>
>   Sometimes I feel a little like Frost. Two years ago I decide to come to this
> country. That were the biggest decision of my life.

Simple Past Tense:
Negative Statements and Questions

THE DAILY NEWS

DID SHE CRASH???

—LAE, NEW GUINEA, JULY 2, 1937. Amelia Earhart's small plane left the island of Lae at exactly 12:00 midnight. She **was not** alone on the flight, but she and Fred Noonan, her navigator, were very tired. She reported her last position at 8:14 P.M. After that, she **did not make** radio contact again. Why **did** they **disappear**? **Were** they exhausted? **Did** they **run out** of gas? The U.S. Coast Guard started its search for the answer at 10:15 P.M.

CHECK *POINT*

Circle T (True), F (False), or ? (the article doesn't say).

T F ? The plane crashed.

T F ? Earhart made radio contact after 8:14 P.M.

T F ? Earhart had a navigator with her.

SIMPLE PAST TENSE: NEGATIVE STATEMENTS

CHART CHECK 1

Check the correct answers.

What word do you add to **be** to form a negative statement?

☐ *not*   ☐ *did not*

What do you add to other verbs to form a negative statement?

☐ *not*   ☐ *did not*

BE			
SUBJECT	**BE**	**NOT**	
I/He/She/It	**was**	**not**	here last year.
We/You*/They	**were**		

You is both singular and plural.

CONTRACTIONS
was not = **wasn't**
were not = **weren't**

REGULAR AND IRREGULAR VERBS			
SUBJECT	**DID NOT**	**BASE FORM OF VERB**	
I/He/She/It We/You/They	**did not**	**call** **fly**	last night.

CONTRACTIONS
did not = **didn't**

SIMPLE PAST TENSE: QUESTIONS

CHART CHECK 2

Check the correct answer.

Which word(s) can begin *yes/no* questions with **be**?

❏ *was*

❏ *were*

❏ *did*

Which word(s) can begin *yes/no* questions with other verbs?

❏ *was*

❏ *were*

❏ *did*

YES/NO QUESTIONS: *BE*

BE	SUBJECT	
Was	she	here last year?
Were	they	

SHORT ANSWERS

AFFIRMATIVE			NEGATIVE		
Yes,	she	**was.**	**No,**	she	**wasn't.**
	they	**were.**		they	**weren't.**

WH- QUESTIONS: *BE*

WH- WORD	BE	SUBJECT	
Why	**was**	she	here last year?
	were	they	

YES/NO QUESTIONS: OTHER VERBS

DID	SUBJECT	BASE FORM	
Did	she	**fly**	to Mexico?

SHORT ANSWERS

AFFIRMATIVE	NEGATIVE
Yes, she **did**.	**No**, she **didn't**.

WH- QUESTIONS: OTHER VERBS

WH- WORD	DID	SUBJECT	BASE FORM
Why	**did**	it	**disappear?**

EXPRESS CHECK

Unscramble these words to form a question and an answer.

navigator • she • have • Did • a _____

fly • She • didn't • alone _____

Grammar Explanations

Examples

1. Use the **simple past tense** to make **negative statements** about actions or situations that are now <u>finished</u>.

Now

Past ·······**X**·········┊·············➤ Future
  wasn't alone

- She **wasn't** alone.
- They **weren't** on an island.
- They **didn't find** the plane.
- He **didn't call** that night.

2. Use the **simple past tense** to ask **questions** about actions or situations that are now <u>finished</u>.

- **Was** she alone in the plane?
- Where **did** she **leave** from?

Check it out!

For questions about the subject, see Unit 24 on pages 102–103.

READ • *Look at some facts about Amelia Earhart.*

- She was born in the United States.
- She didn't complete college.
- She didn't keep her first airplane.
- She flew across the Atlantic Ocean.
- She received many awards.
- She married George Palmer Putnam.
- She didn't have any children.
- She wrote three books.

ANSWER • *Put a check in the correct box.*

		Yes	No
1.	Did she get many awards?	☑	☐
2.	Was she a college graduate?	☐	☐
3.	Was she an American citizen?	☐	☐
4.	Did she keep her first plane?	☐	☐
5.	Was she an author?	☐	☐
6.	Did she have a husband?	☐	☐
7.	Was she a parent?	☐	☐

2 **ASK & ANSWER** • *Use the cues to ask questions about Amelia Earhart. Then answer the questions with the information in the box.*

| ~~1928~~ 1937 American Columbia University two years New Guinea three |

1. When / she / cross the Atlantic Ocean?

   When did she cross the Atlantic Ocean?   In 1928.

2. Where / she / study?

   _____   _____

3. How long / be / she / a social worker?

   _____   _____

4. Where / her last flight / leave from?

   _____   _____

5. How many books / she / write?

   _____   _____

6. What / be / her nationality?

   _____   _____

7. When / she / disappear?

   _____   _____

3 **COMPLETE** • *The magazine* **Flying High** *(FH) interviewed a young pilot. Complete the interview with the correct form of the verbs in parentheses and with short answers.*

FH: _____Did_____ you always _____want_____ to be a pilot?
1. (want)

SUE: _____Yes_____, I _____did_____. I saw a documentary about Amelia
2.
Earhart when I was six. She became my role model.

FH: _____ your parents happy with your decision?
3. (Be)

SUE: _____, they _____. They _____ me to fly.
4. **5. (not want)**

FH: Why not? _____ they _____ it was too dangerous?
6. (feel)

SUE: _____, they _____. But I was very determined, and
7.
they _____ me from pursuing my dream.
8. (not keep)

FH: _____ you ever _____ of flying around the world?
9. (dream)

SUE: Of course. But I _____ it would happen so soon.
10. (not think)

FH: _____ you alone on the flight?
11. (Be)

SUE: _____, I _____. I had a co-pilot.
12.

FH: _____ it difficult to find a co-pilot for this flight?
13. (Be)

SUE: _____, it _____. She's my roommate.
14.

4 **EDIT** • *Read this postcard. Find and correct six mistakes in the use of the simple past tense. The first mistake is already corrected.*

receive
Hi! Did you ~~received~~ my last letter? I didn't knew your new address so I sent it to your old one. When you moved? Did your roommate move with you? Right now I'm on board a plane flying to El Paso to visit Ana. Did you met her at the conference last year? I wanted to visit her in June, but I no had the time. At first I was going to drive from Los Angeles, but I decided to fly instead. This is only my third flight, but I love flying! I didnt know flying could be so much fun! Hope to hear from you.
—M.

To: Sue Avila
1210 Bayview Place
Tampa, FL 33601

Used to

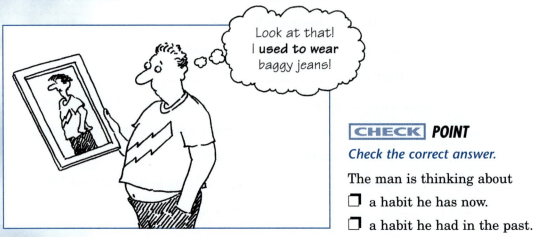

Look at that! I **used to** wear baggy jeans!

CHECK *POINT*

Check the correct answer.

The man is thinking about

☐ a habit he has now.

☐ a habit he had in the past.

CHART CHECK 1

Circle T (True) or F (False).

T F   In affirmative statements, **used to** is used with all subjects.

AFFIRMATIVE STATEMENTS

SUBJECT	USED TO	BASE FORM OF VERB
I She They	**used to**	**wear** jeans.

NEGATIVE STATEMENTS

SUBJECT	DIDN'T USE TO	BASE FORM OF VERB
I She They	**didn't use to**	**wear** jeans.

CHART CHECK 2

Check the correct answer.

In questions, what form of **used to** is used?

☐ *did . . . used to*

☐ *did . . . use to*

YES/NO QUESTIONS

DID	SUBJECT	USE TO	BASE FORM
Did	you she they	**use to**	**wear** jeans?

SHORT ANSWERS

AFFIRMATIVE			NEGATIVE		
Yes,	I she they	**did.**	**No,**	I she they	**didn't.**

WH- QUESTIONS

WH- WORD	DID	SUBJECT	USE TO	BASE FORM
What	**did**	you she they	**use to**	**wear**?

EXPRESS CHECK

Circle the words to complete these sentences.

• He <u>used to / uses to</u> wear baggy jeans.

• Did you <u>use to / used to</u> shop for clothes with your friends?

• What did your parents use to <u>saying / say</u> about your clothes?

Grammar Explanations

Examples

1. Use *used to* + base form of the verb to talk about **past habits** or **past situations** that <u>no longer exist in the present</u>.

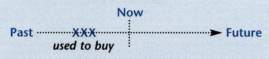

▶ **BE CAREFUL!** *Used to* always has a past meaning. There is <u>no present tense form</u>.

- Leo **used to buy** baggy jeans.
  (In the past, he often bought baggy jeans. He doesn't buy baggy jeans anymore.)

- In his youth, Leo **used to be** thin.
  NOT <s>Today Leo used to be thin.</s>

2. We usually use *used to* in sentences that **contrast the past and the present**. We often emphasize this contrast by using time expressions such as *now*, *no longer*, and *not anymore* with the present tense.

- Jeans **used to come** only in blue. *Now* you can buy them in any color.

- They **used to live** in Genoa, but they *no longer* live there.

- She **used to wear** a size 6, but she does*n't anymore*.

3. **BE CAREFUL!** Form **questions** with *did* + *use to*.

Form the **negative** with *didn't* + *use to*.

USAGE NOTE: *Used to* is more common in affirmative statements than in negative statements or questions.

- **Did** you **use to** wear jeans?
  NOT <s>Did you used to wear jeans?</s>

- They **didn't use to** come in different colors.
  NOT <s>They didn't used to come . . . .</s>

4. **BE CAREFUL!** Do not confuse *used to* + base form of the verb with the following expressions:

be used to (be accustomed to)

get used to (get accustomed to)

- I **used to wear** tight jeans.
  (It was my past habit to wear tight jeans.)

- I**'m used to wearing** tight jeans.
  (It is normal for me to wear tight jeans.)

- I **got used to wearing** tight jeans last year.
  (I got accustomed to wearing tight jeans.)

1 IDENTIFY • *Read this fashion article. Underline all the examples of* **used to** *that refer to a habit in the past.*

In many ways, fashion <u>used to be</u> much simpler. Women didn't use to wear pants to the office, and men's clothes never used to come in bright colors. People also used to dress in special ways for different situations. They didn't use blue jeans as business clothes or wear jogging suits when they traveled. Today you can go to the opera and find some women in evening gowns while others are in blue jeans. Even buying jeans used to be easier—they came only in blue denim. I'm still not used to buying green jeans and wearing them to work!

2 CHOOSE & COMPLETE • *Look at these pictures from an old magazine. Use the verbs in the box with* **used to**. *Write one sentence about each picture.*

| ~~be~~ carry dance dress have wear |

1. Women's skirts _____used to be_____ long and formal.

2. All men _____ long hair.

3. Children _____ like adults.

4. Men and women _____ at formal balls.

5. Women _____ many petticoats under their skirts.

6. Men _____ walking sticks.

3 **ASK & ANSWER •** *Look at the information about sneakers from 1922. Complete the FAQs*. Use the correct form of* **used to***.*

Style	High-top	Low-top
Men's	98¢	89¢
Women's	38¢ WHITE 95¢ BLACK	79¢
Boys' and Girls'	85¢ SMALL 89¢ LARGE	73¢ SMALL 79¢ LARGE
Children's	—	65¢

1. **Q:** <u>Did sneakers use to come in many colors?</u>
   (sneakers / come in many colors?)

   A: <u>No. Only in white and black.</u>

2. **Q:** How many styles did they use to come in?

   A: _____

3. **Q:** _____
   (How much / pair of men's high-tops / cost?)

   A: _____

4. **Q:** What about women's sneakers? Did they use to cost the same as men's?

   A: _____

5. **Q:** What kind of sneakers did children use to wear?

   A: _____

6. **Q:** How many sizes did there use to be for boys and girls?

   A: _____

*FAQs = Frequently Asked Questions

4 **EDIT •** *Read this student's journal. Find and correct five mistakes in the use of* **used to***. The first mistake is already corrected.*

>   ^{use}
> When I was younger, clothing didn't ~~used~~ to be a problem. All the girls at my school used to wore the same uniform. I used to think that it took away from my freedom of choice. Now I can wear what I want, but clothes cost so much! Even blue jeans, today's "uniform," used to be cheaper. My mom uses to pay less than $20 for hers. I guess they didn't used to sell designer jeans back then. You know, I was used to be against school uniforms, but now I'm not so sure!

UNIT 9

Past Progressive

I was snowboarding.

CHECK POINT

Check the correct answer.

The girl in the hospital bed is giving her version of

❏ what she usually did in the past.

❏ what she was doing at the time of her accident.

CHART CHECK 1

Circle T (True) or F (False).

T   F   The past progressive is made up of the past tense of **be** + base form of the verb.

STATEMENTS			
SUBJECT	**BE**	**(NOT)**	**BASE FORM OF VERB + -ING**
I/He/She/It	**was**	**(not)**	**jumping.** **falling.**
We/You*/They	**were**		

You is both singular and plural.

CHART CHECK 2

Check the correct answer.

In questions, the verb **be** comes:

❏ after the subject

❏ before the subject

YES/NO QUESTIONS		
BE	**SUBJECT**	**BASE FORM + -ING**
Was	she	**jumping?** **falling?**
Were	you	

SHORT ANSWERS						
AFFIRMATIVE			**NEGATIVE**			
Yes,	she	**was.**	**No,**	she	**wasn't.**	
	we	**were.**		we	**weren't.**	

WH- QUESTIONS			
WH- WORD	**BE**	**SUBJECT**	**BASE FORM + -ING**
Where When	**was**	she	**jumping?** **falling?**
Why How long	**were**	you	

EXPRESS CHECK

Complete this conversation with the past progressive form of the verb **stay**.

A: Where _____ you _____?

B: I _____ at a resort in Colorado.

Grammar Explanations

Examples

---

1. Use the **past progressive** to describe an action that was <u>in progress at a specific time in the past</u>. The action began before the specific time and may or may not continue after the specific time.

▶ **BE CAREFUL!** Non-action verbs are not usually used in the progressive.
(For a list of common non-action verbs, see Appendix 2 on page 337.)

A: What **were** you **doing** at 3:00?
B: We **were skiing**.
C: I **was eating** lunch at 3:00.

- I **had** a headache last night.
  NOT ~~I was having a headache last night.~~

---

2. Use the **past progressive with** *while* to talk about <u>two actions in progress at the same time in the past</u>. Use the past progressive in both clauses.

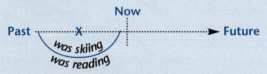

USAGE NOTE: In informal conversation, some people use *when* with the past progressive.

- *While* he **was skiing**, I **was reading**.
  OR
- I **was reading** *while* he **was skiing**.

- Sorry, I **wasn't listening** *when* you **were talking**.

---

3. Use the **past progressive** to focus on the <u>duration</u> of an action, not its completion.

Use the **simple past tense** to focus on the <u>completion</u> of an action.

- Sheila **was reading** a book last night.
  (We don't know if she finished the book.)

- Sheila **read** a book last night.
  (She probably finished the book.)

1   **TRUE OR FALSE** • *Read each numbered sentence. Write T (True) or F (False) for the statement that follows. Write a question mark (?) if there is not enough information.*

1. While Tanya was watching the Winter Olympics on TV, Mikael was shoveling snow.

   F   First Mikael finished shoveling snow. Then Tanya started watching TV.

2. In this photo, I was putting on my boots.

   _____ I was wearing boots in the photo.

3. At 5:00, they were drinking hot chocolate by the fire.

   _____ We don't know when they started drinking hot chocolate.

4. Last night, I was reading an article about skiing in Morocco.

   _____ I finished the article.

5. At 10:00, he drank a cup of coffee.

   _____ He finished the coffee.

6. It was snowing while she was taking the photograph.

   _____ First she took the photograph. Then it started to snow.

2   **DESCRIBE** • *Fritz and Karyn were at a ski café. Write about the picture. Use the past progressive.*

1. Fritz _____ **was wearing a hat.** _____
                         (wear / a hat)

2. Karyn _____ **wasn't wearing a hat.** _____
                         (wear / a hat)

3. They _____
                 (sit / outside)

4. It _____
              (snow)

5. They _____
               (wear / sunglasses)

6. They _____
               (wear / their gloves)

7. The waiter _____
               (serve / drinks)

8. He _____
              (serve / lunch)

9. Karyn _____
              (smile)

10. She _____
             (hold / a cell phone)

3 **COMPLETE** • Mountain Sports Magazine (MS) *interviewed the snowboarding champion, Rosie Happ (RH). Complete the interview with the correct form of the verbs in parentheses and with short answers.*

MS: Congratulations! You just became a semi-finalist for the Olympic snowboarding

team. _____Were_____ you _____expecting_____ to get this far in
1. (expect)

the competition?

RH: No, I _____wasn't_____. During the trials, I _____ from a
2.   **3.** (recover)

bad cold. By the last day, I _____ very well. That's what
4. (not perform)

I thought, anyway.

MS: What _____ you _____ while you _____
5. (think)   **6.** (wait)

for the announcement?

RH: Actually, I _____ about the competition at all. Some friends
7. (not think)

and I _____ a movie.
8. (watch)

MS: You're pretty new to this sport. Where _____ you _____
9. (snowboard)

at this time last year?

RH: In Switzerland. I _____ Barrett Christie and _____
10. (watch)   **11.** (dream)

about being that good.

MS: _____ he _____ for the Olympics at that time?
12. (practice)

RH: Yes, he _____. And he was amazing.
13.

4 **EDIT** • *Read this journal entry. Find and correct eight mistakes in the use of the past progressive. The first mistake is already corrected.*

                                                  were

Tonight, Sheila and I ~~was~~ looking at some photographs from my snowboarding trip with

Fritz's family last year. By the end of the evening, we laughing like crazy. That was my first

experience on a snowboard, so the pictures were pretty embarrassing. In one shot, I was came

down the slope on my back. In another one, my board were falling out of the ski lift while I was

riding up the slope. Fritz was taking that picture from the lift entrance. Good thing he not

standing right under me! Where was I when Fritz was falling down the slope? I guess I wasn't

carry my camera. It was amazing how fast Fritz's girlfriend, Karyn, learned that weekend.

She was doing jumps by the second day. By that time, I spent a lot of time at the ski café.

Past Progressive and Simple Past Tense

Did you see the accident?

Yeah . . . The guy in the sports car was talking on his cell phone when he hit the other car.

CHECK POINT

Number these statements in the correct time order.

_____ There was a car accident.

_____ The driver of the sports car was on the phone.

CHART CHECK

Circle T (True) or F (False).

Use **while** to introduce

T   F   a simple past tense action.

T   F   a past progressive action.

PAST PROGRESSIVE AND SIMPLE PAST TENSE		
PAST PROGRESSIVE	**WHEN**	**SIMPLE PAST TENSE**
He **was speeding**	when	the accident **happened**.

SIMPLE PAST TENSE AND PAST PROGRESSIVE		
SIMPLE PAST TENSE	**WHILE**	**PAST PROGRESSIVE**
The accident **happened**	while	you **were driving**.

SIMPLE PAST TENSE AND SIMPLE PAST TENSE		
SIMPLE PAST TENSE	**WHEN**	**SIMPLE PAST TENSE**
The police **came**	when	the accident **happened**.

PAST PROGRESSIVE AND PAST PROGRESSIVE		
PAST PROGRESSIVE	**WHILE**	**PAST PROGRESSIVE**
They **were talking**	while	they **were driving**.

EXPRESS CHECK

Circle the correct words to complete these sentences.

• <u>When / While</u> the car crashed, he hit his head.

• How fast <u>was he driving / did he drive</u> when the accident occurred?

Grammar Explanations	Examples
1. Use the **past progressive with the simple past tense** to talk about <u>an action that was interrupted by another action</u>. Use the simple past tense for the interrupting action.  Use **when** to introduce the simple past tense action OR use **while** to introduce the past progressive action.	■ I **was crossing** the street when the driver **honked** his horn. ■ They **were driving** too fast when they **crashed**. ■ He was speeding **when** the light **turned** red. ■ **While** he **was speeding**, the light **turned** red.
2. **BE CAREFUL!** Notice the <u>difference in meaning</u> between these two different sentences. 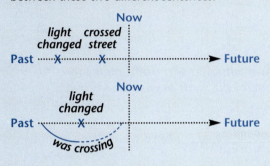	 ■ **When** the light **changed**, I **crossed** the street. *(First the light changed. Then I crossed the street.)* ■ **When** the light **changed**, I **was crossing** the street. *(First I was crossing the street. Then the light changed.)*
3. Use the **past progressive with *while*** to talk about <u>two actions in progress at the same time in the past</u>. Use the past progressive in both clauses. 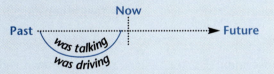	■ Lin **was talking** on the phone **while** he **was driving**. ■ They **weren't paying** attention **while** they **were crossing** the street.
4. The **time clause** (the part of the sentence beginning with **when** or **while**) can come at <u>the beginning or the end</u> of the sentence. The meaning is the same. Use a **comma** after the time clause when it comes at the <u>beginning</u> of the sentence.	■ **When you called**, I was leaving. ■ I was leaving **when you called**. ■ **While he was driving**, he was talking. ■ He was talking **while he was driving**.

1 **TRUE OR FALSE** • *Read each numbered sentence. Write T (True) or F (False) for the statement that follows.*

1. When our friends arrived, we ate lunch.

   ___T___ Our friends arrived before lunch.

2. While we were talking on the phone, I was driving to school.

   _____ We finished the conversation. Then I drove to school.

3. Lori heard about the accident while she was driving to work.

   _____ Lori knew about the accident by the time she got to work.

4. When they exited the freeway, it started to rain.

   _____ It was raining while they were on the freeway.

5. When Zoe got to school, her class was taking a test.

   _____ Zoe was late to class.

2 **COMPLETE** • *A police officer is interviewing two witnesses of a traffic accident. Complete the interview with the correct form of the verbs in parentheses and with short answers.*

OFFICER: _____Were_____ you _____standing_____ here when the accident
1. (stand)

_____occurred_____ ?
2. (occur)

WITNESS 1: Yes, we _____were_____. We _____ at the bus stop
3.   **4. (wait)**

when we first _____ the car.
5. (notice)

OFFICER: _____ the car _____ when it
6. (speed)

_____ to the intersection?
7. (get)

WITNESS 1: Yes, it _____. It _____ very fast when it
8.   **9. (go)**

_____ the corner.
10. (reach)

WITNESS 2: No, it _____! Those men _____ against a red
11.   **12. (cross)**

light when the car _____ them.
13. (hit)

OFFICER: _____ the driver _____ when he
14. (stop)

_____ the men?
15. (see)

WITNESS 1: No, he _____. He _____ on his cell phone
16.   **17. (talk)**

while he _____. That's why he _____ in time.
18. (drive)   **19. (not stop)**

WITNESS 2: But the men _____ attention while they _____.
20. (not pay)   **21. (walk)**

CHART CHECK 2

Check the correct answer.

For is used with:
☐ a point of time
☐ a length of time

WH- QUESTIONS

WH- WORD	HAVE	SUBJECT	PAST PARTICIPLE	
How long	**have**	they	**lived**	here?
	has	he	**been**	

SHORT ANSWERS

Since January.
For a few months.

EXPRESS CHECK

Look at the past participles. Check the correct column.

	Regular	Irregular			Regular	Irregular
driven	☐	☐		won	☐	☐
competed	☐	☐		tried	☐	☐

Grammar Explanations

Examples

1. Use the **present perfect** with *since* or *for* to talk about something that <u>began in the past and continues into the present</u> (and may continue into the future).

```
                    Now
     1994            :
     Past ·X·················:·····──────► Future
                    :
          has been  :     - - - -
```

- Martina Hingis **has been** a professional tennis player *since* 1994.

- She **has been** a professional tennis player *for* years.

  (She began her professional career years ago, and she is still a professional player.)

---

2. Use the present perfect with *since* + **point in time** *(since 5:00, since Monday, since 1994)* to show <u>when something started</u>.

- She **has earned** millions of dollars *since 1994*.

---

3. *Since* can also introduce a **time clause**.

When the action in the time clause ended in the past, use the <u>simple past tense</u>.

When the action in the time clause began in the past but continues into the present, use the <u>present perfect</u>.

- Martina **has loved** sports *since she was a child*.

- She has won many tennis tournaments *since* she **moved** from Slovakia.
  (She doesn't live there anymore.)

- She has become extremely successful *since* she **has been** in Switzerland.
  (She still lives in Switzerland.)

---

4. Use the present perfect with *for* + **length of time** *(for ten minutes, for two weeks, for years, for a long time)* to show <u>how long a present condition has lasted</u>.

- Martina's mother **has been** her coach *for many years*.

1 **IDENTIFY** • *Read about tennis star Martina Hingis. Underline all the verbs in the present perfect. Circle all the time expressions with **since** or **for**.*

Martina Hingis picked up her first tennis racket at the age of two. (Since then), she <u>has become</u> one of the greatest tennis players in the world. Born in Slovakia, she has lived in Switzerland for many years. She became the outdoor Swiss champion at age nine. Since then she has won many international competitions including Wimbledon, the U.S. Open, and the Australian Open.

For young stars like Martina, life has its difficulties. They are under constant pressure to win, and they don't have time to just hang out with classmates. In fact, Martina hasn't attended school since 1994, and she has been in the public spotlight for years. But she seems to be handling her success well. Since she turned professional, she has played tennis all over the world and has earned millions of dollars. She sees her life as normal because tennis has been the most important thing to her since she was a little girl.

2 **COMPLETE & CHOOSE** • *Read this magazine excerpt about a child genius. Complete it with the present perfect form of the verbs in parentheses. Choose between **since** and **for**.*

Thirteen-year-old Ronnie Segal _____has loved_____ math _____since_____ he
                              1. (love)   **2.** (since / for)
was a little boy. "I _____ interested in numbers _____
                    3. (be)   **4.** (since / for)
nine years, five months, three weeks, and two days," says Ronnie. _____
                                                                   5. (Since / For)
the past year, Ronnie _____ graduate-level classes at the university.
                      6. (attend)
He _____ badly. _____ January he _____
   7. (not do)   **8.** (Since / For)   **9.** (take)
five exams and _____ a grade of less than 100 on any of them.
               10. (not get)
_____ Ronnie began classes, he _____ an average of
11. (Since / For)   **12.** (meet)
1.324 people a month. And his future? Young Ronnie _____ about it
                                                   13. (not think)
for years. He _____ _____ he was a little boy that he is
              14. (know)   **15.** (since / for)
going to become a famous sports announcer, get married, and have exactly 2.2 kids.

3 **ASK & ANSWER** • *Complete the interview about Martina Hingis. Use the words in parentheses to write questions. Then answer the questions with information from Exercise 1.*

1. (How long / she / play tennis?)

Q: ___How long has she played tennis?___

A: ___Since she was two.___

2. (How long / she / live in Switzerland?)

Q: _____

A: _____

3. (she / win any competitions / since the outdoor Swiss championship?)

Q: _____

A: _____

4. (she / attend school / since 1994?)

Q: _____

A: _____

5. (How much money / she / earn / since she began her career?)

Q: _____

A: _____

6. (How long / tennis / be important to her?)

Q: _____

A: _____

4 **EDIT** • *Read this student's paragraph. Find and correct seven mistakes in the use of the present perfect. The first mistake is already corrected.*

> have been
> I ~~am~~ in Ms. Rodriguez's physical education class since two months. I enjoy it a lot
> and have only miss two classes since the beginning of the semester. I especially
> like tennis, but since September we don't play because the weather have been too
> cold. I also like volleyball, and my team has win two games since we have started to
> compete with Lincoln High School. I'm looking forward to the next game.

Present Perfect:
Already and *Yet*

As you can see, the flu season **has already begun. Have** you **gotten** your flu shot **yet**? It's never too late!

Well, almost never . . .

CHART CHECK 1

Check the correct answer.

To say that something has happened before now,

☐ use *already*.

☐ use *yet*.

To say that something has <u>not</u> happened before now,

☐ use *already*.

☐ use *not . . . yet*.

AFFIRMATIVE STATEMENTS: *ALREADY*				
SUBJECT	**HAVE**	**ALREADY**	**PAST PARTICIPLE**	
They	**have**	*already*	**developed**	a new flu vaccine.
It	**has**		**saved**	many lives.

NEGATIVE STATEMENTS: *YET*				
SUBJECT	**HAVE NOT**	**PAST PARTICIPLE**		**YET**
They	**haven't**	**finished**	the interview	*yet*.
It	**hasn't**	**ended**		

CHART CHECK 2

Circle T (True) or F (False).

T F *Yet* is used in questions.

YES/NO QUESTIONS: *YET*				
HAVE	**SUBJECT**	**PAST PARTICIPLE**		**YET**
Have	they	**tested**	the new vaccine	*yet*?
Has	it	**gotten**	approval	

SHORT ANSWERS					
AFFIRMATIVE			**NEGATIVE**		
Yes,	they	**have**.	**No,**	they	**haven't**.
	it	**has**.		it	**hasn't**.

EXPRESS CHECK

Unscramble these words to form a question. Answer the question.

you • have • yet • lunch • had

_____?

_____

Grammar Explanations

Examples

1. We often use the **present perfect** with *already* to talk about things that <u>have happened before now</u>.

▶ **BE CAREFUL!** Do not use the present perfect with *already* when you mention a specific time in the past.

Already usually comes between *have* and the past participle.

Already can also come at the end of the clause.

A: Is your daughter going to get her flu shot?
B: She's *already* **gotten** it.

DON'T SAY: ~~She's already gotten it last month~~.

■ Researchers **have** *already* **discovered** cures for many diseases.

■ They'**ve made** a lot of progress *already*.

2. Use the **present perfect** with *not yet* to talk about things that <u>have not happened before now</u>.

Notice that *yet* usually comes at the end of the clause.

Yet can also come between *have not* and the past participle.

■ They **have***n't* **discovered** a cure for the common cold *yet*, but they hope to discover one in the future.

■ The flu season **hasn't arrived** *yet*.

■ They **haven't** *yet* **discovered** a cure for the common cold.

3. We usually use *yet* **in questions** to find out if something has happened <u>before now</u>.

USAGE NOTE: Sometimes we use *already* **in a question** to express surprise that something happened sooner than expected.

■ **Has** your son **gotten** his flu shot *yet*?

■ **Has** he *already* **gotten** his flu shot? The flu season hasn't begun yet.

1 **MATCH •** *Each cause has a probable result. Match the cause with the appropriate result.*

Cause		Result
_e_ **1.** Tom has already gotten his flu shot, so he probably		**a.** is really hungry.
		b. may get the flu.
____ **2.** Dr. Meier has already finished his interview, so he		**c.** has left the TV studio.
		d. isn't very hungry.
____ **3.** Dr. Meier hasn't had lunch yet, so he		**e.** won't get the flu this year.
____ **4.** Randy hasn't gotten his shot yet, so he		
____ **5.** Randy has already had lunch, so he		

2 **COMPLETE •** *Read these questions and answers from a magazine article. Complete them with the present perfect form of the verbs in parentheses plus **already** or **yet**. Use short answers.*

smallpox vaccine	tetanus vaccine	flu vaccine	polio vaccine	measles vaccine	world smallpox vaccination program	last case of smallpox	AIDS vaccine	cancer vaccine	malaria vaccine	common cold vaccine
1796	1880	1945	1954	1963	1966	1980	NOW			

Q: We plan to travel to the rain forest next year. _____Have_____ they

_____found_____ a malaria vaccine _____yet_____?
1. (find)

A: _____No_____, they _____haven't_____. Talk to your doctor about ways to
2.

prevent this disease.

Q: My doctor told me I won't need another smallpox vaccination. I was surprised.

_____ smallpox completely _____?
3. (disappear)

A: _____, it _____.
4.

Q: They _____ vaccines against the flu. What about the common cold?
5. (develop)

A: No. Because there are so many different cold viruses, they _____ to
6. (not be able)

develop a vaccine _____.

Q: There has been so much cancer research. _____ anyone

_____ a successful vaccine _____?
7. (make)

A: _____ they _____. Researchers *have* made a lot of
8.

progress in recent years, however.

DESCRIBE • *Dr. Helmut Meier and his wife, Gisela, are planning a party. Look at their To Do lists and the pictures of their kitchen and dining room. Cross out the chores they have already done. Then write sentences about each item on their To Do lists.*

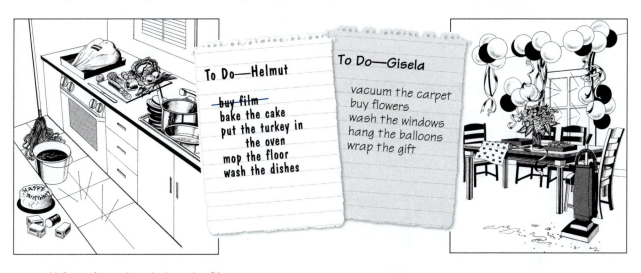

To Do—Helmut

~~buy film~~
bake the cake
put the turkey in
    the oven
mop the floor
wash the dishes

To Do—Gisela

vacuum the carpet
buy flowers
wash the windows
hang the balloons
wrap the gift

1. Helmut has already bought film. _____

2. Gisela hasn't vacuumed the carpet yet. _____

3. _____

4. _____

5. _____

6. _____

7. _____

8. _____

9. _____

10. _____

EDIT • *Read this note from Gisela to Helmut. Find and correct six mistakes in the use of the present perfect with* **already** *and* **yet**. *The first mistake is already corrected.*

>   gone
> Helmut—I'm in a hurry. I haven't ~~went~~ shopping already, but I'll do it on the way home. Rita
> have already had dinner and she's already had her bath. Have you call Mr. Jacobson yet?
> He's called already three times today. His daughter has gotten her flu shot yet. Is it too
> late? See you later.   G.

UNIT 13

Present Perfect:
Indefinite Past

What's new on "Feldstein"?

Tune in Channel 4 tonight at 8:00 and find out!

*I've recently **moved** in with my parents.*

*I've just **thought** of this crazy new idea!*

*Have you **ever** met anyone like us before?*

*I've **met** someone new. Again.*

CHECK **POINT**

Check the correct answer.

The "Feldstein" cast is talking about things of importance to them

☐ now.

☐ in the past.

CHART CHECK 1

Circle T (True) or F (False).

T F You can use the present perfect without mentioning a specific time.

STATEMENTS				
SUBJECT	**HAVE**	**(NOT)**	**PAST PARTICIPLE**	
They	have	(not)	**appeared**	on TV.
It	has		**been**	

For a complete presentation of present perfect forms, see Unit 11, pages 46–47.

CHART CHECK 2

Check the correct answer.

Never and ***just*** come:

☐ before the past participle

☐ at the end of the statement

STATEMENTS WITH ADVERBS					
SUBJECT	**HAVE (NOT)**	**ADVERB**	**PAST PARTICIPLE**		**ADVERB**
They	have	*never* *just* *recently*	**appeared**	on TV.	
It	has		**been**		
They	have (not)		**appeared**	on TV	*lately.* *recently.*
It	has (not)		**been**		

54

CHART CHECK 3 →

Circle T (True) or F (False).

T   F   *Ever* has to be used in *yes/no* questions.

YES/NO QUESTIONS			
HAVE	SUBJECT	(*EVER*)	PAST PARTICIPLE
Have	they	(*ever*)	**acted**?
Has	she		**won**?

SHORT ANSWERS					
AFFIRMATIVE			NEGATIVE		
Yes,	they	**have.**	No,	they	**haven't.**
	she	**has.**		she	**hasn't.**

WH- QUESTIONS				
WH- WORD	*HAVE*	SUBJECT	PAST PARTICIPLE	
How often	**have**	they	**acted**	on this show?
Why	**has**	it	**won**	an award?

EXPRESS `CHECK`

Unscramble these words to form a question. Answer the question.

you • watched • Have • "The Simpsons" • ever

_____? _____

Grammar Explanations

1. Use the **present perfect** to talk about things that happened at an <u>indefinite time in the past</u>. You can use the present perfect when you don't know when something happened or when the specific time is not important.

2. You can use *ever* with the **present perfect** to <u>ask questions</u>. It means at *any time up until now*.

Use *never* to <u>answer negatively</u>.

3. Use the **present perfect** with *just*, *recently*, or *lately* to talk about events in the <u>very recent past</u>.

USAGE NOTE: In <u>spoken American English</u> people often use *just* and *recently* with the simple past tense to talk about indefinite time.

▶ **BE CAREFUL!** Do not use *just*, *recently*, or *lately* with the present perfect and a specific past time expression.

Examples

- They**'ve won** several awards.
- I**'ve interviewed** the whole cast.
- She**'s been** in a Hollywood movie.
- I**'ve seen** his show many times.

A: Have you **won** an award?
OR
Have you *ever* **won** an award?
B: No, I**'ve** *never* **won** one.
OR
No, *never*.

- We**'ve** *just* **gotten** back from Los Angeles.
- I**'ve** *recently* **signed** a contract to write a book.
- He **hasn't had** time *lately*.

- We *just* **got** back from Los Angeles.

- I**'ve** *recently* **gotten** back from Los Angeles.
NOT I've recently gotten back from Los Angeles last Monday.

1 **TRUE OR FALSE** • *Read each numbered sentence. Write T (True) or F (False) for the statement that follows.*

1. I've recently joined the show.

___T___ I am a new cast member.

2. I have never been to Los Angeles.

_____ I went to Los Angeles a long time ago.

3. I've just finished Jimmy's book.

_____ I finished it a little while ago.

4. Have you ever seen this movie?

_____ I want to know when you saw the movie.

5. Arlene asks you, "Have you read any good books lately?"

_____ Arlene wants to know about a book you read last year.

6. She's visited New York several times.

_____ This is her first visit to New York.

7. She has become very popular.

_____ She is popular now.

2 **CHOOSE & COMPLETE** • *Read this script from a scene from "Feldstein." Complete it with the present perfect form of the verbs in the box. Some verbs are used more than once.*

have	make	stop	talk	travel	want

URSULA: This is a nice restaurant. _____Have_____ you _____had_____ the steak?
                                                                            1.

JIMMY: No, but I _____ the spaghetti. I always have that. Actually
                        2.

I _____ eating meat. It's not that I love animals. I just hate
        3.

plants. _____ you ever really _____ to a plant?
                                                          4.

They have absolutely nothing to say.

URSULA: Right. So, _____ you ever_____ to live outside
                                                        5.

of New York?

JIMMY: Outside of New York? Where's that? But seriously, I _____

never _____ to try another place. I love it here.
          6.

URSULA: But _____ you ever _____ to a different city?
                                                  7.

JIMMY: No. Why should I do that? You like it here too, right?

URSULA: It's OK, but I _____ to other places too. It's a big world!
                          8.

JIMMY: I like it right here. Say, _____ you _____ plans
                                                                    9.

for tomorrow night? How about dinner? Same time, same place . . .

3 **ASK & ANSWER •** *Complete the XYZ Network online interview with Jake Stewart, the actor who plays the part of Gizmo on Jimmy's show. Use the words in parentheses and the present perfect form of the verb.*

XYZ: Welcome to Live Studio, Jake. You've become very famous.

       <u>How many online interviews have you done?</u>
               1. (How many / online interviews / do?)

JAKE: None! _____. Very exciting!
              2. (never even / be/ in a chat room)

XYZ: _____
              3. (How / change / as an actor?)

JAKE: I work with a group, so _____
              4. (become / a better team player lately)

XYZ: As a comic actor, _____
              5. (who / be / your role model?)

JAKE: Hard to say. _____
              6. (Charlie Chaplin / have / great influence on me)

XYZ: _____
              7. (What / be / your best moment on this show?)

JAKE: Well, you know, _____. That was fantastic.
              8. (Jimmy / just / win / the Emmy)

XYZ: All in all, _____
              9. (what / find / most rewarding about this experience?)

JAKE: Free coffee! No, really, _____
              10. (meet / some fantastic people on this show)

4 **EDIT •** *Read this message from an online message board. Find and correct seven mistakes in the use of the present perfect. The first mistake is already corrected.*

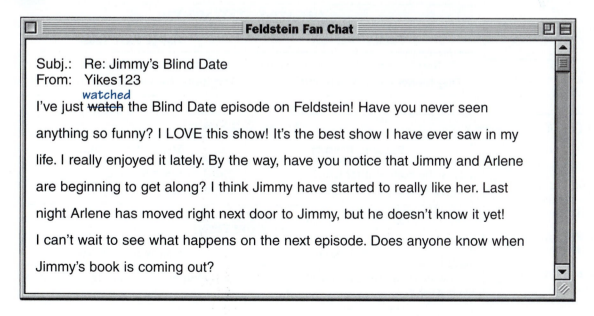

Feldstein Fan Chat

Subj.: Re: Jimmy's Blind Date
From: Yikes123

I've just ~~watch~~ ^{watched} the Blind Date episode on Feldstein! Have you never seen anything so funny? I LOVE this show! It's the best show I have ever saw in my life. I really enjoyed it lately. By the way, have you notice that Jimmy and Arlene are beginning to get along? I think Jimmy have started to really like her. Last night Arlene has moved right next door to Jimmy, but he doesn't know it yet! I can't wait to see what happens on the next episode. Does anyone know when Jimmy's book is coming out?

UNIT 14

Present Perfect and Simple Past Tense

I can't stand this commuter marriage! I've only seen you twice this month.

Yeah . . . This month has been bad . . . But last month was better. We saw each other four times!

Circle T (True) or F (False).

T F The husband and wife live in different cities.

CHART CHECK 1

Check the correct answer.

Use **have** to form

☐ the simple past tense.

☐ the present perfect.

AFFIRMATIVE STATEMENTS

PRESENT PERFECT	SIMPLE PAST TENSE
She**'s owned** the business since 1996. They**'ve met** twice this month.	She **owned** the business from '96 to '98. They **met** twice last month.

NEGATIVE STATEMENTS

PRESENT PERFECT	SIMPLE PAST TENSE
She **hasn't owned** the business for long. They **haven't met** this month.	She **didn't own** the business for long. They **didn't meet** last month.

CHART CHECK 2

Check the correct answer.

Questions in the present perfect are formed with:

☐ **have** + base form of verb

☐ **have** + past participle

YES/NO QUESTIONS

PRESENT PERFECT	SIMPLE PAST TENSE
Has she **owned** it for long? **Have** they **met** this month?	**Did** she **own** it for long? **Did** they **meet** last month?

WH- QUESTIONS

PRESENT PERFECT	SIMPLE PAST TENSE
How long **has** she **owned** it? When **have** they **met** this month?	How long **did** she **own** it? When **did** they **meet** last month?

58

EXPRESS CHECK

Circle the correct words to complete these sentences.

They <u>have met / met</u> in 1989. They <u>have been / were</u> married since 1990.

Grammar Explanations	**Examples**

1. The **present perfect** is used to talk about things that started in the past, <u>continue up to the present</u>, and may continue into the future.

The **simple past tense** is used to talk about things that happened in the past and <u>have no connection to the present</u>.

- ■ They **have lived** apart for the past three years. *(They started living apart three years ago, and they are still living apart.)*

- ■ They **lived** apart for three years. *(They lived apart until 2000. They no longer live apart.)*

2. The **present perfect** is used to talk about things that happened at <u>an unspecified time in the past</u>.

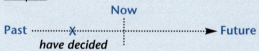

The **simple past tense** is used to talk about things that happened <u>at a specific past time</u>. The time is often stated.

- ■ They **have decided** to travel back and forth. *(We don't know exactly when they decided, or the time is not important.)*

- ■ They **lived** apart *in 1998*. *(We know when they lived apart and can state the exact time.)*

3. The **present perfect** is used to talk about things that have happened in a <u>period of time that is not finished</u>, such as *today*, *this month*, *this year*.

The **simple past tense** is used to talk about things that happened in a <u>period of time that is finished</u>, such as *yesterday*, *last month*, *last year*, and *this morning* when it is after 12 P.M.

- ■ I**'ve had** three cups of coffee *this morning*. *(It's still this morning. I might have more.)*

- ■ I **had** three cups of coffee *yesterday*. *(Yesterday is finished.)*

- ■ I **had** three cups of coffee *this morning*. *(It's now 2 P.M. This morning is finished.)*

1 **IDENTIFY** • *Read about Joe and Maria. Circle the verbs in the present perfect. Underline the simple past tense verbs.*

Many modern marriages are finding interesting solutions to difficult problems. Joe and Maria, for example, (have been) married since 1995. After their wedding, the couple <u>settled</u> down in Boston, where Maria opened an accounting business. Then in 1997 Joe lost his job. By that time, Maria's new business was booming, so they didn't consider moving. Joe never found a new job in Boston, but in 1998, he got a great offer on the other side of the country—in Los Angeles. The couple has lived apart ever since. How have they handled this "commuter marriage" up to now? Joe notes, "It certainly hasn't been easy. We've been geographically separated, but we've grown a lot closer emotionally. For that reason, it's been worth it."

TRUE OR FALSE • *Now write T (True) or F (False) for each statement.*

__F__ **1.** Joe and Maria are divorced.

_____ **2.** Maria started her own business in Boston.

_____ **3.** The couple used to live apart.

_____ **4.** In 1997, they thought about moving.

_____ **5.** The couple is now closer emotionally.

2 **COMPLETE** • *Joe is calling Maria. Complete their conversation with the correct form of the verbs in parentheses and with short answers. Choose between the present perfect and the simple past tense.*

JOE: Hi, honey. _____Did_____ you _____finish_____ that report yesterday?
                                          1. (finish)

MARIA: ___No, I didn't___. I'm still writing it, and I _____ worrying
            2.   **3.** (not stop)
about it all week.

JOE: Besides that, how _____ the week _____ so far?
                                                        4. (be)

MARIA: OK, I guess. I'm a little tired. I only _____ a few hours last night.
                                                  5. (sleep)

JOE: It sounds like you _____ much rest this week. Listen—we
                              6. (not get)
_____ each other only twice this month. I'll come tomorrow.
7. (see)

MARIA: OK, but I still have to work. Last time I _____ any work.
                                                    8. (not do)

JOE: Right! And it _____ us at all, remember? Listen, why don't you

9. (not bother)

relax now? _____ you _____ that special coffee yet?

10. (try)

MARIA: _____. In fact, I _____ five cups today, and it's still

11.   12. (drink)

early. And yesterday I _____ at least six. I'm really wired now.

13. (drink)

JOE: Then have some herbal tea, and I'll see you tomorrow.

3   **ASK & ANSWER** • Lifestyle Magazine (LM) *is interviewing Joe and Maria. Complete the interview using the words in parentheses and information from Exercise 1. Choose between the present perfect and the simple past tense.*

LM: When did you get married? _____

1. (When / get married?)

JOE: We got married in 1995. _____

2.

LM: Did you live in Boston after that? _____

3. (live / in Boston after that?)

MARIA: Yes, we did. _____

4.

LM: _____

5. (start your business / before your marriage?)

MARIA: _____

6.

LM: _____

7. (How long / own your own business?)

MARIA: _____

8.

LM: _____

9. (When / you / find your job in Los Angeles?)

JOE: _____

10.

LM: _____

11. (your commuter marriage / be very difficult?)

MARIA: _____!

12.

4   **EDIT** • *Read this entry from Maria's journal. Find and correct six mistakes in the use of the present perfect and the simple past tense. The first mistake is already corrected.*

Thursday, December 28

       's been

It's 8:00 P.M. It ~~was~~ a hard week, and it's not over yet! I still have to finish that report. I've started

it last Monday, but so far, I've wrote only five pages. And it's due next week! Work was so difficult

lately. I've worked late every night this week. I'm tired, and I haven't gotten much sleep last night.

I miss Joe. I've seen him last weekend, but it seems like a long time ago.

Present Perfect Progressive

You've been **playing** with Patti the Platypus again!

Ty Warner **has been making** Beanie Babies since 1993, and people **have been collecting** them since then.

CHECK POINT

Check the correct sentence.

☐ Ty Warner doesn't make Beanie Babies anymore.

☐ People are still collecting Beanie Babies.

CHART CHECK 1

Circle T (True) or F (False).

T F The present perfect progressive always has the word **been**.

STATEMENTS

SUBJECT	HAVE	(NOT)	BEEN	BASE FORM OF VERB + -ING		SINCE/FOR
I/We/You*/They	**have**	(not)	**been**	**collecting** **making**	toys them	**since** 1992. **for** a long time.
He/She/It	**has**					

You is both singular and plural.

CHART CHECK 2

Check the correct answer.

In questions, which parts of the verb come after the subject?

☐ *have been*

☐ *been* + base form + *-ing*

YES/NO QUESTIONS

HAVE	SUBJECT	BEEN	BASE FORM + -ING		SINCE/FOR
Have	you	**been**	**collecting** **making**	toys them	**since** 1992? **for** a long time?
Has	he				

SHORT ANSWERS

AFFIRMATIVE			NEGATIVE		
Yes,	we	**have.**	**No,**	we	**haven't.**
	he	**has.**		he	**hasn't.**

WH- QUESTIONS					
WH- WORD	**HAVE**	**SUBJECT**	**BEEN**	**BASE FORM + -ING**	
How long	**have**	you	**been**	**collecting**	toys?
	has	he		**making**	them?

EXPRESS CHECK

Complete these conversations.

A: How long _____ he been living here?

B: _____ a long time.

A: I've _____ collecting coins since last year.

B: Really? Have you been _____ foreign coins?

Grammar Explanations

Examples

1. Use the **present perfect progressive** to talk about things that started in the past and <u>continue up to the present</u>. The situation is usually not finished, and it will probably continue into the future.

Now

Past ···▶ Future
have been collecting

REMEMBER! Non-action verbs are usually not used in the progressive.

■ I**'ve been collecting** Beanie Babies for four years. *(I started collecting them four years ago, and I'm still collecting them.)*

■ I**'ve owned** this doll for years. NOT I've been owning this doll for years.

2. Use the **present perfect progressive** to describe things that have <u>stopped very recently</u>. The action is not happening right now, but you <u>can still see the results</u> of the action.

■ The kids **have been playing** here. Their toys are all over the room.
■ It**'s been raining**. The streets are still wet.

Check it out!
For a list of common non-action verbs, see Appendix 2 on page 337.

1 **CHOOSE** • *Read each numbered statement. Then circle the letter of the sentence (a) or (b) that best describes the information in the statement.*

1. Gina has been collecting stamps since high school.

    a. Gina stopped collecting stamps.

    (b.) Gina still collects stamps.

2. Enrico has been writing an article about toys.

    a. The article is finished.

    b. The article isn't finished yet.

3. They've been selling a lot of Pokémon toys.

    a. People are still buying Pokémon toys.

    b. The Pokémon fad is finished.

4. Enrico looked out the window and said, "It's been raining."

    a. It's definitely still raining.

    b. It's possible that it stopped raining a little while ago.

5. It's been raining since 6:00.

    a. It's still raining.

    b. It stopped raining a little while ago.

6. They've been playing for hours.

    a. They stopped playing.

    b. They're still playing.

2 **COMPLETE** • *Enrico Sanchez (ES) interviewed the manager of Toys and Us (TAU). Complete the interview with the present perfect progressive form of the verbs in parentheses. Use short answers when appropriate.*

ES: So, _____ have _____ you _____ been selling _____ a lot of toys this season?
    1. (sell)

TAU: _____ Yes, we have _____, Enrico. In fact, Pokémon toys and games _____
    2.   **3.** (fly)

out of the store. They're our most popular item right now.

ES: In case one of our viewers _____ on Mars, could you explain
    4. (live)

what Pokémon toys are?

TAU: Haha. I bet the company _____ Pokémon to Mars too. This product
    5. (send)

started out in Japan as a computer game. Since 1996, the characters

_____ in collectors' cards, board games—you name it.
    6. (appear)

ES: Why _____ this fad _____ people all over the world?
    7. (attract)

TAU: Well, my husband _____ these products for our children because
    8. (choose)

the characters are cute and not violent. Maybe that's why.

ES: How about Power Rangers? _____ people _____ in
    9. (stand)

line for them?

TAU: _____. People _____ for Power Rangers very
    10.   **11.** (not ask)

much anymore.

3 **DESCRIBE •** *Look at the two pictures of journalist Enrico Sanchez. Write sentences describing what has been going on. Use the present perfect progressive form of the verbs in parentheses. Choose between affirmative and negative forms.*

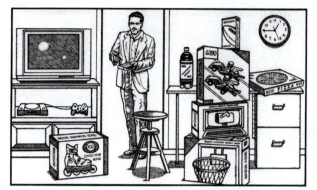

1. He's been doing research on new toys.
   _____
   (do research on new toys)

2. _____
   (test the inline skates)

3. _____
   (shoot baskets)

4. _____
   (eat pizza)

5. _____
   (drink soda)

6. _____
   (build a racing car)

7. _____
   (play video games)

8. _____
   (send e-mail messages)

4 **EDIT •** *Read the thank-you note. Find and correct six mistakes in the use of the present perfect progressive. The first mistake is already corrected.*

> Dear Aunt Toni,
>
> Thank you very much for the Pokémon cards. My friend and I have been ~~play~~ *playing*
>
> with them all day. So far, I am been winning. I really love Pokémon. My Mom been
>
> buying the toys for us because she thinks they're cute too. All my friends were
>
> collecting the cards for months now. Tonya loves the computer game you sent
>
> too. She've been asking me to play with her, but I've been having too much fun
>
> with my cards. How have you been? I've been thought about you a lot. I hope
>
> you can come and visit us soon.
>
> Love,
>
> Patrick

Present Perfect and Present Perfect Progressive

That woman has no manners. She**'s been following** me all day. She**'s taken** 100 rolls of film and **written** 42 pages of notes. But she **hasn't** even **given** me a single peanut!

CHECK *POINT*

Circle T (True) or F (False).

The woman is finished

T F following the elephant.

T F taking 100 rolls of film.

CHART CHECK

Circle T (True) or F (False).

T F In some sentences you can use either the present perfect or the present perfect progressive.

PRESENT PERFECT

Elephants **have roamed** the earth for thousands of years.

I**'ve read** two books about elephants.

Dr. Owen **has written** many articles.

She**'s lived** in many countries.

PRESENT PERFECT PROGRESSIVE

Elephants **have been roaming** the earth for thousands of years.

I**'ve been reading** this book since Monday.

She**'s been writing** articles since 1990.

She**'s been living** in France for a year.

EXPRESS CHECK

*Complete this conversation with the verb **eat** and a short answer.*

A: He's been _____ all morning!

B: What _____ he _____ eating?

A: Peanuts. He _____ eaten five bags of peanuts!

B: _____ he eaten the whole supply?

A: _____, he _____. There are still ten bags left.

Grammar Explanations	Examples
1. The **present perfect** often shows that something is <u>finished</u>. It focuses on the <u>result</u> of the action.  The **present perfect progressive** often shows that an activity is <u>unfinished</u>. It focuses on the <u>continuation</u> of an action. 	■ I**'ve read** a book about elephants. *(I finished the book.)* ■ She**'s written** an article. *(She finished the article.)* ■ I**'ve been reading** a book about elephants. *(I'm still reading it.)* ■ She**'s been writing** an article. *(She's still writing it.)*
2. We often use the **present perfect** to talk about — <u>how much</u> someone has done. — <u>how many times</u> someone has done something. — <u>how many things</u> someone has done. We often use the **present perfect progressive** to talk about <u>how long</u> something has been happening. ▶ **Be careful!** We usually do not use the present perfect progressive when we mention a <u>number</u> of completed events.	■ I**'ve read** *a lot* about it. ■ I**'ve been** to Africa *twice*. ■ She**'s written** *three* articles. ■ I**'ve been reading** books on elephants *for two months*. ■ I**'ve read** that book *twice*. Not ~~I've been reading that book twice.~~
3. Sometimes you can use either the **present perfect** OR the **present perfect progressive**. The meaning is basically the same. This is especially true when you use verbs such as *live*, *work*, *study*, and *teach* with *for* or *since*.	■ She**'s studied** elephants *for* two years. OR ■ She**'s been studying** elephants *for* two years. *(In both cases, she started studying elephants two years ago and she is still studying them.)*

TRUE OR FALSE • *Read each numbered sentence. Write T (True) or F (False) for the statement that follows.*

1. Professor Owen has been reading a book about elephants.

    __F__   She finished the book.

2. She's read a book about elephants.

    _____   She finished the book.

3. She's written a magazine article about the rain forest.

    _____   She finished the article.

4. She's been waiting for some supplies.

    _____   She received the supplies.

5. They've lived in Uganda since 1992.

    _____   They are still in Uganda.

6. They've been living in Uganda since 1992.

    _____   They still live in Uganda.

CHOOSE • *Here are some statements about Professor Owen's work. Circle the correct form of the verbs to complete these statements. In some cases, both forms are correct.*

1. Professor Owen is working on two articles for *National Wildlife Magazine*. She has written / (has been writing) these articles since Monday.

2. *National Wildlife Magazine* has published / has been publishing its annual report on the environment. It's an excellent report.

3. Five hundred and sixty African elephants have already died / have been dying this year.

4. Professor Owen has given / has been giving many talks about wildlife preservation in past lecture series.

5. She has spoken / has been speaking at our school many times.

6. Professor Owen was late for a meeting. When she arrived the chairperson said, "At last, you're here. We have waited / have been waiting for you."

7. Professor Owen has lived / has been living in England for the last two years.

8. She has worked / has been working with environmentalists in England and France.

9. Congress has created / has been creating a new study group to discuss the problem of endangered animals. The group has already met twice.

3 **COMPLETE** • *Read this entry from Dr. Owen's field journal about an elephant she calls Grandad. Use the present perfect or the present perfect progressive form of the verbs in parentheses.*

We _____ **'ve been hearing** _____ about Grandad since we arrived here in
    1. (hear)

Amboseli Park. He is one of the last "tuskers." Two days ago, we finally saw him. His tusks

are more than seven feet long. I _____ never _____ anything like them.
    2. (see)

Grandad _____ here for more than sixty years. He
    3. (live)

_____ everything, and he _____
    4. (experience)   **5. (survive)**

countless threats from human beings. Young men _____ their
                          6. (test)

courage against him, and poachers _____ him for his ivory.
                        7. (hunt)

His experience and courage _____ him so far.
                   8. (save)

For the last two days, he _____ slowly through the tall
                9. (move)

grass. He _____ and _____.
    10. (eat)   **11. (rest)**

Luckily, it _____ a lot this year, and even the biggest elephants
    12. (rain)

_____ enough food and water.
    13. (find)

4 **EDIT** • *Read this student's report. Find and correct six mistakes in the use of the present perfect and present perfect progressive. The first mistake is already corrected.*

                              living
    Elephants and their ancestors have been ~~live~~ on this planet for 5 million years.

Scientists have found their bones in many places, from Asia to North America.

Present-day elephants has also survived in different kinds of environments, including

very dry areas in Niger, grasslands in East Africa, and forests in West Africa.

    Because of their great size and strength, elephants have always fascinating

humans. Our fascination has almost caused African elephants to become extinct. Poachers

(illegal hunters) have already been killing hundreds of thousands of elephants for the

ivory of their tusks. After 1989 it became illegal to sell ivory. Since then, the elephant

population has been grown steadily. Recently several countries have been protecting

elephants in national parks, and herds have became larger and healthier.

Past Perfect

By the time I turned twelve, I **had** already **decided** on a career. I wanted to be paid to talk!

Talk-show host Oprah Winfrey with her TV audience.

CHECK POINT

Check the event that happened first.

☐ Oprah turned twelve.

☐ Oprah decided on a career.

CHART CHECK 1

Circle T (True) or F (False).

T F The past perfect uses **had** for all subjects.

STATEMENTS			
SUBJECT	**HAD (NOT)**	**PAST PARTICIPLE**	
I/He/She/We/You*/They	had (not)	**decided**	by then.
It		**been**	easy.

*You is both singular and plural.

CHART CHECK 2

Check the correct answer.

In past perfect questions, where does **had** go?

☐ before the subject
☐ after the subject

YES/NO QUESTIONS			
HAD	**SUBJECT**	**PAST PARTICIPLE**	
Had	she	**decided**	by then?
	it	**been**	easy?

SHORT ANSWERS					
AFFIRMATIVE			**NEGATIVE**		
Yes,	she / it	had.	No,	she / it	hadn't.

WH- QUESTIONS				
WH- WORD	**HAD**	**SUBJECT**	**PAST PARTICIPLE**	
Why	had	she	**decided**	to be a talk-show host?
		it	**been**	easy?

EXPRESS CHECK

Complete this conversation with the verb **arrive**.

A: Had she _____ by 9:00?

B: No, she _____ .

Grammar Explanations

Examples

1. Use the **past perfect** to show that something happened <u>before a specific time in the past</u>. *became famous* **Now** Past ┈┈x┈┈┈┈x┄┊┈┈┈┈┈➤ Future 　　　　　　　*1988*	■ By 1988 Oprah Winfrey **had become** famous. ■ It was 1985. She **had** already **been** in a Hollywood film.
2. The **past perfect** always shows a <u>relationship with another past event</u>. Use the <u>past perfect for the earlier event</u>. Use the simple past tense for the later event. ▶ **BE CAREFUL!** In these sentences with *when*, notice the <u>difference in meaning</u> between the simple past tense and the past perfect.	■ In 1990 Oprah *invited* Matt on the show. He **had been** an author for two years. *(He was an author before 1990.)* ■ By the time Jill *got* home, "The Oprah Winfrey Show" **had finished**. ■ **When** the show ended, she **left**. *(First the show ended. Then she left.)* ■ **When** the show ended, she **had left**. *(First she left. Then the show ended.)*
3. *Already*, *yet*, *ever*, and *never* are often used with the past perfect to <u>emphasize the event which occurred first</u>.	■ I saw *The Color Purple* last night. I **had** *never* **seen** it before. ■ Jason **had** *already* **seen** it.
4. When the time relationship between two past events is clear, you can use the **simple past tense for both events**. The meaning is usually clear when you use *after*, *before*, or *as soon as* to connect the events.	■ *After* Oprah **had appeared** in *The Color Purple*, she **got** a part in another movie. OR ■ *After* Oprah **appeared** in *The Color Purple*, she **got** a part in another movie.
5. We often use the **past perfect** with *by* (a certain time).	■ *By 1966* Oprah **had decided** on a career.

1 **TRUE OR FALSE** • *Read each numbered sentence. Write T (True) or F (False) for the statement that follows.*

1. When I got home, "The Oprah Winfrey Show" started.

   __F__ First the Oprah show started. Then I got home.

2. When I got home, "The Oprah Winfrey Show" had started.

   _____ First the Oprah show started. Then I got home.

3. Oprah's guest had lost 100 pounds when she interviewed him.

   _____ The guest lost the weight before the interview.

4. By the end of the show, I had fallen asleep.

   _____ I fell asleep after the show.

5. When I went to bed, I had turned off the radio.

   _____ I turned off the radio after I went to bed.

6. By midnight, I had finished the magazine article.

   _____ I finished the article before midnight.

2 **COMPLETE** • *Look at some important events in Oprah Winfrey's career. Then complete the sentences below. Use the past perfect with **already** or **not yet**.*

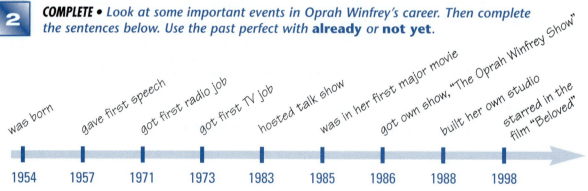

1. By 1958 Oprah _____had already given_____ her first speech.

2. By 1971 she _____ her first TV job.

3. By 1972 she _____ her first radio job.

4. By 1972 she _____ in a major movie.

5. By 1985 she _____ her own TV show.

6. By 1986 she _____ in a major movie.

7. By 1987 she _____ her own studio.

8. By 2000 she _____ in the film *Beloved*.

3 **ASK & ANSWER** • *Look at this typical daily schedule for a TV talk-show host. Complete the questions about his schedule. Use the past perfect and give short answers.*

7:00 A.M.	Arrive at studio
8:00	Review day's schedule
11:00	Discuss future shows with assistant producers
2:00 P.M.	Hair and makeup
2:30	Meet the day's guests
3:00	Tape the show
4:30	Work out with trainer

1. It was 7:45. The host was on schedule.

   A: ___Had he arrived___ at the studio yet?   **B:** ___Yes, he had.___

2. At 7:30 the host was at his desk.

   A: _____ the day's schedule yet?   **B:** _____

3. At 10:55 he was having coffee.

   A: _____ the schedule by that time?   **B:** _____

4. It was 2:00. He was on his way to makeup.

   A: _____ the day's guests by then?   **B:** _____

5. At 4:00 he had a late lunch.

   A: _____ the show yet?   **B:** _____

6. He went to bed at 10:30.

   A: _____ with his trainer that day?   **B:** _____

4 **EDIT** • *Read this student's report. There are six mistakes in the use of the past perfect. Find and correct them. The first mistake is already corrected.*

Oprah Winfrey is an amazing person! By the time she was twelve, she ~~has~~ already
                                                                          had
decided on a career. Not long afterward, she got her first radio job. Although she hadn't

have any experience, she became a news reporter. When she got her own TV talk show,

she has already acted in a major Hollywood movie. By the late 1980s "Oprah Winfrey"

had became a household word. Then in 1994 she decided to improve the quality of

talk-show themes. She also made a personal change. She had always had a weight

problem, but in 1995 TV viewers saw a new Winfrey. She had lost almost ninety

pounds as a result of dieting and working out. She had also compete in a marathon.

She has really been an inspiration to many people.

Past Perfect Progressive

By the time the last runner crossed the finish line, he **had been running** 7 hours, 16 minutes, and 24 seconds.

CHECK *POINT*

Circle T (True) or F (False).

T F   The race is finished.

CHART CHECK

Check the correct answer.

What form of **be** does the past perfect progressive always use?

☐ **was** or **were**

☐ **is**, **am**, or **are**

☐ **been**

STATEMENTS			
SUBJECT	**HAD (NOT) BEEN**	**BASE FORM OF VERB + -ING**	
I/He/She/It/We/You*/They	**had (not) been**	**running working**	all day.

You is both singular and plural.

YES/NO QUESTIONS				
HAD	**SUBJECT**	**BEEN**	**BASE FORM + -ING**	
Had	she	**been**	**running working**	all day?

SHORT ANSWERS	
AFFIRMATIVE	**NEGATIVE**
Yes, she **had**.	**No**, she **hadn't**.

WH- QUESTIONS				
WH- WORD	**HAD**	**SUBJECT**	**BEEN**	**BASE FORM + -ING**
How long Why	**had**	she	**been**	**running?** **working?**

EXPRESS CHECK

Complete this conversation with the past perfect progressive form of the verb **practice***.*

A: How long _____ she _____ when she entered the race?

B: She _____ for more than two years.

A: _____ she _____ alone?

B: No, she _____ . She _____ with a partner.

Grammar Explanations

Examples

1. Use the **past perfect progressive** to talk about an action that was <u>in progress before a specific time in the past</u>. The progressive emphasizes the <u>continuation</u> of an action, not the end result.

REMEMBER! Non-action verbs are not usually used in the progressive.

- It was 2:00 P.M. The runners **had been running** since 10:48 A.M.
- I finally saw Rob at 4:00 P.M. I **had been waiting** for hours.
- One runner fainted. She **hadn't been drinking** enough water.

- It was 5:00 P.M. He **had had** a headache all day. NOT He ~~had been having~~ a headache all day.

2. The **past perfect progressive** always shows a <u>relationship with another past event</u>.

Use the past perfect progressive for the <u>earlier event</u>. Use the simple past tense for the later event.

- She **had been practicing** for three years when she **entered** the race.
  (First she practiced. Then she entered the race.)

3. We often use the **past perfect progressive** to <u>draw conclusions</u> about past events based on evidence.

- She was out of breath. It was clear that she **had been running**.
- The streets were wet. It **had been raining**.

4. BE CAREFUL! In these sentences with **when**, notice the <u>difference in meaning</u> between the past progressive and the past perfect progressive.

- **When** the race started, it **was raining** and the streets were wet.
  (It was still raining during the race.)

- **When** the race started, it **had been raining** and the streets were wet.
  (It wasn't raining during the race. It had already stopped.)

1 **MATCH** • *Each result has a cause. Match the result with the correct cause.*

Result

b **1.** She was out of breath.

_____ **2.** The ground was wet.

_____ **3.** Her eyes were red.

_____ **4.** There was an open book on the couch.

_____ **5.** There were empty cans on the floor.

_____ **6.** The TV was on.

Cause

a. He had been reading.

b. She had been running.

c. They had been watching the race.

d. She had been crying.

e. It had been raining.

f. They had been drinking soda.

2 **COMPLETE** • *Read this story from a magazine article. Complete it with the past perfect progressive form of the verbs in parentheses.*

🏃 MARATHON RUNNING

BY BERNADINE MARTIN

On October 23, I ran the Boston Marathon with a partner, Marcia Davis. We ____**had been training**____
1. (train)
together since last year, and we

_____ to enter
2. (plan)
the race ever since we saw Oprah

in the Washington Marathon. The start of the race was dramatic. Up to that point, we

_____, but we were very serious when we lined up. I was so nervous
3. (joke and laugh)
I couldn't breathe. Marcia and I _____ on those same streets for a
4. (practice)
couple of weeks, so at the beginning we did well. By the time we got to Heartbreak Hill,

we _____ for almost four hours, and I really believed we could
5. (run)
finish. Then, halfway up the hill, Marcia stopped. She just couldn't run anymore.

We _____ to this race for so long that I didn't want to go on
6. (look forward)
alone, but Marcia wanted me to finish. When I got to the finish line, I saw Marcia. She

_____ for me for three hours. First we cried. Then we started talking
7. (wait)
about next year's marathon.

3 **CHOOSE & COMPLETE** • *The magazine* Runner's World *(RW) is interviewing marathon winner Paolo Esposito (PE). Complete the interview with the past perfect progressive form of the correct verbs from the box. Use short answers where appropriate.*

date	expect	live	~~practice~~	run

RW: You just won the marathon. _____Had you been practicing_____ long for it?
1.

PE: _____Yes, I had_____. For more than five years. First in Madrid,
2.
then in Rome.

RW: You tripped during the race. How long _____ when
3.
that happened?

PE: It was in the last hour. Luckily it didn't keep me from winning.

RW: I understand that you recently married your trainer, Emilia Leale. How long

_____ each other when you decided to get married?
4.

PE: About six months. We met in Rome and knew right away that we wanted to

be together.

RW: _____ in Rome for a long time when you met?
5.

PE: _____. In fact, I had just moved there.
6.

RW: When you crossed the finish line you looked very calm.

_____ to win?
7.

PE: _____! I was really surprised. And very happy.
8.

4 **EDIT** • *Read part of an entry from a runner's journal. Find and correct five mistakes in the use of the past perfect progressive. The first mistake is already corrected.*

October 19,

I just got back from the marathon! I'm tired but very happy. When I crossed the finish
                    had
line, I ~~have~~ been running for four hours and twenty-five minutes. Jeremy was standing

there. He had been waited for me the whole time. We were both soaking wet—I, because

I had been sweating; he, because it has been raining just a little while before. I was so

glad to see him. I had been look forward to this day for so long and hoping that I could

finish the race in less than four and a half hours. When I got home, I called my parents.

They had watching the marathon on TV and had actually seen me cross the finish line!

SelfTest

Circle the letter of the correct answer to complete each sentence.

EXAMPLE:

Jennifer never _____ coffee.   **A Ⓑ C D**
(A) drink   (C) is drinking
(B) drinks   (D) was drinking

---

1. He _____ for the Olympics since 1998.   **A B C D**
   (A) practiced   (C) has been practicing
   (B) practices   (D) was practicing

2. We've known Sally _____ a long time.   **A B C D**
   (A) since   (C) while
   (B) by   (D) for

3. We've been living in Montreal since we _____.   **A B C D**
   (A) have graduated   (C) graduated
   (B) have been graduating   (D) graduate

4. They haven't _____ an AIDS vaccine.   **A B C D**
   (A) yet developed   (C) developed already
   (B) developed yet   (D) already develop

5. _____ you reserved your hotel room yet?   **A B C D**
   (A) Did   (C) Do
   (B) Have   (D) Has

6. She hasn't _____ very often.   **A B C D**
   (A) flew   (C) flown
   (B) flies   (D) flying

7. It _____ and the ground was still white.   **A B C D**
   (A) snows   (C) would snow
   (B) had been snowing   (D) has snowed

8. Tina _____ last week.   **A B C D**
   (A) has arrived   (C) has been arriving
   (B) arrived   (D) arrives

9. They _____ here for three years before they moved.   **A B C D**
   (A) live   (C) had lived
   (B) have lived   (D) have been living

10. The show has _____ won an award.   **A B C D**
    (A) just   (C) lately
    (B) ever   (D) yet

11. Professor Kidd _____ three books since 1999, and she's working on her fourth. A B C D
   (A) has been writing   (C) wrote
   (B) has written   (D) writes

12. We _____ to buy that car yet. A B C D
   (A) haven't decided   (C) have decided
   (B) decided   (D) are deciding

13. —Has Maria called yet?
   —Yes, she _____. But she didn't leave a message. A B C D
   (A) did   (C) hasn't
   (B) called   (D) has

14. Since I _____ school, I haven't had much spare time. A B C D
   (A) begun   (C) have begun
   (B) began   (D) begin

SECTION TWO

Each sentence has four underlined words or phrases. The four underlined parts of the sentence are marked A, B, C, and D. Circle the letter of the one underlined word or phrase that is NOT CORRECT.

> **EXAMPLE:**
> Mike usually drives to school, but today he walks. A B C (D)
>   A   B   C   D

15. When she was younger, she has played tennis every day. A B C D
      A   B   C   D

16. It's already 10:00, but Teri hasn't finished her homework already. A B C D
      A   B   C   D

17. I've been worrying about you because you haven't been seeming A B C D
        A   B   C
   well lately.
       D

18. I've read a good book recently, but I haven't finished it yet. A B C D
      A   B   C   D

19. Did you written your paper, or have you been watching TV? A B C D
     A   B   C   D

20. Karl has been driving since ten years. A B C D
        A   B   C   D

21. We've been here only one day, but we've been taking three rolls of film. A B C D
       A   B   C   D

22. This hotel has been already in business for fifty years. A B C D
         A   B   C   D

23. How much coffee did you been drinking last night? A B C D
      A   B   C   D

24. I've been studying French since I've started high school. A B C D
         A   B   C   D

25. Before she became a film star, she has been a stand-up comedian. A B C D
         A   B   C   D

UNIT 19

Future:
Be going to and *Will*

Oh, no. It's going to rain! I'll get all wet!

WELCOME! SMART TRANSPORT CONFERENCE

CHECK **POINT**

Check the main point of the cartoon.

☐ The man forgot his umbrella.

☐ The man is going to fall into the hole.

CHART CHECK 1

Check the correct answer.

How many forms does *be* have in *be going to*?

☐ one

☐ two

☐ three

STATEMENTS: *BE GOING TO*				
SUBJECT	**BE***	**(NOT) GOING TO**	**BASE FORM OF VERB**	
I	**am**			
He/She/It	**is**	**(not) going to**	**leave**	soon.
We/You†/They	**are**			

*For contractions with *be*, see Appendix 24 on page 345.
†*You* is both singular and plural.

CHART CHECK 2

Circle T (True) or F (False).

T F In questions, a form of *be* goes after the subject.

YES/NO QUESTIONS: *BE GOING TO*			
BE	**SUBJECT**	**GOING TO**	**BASE FORM**
Am	I		
Is	he	**going to**	**leave** soon?
Are	you		

SHORT ANSWERS					
AFFIRMATIVE			**NEGATIVE**		
Yes,	you	**are.**	**No,**	you	**aren't.**
	he	**is.**		he	**isn't.**
	I	**am.**		I	**'m not.**

WH- QUESTIONS: *BE GOING TO*				
WH- WORD	**BE**	**SUBJECT**	**GOING TO**	**BASE FORM**
When Why	**am**	I		
	is	he	**going to**	**leave?**
	are	you		

CHART CHECK 3

Circle T (True) or F (False).

T F The form of **will** is the same for all subjects.

STATEMENTS: *WILL*			
SUBJECT	***WILL*** (NOT)	**BASE FORM**	
I/He/She/It/We/You/They	**will (not)**	**leave**	soon.

*For contractions with *will*, see Appendix 24 on page 345.

YES/NO QUESTIONS: *WILL*			
WILL	**SUBJECT**	**BASE FORM**	
Will	he	**leave**	soon?

SHORT ANSWERS	
AFFIRMATIVE	**NEGATIVE**
Yes, he **will**.	**No**, he **won't**.

WH- QUESTIONS: *WILL*			
WH- WORD	***WILL***	**SUBJECT**	**BASE FORM**
When	**will**	he	**leave**?

EXPRESS CHECK

Unscramble these words to form two sentences.

to • rain • It's • going _____

an • get • I'll • umbrella _____

Grammar Explanations

Examples

1. You can use **be going to** or **will** to talk about future <u>plans</u> or <u>predictions</u>.

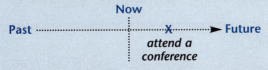

■ Professor Vroom **is going to attend** a conference next week.

OR

■ Professor Vroom **will attend** a conference next week.

■ I think it**'s going to be** very interesting.

OR

■ I think it**'ll be** very interesting.

2. Use **be going to** when there is <u>something in the present that leads to the prediction</u>.

Use **will** when you decide something at the <u>moment of speaking</u>.

■ Look at those dark clouds! It**'s going to rain**. NOT Look at those dark clouds! ~~It'll rain.~~

A: Professor Vroom is speaking at noon.
B: Oh. I think I**'ll go** to his talk.

PRONUNCIATION NOTE
In informal speech, **going to** is often pronounced "gonna." Do not write *gonna*.

Check it out!
There are other ways to talk about the future. See Unit 20, pages 84–85.

1 **READ** • *Look at Professor Harry Vroom's e-mail message.*

Harry's Travel Plans

Greg—Just a quick note to let you know my plans. I hear you're going to be in Madison next weekend. Unfortunately, I won't be there. That means I won't be able to go fishing with you on Saturday. I'm going to be in Chicago giving a speech at the Smart Transport conference. I attend every year, but this is the first time I'm going to give a speech. The conference is over on Saturday, but I'm not going to return to Madison until Sunday night. I'm going to take the train instead of driving, so I can get some work done. So, it doesn't look like we'll get to see each other this time. I hope next time works out better. —Harry

---

ANSWER • *Check all the things Harry Vroom is going to do next weekend.*

1. ☐ be in Madison
2. ☑ be in Chicago
3. ☐ go fishing

4. ☐ attend a conference
5. ☐ give a speech
6. ☐ return on Saturday

7. ☐ drive to Madison
8. ☐ see Greg

2 **DESCRIBE** • *Look at the pictures. They show events from a day in Professor Vroom's life. Write predictions or guesses. Use the words in the box and a form of **be going to** or **not be going to**.*

| answer the phone | drive | give a speech | ~~rain~~ | take a trip | watch TV |

1. It's going to rain.

2. _____

3. _____

4. _____

5. _____

6. _____

3 **COMPLETE •** *After his speech, Professor Vroom answered questions from the audience. Complete the questions and answers. Use the words in parentheses and **will** or **won't**.*

WOMAN 1: My question is this, Professor Vroom: _____ Will _____ the car of the

future _____ run _____ on gasoline?
1. (run)

VROOM: No, it _____ won't _____. It _____ probably
2.

_____ solar energy.
3. (use)

WOMAN 2: _____ we still _____ flat tires?
4. (get)

VROOM: No, we _____. By the year 2010, tires _____
5. **6. (have)**

a special seal so that they _____ themselves.
7. (repair)

MAN 1: In what other ways _____ cars _____ different?
8. (be)

VROOM: Well, instead of keys, cars _____ smart cards. These
9. (have)

_____ a lot like credit cards. They _____ doors
10. (look) **11. (open)**

and they _____ the seats, mirrors, and steering wheels. They
12. (adjust)

_____ even _____ the inside temperature.
13. (control)

MAN 1: _____ they _____ car thefts?
14. (prevent)

VROOM: Yes, they _____! Next question? That gentleman in the back.
15.

MAN 2: How much _____ these cars _____?
16. (cost)

VROOM: I don't know exactly, but they certainly _____ cheap.
17. (be)

 4 **EDIT •** *Read this e-mail message to Professor Vroom. Find and correct nine mistakes in the use of the future with **will** and **be going to**. The first mistake is already corrected.*

Re: Travel Plans

won't
Harry—I'm sorry that we ~~will no~~ be able to get together in Madison. Martha, too, will

misses you. Perhaps we can get together sometime next month. Martha and I am going

to be in Minneapolis until July 15. After that, we are going visit our son in Phoenix. His

wife is pregnant and will have a baby the first week in July. It's hard to believe that we're

gonna be grandparents!

How exciting that you going to talk at the conference! I'm sure it wills be great.

I've got to run now. The sky is getting really dark and it'll storm. I want to get out of this

office before then. More later. —Greg

Future: Contrast

CHART CHECK

Circle T (True) or F (False).

T F There are several ways to talk about the future.

T F You can't use the present tense to talk about the future.

AFFIRMATIVE STATEMENTS

We**'re going to leave**	
We**'ll leave**	
We**'re leaving**	for Mars soon.
We **leave**	

NEGATIVE STATEMENTS

We **aren't going to leave**	
We **won't leave**	
We **aren't leaving**	until 1:00.
We **don't leave**	

YES/NO QUESTIONS

Is she **going to leave**	
Will she **leave**	
Is she **leaving**	for Mars soon?
Does she **leave**	

SHORT ANSWERS

	she **is.**		she **isn't.**
Yes,	she **will.**	**No,**	she **won't.**
	she **is.**		she **isn't.**
	she **does.**		she **doesn't.**

WH- QUESTIONS

When **is** she **going to leave**	
When **will** she **leave**	
When **is** she **leaving**	for Mars?
When **does** she **leave**	

EXPRESS CHECK

Check the sentences that refer to the future.

☐ I'm leaving in five minutes.

☐ What time do you normally leave the office?

☐ Are you going to the conference in May?

☐ At the moment, I'm working on a report.

Grammar Explanations

Examples

1. Use *be going to*, *will*, the **present progressive**, and the **simple present tense** to talk about things in the future.

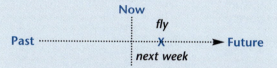

- ■ I**'m going to fly** to Mars next week.
- ■ I**'ll fly** to Mars next week.
- ■ I**'m flying** to Mars next week.
- ■ I **fly** to Mars next week.

2. USAGE NOTES: Sometimes only one form of the future is appropriate, but in many cases more than one form is possible.

   a. Use *be going to* or *will* to make <u>predictions or guesses</u>.

- ■ In a few years people **are going to fly** to Mars.
- ■ In a few years people **will fly** to Mars.

   b. Use *be going to* (not *will*) when <u>something in the present leads to a prediction</u>.

- ■ Look at that spaceship! It**'s going to land**! NOT ~~It will land~~.

   c. Use *be going to*, *will*, or the **present progressive** to talk about <u>future intentions or plans</u>.

- ■ Dr. Green **is going to speak** tomorrow.
- ■ Dr. Green **will speak** tomorrow.
- ■ Dr. Green **is speaking** tomorrow.

   d. We often use *will* when we decide something at the <u>moment of speaking</u>. We also use *will* to <u>make offers</u>.

- **A:** Dr. Green is giving a talk tomorrow.
- **B:** Oh! Maybe I**'ll go**.
- **A:** Great! I**'ll get** you a ticket.

   e. We often use the **present progressive** when we talk about <u>future plans that have already been arranged</u>. There is usually some reference to the future that shows that the event is not happening now.

- ■ I**'m flying** to Mars *next week*. I've already gotten a ticket.

   f. Use the **simple present tense** to talk about <u>scheduled future events</u> such as timetables, programs, and schedules.

- ■ The shuttle to Mars **leaves** at 10:00 A.M. *tomorrow*.
- ■ We **land** at midnight.

IDENTIFY • Professor Green is attending a conference this week. Read her conversation with Professor Russ. Underline all the verbs that refer to the future.

RUSS: Ellen! It's nice to see you. <u>Are</u> you <u>presenting</u> a paper this week?

GREEN: Hi, Rick. Yes. In fact, my talk starts at two o'clock.

RUSS: Oh, maybe I'll go. What are you going to talk about? Robots?

GREEN: Yes. I'm focusing on personal robots for household work.

RUSS: I'd like one of those! Where's your son, by the way? Is he here with you?

GREEN: No. Tony stays in Denver with his grandparents in the summer. I'm going to visit him after the conference. So, what are you working on these days?

RUSS: I'm still with the Mars Association. In fact, we're going to be holding a news conference next month about the Mars shuttle launch.

GREEN: That's exciting. Maybe I'll see you there.

RUSS: Great. The conference begins at noon on the tenth.

CHOOSE • Circle the most appropriate words to complete these conversations.

1. **GREEN:** Which project <u>do you work</u> / (are you going to work) on next?

   RUSS: I haven't decided for sure. Probably the Spacemobile.

2. **RUSS:** Look at those dark clouds!

   GREEN: Yes. It looks like <u>it's raining</u> / <u>it's going to rain</u> any minute.

3. **GREEN:** I'd better get back to my hotel room before the storm.

   RUSS: OK. <u>I'm seeing</u> / <u>I'll see</u> you later.

4. **DESK:** Professor Green, your son just called.

   GREEN: Oh, good. <u>I'll call</u> / <u>I'm calling</u> him back right away.

5. **GREEN:** Hi, honey. How's it going?

   TONY: Great. <u>I go</u> / <u>I'm going</u> fishing with Grandpa tomorrow.

6. **GREEN:** Have fun, but don't forget. You still have to finish that paper.

   TONY: I know, Mom. <u>I mail</u> / <u>I'm mailing</u> it tomorrow. I already have the envelope.

7. **TONY:** How's the conference?

   GREEN: Good. <u>I'm giving</u> / <u>I'll give</u> a talk this afternoon.

8. **TONY:** Good luck. When <u>are you</u> / <u>will you be</u> here?

   GREEN: Tomorrow. My plane <u>lands</u> / <u>will land</u> at 7:00, so <u>I see</u> / <u>I'll see</u> you about 8:00.

3 **COMPLETE** • *Read these conversations. Complete them with an appropriate form of the verbs in parentheses. (There is more than one correct answer for some items.)*

1. **A:** Hurry up! The shuttle _____ **leaves** _____ in just a few minutes.
   (leave)

   B: Oh, I'm sure they _____ for us.
   (wait)

2. **A:** Look at those storm clouds! Do you think it _____?
   (rain)

   B: I don't know. I _____ the weather forecast.
   (check)

3. **A:** When _____ we _____ the shuttle?
   (board)

   B: We _____ first class, so we should be among the first
   (fly)

   to board.

4. **A:** Wow! This suitcase is heavy.

   B: I _____ it for you. Give it to me.
   (carry)

5. **A:** What time _____ we _____ on Mars?
   (land)

   B: According to the schedule, at 9:00 A.M., but I think we _____
   (be)

   a little late.

6. **A:** I'm hungry. I hope we _____ some food soon.
   (get)

   B: Me too. I _____ the seafood special. I ordered it
   (have)

   in advance.

7. **A:** Look! The flight attendant is getting ready to announce something.

   B: Great. That means we _____ boarding soon.
   (start)

4 **EDIT** • *Read this flight announcement on the shuttle to Mars. Find and correct seven mistakes in the use of the future. The first mistake is already corrected. (There is often more than one way to correct a mistake).*

"Good evening, ladies and gentlemen. This ~~will be~~ your captain speaking. We be going
                                        is
to leave the Earth's gravity field in about fifteen minutes. At that time, you are able

to unbuckle your seat belts and float around the cabin. Host robots take orders for

dinner soon. After these storm clouds, we are having a smooth trip. The shuttle

arrives on Mars tomorrow at 9:00. Tonight's temperature on the planet is a mild

minus 20 degrees Celsius. By tomorrow morning the temperature is 18 degrees, but it

is feeling more like 28 degrees. Enjoy your flight."

UNIT 21

Future Time Clauses

When I grow up, I'm going to be a ballet dancer.

CHECK POINT

Check the correct answer.

☐ The child is talking about a present habit.

☐ The child is planning her future.

CHART CHECK

Circle T (True) or F (False).

T F The verb in the main clause is in the future.

T F The verb in the time clause is in the future.

STATEMENTS	
MAIN CLAUSE	**TIME CLAUSE**
I'**m going to be** a ballet dancer	*when* I **grow up**.
She'**ll join** a ballet company	*after* she **graduates**.

YES/NO QUESTIONS	
MAIN CLAUSE	**TIME CLAUSE**
Are you **going to be** a ballet dancer	*when* you **grow up**?
Will she **join** a ballet company	*after* she **graduates**?

SHORT ANSWERS			
AFFIRMATIVE		**NEGATIVE**	
Yes,	I **am**.	**No,**	I'**m not**.
	she **will**.		she **won't**.

WH- QUESTIONS		
MAIN CLAUSE		**TIME CLAUSE**
What	**are** you **going to be**	*when* you **grow up**?
	will she **do**	*after* she **graduates**?

EXPRESS CHECK

Unscramble these words to form a question and an answer.

be • What • grows up • she • when • will • she

_____

to • scientist • a • going • She's • be

_____

Grammar Explanations

Examples

1. When a sentence about future time has two clauses, the verb in the <u>main clause</u> is often in the **future** (*will* or *be going to*). The verb in the <u>time clause</u> is often in the **present tense**.

main clause   time clause
■ He'**ll look** for a job *when* he **graduates**.

▶ **BE CAREFUL!** Do not use *will* or *be going to* in a future time clause.

main clause   time clause
■ I'm going to work *after* I **graduate**.
NOT ~~after I will graduate~~.

The **time clause** can come at the beginning or the end of the sentence. The meaning is the same. Use a **comma** after the time clause when it comes at the <u>beginning</u>. Do not use a comma when it comes at the end.

■ *Before she applies*, she'll visit schools.
OR
■ She'll visit schools *before she applies*.
NOT ~~She'll visit schools, before she applies~~.

2. Here are some **common time expressions** you can use to begin future time clauses.

  a. *When*, *after*, and *as soon as* often introduce the <u>event that happens first</u>.

Now

graduate   look for a job

Past ⋯⋯⋯⋯⋯⋯X⋯⋯⋯⋯⋯⋯X⋯⋯⋯▶ Future

■ *When* I graduate, I'll look for a job.
■ *After* I graduate, I'll look for a job.
■ *As soon as* I graduate, I'll look for a job.
  (*First I'm going to graduate. Then I'll look for a job.*)

  b. *Before*, *until*, and *by the time* often introduce the <u>event that happens second</u>.

Now

finish school   get a job

Past ⋯⋯⋯⋯⋯⋯⋯⋯X⋯⋯⋯⋯X⋯⋯▶ Future

■ *Before* I get a job, I'll finish school.
■ *Until* I get a job, I'll stay in school.
■ *By the time* I get a job, I'll be out of school.
  (*First I'll finish school. Then I'll get a job.*)

  c. *While* introduces an event that will happen <u>at the same time</u> as another event.

Now

Past ⋯⋯⋯⋯⋯⋯⋯⋯⋯⋯⋯⋯⋯▶ Future

look for a job
continue to study

■ *While* I look for a job, I'll continue to study.
  (*I will look for a job and study during the same time period.*)

TRUE OR FALSE • *Read each numbered sentence. Write T (True) or F (False) for the statement that follows.*

1. Amber will open her own business when she finishes school.

   __F__ Amber will open her own business. Then she'll finish school.

2. Denzell won't quit until he finds another job.

   _____ Denzell will find another job. Then he'll quit.

3. Jake will retire as soon as he turns sixty.

   _____ Jake will retire. Then he'll turn sixty.

4. Marisa will call you when she gets home.

   _____ Marisa will get home. Then she'll call you.

5. While Li-jing is in school, she'll work part-time.

   _____ Li-jing will finish school. Then she'll get a part-time job.

6. By the time Marta gets her diploma, she'll be twenty-one.

   _____ Marta will turn twenty-one. Then she'll get her diploma.

2 **COMBINE** • *Read about Sandy and Jeff. Combine the sentences.*

1. Sandy and Jeff will get married. Then Sandy will graduate.

   __Sandy and Jeff will get married__ before __Sandy graduates.__

2. Jeff is going to get a raise. Then they are going to move to a larger apartment.

   _____ as soon as _____

3. They're going to move to a larger apartment. Then they're going to have a baby.

   After _____

4. They'll have their first child. Then Sandy will get a part-time job.

   _____ after _____

5. Their child will be two. Then Sandy will go back to work full-time.

   By the time _____

6. Sandy will work full-time. At the same time, Jeff will go to school.

   _____ while _____

7. Jeff will graduate. Then he'll find another job.

   _____ when _____

3 **COMPLETE** • *Look at this student's worksheet. Complete it with the correct form of the verbs in parentheses.*

GOAL PLANNING WORKSHEET

I. **Write your major goal.**

I __'ll get__ a job after I _____ .
   (get)   (graduate)

II. **List three benefits of achieving your goal.**

1. When I _____ a job, I _____ more money.
            (get)   (have)

2. When I _____ enough money, I _____ a used car.
            (save)   (buy)

3. I _____ happier when I _____ employed.
        (feel)   (be)

III. **How will you reach your goal? Write down smaller goals.**

1. As soon as I _____ in the morning, I _____ the
                 (get up)   (buy)
newspaper to look at the employment ads.

2. When I _____ to my friends, I _____ them if they
            (speak)   (ask)
know of any jobs.

3. I _____ at the job notices board when I _____ to
        (look)   (go)
the supermarket.

4. Before I _____ on an interview, I _____ my
              (go)   (improve)
computer skills.

---

4 **EDIT** • *Read this dancer's journal entry. Find and correct seven mistakes in the use of future time clauses. The first mistake is already corrected. Don't forget to check for commas!*

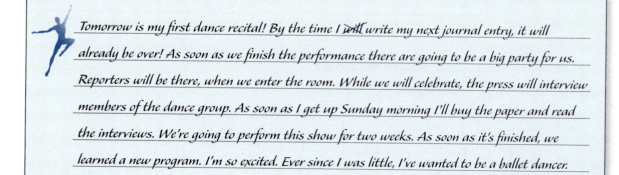

Tomorrow is my first dance recital! By the time I ~~will~~ write my next journal entry, it will already be over! As soon as we finish the performance there are going to be a big party for us. Reporters will be there, when we enter the room. While we will celebrate, the press will interview members of the dance group. As soon as I get up Sunday morning I'll buy the paper and read the interviews. We're going to perform this show for two weeks. As soon as it's finished, we learned a new program. I'm so excited. Ever since I was little, I've wanted to be a ballet dancer.

Future Progressive

*I'm sorry. I won't be here at 12:00. I'll **be** out **walking** the dog.*

CHECK *POINT*

Check the correct answer.

When will Robo take the dog out for a walk?

❏ before 12:00

❏ at 12:00

❏ after 12:00

CHART CHECK

Circle T (True) or F (False).

T F You can form the future progressive with **be going to** or **will** plus **be** and the base form of the verb + **-ing**.

STATEMENTS

SUBJECT	BE (NOT) GOING TO/ WILL (NOT)	BE + BASE FORM + -ING	
I	am (not) going to	be working	tomorrow.
He/She/It	is (not) going to	be working	
We/You/They	are (not) going to		
I/He/She/It/We/You/They	will (not)	be working	tomorrow.

YES/NO QUESTIONS

BE/WILL	SUBJECT	GOING TO	BE + BASE FORM + -ING	
Am	I	going to	be working	tomorrow?
Is	she			
Are	you			
Will	you		be working	tomorrow?

SHORT ANSWERS

AFFIRMATIVE		NEGATIVE	
Yes,	you **are**.	No,	you **aren't**.
	she **is**.		she **isn't**.
	I **am**.		I'm **not**.
	we **will**.		we **won't**.

WH- QUESTIONS				
WH- WORD	BE/WILL	SUBJECT	GOING TO	BE + BASE FORM + -ING
Where When	**is**	he	**going to**	**be working**?
	will	she		**be working**?

EXPRESS CHECK

Unscramble these words to form two questions. Answer the questions.

working • be • Will • tomorrow • you

_____?

_____.

you • be • What • doing • are • to • going

_____?

_____.

Grammar Explanations

Examples

1. Use the **future progressive** with **be going to** or *will* to talk about things that will be <u>in progress at a specific time in the future</u>.

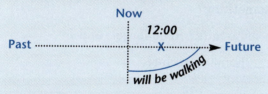

REMEMBER! Non-action verbs are not usually used in the progressive.

■ Robo **is going to be walking** the dog at noon.

OR

■ Robo **will be walking** the dog at noon.

■ You**'re going to have** a headache tomorrow morning.
NOT You're going to be having a headache tomorrow morning.

2. USAGE NOTE: We often use the future progressive to <u>hint that we would like someone to do us a favor</u>.

A: **Will** you **be going** by the post office tomorrow?
B: Yes. Do you need stamps?
A: Yes. Could you get me some?

3. Remember that if the sentence has a **time clause**, use the <u>simple present tense</u> or <u>present progressive</u> in the time clause, not the future or future progressive.

■ I**'ll be cooking** *while* the robot **is cleaning**.
NOT I'll be cooking while the robot will be cleaning.

1   **IDENTIFY** • *Read this paragraph. Underline all the future progressive forms.*

Today we find most robots working in factories around the world. But what <u>will</u> robots of the future <u>be doing</u>? One Massachusetts Institute of Technology designer predicts that in just a few years, small, intelligent robots are going to be taking care of all the household chores. This is going to make life a lot easier. While one robot is cooking dinner, another one will be vacuuming the floor. But what about outside the home? Will robots be playing football or fighting wars? Scientists aren't sure. What is certain, however, is that robots will be playing a more and more significant role in our lives.

2   **COMPLETE** • *Read these conversations. Complete them with the future progressive form of the words in parentheses and with short answers.*

1. **STUDENT:** _____Will_____ you _____be having_____ office
         a. (Will / have)
     hours today? I'd like to talk to you about my robotics paper.

    TEACHER: _____Yes, I will_____. I _____ to lunch
            b.   **c. (will / go)**
     at 2:00. But stop in anytime before then.

2. **MRS. GEE:** When _____ you _____ the office?
              a. (be going to / leave)

    MR. GEE: At 2:00. Why? Do we need something?

    MRS. GEE: Would you mind picking up some milk? Robo forgot, and I
     _____ home until late.
        b. (won't / get)

3. **TONY:** Dad, what time _____ you _____
              a. (be going to / come)
     home today? I need some help with my science project.

    MR. GEE: I _____ Mia to the dentist after work, but
       b. (will / take)
     I'll be back by 4:00.

    TONY: _____ we _____ dinner before
            c. (Be going to / have)
     Mom comes home?

    MR. GEE: _____. You know we always wait for Mom.
         d.

4. **SALESMAN:** I'm calling from Robotronics Inc. I _____ your
              a. (be going to / visit)
     neighborhood soon to demonstrate our new robot.

    ROBO: I'm sorry. The Gee family _____ a new robot
            b. (won't / buy)
     for a while.

3 **COMPLETE** • *Look at Robo's and Robota's schedules for tomorrow. Complete the statements.*

Robo	
8:00	make breakfast
9:00	dust bedrooms
10:00	do laundry
12:00	make lunch
1:00	give Mr. Gee a massage
5:00	help Tony with homework
7:00	play chess with Tony

Robota	
8:00	pay bills
9:00	vacuum living room
10:00	repaint kitchen
12:00	recycle the garbage
1:00	shop for food
5:00	make dinner
7:00	walk the dog

1. While Robo _____*is making breakfast*_____, Robota _____*will be paying bills.*_____

2. Robo _____ the bedrooms while Robota _____

3. Robota _____ the kitchen while Robo _____

4. While Robo _____ lunch, Robota _____

5. Robo _____ a massage while Robota _____

6. Robota _____ dinner while Robo _____

7. While Robo _____ chess, Robota _____

4 **EDIT** • *Read this student's paragraph. Find and correct seven mistakes in the use of the future progressive. The first mistake is already corrected.*

In the future, robots will be ~~perform~~ ^{performing} more and more tasks for humans. This will be having both positive and negative effects. On the one hand, while robots will be doing the boring and dangerous jobs, humans will be devoting more time to interesting pursuits. In this way robots is going to be making life a lot easier for humans. On the other hand, the widespread use of robots is going create a lot of future unemployment. People will losing their jobs as robots fill their positions. And some robots could even become dangerous. I'm afraid that in the not-too-distant future, robots will be operating nuclear power stations! And before too long, robots are going to be fight in wars. Although, on second thought, that will be better than humans killing each other!

UNIT 23

Future Perfect and Future Perfect Progressive

By February, he'll **have been saving** for three years and I'll be rich!

By February, I'll **have traded** Piggy for a shiny new Jaguar!

CHECK POINT

Check the correct answer.

☐ It's February.

☐ He hasn't been saving for three years yet.

CHART CHECK 1

Circle T (True) or F (False).

T F Both the future perfect and the future perfect progressive use **will have been**.

FUTURE PERFECT STATEMENTS

SUBJECT	WILL (NOT)	HAVE + PAST PARTICIPLE
I/He/She/It/We/You*/They	**will (not)**	**have saved** enough money by then.

You is both singular and plural.

FUTURE PERFECT PROGRESSIVE STATEMENTS

SUBJECT	WILL (NOT)	HAVE BEEN + BASE FORM + -ING
I/He/She/It/We/You/They	**will (not)**	**have been saving** for three years.

CHART CHECK 2

Circle T (True) or F (False).

T F Short answer forms are the same for the future perfect and the future perfect progressive.

FUTURE PERFECT YES/NO QUESTIONS

WILL	SUBJECT	HAVE + PAST PARTICIPLE
Will	he	**have saved** enough by then?

SHORT ANSWERS

AFFIRMATIVE	NEGATIVE
Yes, he **will**.	**No**, he **won't**.

FUTURE PERFECT PROGRESSIVE YES/NO QUESTIONS

WILL	SUBJECT	HAVE BEEN + BASE FORM + -ING
Will	he	**have been saving** for long?

SHORT ANSWERS

AFFIRMATIVE	NEGATIVE
Yes, he **will**.	**No**, he **won't**.

EXPRESS CHECK

Complete these sentences with the verb **drive***. Use one word for each blank.*

• By June, I'll have been _____ my new car for a year.

• I'll have _____ 10,000 miles by then.

Grammar Explanations

Examples

1. When we use the **future perfect**, we imagine a certain point of time in the future, and we <u>look back at events that will be completed by that time</u>.

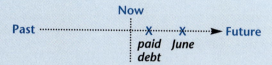

Use **by** + **time expression** to identify the point in time in the future.

Use **already** and **yet** to emphasize whether an event will have happened by a point in time.

■ By June, he **will have paid** his debt.
■ We **won't have saved** enough by then.

■ *By June*, she**'ll have bought** a used car.
■ She**'ll have looked** at a lot of cars *by then*.

■ By May, he**'ll have** *already* saved $1,000.
■ By May, he **won't have saved** $2,000 *yet*.

2. When we use the **future perfect progressive**, we imagine a certain point in the future, and we <u>look back on things already in progress</u>.

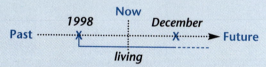

The **future perfect progressive** focuses on *how long* and often includes <u>the length of time</u>.

REMEMBER! Non-action verbs are not usually used in the progressive.

■ We moved here in 1998. By next December we **will have been living** here for several years.

■ We're moving to Paris next year. By 2005 we **will have been living** there for several years, and it should feel like home.

■ You**'ll have been speaking** French *for ten years* by then.

■ By May, he**'ll have owned** his car for a year. NOT ~~he'll have been owning his car . . .~~

3. Use the future perfect or the future perfect progressive **with the simple present tense** to show <u>the order of events</u>:

FIRST EVENT: future perfect (progressive)

SECOND EVENT: simple present tense

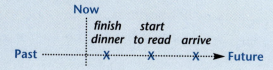

■ By the time you *arrive*, I**'ll have finished** dinner. NOT ~~By the time you will arrive,~~ I'll have finished dinner.

■ By the time you *arrive*, I**'ll have been reading** for an hour.

1 **TRUE OR FALSE** • *Read each numbered sentence. Write T (True) or F (False) for the statement that follows.*

1. By this time tomorrow, I'll have decided which car to buy.

   ___T___ I haven't decided yet which car I'm going to buy.

2. We'll have already finished the grocery shopping by the time you get home.

   _____ You will get home while we are shopping.

3. By next year, Mary will have been working at the newspaper for five years.

   _____ Next year, Mary can celebrate her fifth anniversary at the newspaper.

4. By ten o'clock, she won't have finished writing her column yet.

   _____ She will finish writing at ten o'clock.

5. We will have moved to a larger office by the year 2010.

   _____ We will move to a larger office after the year 2010.

6. By next year, we'll have been publishing the newsletter for fifteen years.

   _____ We started the newsletter less than fifteen years ago.

2 **COMPLETE** • *Look at the time line and complete the sentences about Tom and Linda's future accomplishments. Use the future perfect or the future perfect progressive form of the words in parentheses. Choose between affirmative and negative.*

| 2010 | 2011 | 2012 | 2013 | 2015 | 2017 | 2018 | 2022 |

1. By 2012, they _____'ll have bought_____ a new car.
                        (buy)
2. By 2015, they _____'ll have been living_____ in their own house for three years.
                        (live)
3. By Travis's first birthday, Tom _____.
                                        (graduate)
4. By 2017, Tom _____ school for four years.
                    (attend)
5. By 2019, they _____ another car.
                    (buy)
6. They _____ their old car for eight years by then.
              (drive)
7. By 2020, Linda _____ her business.
                      (open)
8. They _____ for two years by 2020.
              (save)
9. By retirement, the couple _____ a lot.
                                  (accomplish)

3 **COMPLETE** • *Read Linda Leone's (LL) interview with* Teenage Couples Magazine *(TC). Complete the interview with the correct form of the verbs in parentheses. Use the progressive form when possible. Use* **already** *or* **yet** *when appropriate.*

TC: You two are amazing! By the time you _____*get*_____ married,
1. (get)

you _____*'ll have already planned*_____ your whole life together!
2. (plan)

LL: Well, we've been dating since middle school. By the time we _____
3. (graduate)

from high school, we _____ about our marriage for a long time.
4. (think)

TC: When Travis _____, Tom _____
5. (be born) **6. (not graduate)**

from college _____. How will you manage with Tom still in school?

LL: It won't be easy, but we've got a plan. Tom _____ most
7. (finish)

of his courses by then. He'll stay home with the baby during the day and go to

night school.

TC: By the time you _____ your tenth wedding anniversary,
8. (celebrate)

you _____ your business _____.
9. (not start)

You have a lot of patience.

LL: Not really. I _____ years of practice on my job
10. (get)

by then. When I _____ the doors of Linda, Inc.,
11. (open)

I _____ a very experienced Web page designer.
12. (become)

TC: Well, good luck to you, and thanks for the interview.

 4 **EDIT** • *Read this journal entry. Find and correct six mistakes in the use of the future perfect and the future perfect progressive. The first mistake is already corrected.*

> have been
> By August I'll ~~be~~ a word processor for ten years. And I'll earn almost the same salary for three
>
> years! That's why I've made a New Year's resolution to go back to school this year. First I'm
>
> going to write for school catalogs and start saving for tuition. By March, I'll have figure out
>
> how much tuition will cost. Then I'll start applying. By summer, I had received acceptance
>
> letters. In August, I'll talk to my boss about working part-time and going to school part-time.
>
> By that time, I'll have saved already enough to pay for a semester's tuition. By next New
>
> Year's Day, I'll have been study for one whole semester!

SelfTest

Circle the letter of the correct answer to complete each sentence.

> **EXAMPLE:**
> Jennifer never _____ coffee.   **A (B) C D**
> (A) drink   (C) is drinking
> (B) drinks   (D) was drinking

1. It _____ tomorrow.   **A B C D**
   (A) rains   (C) 's going to rain
   (B) rained   (D) 's raining

2. The package will _____ on Monday.   **A B C D**
   (A) arrive   (C) arriving
   (B) arrives   (D) be going to arrive

3. Goodnight. I _____ you in the morning.   **A B C D**
   (A) 'll see   (C) 'm seeing
   (B) 'm going to see   (D) see

4. Hurry. The next bus _____ at 7:15.   **A B C D**
   (A) leave   (C) leaving
   (B) leaves   (D) will have been leaving

5. Bill will be _____ to Taipei tomorrow.   **A B C D**
   (A) flies   (C) fly
   (B) flying   (D) have flown

6. We _____ a new VCR soon.   **A B C D**
   (A) have owned   (C) 're owning
   (B) 'll own   (D) own

7. They'll be making copies while he _____ the report.   **A B C D**
   (A) finishes   (C) 'll finish
   (B) 'll be finishing   (D) 's been finishing

8. She'll _____ almost $1,000 by then.   **A B C D**
   (A) save   (C) have been saving
   (B) have saved   (D) be saving

9. By next year, Roger will _____ here for ten years.   **A B C D**
   (A) live   (C) have been living
   (B) be living   (D) be going to live

10. Will you buy an electric car when they _____ available?   **A B C D**
    (A) become   (C) are becoming
    (B) became   (D) will become

11. She'll have gotten married _____ June.

(A) already   (C) since

(B) by   (D) until

A B C D

12. Where _____ be living?

(A) they   (C) will they

(B) they will   (D) are they

A B C D

13. Look at those cars! They _____!

(A) will crash   (C) 're going to crash

(B) will be crashing   (D) will have crashed

A B C D

14. How _____ for college?

(A) should pay   (C) she pays

(B) will she pay   (D) she's going to pay

A B C D

SECTION TWO

Each sentence has four underlined words or phrases. The four underlined parts of the sentence are marked A, B, C, and D. Circle the letter of the one underlined word or phrase that is NOT CORRECT.

> **EXAMPLE:**
>
> Mike <u>usually</u> <u>drives</u> to school, but <u>today</u> he <u>walks</u>.
>   A   B   C   D
>
> **A B C ⒟**

15. <u>Will</u> you <u>been</u> <u>going</u> to the drugstore <u>tonight</u>?
   A   B   C   D

A B C D

16. The movie <u>starts</u> <u>at</u> 7:30, so I <u>think</u> I <u>go</u>.
           A   B   C   D

A B C D

17. We <u>are going</u> to <u>study</u> tonight <u>until</u> we <u>will finish</u> this chapter.
        A   B   C   D

A B C D

18. <u>By</u> April, I'll <u>have</u> been <u>driven</u> my new car <u>for</u> a year.
   A   B   C   D

A B C D

19. We'll <u>travel</u> <u>for</u> a couple of days, so you <u>won't</u> <u>be able to</u> call us.
         A   B   C   D

A B C D

20. Jan <u>finished</u> school <u>by</u> next summer, so <u>we're going</u> to <u>visit</u> her.
         A   B   C   D

A B C D

21. Which project <u>will</u> he <u>works</u> on <u>after</u> he <u>finishes</u> this job?
                A   B   C   D

A B C D

22. <u>By</u> January, he'<u>ll</u> have <u>yet</u> <u>saved</u> $1,000.
   A   B   C   D

A B C D

23. Where <u>you will</u> <u>be</u> <u>staying</u> when you <u>go</u> to Morocco?
           A   B   C   D

A B C D

24. I'<u>ll</u> <u>be studying</u> <u>while</u> Ana <u>will be</u> sleeping.
   A   B   C   D

A B C D

25. She <u>will not</u> <u>has</u> <u>graduated</u> <u>by</u> June.
         A   B   C   D

A B C D

Wh- Questions:
Subject and Predicate

> What happened on the night of May 12th? **Where did** you **go**? **Who did** you **see**? **Who saw** you?

> **Why did** I **get** out of bed this morning?

CHECK *POINT*

Check the correct answers.

The lawyer wants to know

☐ the events on the night of May 12th.

☐ the witness's profession.

☐ the names of people who saw the witness.

CHART CHECK 1

Circle T (True) or F (False).

T F *Wh-* questions about the subject have the same word order as statements.

QUESTIONS ABOUT THE SUBJECT

Wh- Word Subject	Verb	Predicate
Who	**saw**	you?

ANSWERS (STATEMENTS)

Subject	Verb	Predicate
He	saw	me.

CHART CHECK 2

Circle T (True) or F (False).

T F *Wh-* questions about the predicate have the same word order as statements.

T F Questions about the predicate can include a form of the verb *do*.

QUESTIONS ABOUT THE PREDICATE

Wh- Word Predicate	Auxiliary Verb	Subject	Verb
Who(m)	**did**	you	**see**?

ANSWERS (STATEMENTS)

Subject	Verb	Predicate
I	saw	**him**.

EXPRESS CHECK

Unscramble these words to form two questions.

night • happened • What • last _____?

do • did • What • next • you _____?

Grammar Explanations

Examples

1. Use *wh-* **questions** to <u>ask for specific information</u>.

Wh- questions begin with question words such as *who, what, where, when, why, which, whose, how, how many, how much,* and *how long*.

- **Who** did you see at Al's Grill?
- **Why** did you go there?
- **How many** people saw you there?
- **How long** did you stay there?

2. When you are **asking about the subject** (usually the first part of the sentence), use a *wh-* question word in place of the subject. The <u>word order is the same as in a statement</u>.

<u>Someone</u> saw you.
↓
- **Who** saw you?

3. When you are **asking about the predicate** (usually the last part of the sentence), the question begins with a *wh-* word, but the <u>word order is the same as in a *yes/no*</u> question.

You saw <u>someone</u>.
Did you see <u>someone</u>?
↓
- **Who** did you see?

▶ **BE CAREFUL!** When you ask a *wh-* question about something in the predicate, you need either

  a. a form of the verb *be*.

  OR

  b. a form of an **auxiliary** ("helping") verb such as *do, have, can, will*.

- Who **is** Harry Adams?
- Why **was** he at Al's Grill?

- Why **does** she want to testify?
  NOT ~~Why she wants to testify?~~

4. **USAGE NOTE:** In very formal English when asking about people in the predicate, *whom* is sometimes used instead of *who*.

VERY FORMAL
- **Whom** did you see?

INFORMAL
- **Who** did you see?

▶ **BE CAREFUL!** If the main verb is a form of *be*, you cannot use *whom*.

- **Who** *is* the next witness?
  NOT ~~Whom is the next witness?~~

1 **MATCH** • *Each question goes with an answer. Match each question with the correct answer.*

Question		Answer
__f__	**1.** Who did you see?	**a.** His wife saw me.
_____	**2.** Who saw you?	**b.** She hit a car.
_____	**3.** What hit her?	**c.** I gave the money to Harry.
_____	**4.** What did she hit?	**d.** A car hit her.
_____	**5.** Which man did you give the money to?	**e.** Harry gave me the money.
_____	**6.** Which man gave you the money?	**f.** I saw the defendant.

2 **COMPLETE** • *Read this cross-examination. Complete it by writing the lawyer's questions.*

1. LAWYER: ___What time did you return home?___
(What time / you / return home?)

WITNESS: I returned home just before midnight.

2. LAWYER: _____
(How / you / get home?)

WITNESS: Someone gave me a lift.

3. LAWYER: _____
(Who / give / you / a ride?)

WITNESS: A friend from work.

4. LAWYER: _____
(What / happen / next?)

WITNESS: I opened my door and saw someone on my living room floor.

5. LAWYER: _____
(Who / you / see?)

WITNESS: Deborah Collins.

6. LAWYER: _____
(Who / be / Deborah Collins?)

WITNESS: She's my wife's boss. I mean she *was* my wife's boss. She's dead now.

7. LAWYER: _____
(What / you / do?)

WITNESS: I called the police.

8. LAWYER: _____
(How many / people / call / you?)

WITNESS: No one called me. Why?

3 **ASK** • *Read these statements. Then ask questions about the underlined words.*

1. The witness recognized Harry Adams.

Who recognized Harry Adams?

2. The witness recognized Harry Adams.

Who did the witness recognize?

3. Court begins at 9:00 A.M.

4. Five witnesses testified.

5. The jury found Adams guilty because he didn't have an alibi.

6. Something horrible happened.

7. The trial lasted two weeks.

8. The judge spoke to the jury.

9. Adams paid his lawyer $2,000.

10. The district attorney questioned the restaurant manager.

 4 **EDIT** • *Read this list of questions. There are six mistakes in the use of wh- questions. Find and correct them. The first mistake is already corrected.*

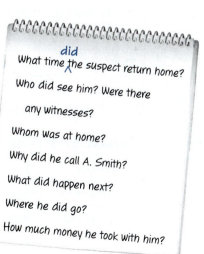

did
What time ʌ the suspect return home?

Who did see him? Were there

any witnesses?

Whom was at home?

Why did he call A. Smith?

What did happen next?

Where he did go?

How much money he took with him?

Tag Questions

WITH *BE* AS THE MAIN VERB

AFFIRMATIVE	NEGATIVE	NEGATIVE	AFFIRMATIVE
STATEMENT	**TAG**	**STATEMENT**	**TAG**
You're from L.A.*,	**aren't you?**	**You're not** from L.A.,	**are you?**

*L.A. = Los Angeles

WITH ALL AUXILIARY VERBS EXCEPT *DO*

AFFIRMATIVE	NEGATIVE	NEGATIVE	AFFIRMATIVE
STATEMENT	**TAG**	**STATEMENT**	**TAG**
You're moving,	**aren't you?**	**You're not** moving,	**are you?**
He's been here,	**hasn't he?**	**He hasn't** been here,	**has he?**
They can move,	**can't they?**	**They can't** move,	**can they?**

WITH *DO* AS AN AUXILIARY VERB

AFFIRMATIVE	NEGATIVE	NEGATIVE	AFFIRMATIVE
STATEMENT	**TAG**	**STATEMENT**	**TAG**
You live here,	**don't you?**	**You don't** live here,	**do you?**
They moved,	**didn't they?**	**They didn't** move,	**did they?**

EXPRESS CHECK

Unscramble these words to form a tag question.

actor • you • an • aren't • You're _____, _____?

Grammar Explanations	Examples

1. We often use **tag questions** to:

  a. check information we believe to be true

     OR

  b. comment on a situation

■ Tom lives in L.A., **doesn't he?**
(The speaker believes that Tom lives in L.A. and wants to check this information.)

■ It's a nice day, **isn't it?**
(The speaker is commenting on the weather.)

---

2. Tag questions have **a statement and a tag**. Forms of tag questions vary, but their meaning is always similar. The statement expresses an assumption. The tag means *Right?*

  a. If the statement verb is affirmative, the tag verb is negative.

  b. If the statement verb is negative, the tag verb is affirmative.

              statement   tag
■ You're not from L.A., **are you?**
■ You're Jack La Costa, **aren't you?**
■ You don't drive much, **do you?**

        affirmative   negative
■ You **work** on Fridays, **don't** you?

           negative   affirmative
■ You **don't work** on Fridays, **do** you?

---

3. The **tag** always uses a form of *be* or an auxiliary verb (*be*, *have*, *do*, or *will*, or a modal such as *can*, *could*, or *should*).

USAGE NOTE: Notice the tag for *I am*.

▶ **BE CAREFUL!** In the tag, only use pronouns.

When the subject of the statement is *this* or *that*, the subject of the tag is *it*.

■ It's a nice day, **isn't** it?
■ You've lived here a long time, **haven't** you?
■ You come from New York, **don't** you?
■ You can drive, **can't** you?

■ I'm next, **aren't** I?

■ *Tom* works here, doesn't **he?**
NOT Tom works here, ~~doesn't Tom?~~

■ *That's* a good idea, isn't **it?**
NOT That's a good idea, ~~isn't that?~~

---

4. When you use a tag question to **check information** or to **comment on a situation**, your voice falls on the tag. You expect the listener to agree or just show that he or she is listening.

Tag questions can also be used to **get information**. As with *yes/no* questions, your voice rises at the end, and you expect to get an answer (*Yes* or *No*).

A: It's getting warmer, **isn't it?**
B: Yeah. Seems more like summer.

A: You're not moving, **are you?**
B: Yes. We're returning to L.A.
              OR
No. We're staying here.

IDENTIFY • *Read this conversation. Underline all the tags.*

KAY: Hi, Tom. It's a nice day, <u>isn't it?</u>

TOM: Sure is. Not a cloud in the sky. How are you doing?

KAY: Good, thanks. You don't know of any vacant apartments, do you? My son is looking for one.

TOM: He is? I thought he was staying with you.

KAY: Well, he really wants a place of his own. Do you know of anything?

TOM: As a matter of fact, I do. You know the Sobotas, don't you? Well, I just found out that they're moving to New York next month.

KAY: They are? What kind of apartment do they have?

TOM: A one-bedroom.

KAY: It's not furnished, is it?

TOM: No. Why? He doesn't need a furnished apartment, does he?

KAY: Well, he doesn't have furniture. But I guess he can always rent some, can't he?

TOM: Why don't you give your son my number, and I'll give him some more information?

KAY: Will you? Thanks, Tom.

MATCH • *Each statement goes with a tag. Match each statement with the correct tag.*

	Statement	Tag
__i__	**1.** You've called the movers,	**a.** can't we?
_____	**2.** They're coming tomorrow,	**b.** do we?
_____	**3.** This isn't going to be cheap,	**c.** is he?
_____	**4.** You haven't finished packing,	**d.** isn't it?
_____	**5.** We don't need any more boxes,	**e.** are they?
_____	**6.** Paul is going to help us,	**f.** have you?
_____	**7.** We can put some things in storage,	**g.** isn't he?
_____	**8.** Jack isn't buying our bookcases,	**h.** is it?
_____	**9.** The movers aren't packing the books for us,	**i.** haven't you?
_____	**10.** Moving is hard,	**j.** aren't they?

3 **COMPLETE** • *A radio talk-show host is interviewing one of her guests, a Hollywood screenplay writer. Complete the interview with appropriate tags.*

HOST: You've lived in Hollywood for many years, <u>haven't you</u> ?
1.

GUEST: Since I was eighteen and came here to write my first screenplay.

HOST: You didn't know anyone here at first, _____?
2.

GUEST: No. And I didn't have a cent to my name. Just some ideas and a lot of hope. It
sounds crazy, _____?
3.

HOST: But things have worked out for you, _____?
4.
You're working on another screenplay now, _____?
5.

GUEST: Yes. It's a comedy about some kids who become invisible.

HOST: Speaking of kids, you have some of your own, _____?
6.

GUEST: Two boys and a girl—all very visible!

HOST: I know what you mean. Do you ever wish they were invisible?

GUEST: Now, that's an interesting thought, _____?
7.

 4 **EDIT** • *Read this part of a movie script. Find and correct seven mistakes in the use of tag questions. The first mistake is already corrected.*

Ben: It's been a long time, Joe, ~~haven't~~ ^{hasn't} it?

Joe: That depends on what you mean by a long time, doesn't that?

Ben: What are you doing around here, anyway? It's dangerous.

Joe: I can take care of myself. I'm still alive, amn't I?

Ben: Yes, but you're still wanted by the police, are you?

Joe: Look, I need a place to stay. You have a place, don't you? Just for one night.

Ben: I have to think of my wife and kids. You can find someplace else, can you?

Joe: No. You've got to help me!

Ben: I've already helped you plenty. I went to jail for you, haven't I?

Joe: Yeah, OK, Ben. You remember what happened in Vegas, do you?

Ben: OK, OK. I can make a call.

UNIT 26

Additions with *So, Too, Neither,* and *Not either*

HERALD SUN

Twins Separated at Birth Are Reunited!

Mark likes hunting, fishing, and Chinese food.
So does Gerald.

| CHECK | POINT

Check the correct answer.

☐ The men like different things.
☐ The men like the same things.

WITH *BE* AS THE MAIN VERB

CHART CHECK

Circle T (True) or F (False).

T F There is more than one way to make an addition.

T F Use *so* or *too* with negative statements.

T F When a statement does not have a form of *be* or an auxiliary verb, use a form of *do* in the addition.

AFFIRMATIVE		NEGATIVE	
STATEMENT	**ADDITION**	**STATEMENT**	**ADDITION**
Amy **is** a twin,	**and so is** Sue. **and** Sue **is too.**	Amy **isn't** very tall,	**and neither is** Sue. **and** Sue **isn't either.**

WITH ALL AUXILIARY VERBS EXCEPT *DO*

AFFIRMATIVE		NEGATIVE	
STATEMENT	**ADDITION**	**STATEMENT**	**ADDITION**
Amy **can** swim,	**and so can** Sue. **and** Sue **can too.**	Amy **can't** ski,	**and neither can** Sue. **and** Sue **can't either.**

WITH VERBS USING *DO* AS AN AUXILIARY VERB

AFFIRMATIVE		NEGATIVE	
STATEMENT	**ADDITION**	**STATEMENT**	**ADDITION**
Amy **likes** dogs,	**and so does** Sue. **and** Sue **does too.**	Amy **doesn't** like cats,	**and neither does** Sue. **and** Sue **doesn't either.**

EXPRESS CHECK

Unscramble these words to form additions.

is • Mark • and • neither   does • Gerald • so • and

Gerald isn't married, _____. Mark fights fires, _____.

Grammar Explanations

Examples

1. **Additions** are phrases or short sentences that follow a statement. Use an addition to avoid repeating the information in the statement.	■ Gerald is a firefighter, **and so is Mark**. *(Gerald is a firefighter, and Mark is a firefighter.)*
2. Use *so* or *too* if the addition follows an <u>affirmative</u> statement.	■ Gerald **is** a firefighter, and *so is* Mark. <div align="center">OR</div> ■ Gerald **is** a firefighter, and Mark **is** *too*.
Use *neither* or *not either* if the addition follows a <u>negative</u> statement.	■ Gerald **didn't** get married. *Neither* **did** Mark. <div align="center">OR</div> ■ Gerald **didn't** get married. Mark **did***n't either*.
▶ **BE CAREFUL!** Notice the <u>word order</u> after *so* and *neither*. The verb comes before the subject.	■ So **is Mark**. NOT ~~So Mark is.~~ ■ Neither **did Mark**. NOT ~~Neither Mark did.~~
3. **Additions** always use a form of *<u>be</u>* or an <u>auxiliary verb</u> (*be, have, do, will,* or a modal verb such as *can, could, should, would*).	
a. If the statement uses a form of *be*, <u>use a form of *be*</u> in the addition too.	■ I**'m** a twin, and so **is** my cousin.
b. If the statement uses an auxiliary verb, <u>use the same auxiliary verb</u> in the addition.	■ Gerald **had** quit his job, and so **had** Mark. ■ I **can't** drive, and neither **can** my twin.
c. If the statement has a verb that uses *do* as an auxiliary verb, <u>use the appropriate form of *do*</u> in the addition.	■ Gerald **owns** a dog, and so **does** Mark. ■ Gerald **bought** a jeep, and so **did** Mark.
4. In conversation, you can use short **responses** with *so, too, neither,* and *not either* to <u>agree</u> with another speaker.	**A:** I have a twin sister. **B:** *So do I.* OR *I do too.* **A:** I don't have any brothers or sisters. **B:** *Neither do I.* OR *I don't either.*
USAGE NOTE: In informal speech, people say *Me too* and *Me neither* to express similarity or agreement.	**A:** I'm left-handed. **B:** *Me too.* **A:** I've never heard of these twins. **B:** *Me neither.*

1 **TRUE OR FALSE** • *Read these short conversations between reunited twins. Write T (True) or F (False) for the statement that follows each conversation.*

1. **MARK:** I like Chinese food.
    GERALD: So do I.

    __T__ Gerald likes Chinese food.

2. **ANDREA:** I don't want to go out.
    BARBARA: Neither do I.

    _____ Barbara wants to go out.

3. **JEAN:** I'm not hungry.
    JOAN: I'm not either.

    _____ Joan isn't hungry.

4. **AMY:** I've always felt lucky.
    KERRIE: So have I.

    _____ Kerrie has felt lucky.

5. **MIA:** I don't eat meat.
    BOB: I don't either.

    _____ Bob eats meat.

6. **JIM:** I have a headache.
    BILL: I do too.

    _____ Both Jim and Bill have
    headaches.

7. **NORA:** I can't swim.
    DINA: Me neither.

    _____ Dina can swim.

8. **CHET:** I shouldn't work so much.
    TODD: Neither should I.

    _____ Todd wants to work less.

9. **JASON:** I'd like to leave now.
    TYLER: Me too.

    _____ Tyler wants to leave.

 2 **CHOOSE** • *Circle the correct words to complete this paragraph.*

Sometimes being a twin can cause trouble. In high school, I was in Mr. Jacobs's

history class. Neither /(So) was my brother. One day we took a test. I got questions 18
                              1.

and 20 wrong. My brother did so / too. I didn't spell *Constantinople* correctly, and
                                  2.

either / neither did he. The teacher was sure we had cheated. As a result, I got an F
3.

on the test, and so did / got my brother. We tried to convince Mr. Jacobs of our
                      4.

innocence, but he didn't believe us. The principal didn't either / too. We finally
                                                              5.

convinced them to give us another test. This time I got items 3 and 10 wrong.

Guess what? Neither / So did my brother. Our teacher was astounded. So / Too was
                 6.   **7.**

the principal. We weren't. We were just amused.

3 **COMPLETE •** *Marta and Carla are twins. They agree on everything. Complete their conversation with responses.*

MARTA: I'm so happy we finally found each other.

CARLA: So _____*am I*_____ . I always felt like something was missing from my life.
  1.

MARTA: So _____ . I always knew I had a double somewhere out there.
  2.

CARLA: I can't believe how similar we are.

MARTA: Neither _____ . It's like always seeing myself in the mirror.
  3.

CARLA: Not only do we look identical, but we like and dislike all the same things.

MARTA: Right. I hate lettuce.

CARLA: I _____ . And I detest liver.
  4.

MARTA: So _____ . I *love* pizza, though.
  5.

CARLA: So _____ . But only with tomato and cheese. I don't like pepperoni.
  6.

MARTA: Neither _____ .
  7.

CARLA: This is amazing! I wonder if our husbands have so much in common.

MARTA: Me _____ !
  8.

4 **EDIT •** *Read this student's composition. There are six mistakes in the use of sentence additions. Find and correct them. The first mistake is already corrected.*

My Brother and I

My brother is just a year older than I am. We have a lot of things in common.

First of all, we look alike. I am 5'10", and so ~~he is.~~ *is he* I have straight black hair and dark brown eyes, and so does he. We share many of the same interests too. I love to play soccer, and he too. Both of us swim every day, but I can't dive, and either can he.

Sometimes being so similar has its problems. For example, last night I wanted the last piece of chocolate cake, and so does he. Often I won't feel like doing the dishes, and neither won't he. Worst of all, sometimes I'm interested in dating a certain schoolmate, and so he is. However, most of the time I feel our similarities are really nice. So does my brother.

SelfTest

SECTION ONE

Circle the letter of the correct answer to complete each sentence.

> **Example:**
> Jennifer never _____ coffee.   **A (B) C D**
> (A) drink   (C) is drinking
> (B) drinks   (D) was drinking

1. Where _____?   **A B C D**
   (A) does she live   (C) she does live
   (B) she lives   (D) she lived

2. _____ lost this wallet?   **A B C D**
   (A) Whom   (C) Who
   (B) Whose   (D) Who did

3. You're Cynthia, _____ you?   **A B C D**
   (A) aren't   (C) didn't
   (B) are   (D) were

4. Laura loves soap operas, and _____.   **A B C D**
   (A) Jane does too   (C) Jane loves too
   (B) so Jane does   (D) so loves Jane

5. I didn't like sports, and _____ my brother.   **A B C D**
   (A) either did   (C) so did
   (B) neither does   (D) neither did

6. —That isn't Sam, is it?   **A B C D**
   —No, _____. Sam's taller.
   (A) it is   (C) it wasn't
   (B) it doesn't   (D) it isn't

7. We didn't eat here last week, _____ we?   **A B C D**
   (A) didn't   (C) do
   (B) haven't   (D) did

8. —Who _____ your bike?   **A B C D**
   —Mike did.
   (A) did give you   (C) you gave
   (B) did you give   (D) gave you

9. —Who _____ at the party?   **A B C D**
   —I saw Stefan.
   (A) saw you   (C) you saw
   (B) did you see   (D) you see

10. —I hate cabbage.

—Me _____. I can't even look at it.   A B C D

(A) too   (C) neither
(B) either   (D) do too

11. _____ washing the dishes tonight?   A B C D

(A) Whose   (C) Who are
(B) Who's   (D) Who does

12. Liam was born in Ireland, and so _____ his brother.   A B C D

(A) wasn't   (C) was
(B) didn't   (D) did

SECTION TWO

Each sentence has four underlined words or phrases. The four underlined parts of the sentence are marked A, B, C, and D. Circle the letter of the one underlined word or phrase that is NOT CORRECT.

> **EXAMPLE:**
>
> Mike <u>usually</u> <u>drives</u> to school, but <u>today</u> he <u>walks</u>.   A B C ⓓ
>   A   B   C   D

13. <u>This</u> is <u>a</u> good school, <u>wasn't</u> <u>it?</u>   A B C D
    A   B   C   D

14. <u>We</u> <u>went</u> to Stan's holiday party last year, <u>hadn't</u> <u>we</u>?   A B C D
    A   B   C   D

15. Kevin <u>has</u> always <u>been</u> a great student, <u>and so</u> <u>his brother has</u>.   A B C D
        A   B   C   D

16. My sister <u>has</u> never <u>gone</u> skiing, and <u>neither</u> <u>did</u> I.   A B C D
         A   B   C   D

17. Where <u>you worked</u> last year <u>when</u> you <u>were</u> <u>going</u> to school?   A B C D
        A   B   C   D

18. <u>That</u> sign is too small <u>to read</u>, <u>isn't</u> <u>that</u>?   A B C D
   A   B   C   D

19. English <u>isn't</u> an easy language <u>to learn</u>, <u>is</u> <u>it.</u>   A B C D
        A   B   C D

20. My <u>parents</u> <u>are</u> both good cooks, <u>and</u> <u>me too</u>.   A B C D
     A   B   C   D

21. Tom and Fred <u>hadn't been</u> to Florida <u>before</u> then, <u>had</u> <u>he</u>?   A B C D
           A   B   C D

22. <u>I'm</u> <u>usually</u> right about the weather, <u>amn't</u> <u>I</u>?   A B C D
   A   B   C   D

23. <u>Paul</u> <u>likes</u> Italian food, <u>doesn't</u> <u>Paul</u>?   A B C D
   A   B   C   D

24. <u>Where</u> <u>did</u> they <u>went</u> <u>yesterday</u>?   A B C D
     A   B   C   D

25. <u>Why</u> <u>you</u> <u>call</u> me so <u>late</u> last night?   A B C D
     A   B   C   D

UNIT 27

Ability:
Can, Could, Be able to

Can you **do** spreadsheets?

CHECK POINT

Circle T (True) or F (False).

T F The father wants to know if his daughter has permission to do spreadsheets.

CHART CHECK 1

Circle T (True) or F (False).

T F The form for **can** and **could** is the same for all subjects.

STATEMENTS: CAN/COULD

SUBJECT	CAN/COULD*	BASE FORM OF VERB	
I/He/She/It/We/You/They	can (not)	do	spreadsheets now.
	could (not)	use	a computer last year.

*Can and could are modals. They do not have -s in the third person singular.

YES/NO QUESTIONS: CAN/COULD

CAN/COULD	SUBJECT	BASE FORM	
Can	she	do	them?
Could	they	use	one?

SHORT ANSWERS

AFFIRMATIVE		NEGATIVE	
Yes,	she **can**.	No,	she **can't**.
	they **could**.		they **couldn't**.

WH- QUESTIONS: CAN/COULD

WH- WORD	CAN/COULD	SUBJECT	BASE FORM	
How well	can	she	do	spreadsheets?
	could	they	use	a computer?

CHART CHECK 2

Check the correct answer.

Which part of **be able to** changes for different subjects?

☐ **be**   ☐ **able to**

STATEMENTS: BE ABLE TO

SUBJECT	BE	ABLE TO	BASE FORM	
I	am			
He/She/It	is	(not) able to	do	spreadsheets.
We/You/They	are			

CHART CHECK 3

Check the correct answer.

In questions with *be able to*, what comes before the subject?

☐ a form of *be*

☐ a form of *able to*

YES/NO QUESTIONS: *BE ABLE TO*

BE	SUBJECT	ABLE TO	BASE FORM	
Are	you	**able to**	**do**	spreadsheets?
Is	she			

SHORT ANSWERS

AFFIRMATIVE		NEGATIVE	
Yes,	I **am**.	**No,**	I**'m not**.
	she **is**.		she **isn't**.

WH- QUESTIONS: *BE ABLE TO*

WH- WORD	BE	SUBJECT	ABLE TO	BASE FORM	
How well	**are**	you	**able to**	**do**	spreadsheets?
	is	she			

EXPRESS CHECK

Complete these sentences with **can** *or* **be able to**. *Use one word for each blank.*

A: _____ she able _____ use a computer already?

B: Yes, she _____, and she _____ type and do spreadsheets too.

Grammar Explanations

Examples

1. Use *can* or *be able to* to talk about <u>ability in the present</u>.

   USAGE NOTE: In everyday speech, *can* is <u>more common</u> than *be able to* in the <u>present tense</u>.

- She **can do** computer graphics.
- She**'s able to do** computer graphics.

2. Use either *could* or *was/were able to* to talk about <u>ability (but not a specific achievement) in the past</u>.

   ▶ **BE CAREFUL!** Use only *was/were able to* to talk about <u>a specific achievement or a single event in the past</u>.

   Use either *could* or *was/were able to* in <u>negative sentences about past ability</u>.

- Sami **could read** when he was four.
- He **was able to use** a computer too.

- He **was able to win** the Math Prize last year. NOT He could win the Math Prize . . .

- I **couldn't win** the Math Prize last year.
- I **wasn't able to do** one problem.

3. For forms and tenses <u>other than the present or past</u>, use *be able to*.

- Jen wants **to be able to write** programs. *(infinitive)*

- By June she **will be able to complete** her computer class. *(future)*

1 **IDENTIFY •** *Read part of an article about some talented young business people. Underline the words that express ability.*

A surprising number of young people <u>have been able to create</u> successful Web-based businesses. One young entrepreneur is Sam Roberts. Sam could design Web pages when he was eight, but he got his break at twelve when a writer hired him to design a Web site. Sam's first business failed because he and his partner weren't able to get along. However, his new business, Webman, is up and running. Another young businessman, Jay

WEB BUSINESSES FOR FUN AND PROFIT

Leibowitz, was able to sell two software programs when he was fourteen. He made $30,000 on the deal and now Jay runs his own Web site. Dan Finley writes reviews of new software. He started his business at sixteen. A full-time college student, Dan can pay a staff of writers and still earn $500 a month. Although they all make money, all three started out to have fun at their hobby, not to make a profit.

COMPLETE • *Read each description. Complete it with a name from the article.*

1. _____Jay_____ sold software programs at the age of fourteen.

2. _____ didn't agree with his partner.

3. _____ earns money reviewing software.

4. _____ was able to design a Web page for a writer.

2 **COMPLETE •** *Read these paragraphs. Complete them with* **can**, **could**, *or* **be able to**. *Use* **can** *or* **could** *when possible. Choose between affirmative and negative.*

1. Stefan is enjoying his computer class. Two weeks ago, he _____couldn't_____ even use the mouse, but now he _____ edit his homework. By next week, he _____ do research on the Internet.

2. Eleni misses her family in Greece. She _____ visit them for years, but they just got an e-mail account, so now they _____ keep in touch daily.

3. I _____ understand how to set up a presentation. The software instructions don't help. I think I'll take a professional development course. In a few months maybe I _____ make that presentation.

4. Mike and I _____ get along since we started this business. He _____ work alone (he needs people), and I _____ work in a group (I have to work alone). I hope we _____ work out our problems soon.

3 | **COMPLETE** • *Read this advertisement. Complete it with the appropriate form of* **can**, **could**, *or* **be able to** *plus the verbs in parentheses. Use* **can** *or* **could** *when possible.*

WILL B. HAPPY®
Professional Development Courses

Time Management   Presentations   Career Development   Teamwork

Think about your last presentation: _____*Were*_____ you _____*able to prepare*_____ on time?
                                                                    1. (prepare)

_____ you _____ your ideas?
                            2. (communicate)

***Will B. Happy*®** has helped others, and he _____ YOU!
                                                        3. (help)

"Before I took Will B. Happy's course, my work was always late because

I _____ a schedule. I also had big piles on my desk because I
      4. (follow)

_____ what was important. Now I _____ my time
   5. (decide)   **6.** (manage)

effectively. Next month, when my workload gets heavy, I _____ it
                                                               7. (organize)

and do the important things first."
                                                        —*Scott Mathis, student*

"I didn't use to _____ in front of groups. Now I can!"
                        8. (speak)

                                                        —*Mary Zhang, sales manager*

---

4 | **EDIT** • *Read this student's journal. Find and correct seven mistakes in expressing ability. The first mistake is already corrected.*

Today in my Will B. Happy Teamwork course, I learned about work styles—"Drivers" and
                                                                    to
"Enthusiasts." I'm a Driver, so I can make decisions, but I'm not able ⋀listen to other

people's ideas. The Enthusiast in our group can communicates well, but you can't

depend on her. Now I understand what was happening in my business class last year,

when I couldn't felt comfortable with my team. I thought that they all talked too much

and didn't able to work efficiently. I could get an A for the course, but it was hard. I can

do a lot more alone, but some jobs are too big for that. Our instructor says that soon

the Drivers will able to listen and the Enthusiast could be more dependable.

Permission:
May, Can, Could, Do you mind if . . . ?

> I think I have something in my eye. **Could** I **take** the test tomorrow?

CHECK *POINT*

Check the sentence that describes what's happening in the cartoon.

☐ The student wants to know if his eye will be better tomorrow.

☐ The student is asking the teacher to allow him to take the test tomorrow.

CHART CHECK 1

Check the correct answer.

Which modal is used in questions but NOT in short answers about permission?

☐ *may*

☐ *can*

☐ *could*

QUESTIONS: *MAY/CAN/COULD*

MAY/CAN/COULD*	SUBJECT	BASE FORM OF VERB	
May **Can** **Could**	I/we/he/she/it/they	**start**	now?

*May, can, and *could* are modals. They do not have *-s* in the third person singular.

SHORT ANSWERS

AFFIRMATIVE			NEGATIVE		
Yes,	you/he/she/it/they	**may.** **can.**	**No,**	you/he/she/it/they	**may not.** **can't.**

CHART CHECK 2

Circle T (True) or F (False).

T F After *Do you mind if . . . ?* the verb is the same for all subjects.

T F The answer *Not at all* gives permission.

QUESTIONS: *DO YOU MIND IF . . . ?*

DO YOU MIND IF	SUBJECT	VERB
Do you mind if	I/we/they	**start?**
	he/she/it	**starts?**

SHORT ANSWERS

AFFIRMATIVE	NEGATIVE
Not at all.	
No, I **don't.**	**Yes,** I **do.**

STATEMENTS: *MAY/CAN*

SUBJECT	MAY/CAN	BASE FORM
I/He/She/It/We/You/They	**may (not)** **can (not)**	**start.**

EXPRESS CHECK

Circle the correct words to complete this conversation.

A: Do you mind if he <u>help / helps</u> me with my homework?

B: <u>Not at all / Yes I do</u>. He can <u>help / helps</u> you, but you should do most of the work.

Grammar Explanations

| Examples |

1. Use *may*, *could*, and *can* to <u>ask for permission</u>.

- **May** I **call** you next Friday?
- **Could** we **use** our dictionaries?
- **Can** he **come** to class with me?

USAGE NOTE: *May* is a little more <u>formal</u> than *can* and *could*.

- **May** I **leave** the room, Professor Lee?

▶ **BE CAREFUL!** Requests for permission always <u>refer to the present or the future</u>. When you use *could* to ask for permission, it is not past tense.

A: **Could** I take the test *tomorrow*?
B: Certainly. The test starts at 9:00 A.M.

2. We often say *please* when we ask for permission. Note the possible word orders.

- **Could** I ask a question, *please*?
- **Could** I *please* ask a question?

3. Use *Do you mind if . . . ?* to ask for permission when your action might bother someone.

A: **Do you mind if** I clean up tomorrow?
B: Yes, actually, I do mind. I hate to see a mess.

▶ **BE CAREFUL!** A <u>negative answer</u> to the question *Do you mind if . . . ?* <u>gives permission</u> to do something. It means, *It's OK. I don't mind.*

A: **Do you mind if** I leave the room?
B: *Not at all*.
   (You may leave the room.)

4. Use *may* or *can* in <u>answers</u>. Do not use *could*.

A: **Could** I borrow this pencil?
B: Yes, of course you **can**.
   NOT ~~Yes, you could.~~

▶ **BE CAREFUL!** Do not contract *may not*.

- No, you **may not**.
   NOT ~~No, you mayn't.~~

We often use **polite expressions** instead of modals to answer requests for permission.

A: **Could** I close the window?
B: *Sure*.
   Certainly.
   Go ahead.
   No, please don't. It's hot in here.

5. When people **refuse permission**, they often give <u>an apology and an explanation</u>.

A: Can I please have a little more time?
B: *I'm sorry, but the time is up*.

If the <u>rules are very clear</u>, someone may refuse without an apology or explanation.

DRIVER: Can I park here?
OFFICER: *No, you can't*.

1

MATCH • *Each request for permission goes with a response. Match each request with the correct response.*

Request

___d___ **1.** May we come in now?

_____ **2.** Could I see your tickets, please?

_____ **3.** May I please speak to Harry?

_____ **4.** Could they come with us?

_____ **5.** Can I park here?

_____ **6.** Do you mind if I have more tea?

Response

a. No, you can't. It's a bus stop.

b. Not at all. There's plenty of time.

c. Sure they can. We have room.

d. Yes, you may. The test starts soon.

e. I'm sorry, he's not in.

f. Certainly. Here they are.

2

COMPLETE • *Mr. Hamad is supervising a test. Complete his conversations with his students. Use a pronoun plus the correct form of the words in parentheses and short answers.*

AHMED: _____Could we come_____ into the test room now?
 1. (Could / come)

MR. H: Yes, _____certainly_____. Please show your registration form
 2.
as you come in.

SOFIA: My brother isn't taking the test. _____ in the
 3. (Do you mind / stay)
room with me?

MR. H: Yes, _____. Sorry, only people with tickets are
 4.
permitted inside.

ROSA: _____ a pen to write my name on the test
 5. (May / use)
booklet?

MR. H: No, _____. You must use a pencil. And everyone
 6.
please remember, _____ the test until I tell you to.
 7. (can't / start)

ROSA: Jamie, _____ this pencil? I only brought a pen.
 8. (do you mind if / borrow)

JAMIE: _____. Take it. I brought a few.
 9.

MR. H: OK, _____ your test booklets and read the
 10. (may / open)
instructions now.

JEAN: I'm late because my train broke down. _____ in?
 11. (Can / come)

MR. H: No, _____. We've already started the test.
 12.

3 **ASK** • *Lucy and Carl are going to a concert. Read each situation. Write questions to ask for permission. Use the words in parentheses.*

1. Carl wants his friend Bob to come.

   CARL: I have an extra ticket. _____ Do you mind if Bob comes? _____
   (Do you mind if)

2. Carl wants to use Lucy's phone to call Bob.

   CARL: Great. I'll call him right now. _____
   (Could)

3. Carl wants to park in front of the stadium.

   CARL: We're going to the concert, Officer. _____
   (May)

4. Lucy, Bob, and Carl want to move up a few rows. Bob asks an usher.

   BOB: All those seats are empty. _____
   (Could)

5. Carl wants to tape the concert. Lucy asks the usher first.

   LUCY: My friend brought a tape recorder. _____
   (Can)

6. Lucy hates the music. She wants to leave.

   LUCY: This music is giving me a headache. _____
   (Do you mind if)

4 **EDIT** • *This exercise is similar to part of the TOEFL®. Find the mistake in each item and fill in the space that corresponds to the letter of the incorrect word or phrase. Then go one step beyond the TOEFL® and correct the mistake.*

1. $\overset{come}{\underset{A}{\text{Can}}}$ he $\underset{B}{\text{comes}}$ on the train with me or $\underset{C}{\text{does}}$ he $\underset{D}{\text{need}}$ a ticket? Ⓐ ●Ⓑ Ⓒ Ⓓ

2. I'm $\underset{A}{\text{sorry}}$, he $\underset{B}{\text{couldn't}}$. Only passengers $\underset{C}{\text{can}}$ $\underset{D}{\text{board}}$ the train. Ⓐ Ⓑ Ⓒ Ⓓ

3. $\underset{A}{\text{Could}}$ I $\underset{B}{\text{changed}}$ seats with $\underset{C}{\text{you}}$? I'd like to $\underset{D}{\text{sit}}$ next to my son. Ⓐ Ⓑ Ⓒ Ⓓ

4. Yes, $\underset{A}{\text{you}}$ $\underset{B}{\text{could}}$. Go right $\underset{C}{\text{ahead}}$. I'm $\underset{D}{\text{getting}}$ off soon. Ⓐ Ⓑ Ⓒ Ⓓ

5. Mom, $\underset{A}{\text{may}}$ $\underset{B}{\text{I}}$ $\underset{C}{\text{to have}}$ some candy? $\underset{D}{\text{I'm}}$ hungry. Ⓐ Ⓑ Ⓒ Ⓓ

6. No, you $\underset{A}{\text{mayn't}}$. I'm sorry, $\underset{B}{\text{but}}$ you've $\underset{C}{\text{already}}$ had $\underset{D}{\text{enough}}$ candy. Ⓐ Ⓑ Ⓒ Ⓓ

7. $\underset{A}{\text{Do}}$ $\underset{B}{\text{you}}$ mind $\underset{C}{\text{if}}$ he $\underset{D}{\text{play}}$ his computer game? Ⓐ Ⓑ Ⓒ Ⓓ

8. Yes, $\underset{A}{\text{I do}}$. He can $\underset{B}{\text{play}}$ if he $\underset{C}{\text{wants}}$. It $\underset{D}{\text{won't}}$ bother me. Ⓐ Ⓑ Ⓒ Ⓓ

9. I'm still $\underset{A}{\text{hungry}}$. $\underset{B}{\text{Can}}$ $\underset{C}{\text{we'll}}$ $\underset{D}{\text{get}}$ a sandwich soon? Ⓐ Ⓑ Ⓒ Ⓓ

10. $\underset{A}{\text{Not at all}}$. $\underset{B}{\text{We}}$ $\underset{C}{\text{can}}$ $\underset{D}{\text{go}}$ find the club car. Ⓐ Ⓑ Ⓒ Ⓓ

Requests:
Will, Can, Would, Could, Would you mind . . . ?

"Miss Fleming, would you mind dialling 911 for me?"

CHECK POINT

Check the correct answer.

The businessman is

☐ giving an order.

☐ asking someone to do something.

☐ asking for information.

NOTE: 911 is the emergency telephone number in the United States and Canada.

CHART CHECK 1

Circle T (True) or F (False).

T F You can use **would** and **could** in questions but NOT in short answers to requests.

QUESTIONS: *WILL/CAN/WOULD/COULD*			
WILL/CAN/ WOULD/COULD*	**SUBJECT**	**BASE FORM OF VERB**	
Will **Can** **Would** **Could**	you	**mail**	this for me?

*These words are modals. They do not have *-s* in the third person singular.

SHORT ANSWERS		
AFFIRMATIVE		**NEGATIVE**
Sure Certainly	(I **will**). (I **can**).	I'm sorry, but I **can't**.

QUESTIONS: *WOULD YOU MIND . . . ?*		
WOULD YOU MIND	**GERUND**	
Would you mind	**mailing**	this for me**?**

CHART CHECK 2

Check the correct answer.

Not at all means:

☐ **OK**   ☐ **no**

SHORT ANSWERS	
AFFIRMATIVE	**NEGATIVE**
No, not at all. I'd be glad to.	I'm sorry, but I **can't**.

EXPRESS CHECK

Complete this conversation.

A: _____ you mind filing these reports now?

B: _____, _____ at all.

A: Thanks. And _____ you answer the phone, please?

B: Sorry, but I _____. My hands are full.

Grammar Explanations

Examples

1. Use **will**, **can**, **would**, and **could** to ask someone to do something.

We often use **will** and **can** for informal requests.

SISTER: **Will** you **answer** the phone?
Can you **turn down** the TV?

We use **would** and **could** to make requests more polite.

BOSS: **Would** you **type** this report?
Could you **make** ten copies?

2. We also use **please** with **will, can, would,** and **could** to make the request even more polite. Note the word order.

■ **Could** you *please* close the door?
OR
■ **Could** you close the door, *please*?

3. We also use **Would you mind** + **gerund** (without *please*) to make polite requests.

Note that a **negative answer** means that you will do what the person requests.

A: **Would you mind waiting** for a few minutes? Mr. Caras is still at a meeting.
B: **Not at all**.
(OK. I'll do it.)

4. People usually expect us to say **yes** to polite requests. When we **cannot say yes**, we usually apologize and give a reason.

▶ **BE CAREFUL!** Do not use **would** or **could** to answer polite requests.

A: **Could** you take this to Susan Lane's office for me?
B: **I'm sorry, I can't**. I'm expecting an important phone call.

A: I'm cold. **Would** you shut the window, please?
B: **Certainly**.
NOT Yes, I would.

1 **IDENTIFY** • *Marcia has a new co-worker. Read their conversations. Underline all the polite requests.*

1. **MARCIA:** Hi. You must be the new office assistant. I'm Marcia Jones. Let me know if you need anything.

   LORNA: Thanks, Marcia. <u>Could you show me the coat closet?</u>

   MARCIA: Certainly. It's right over here.

2. **LORNA:** Marcia, would you explain these instructions for the fax machine?

   MARCIA: Sure. Just put your letter in here and dial the number.

3. **MARCIA:** I'm leaving for lunch. Would you like to come?

   LORNA: Thanks, but I can't right now. I'm really busy.

   MARCIA: Do you want a sandwich from the coffee shop?

   LORNA: That would be great. Can you get me a tuna sandwich and a soda?

   MARCIA: Sure. Will you answer my phone until I get back?

   LORNA: Certainly.

4. **MARCIA:** Lorna, would you mind making some coffee?

   LORNA: I'm sorry, but I can't do it now. I've got to finish this letter before 2:00.

2 **CHOOSE** • *Lorna's roommate, Jana, is having problems today. Check the appropriate response to each of Jana's requests.*

1. Lorna, would you please drive me to class today? My car won't start.

   a. _____ Yes, I would.　　　　　**b.** __✓__ I'd be glad to.

2. Would you mind lending me five dollars? I'm getting paid tomorrow.

   a. _____ Not at all.　　　　　**b.** _____ Yes.

3. Lorna, can you take these books back to the library for me? I'm running late.

   a. _____ I'm late too. Sorry.　　　　　**b.** _____ No, I can't.

4. Could you lock the door on your way out? My hands are full.

   a. _____ Yes, I could.　　　　　**b.** _____ Sure.

5. Can you turn the radio down? I need to study for my math quiz this morning.

   a. _____ Certainly.　　　　　**b.** _____ Not at all.

6. Will you pick up some milk on the way home this afternoon?

   a. _____ No, I won't.　　　　　**b.** _____ Sorry. I'll be at work until 8:00.

3 **CHOOSE AND COMPLETE** • *Use the appropriate imperative from the box to complete these requests. Use* **please** *when possible, and make any necessary changes.*

Buy some cereal.	Call back later.	~~Close the window.~~
File these reports.	Shut the door.	Turn on the lights.

1. Can _____you please close the window?_____ It's freezing in here.

2. Could _____ I've finished reading them.

3. Would you mind _____ It's too dark in here.

4. Will _____ We don't have any left.

5. Could _____ Ms. Cho is on another call right now.

6. Would _____ There's too much noise in the hall!

4 **EDIT** • *Read these requests from Marcia's boss and Marcia's answers (in dark print). Find and correct six mistakes in making and responding to requests. The first mistake is already corrected.*

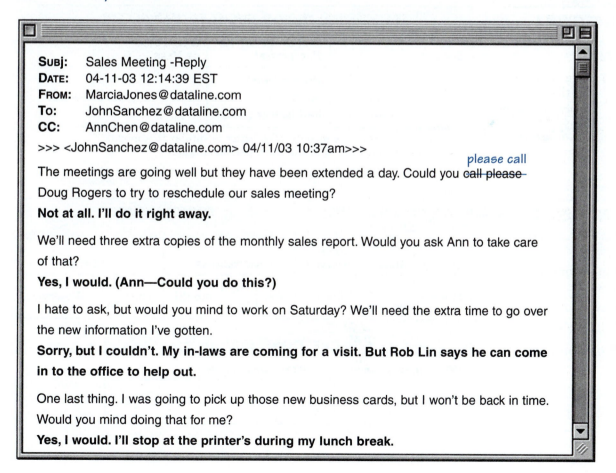

SUBJ: Sales Meeting -Reply
DATE: 04-11-03 12:14:39 EST
FROM: MarciaJones@dataline.com
TO: JohnSanchez@dataline.com
CC: AnnChen@dataline.com
>>> <JohnSanchez@dataline.com> 04/11/03 10:37am>>>

                                                              please call
The meetings are going well but they have been extended a day. Could you ~~call please~~
Doug Rogers to try to reschedule our sales meeting?
Not at all. I'll do it right away.

We'll need three extra copies of the monthly sales report. Would you ask Ann to take care
of that?
Yes, I would. (Ann—Could you do this?)

I hate to ask, but would you mind to work on Saturday? We'll need the extra time to go over
the new information I've gotten.
**Sorry, but I couldn't. My in-laws are coming for a visit. But Rob Lin says he can come
in to the office to help out.**

One last thing. I was going to pick up those new business cards, but I won't be back in time.
Would you mind doing that for me?
Yes, I would. I'll stop at the printer's during my lunch break.

UNIT 30

Advice:
Should, Ought to, Had better

> I really don't mind starting at the bottom and working my way to the top.

> Maybe you **ought to consider** a job as an elevator operator.

CHECK *POINT*

Check the correct answer.

☐ The interviewer is suggesting a type of job for the applicant.

☐ The interviewer is telling the applicant how to be successful.

CHART CHECK 1

Circle T (True) or F (False).

T F The same form of the verb follows *should*, *ought to*, and *had better*.

	STATEMENTS: *SHOULD/OUGHT TO/HAD BETTER*		
SUBJECT	**SHOULD/OUGHT TO/ HAD BETTER***	**BASE FORM OF VERB**	
I/He/She/We/You/They	**should (not)** **ought to** **had better (not)**	**look**	for a new job.

*Should and ought to are modals. Had better is similar to a modal. These forms do not have -s in the third person singular.

NOTE: For contractions of *should not* and *had better*, see Appendix 24 on page 346.

CHART CHECK 2

Check the correct answer.

In questions about advice, we usually use:

☐ *should*

☐ *ought to*

☐ *had better*

YES/NO QUESTIONS: *SHOULD*		
SHOULD	**SUBJECT**	**BASE FORM**
Should	I he	**look**?

SHORT ANSWERS					
AFFIRMATIVE			**NEGATIVE**		
Yes,	you he	**should.**	**No,**	you he	**shouldn't.**

WH- QUESTIONS: *SHOULD*				
WH- WORD	**SHOULD**	**SUBJECT**	**BASE FORM**	
Where	**should**	I he	**look**	for a new job?

EXPRESS CHECK

Complete this conversation.

A: They're looking for a cashier at McDonald's. _____ I apply for the job?

B: _____, you _____. You can get more money working at the bookstore.

Grammar Explanations

Examples

---

1. Use *should* and *ought to* to say that <u>something is advisable</u>.

USAGE NOTE: We do not usually use the negative of *ought to* in American English. We use *shouldn't* instead.

- Mario **should find** a new job.
- He **ought to read** the help wanted ads.

- He **shouldn't quit** school.
  NOT COMMON ~~He ought not to quit.~~

---

2. Use *had better* for <u>urgent advice</u>—when you believe that something bad will happen if the person does not follow the advice.

USAGE NOTE: We usually use the <u>contraction</u> for *had better*.

The negative of *had better* is ***had better not***.

▶ **BE CAREFUL!** *Had better* always refers to the <u>present</u> or the <u>future</u>, never to the past (even though it uses the word *had*).

- You**'d better leave** now, *or you'll be late.*

- You**'d better** apply for more than one job.
  NOT ~~You had better apply . . .~~

- You**'d better not** be late.
  NOT ~~You'd not better be late.~~

- We**'d better take** the bus *now*.
- You**'d better call** them back *tomorrow*.

---

3. Use *should* for <u>questions</u>. We do not usually use *ought to* or *had better* for questions.

- **Should** I **apply** for that job?
- When **should** I **apply**?

---

4. It is usually considered impolite to give **advice to people of equal or higher status** (such as friends or bosses) unless they ask for it.

When we give <u>unasked-for advice</u>, we often soften it with ***maybe***, ***perhaps***, or ***I think***.

FRIEND: **Should** I **shake** hands with the interviewer?
YOU: Yes, you **should**.

BOSS: Where **should** I **take** our client to lunch?
YOU: I think you **should go** to the Tuscan Grill.

- Myra, ***maybe*** you **ought to apply** for this job.

PRONUNCIATION NOTE
Ought to is often pronounced "oughta" in informal speech. Do not write *oughta*.

READ • *Look at these job search tips.*

> • You should tell all your friends that you are looking for a job.
> • You'd better not quit your present job before you find a new one.
> • You shouldn't tell your boss that you are looking for a new job.
> • You ought to apply for several jobs at once.
> • You shouldn't immediately ask an interviewer about job benefits.
> • You should always give the interviewer accurate salary information.

ANSWER • *Check the things that are OK to do according to the tips.*

1. ☑ tell your friends about your job search
2. ☐ tell your boss about your job search
3. ☐ ask about job benefits right away
4. ☐ leave your job during your search
5. ☐ apply for several jobs at once
6. ☐ tell the interviewer your real salary

 CHOOSE • *Read this advice for job seekers. Complete it with the correct words.*

Reader's Weekly   Volume II, Issue 23

ADVICE FOR JOB SEEKERS

Want or need a new job? When's the best time to start looking? Right now!

You _____ **'d better not** _____ delay, or you'll start to feel "stuck."
      1. (ought to / 'd better not)

These tips will help:

☛ A lot of people wait until after the holidays to look for a job. That means less competition for

you right now. You _____ wait!
      2. (shouldn't / should)

☛ Too busy at work to schedule interviews? Early morning interviews have fewer interruptions.

You _____ ask for interviews before nine o'clock.
      3. (should / 'd better not)

☛ If you are laid off, you _____ take a lower-paying job just to
      4. ('d better / shouldn't)

get work. If your new salary is low, your employer won't appreciate your skills. If possible, you

_____ ask for a salary that matches your skills.
      5. ('d better not / should)

☛ However, money isn't everything! You _____ take a position
      6. (ought to / 'd better not)

with a company you dislike, or you won't do a good job there.

☛ Don't talk about salary too soon. You _____ wait—learn about
      7. ('d better / shouldn't)

the job and talk about your skills first.

3 **COMPLETE** • *Kim Yee's boss has invited him to dinner at his home. Complete Kim's conversation with his friend. Use **should**, **ought to**, or **had better** and the words in parentheses. Choose between affirmative and negative.*

KIM: ___How should I dress?_____ In a suit?
           1. (How / dress?)

SCOTT: You don't have to wear a suit. _____,
                                           2. (look / neat)

      but you can wear casual clothes.

KIM: _____
              3. (What time / arrive?)

SCOTT: It's really important to be on time. Your boss and his wife are expecting you

      at 7:00, so _____. It's OK to be a little
                         4. (arrive after 7:15)

      late, but don't make them wait too long for you!

KIM: _____
              5. (bring a gift?)

SCOTT: Yes, but get something small. _____.
                              6. (buy an expensive gift)

      It would embarrass them.

KIM: _____
              7. (What / buy?)

SCOTT: I think _____.
                    8. (get some flowers)

 4 **EDIT** • *Read this letter. Find and correct six mistakes in expressing advice. The first mistake is already corrected.*

Dear Son,

We are so happy to hear about your new job. Congratulations! Just remember—you shouldn't ~~to~~ work too hard. The most important thing right now is your schoolwork. Maybe you only oughta work two days a week instead of three. Also, we think you'd better ask your boss for time off during exams. That way you'll have plenty of time to study. You would better give this a lot of careful thought, OK? Please take good care of yourself. You'd not better start skipping meals, and you definitely shouldn't worked at night. At your age, you will better get a good night's sleep. Do you need anything from home? Should we send any of your books? Let us know.

                                 With love,

                                 Mom and Dad

UNIT 31

Suggestions:
Could, Why don't . . . ?, Why not . . . ?, Let's, How about . . . ?

Let's Travel!

HOSTELLING INTERNATIONAL

Going to Germany?

Why not stay at a youth hostel?

How about a magnificent one like Altena Castle? Altena is also fun and cheap. So, **why don't** you **make** our castle your home?

Altena Castle, Germany

CHECK **POINT**

Circle T (True) or F (False).

T **F** The ad wants to know why many people don't stay at youth hostels.

CHART CHECK 1

Check the correct answer.

The verb after ***could***, ***why don't***, ***why not***, or ***let's***

☐ changes for different subjects.

☐ does not change for different subjects.

COULD				
(MAYBE)	SUBJECT	COULD*	BASE FORM	
(Maybe)	I/he/she/we/you/they	**could**	**stay**	in a castle.

*Could is a modal. It does not have -s in the third person singular.

WHY DON'T . . . ?				
WHY	DON'T	SUBJECT	BASE FORM	
Why	**don't**	I/we/you/they	**stay**	in a castle**?**
	doesn't	he/she		

WHY NOT . . . ?		
WHY NOT	BASE FORM	
Why not	**stay**	there**?**

LET'S		
LET'S (NOT)	BASE FORM	
Let's (not)	**stay**	there.

CHART CHECK 2

Circle T (True) or F (False).

T **F** Suggestions with ***How about . . . ?*** have only one form.

HOW ABOUT . . . ?		
HOW ABOUT	GERUND/NOUN	
How about	**staying**	in a castle**?**
	a castle?	

EXPRESS CHECK

Add the correct punctuation.

Let's take the train_____   Maybe we could take the train_____

Why not take the train_____   How about the train_____

Grammar Explanations	Examples

1. Use *Let's*, *(Maybe)* . . . *could*, *Why don't/ doesn't*, *Why not*, and *How about* to make <u>suggestions</u>.

A: **Let's take** a trip this summer.
B: **Maybe** we **could go** to Germany.
A: **Why don't** we **ask** Luke to go with us?
B: Good idea. **Why doesn't** Tom **call** him tonight?
A: **Why not call** him right now?
B: **How about staying** at a youth hostel?
A: **How about Altena Castle**?

▶ **BE CAREFUL!** When someone uses *Why not* and *Why don't/doesn't* to <u>make a suggestion</u>, these expressions are not information questions. The speaker does <u>not expect to receive information</u> from the listener.

SUGGESTION
A: **Why don't** you **visit** Jill in Hong Kong?
B: That's a good idea.

INFORMATION QUESTION
A: **Why don't** you **eat** meat?
B: Because I'm a vegetarian.

2. *Let's* always <u>includes the speaker</u>. It means: *Here's a suggestion for you and me.*

■ **Let's go** to Hong Kong.
 (I suggest that we go to Hong Kong.)

3. Note the **different forms** to use with these expressions.

BASE FORM OF THE VERB
■ **Let's** *take* the train.
■ **Maybe** we **could** *take* the train.
■ **Why don't** we *take* the train?
■ **Why not** *take* the train?

GERUND OR NOUN
■ **How about** *taking* the train?
■ **How about** *the train*?

4. Notice the **punctuation** at the end of each kind of suggestion.

STATEMENTS
■ **Let's** stay at a hostel**.**
■ **Maybe** we **could** stay at a hostel**.**

QUESTIONS
■ **Why don't** we stay at a hostel**?**
■ **Why not** stay at a hostel**?**
■ **How about** staying at a hostel**?**
■ **How about** a hostel**?**

IDENTIFY • *Emily and Megan are visiting Hong Kong. Read their conversation. Underline all the suggestions.*

EMILY: <u>Why don't we go to the races?</u> I hear they're really exciting.

MEGAN: I'd like to, but I need to go shopping.

EMILY: Then let's go to the Temple Street Market tonight. We might even see some Chinese opera in the street while we're there.

MEGAN: That sounds like fun. If we do that, why not go to the races this afternoon?

EMILY: OK, but let's get something to eat first in one of those floating restaurants.

MEGAN: I don't think we'll have time. Maybe we could do that tomorrow. Right now, how about getting *dim sum* at the Kau Kee Restaurant next door? Then we could take the Star Ferry to Hong Kong Island and the racecourse.

EMILY: Sounds good. Here's an idea for tomorrow. Why not take one of those small boats—*kaido*—to Lantau Island? When we come back, we could have dinner at the Jumbo Palace.

MEGAN: Let's do that. It's a little expensive, but at least it floats!

 COMPLETE • *Read these conversations. Complete them with the appropriate expression in parentheses.*

1. **A:** I feel like having seafood for dinner, but we went to Tai Pak for seafood last night.

   B: _____ **Why not** _____ go again? The food's great, and so is the view.
   (Why not / Let's not)

2. **A:** I'm really tired. _____ resting before we go out?
   (Let's / How about)

   B: That's a good idea. I'm tired too.

3. **A:** I want to explore downtown Hong Kong.

   B: _____ take a minibus? We'll see a lot more that way.
   (Let's not / Why don't we)

4. **A:** A group of foreign students just checked in at the hostel.

   B: _____ ask them to join us for dinner.
   (How about / Maybe we could)

5. **A:** I still need to buy some souvenirs before we leave.

   B: _____ go shopping after dinner.
   (Let's / How about)

6. **A:** I don't want to go home tomorrow. I'm having a really good time here.

   B: So am I. _____ leave tomorrow.
   (Let's not / Why not)

3 **CHOOSE & COMPLETE** • *Read these conversations. Complete the suggestions with phrases from the box. Add pronouns and change the verbs as necessary. Punctuate correctly.*

> take a trip together   try that new seafood place   ~~buy tickets~~
> go to the beach   buy another one

1. **A:** There's an Oasis concert at the Hong Kong Convention Centre next weekend.

   B: We're near there now. Maybe ___*we could buy tickets.*___

2. **A:** It's going to be hot tomorrow.

   B: I know. How about _____

3. **A:** Sweaters are on sale. Maybe we could buy one for Brian's birthday.

   B: We got him a sweater last year. Let's not _____

4. **A:** I don't know what to do on spring vacation. I'm sick of staying in the dorm.

   B: Me too. Why don't _____

5. **A:** I'm hungry.

   B: Let's _____

4 **EDIT** • *Read these notes. Find and correct seven mistakes in the use of suggestions. The first one is already corrected. Don't forget to check punctuation.*

3:00

Emily

I'm going shopping. I'll be back at
5:00. Let's ~~eating~~ *eat* at 7:00. OK?

Megan

Megan   4:00

7:00 for dinner is fine.

How about go to a movie afterward.

See you later.

E.

Emily   5:00

I'm going to be too tired for a movie.
Maybe we could just hanging around
the hostel after dinner. Let's talk
about it later. I'm taking a nap.

M.

M—   6:00

Let's not eat at the same restaurant
tonight? Why don't we trying a new
place? How about Broadway Seafood.
I'll meet you downstairs at 7:00.

E.

Preferences:
Prefer, Would prefer, Would rather

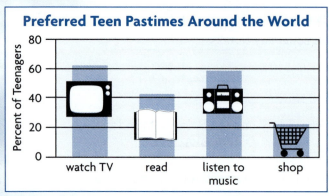

Preferred Teen Pastimes Around the World

Teenagers around the world **prefer watching** TV to all other leisure-time activities.

CHECK *POINT*

Check the main point of the bar graph.

☐ Teenagers like to watch TV, read books, and listen to music.

☐ Teenagers like to watch TV better than they like to do other things.

CHART CHECK 1

Check the correct answer.

Which word(s) can you use with all subjects?

☐ *prefer*

☐ *would prefer ('d prefer)*

STATEMENTS: *PREFER/WOULD PREFER*		
SUBJECT	**(WOULD) PREFER**	**NOUN/GERUND/INFINITIVE**
I/We/You*/They	**prefer**	**newspapers** (to magazines). **reading** newspapers (to reading books). **(not) to read** newspapers.
He/She	**prefers**	
I/He/She/We/You/They	**would prefer 'd prefer**	

*You is both singular and plural.

CHART CHECK 2

Check the correct answer.

Which two forms of the verb can follow **prefer**?

☐ the base form or the gerund

☐ the gerund or the infinitive

YES/NO QUESTIONS: *PREFER/WOULD PREFER*			
DO/WOULD	**SUBJECT**	**PREFER**	**NOUN/GERUND/INFINITIVE**
Do	you/they	**prefer**	**newspapers**? **reading** newspapers? **to read** newspapers?
Does	he/she		
Would	you/they/he/she		

SHORT ANSWERS					
AFFIRMATIVE			**NEGATIVE**		
Yes,	I/we/they	**do.**	**No,**	I/we/they	**don't.**
	he/she	**does.**		he/she	**doesn't.**
	I/we/they/he/she	**would.**		I/we/they/he/she	**wouldn't.**

STATEMENTS: *WOULD RATHER*		
SUBJECT	***WOULD RATHER***	**BASE FORM OF VERB**
I/He/She/We/You/They	**would rather** **'d rather**	**read** newspapers (than read magazines). **(not) read** newspapers.

YES/NO QUESTIONS: *WOULD RATHER*			
WOULD	**SUBJECT**	**RATHER**	**BASE FORM**
Would	she	**rather**	**read**?

SHORT ANSWERS	
AFFIRMATIVE	**NEGATIVE**
Yes, she **would**.	**No**, she **wouldn't**. She'**d rather not**.

EXPRESS CHECK

Circle the correct words to complete this sentence.

I'd rather <u>read / to read</u> <u>than / to</u> shop, but Jo prefers <u>shop / shopping</u>.

Grammar Explanations

Examples

1. Use *prefer*, *would prefer*, and *would rather* to talk about <u>things that you like better</u> than other things.

USAGE NOTE: We often use *prefer* for a <u>general</u> preference and *would prefer* or *would rather* for a preference in a <u>particular</u> situation.

- We usually **prefer *Italian food***.
- I'**d prefer *to have*** Chinese food tonight.
- I'**d rather *cook*** at home.

- Which **do** you **prefer**—chicken or shrimp?
- **Would** you **prefer** chicken or shrimp tonight?

2. *Prefer* and *would prefer* may be followed by a <u>noun</u>, a <u>gerund</u>, or an <u>infinitive</u>.

- I usually **prefer** the *newspaper*. [noun]
- **Does** Bill **prefer *reading*** magazines? [gerund]
- He'**d prefer *to watch*** TV. [infinitive]

Would rather can be followed by only the <u>base form of the verb</u>.

- I'**d rather *stay*** home tonight. [base form]

USAGE NOTE: We often use *I'd rather not*, by itself, <u>to refuse</u> an offer, suggestion, or invitation.

A: Would you like to have some dessert?
B: I'**d rather not**. I've had enough to eat.

▶ **BE CAREFUL!** The negative of *I'd rather* is *I'd rather not.*

- I'**d rather not** have dessert.
NOT ~~I wouldn't rather have dessert.~~

3. A **comparison with *to*** may follow *prefer/would prefer* + noun.

A **comparison with *to*** may also follow *prefer/would prefer* + gerund.

A **comparison with *than*** may follow *would rather* + base form of the verb.

- Lani **prefers** comedies *to* action movies. [noun] [noun]

- I'**d prefer** visiting Lani *to* going to the party. [gerund] [gerund]

- I'**d rather** watch football *than* play it. [base form] [base form]

1 **TRUE OR FALSE** • *Julio ranked some activities from 1 to 8 according to his preferences (1 = his favorite). Look at his list. Then read each numbered sentence and write T (True) or F (False).*

Preferred Activities

__3__	listen to music
__5__	go swimming
__4__	go biking
__1__	watch TV
__8__	bake pies
__6__	play guitar
__7__	hike
__2__	read

__T__ **1.** He prefers listening to music to playing guitar.

_____ **2.** He'd rather hike than go swimming.

_____ **3.** He prefers swimming to biking.

_____ **4.** He'd rather not watch TV.

_____ **5.** He prefers baking pies to reading.

_____ **6.** He prefers watching TV to reading.

_____ **7.** He'd probably prefer a concert to a hike in the woods.

2 **CHOOSE & COMPLETE** • *Julio and Ana are discussing their evening plans. Complete their conversation. Use **would rather (not)** with one of the verbs in the box or by itself in short answers.*

have	cook	see	~~stay~~	go

ANA: Would you like to go to a movie tonight?

JULIO: _____ I'd rather stay _____ home and watch TV.
                                      1.

ANA: Sounds good. Maybe we could make dinner later.

JULIO: _____ tonight. I'm too tired.
                          2.

ANA: OK. _____ you _____ to
                                                              3.
a restaurant instead?

JULIO: Let's order out for some pizza.

ANA: How about a pepperoni pizza?

JULIO: _____. Pepperoni gives me heartburn.
                          4.
_____ mushrooms than pepperoni if that's OK.
                          5.

ANA: No problem. Do you want to watch the Stephen King thriller at 8:00?

JULIO: _____. I don't like his movies.
                          6.

ANA: Well . . . there's a comedy on at 8:00 and a documentary at 8:30.

JULIO: _____ the comedy. I need a laugh.
                          7.

3

COMPLETE • *Read these conversations. Complete them with* prefer, would prefer, *or* would rather. *Use* prefer *to state general preferences. Complete the comparisons with* to *or* than.

1. A: We're going to Rome again next week. _____Would_____ you

_____prefer_____ taking the train _____to_____ flying this time?

B: You know me. I always _____ the plane _____ the train.

2. A: I _____ have the aisle seat _____ the window seat.

B: That's fine with me. I _____ the window seat. That way I can look out.

3. A: Where would you like to stay? In a hotel or a *pensione*?

B: Oh, I _____ to stay in a *pensione* this time. It's more personal.

4. A: I _____ eating in small *trattorias* _____ eating in

big restaurants.

B: Me too. They're less expensive and the food is always delicious.

5. A: Speaking of food, you make the best spaghetti with clam sauce in the world.

B: Thanks, but I _____ order it in a restaurant _____

make it at home!

6. A: When in Rome, _____ you _____ drinking tea or coffee?

B: I definitely _____ coffee _____ tea. You know what

they say, "When in Rome do as the Romans do!"

 4

EDIT • *Read Ana's report. Find and correct six mistakes in the use of* prefer *and* would rather. *The first mistake is already corrected.*

For my study, I interviewed fifty men and women. There was no difference
in men's and women's preferences for TV. I found that everyone prefers
                    to
watching TV ~~than~~ going to movies. Men and women both enjoy news programs
and entertainment specials. However, men would rather watching adventure
programs and science fiction, while women prefer soap operas. Men also like to
watch all kinds of sports, but women would rather see game shows to sports.
Reading preferences differ too. Men prefer to reading newspapers, while women
would rather read magazines and books. When men read books, they prefer read
nonfiction and adventure stories. Women are preferring novels.

SelfTest

Circle the letter of the correct answer to complete each sentence.

> **EXAMPLE:**
> Jennifer never _____ coffee.   A **(B)** C D
> (A) drink   (C) is drinking
> (B) drinks   (D) was drinking

1. —Would you shut the door, please?   A B C D
   —_____
   (A) Certainly.   (C) Yes, I could.
   (B) No, I can't.   (D) Yes, I would.

2. Why _____ a movie tonight?   A B C D
   (A) about seeing   (C) not seeing
   (B) don't we see   (D) we don't see

3. Marcia can't speak German yet, but after a few lessons   A B C D
   she _____ speak a little.
   (A) can   (C) is able to
   (B) could   (D) will be able to

4. In 1998, Tara Lipinski _____ win the gold medal in   A B C D
   figure skating at the Winter Olympics.
   (A) can   (C) will be able to
   (B) could   (D) was able to

5. I _____ make new friends since I moved here.   A B C D
   (A) can't   (C) haven't been able to
   (B) couldn't   (D) 'm not able to

6. She _____ better not arrive late.   A B C D
   (A) did   (C) 'd
   (B) has   (D) would

7. —Do you mind if I borrow a chair?   A B C D
   —_____ Do you need only one?
   (A) I'm sorry.   (C) Yes, I do.
   (B) Not at all.   (D) Yes, I would.

8. Would you mind _____ me tomorrow?   A B C D
   (A) call   (C) to call
   (B) calling   (D) if you call

9. I'd rather _____ the movie. I hear it's very good.   A B C D
   (A) watch   (C) watching
   (B) to watch   (D) not watch

10. You _____ miss the deadline or you'll have to pay a fee.   A B C D
    (A) better not   (C) 'd better not
    (B) 'd better   (D) had no better

11. _____ take the train instead of the bus? It's faster.   A B C D
    (A) How about   (C) Why don't
    (B) Let's   (D) Why not

12. May my sister _____ to class with me tomorrow?   A B C D
    (A) come   (C) coming
    (B) comes   (D) to come

13. I _____ have dessert. I'm trying to lose some weight.   A B C D
    (A) 'd rather   (C) 'd prefer
    (B) 'd rather not   (D) 'd prefer not

14. Jamie prefers working at home _____ working in an office.   A B C D
    (A) more   (C) that
    (B) than   (D) to

SECTION TWO

*Each sentence has four underlined words or phrases. The four underlined parts
of the sentence are marked A, B, C, and D. Circle the letter of the one underlined
word or phrase that is NOT CORRECT.*

> **EXAMPLE:**
> Mike <u>usually</u> <u>drives</u> to school, but <u>today</u> he <u>walks</u>.   A B C (D)
>   A   B   C   D

15. <u>When</u> I was ten, I <u>could</u> swim, but I <u>wasn't</u> <u>able dive</u>.   A B C D
    A   B   C   D

16. Why <u>don't</u> we <u>have</u> dinner and then <u>go</u> see *Possible Dreams.*   A B C D
        A   B   C   D

17. You <u>drove</u> for seven hours today, so <u>maybe</u> you'd <u>not better</u> <u>drive</u> tonight.   A B C D
     A   B   C   D

18. <u>Will</u> you mind <u>bringing</u> your camera to the graduation party <u>tomorrow</u><u>?</u>   A B C D
    A   B   C D

19. Dad, <u>may</u> Jim <u>borrows</u> the car tomorrow or <u>does</u> Mom <u>need</u> it?   A B C D
      A   B   C   D

20. I <u>can't</u> <u>help</u> you, so <u>maybe</u> you should <u>to ask</u> Marta.   A B C D
   A   B   C   D

21. <u>Should</u> I <u>bring</u> flowers to Lisa's or <u>should</u> I <u>giving</u> her candy?   A B C D
    A   B   C   D

22. <u>Maybe</u> you <u>ought</u> <u>than</u> just <u>bring</u> flowers.   A B C D
   A   B   C   D

23. Silva <u>celebrated</u> <u>last year</u> because she <u>could</u> <u>win</u> the race.   A B C D
      A   B   C D

24. <u>It's</u> really late, so <u>let's</u> <u>we</u> <u>go</u> out to dinner tonight.   A B C D
   A   B   C D

25. Why <u>would</u> you <u>rather</u> <u>stay</u> home <u>to</u> go out tonight?   A B C D
    A   B   C   D

UNIT 33

Necessity:
Have (got) to and Must

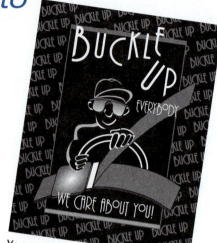

CHECK POINT

Check the correct answer.

Using a seat belt is:

❑ a requirement

❑ a choice

You **must buckle** your seat belt. It's the law.

CHART CHECK 1

Circle T (True) or F (False).

T   F   We use **have got to** in affirmative and negative statements.

AFFIRMATIVE STATEMENTS: *HAVE (GOT) TO*

SUBJECT	HAVE TO/ HAVE GOT TO	BASE FORM OF VERB
I/We/You/They	**have (got) to**	**stop**.
He/She/It	**has (got) to**	

CONTRACTIONS

Have got to = **'ve got to**

Has got to = **'s got to**

NEGATIVE STATEMENTS: *HAVE TO*

SUBJECT	DO NOT	HAVE TO	BASE FORM
I/We/You/They	**don't**	**have to**	**stop**.
He/She/It	**doesn't**		

CHART CHECK 2

Check the correct answer.

In questions with **have to**, what comes before the subject?

❑ a form of **do**

❑ a form of **have to**

YES/NO QUESTIONS: *HAVE TO*

DO	SUBJECT	HAVE TO	BASE FORM
Do	we	**have to**	**stop**?
Does	he		

SHORT ANSWERS

AFFIRMATIVE			NEGATIVE	
Yes,	you	**do.**	**No,**	you	**don't.**
	he	**does.**		he	**doesn't.**

STATEMENTS: *MUST*

SUBJECT	MUST* (NOT)	BASE FORM
I/He/She/It/We/You/They	**must (not)**	**stop**.

CONTRACTION

must not = **mustn't**

*Must is a modal. It does not have *-s* in the third person singular.

EXPRESS CHECK

Complete this conversation. Use <u>one word</u> for each blank.

A: Why _____ she _____ _____ wear her seat belt?

B: It's the law. Everyone _____ wear a seat belt.

Grammar Explanations

Examples

1. Use *have to*, *have got to*, and *must* to express <u>necessity</u>.

  a. *Have to* is the most common expression in <u>everyday use</u>.

■ Everyone **has to pass** a road test before getting a driver's license.

  b. *Have got to* often expresses strong feelings in <u>speaking</u> and <u>informal writing</u>.

■ He**'s got to drive** more slowly. I'm afraid he's going to have an accident.

  c. *Must* is used in <u>writing</u> (forms, signs, notices).

■ You **must stop** completely at a stop sign.

    Must is used in <u>spoken English</u>, when

    • the speaker is in a position of <u>power</u>.

■ Ling-ling, you **must clean** your room. *(mother talking to her young child)*

    • there is <u>urgent necessity</u>.

■ You really **must talk** to your boss about a raise. *(friend talking to a friend)*

  ▶ **BE CAREFUL!** *Don't have to* and *must not* have <u>very different meanings</u>. *(See Unit 34.)*

■ You **don't have to stop** here. *(It isn't necessary to stop here.)*

■ You **must not stop** here. *(You can't stop here. It's not allowed.)*

2. Use the correct form of *have to* for <u>all tenses and forms</u>.

■ After his accident, Sal **had to take** a driver's improvement class. *(past tense)*
■ Sheila **has had to drive** to work for two years. *(present perfect)*
■ I**'ll have to drive** tomorrow. *(future)*

  Use *have got to* and *must* only for the <u>present</u> or the <u>future</u>.

■ I**'ve got to wear** glasses all the time.
■ Everyone **must take** an eye test tomorrow.

3. Use *have to* for most <u>questions</u>. (We rarely use *have got to* or *must* for questions.)

■ **Does** Paul **have to drive**?
■ When **will** he **have to leave**?

PRONUNCIATION NOTE
In informal speech, *have to* is often pronounced "hafta" and *got to* is often pronounced "gotta."
Do not write *hafta* or *gotta*.

1 **IDENTIFY** • *Read Ben Leonard's telephone conversation with a clerk from the California Department of Motor Vehicles (DMV). Underline the words that talk about necessity.*

DMV: Department of Motor Vehicles. May I help you?

BEN: I'm moving to California soon. <u>Will I have to get</u> a California license when I move?

DMV: Yes, you will. California residents must have a California driver's license.

BEN: When will I have to get my California license?

DMV: You have to replace your old license ten days after you become a resident. So come in and apply for your California license right after you get here.

BEN: Do I have to take any tests to exchange my Illinois license for a California license?

DMV: Since you already have an Illinois license, you won't have to take the road test. But you will have to take the written test.

BEN: How about the eye test?

DMV: Oh, everyone has got to take the eye test.

BEN: OK. Thanks a lot. You've been very helpful.

2 **COMPLETE** • *Read this conversation. Complete it with the correct form of **have to** or **have got to** and the verbs in parentheses. Use **have got to** and give short answers whenever possible.*

BEN: When _____do_____ you _____have to use_____ the car?
                                                    1. (use)

ANN: I _____ Jim's school records pretty soon. Why?
                    2. (pick up)

_____ you still _____ the oil?
                                              3. (change)

BEN: No, _____. I did it early this morning. Oh, and
                    4.

I bought some film.

ANN: Oh, you _____ that. I bought three rolls yesterday.
                        5. (not do)

BEN: We _____ lots of pictures on the trip.
                    6. (take)

_____ Jim still _____?
                                        7. (pack)

ANN: No, _____. He finished and went to Sara's to say
                    8.

goodbye. Why?

BEN: He _____ me clean out the car. It's full of his stuff.
                    9. (help)

ANN: I'll call him again. It's hard for him to leave his friends.

I _____ him to come home twice already.
            10. (call)

3 **CHOOSE & COMPLETE** • *Look at these signs. Use the verbs from the box to complete the sentences about things you **must** do and **must not** do.*

turn	drive	ride	walk

1. You _____*must not turn*_____ left.

2. You _____ right.

3. You _____ over 40 mph.

4. You _____ 60 mph.

5. Bicyclists _____ on the right.

6. Pedestrians _____ on the right.

4 **EDIT** • *Read Jim's letter to Sara. Find and correct seven mistakes in expressing necessity. The first mistake is already corrected.*

Dear Sara,

How are you doing? We've been here about six weeks. It's strange living in the suburbs.

There's no public transportation, so you've ~~get~~ ^got to drive everywhere. I had to signs up for driver's ed this semester so I can get my license by summertime. It's the law here that everyone musts wear a seat belt. I used to hate to buckle up, but with the traffic here, I have changed my mind. There are a lot of freeways, and you've gotta know how to change lanes with a lot of fast traffic. Even my Mom have had to get used to it. Dad works at home, so he hasn't has to do a lot of driving.

Have you beaten those computer games yet? I'm having a lot of trouble with "Doom." You got to write to me and tell me how to get past the fifth level!

Jim

UNIT 34

Choice: *Don't have to*
No Choice: *Must not* and *Can't*

*No, we **don't have to stop** and **ask** for directions!*

DRIVERS MUST NOT PARK IN THE CROSSWALK

CHECK *POINT*

Check the correct answer.

The driver can choose to

☐ park in the crosswalk.   ☐ stop to ask for directions.

CHART CHECK 1

Check the correct answer.

Which part of ***do not have to*** changes for different subjects?

☐ **do**   ☐ **have**

DON'T HAVE TO				
SUBJECT	**DO NOT**	**HAVE TO**	**BASE FORM OF VERB**	
I/We/You/They	**don't**	**have to**	**stop**	here.
He/She/It	**doesn't**		**park**	

CHART CHECK 2

Circle T (True) or F (False).

T F   The form of ***must not*** and ***can't*** changes for different subjects.

MUST NOT			
SUBJECT	**MUST* NOT**	**BASE FORM**	
I/He/She/It/We/You/They	**must not**	**stop**	here.

CAN'T			
SUBJECT	**CAN'T***	**BASE FORM**	
I/He/She/It/We/You/They	**can't**	**stop**	here.

*These words are modals. They do not have -*s* in the third person singular.

EXPRESS CHECK

Unscramble these words to form two sentences.

stop • He • have • here • to • doesn't

_____

must • fast • You • not • drive • too

_____

Grammar Explanations

1. *Have to* and *must* have similar meanings. They both express the idea that something is <u>necessary or required</u>.

Don't/Doesn't have to and *must not* have <u>very different meanings</u>.

  a. *Don't/Doesn't have to* expresses that something is <u>not necessary</u>. It means that there is another possibility. There is a **choice**.

  b. *Must not* expresses **prohibition**. It means that something is <u>not allowed</u> or is <u>against the law</u>. There is **no choice**.

2. *Must not* is used to express <u>prohibition in writing</u>, including official forms, signs, and notices.

  Usage Note: In <u>spoken English</u>, we do not usually use *must not* when talking to or about another <u>adult</u>. We use *can't* instead.

  Sometimes people use *must not* to tell a <u>child</u> that there is no choice in a situation.

3. You can use *not have to* for <u>all tenses and forms</u>.

  Must not refers only to the <u>present</u> or the <u>future</u>.

Examples

■ You **have to stop** at the stop sign.
■ You **must stop** at the stop sign.

■ You **don't have to drive**. I can do it.
■ He **doesn't have to turn** here. He can turn at the next intersection.

■ You **must not use** the car without my permission.
■ You **must not drive** without a license. It's against the law.

■ You **must not use** your horn unnecessarily.

■ We **can't park** here. It's a tow-away zone.

■ Jesse, you **mustn't take off** your seat belt while the car is moving.

■ You **don't have to drive**. *(present)*
■ She **won't have to renew** her license next year. *(future)*
■ We **haven't had to pay** a lot of parking fines this year. *(present perfect)*
■ They **didn't have to take** driver's education last year. Now it's required. *(simple past tense)*

■ Drivers **must not pass** on the right.

1 **IDENTIFY** • *Read this article. Underline the words that show that there is a choice about doing something. Circle the words that show that there is no choice.*

A New Alternative to Car Ownership

New drivers are usually excited about their new freedom: "My mom <u>doesn't have to drive</u> me everywhere anymore! I don't have to ask my friends for rides to school!" When you don't have your own car yet, any price seems worth paying. But once you buy a car, you (can't forget) your car payments and insurance premiums, or you won't be a driver for very long. You can't leave gas and maintenance out of the budget either. Car sharing offers an alternative to these problems, however. Members of car-sharing groups have a car when they need one for either short trips or vacations, but they don't have the high expenses of ownership. They pay very little to use a shared car, and they don't have to worry about maintaining the car or paying the insurance. Fees for short trips are only about $3.00 an hour plus $0.50 per mile. Groups do not have strict requirements either. Members must not have bad driving records or poor credit, and they must not return the cars in poor shape or they will pay extra.

2 **COMPLETE** • *Read this conversation. Complete it with **can't** or the correct form of **not have to** and the verb in parentheses.*

JIM: Austin _____doesn't have to sit_____ in a safety seat, but I do. It's not fair.
 1. (sit)

ANN: Jim, you really _____ like that in the car. Your father has
 2. (yell)

to concentrate on driving. Ben, turn left for the restaurant.

BEN: I _____ left. It's a one-way street. I'll go around the block.
 3. (turn)

ANN: There's the restaurant. Uh-oh. You _____ here. It's a bus stop.
 4. (park)

BEN: Maybe I'll park in that indoor garage. That way we _____
 5. (worry)

about our stuff while we're eating. Remind me to buy gas after lunch.

ANN: We _____ gas, do we? The tank is still half full.
 6. (get)

BEN: I know. But we _____ gas for a long time. I'm not sure the
 7. (buy)

gauge is working.

AUSTIN: You _____ that truck into the restaurant, Jim! It's too big.
 8. (bring)

JIM: Mom said OK. Anyway, I _____ to you. Let's eat!
 9. (listen)

3 **READ & COMPLETE** • *Look at this sign at the Holiday Motel swimming pool. Complete each sentence with **must not** or **don't have to** and the correct form of the verb in parentheses.*

 Holiday Motel
Swimming Pool Rules and Regulations
Pool Hours 10:00 A.M.–10:00 P.M.
Children under 12 years NOT ALLOWED in pool without an adult.
Towels available at front desk.

NO
• ball playing
• radios
• diving
• glass bottles
• alcoholic beverages

1. Children under age 12 _____ **must not swim** _____ without an adult.
   (swim)
2. You _____ your own towel.
   (bring)
3. You _____ ball in or around the pool.
   (play)
4. You _____ into the pool.
   (dive)
5. Teenagers _____ with an adult.
   (be)
6. You _____ the pool at 8:00 P.M.
   (leave)

4 **EDIT** • *Read Austin's postcard to his friend. Find and correct five mistakes in expressing necessity. The first mistake is already corrected.*

Holiday Motel, Rte. 55

Hi, Janet!

We got to the motel late this evening because we got lost. But we
were lucky—they kept our room so we ~~must not~~ find another
                didn't have to
motel. Jimmy is really happy because he don't have to go to bed
until after 10:00, when the swimming pool closes. We mustn't leave
until 11:00 tomorrow (checkout time), so we can stay up later.
Yosemite is only four hours away, so we won't had to drive the
whole day tomorrow. It's going to be exciting. My parents say
we absolutely must not to go out by ourselves because there
are bears there. I'd love to see a bear (from the inside of the
car). I'll send a postcard of one.
              Austin

To: Janet Edwards

5500 Amherst Lane

Erie, PA 16506

Expectations:
Be supposed to

Oh no! I **was supposed to prepare** a speech!

He'd better hurry up with these pictures. It**'s supposed to rain**.

Thank goodness I**'m not supposed to pay** for this photographer.

best man   bride's parents   maid of honor   bride   groom   groom's parents

CHECK POINT

Check the correct answers.

The groom's father is thinking about

☐ something he forgot to do.

☐ the usual way something is done at a wedding.

CHART CHECK

Circle T (True) or F (False).

T F You can use ***be supposed to*** in the simple present and simple past tenses.

STATEMENTS				
SUBJECT	**BE**	**(NOT) SUPPOSED TO**	**BASE FORM OF VERB**	
I	am was	(not) supposed to	stand be	here.
He/She/It	is was			
We/You*/They	are were			

You is both singular and plural.

YES/NO QUESTIONS				
BE	**SUBJECT**	**SUPPOSED TO**	**BASE FORM**	
Am Was	I	supposed to	stand	here?
Is Was	he			
Are Were	you			

150

SHORT ANSWERS					
AFFIRMATIVE			**NEGATIVE**		
Yes,	you	**are.** **were.**	**No,**	you	**aren't.** **weren't.**
	he	**is.** **was.**		he	**isn't.** **wasn't.**
	I	**am.** **was.**		I	**'m not.** **wasn't.**

EXPRESS CHECK

Complete these sentences.

A: What _____ we supposed to wear yesterday?

B: Our suits. It _____ supposed to be a dress rehearsal.

A: Oops.

Grammar Explanations

1. Use *be supposed to* to talk about different kinds of expectations:

    a. **rules** and **usual ways** of doing things

    b. **predictions**

    c. **hearsay** (what everyone says)

    d. **plans** or **arrangements**

2. Use *be supposed to* only in the **simple present** tense or in the **simple past** tense.

Use the **simple present** tense to refer to both the present and the future.

USAGE NOTE: The **simple past** tense often suggests that something did not happen.

Examples

- The groom **is supposed to arrive** at the ceremony early. It's a custom.

- It's **not supposed to rain** tomorrow. I heard it on the radio.

- The beach **is supposed to be** beautiful in August. Everyone says so.

- The ceremony **isn't supposed to begin** yet.

- The bride **is supposed to wear** white.
- The ceremony **was supposed to begin** at 7:00.
- It **wasn't supposed to rain**.

- I'm **supposed to be** at the wedding rehearsal *tomorrow*.
  NOT I will be supposed to be there tomorrow.

- Carl **was supposed to bring** flowers, *but* he forgot.

IDENTIFY • *Read this article and underline the phrases that express expectations.*

IT WASN'T SUPPOSED TO BE A BIG WEDDING

PROVIDENCE, JULY 19—The Stricklands wanted a quiet wedding—that's why they eloped to Block Island, off the Atlantic Coast of the United States. The island is quite small, so the Stricklands packed their bikes for the ferry trip. The weather was supposed to be lovely, and they had asked the mayor to marry them on a hill overlooking the ocean.

"When we got there, we found a crowd of cyclists admiring the view," laughed Beth.

When Bill kissed his bride, the audience burst into loud applause and rang their bicycle bells. "We weren't supposed to have fifty wedding guests, but we love cycling, and we're not sorry," Bill said.

While packing the next day, Beth left her wedding bouquet at the hotel. Minutes before the ferry was supposed to leave, Bill jumped on his bike, got the flowers, and made it back to the ferry on time. "Cyclists are supposed to stay fast and fit," he said.

TRUE OR FALSE • *Read the article again. Write T (True) or F (False) for each sentence.*

__F__ 1. The Stricklands planned a big wedding.

_____ 2. The weather forecaster predicted rain.

_____ 3. The Stricklands invited fifty wedding guests.

_____ 4. The ferry followed a schedule.

_____ 5. People think that cyclists are in good shape.

2 **COMPLETE** • *Read these conversations. Complete them with a form of* **be supposed to** *and the verb in parentheses. Give short answers. Choose affirmative or negative.*

1. **A:** Netta, Gary called while you were out.

   B: _____Am_____ I _____supposed to call_____ him back?
   a. (call)

   A: _____No, you aren't_____. He'll call you this afternoon.
   b.

2. **A:** The dress store called too. They delivered your wedding dress to your office.

   _____ they _____ that?
   a. (do)

   B: _____! That's why I stayed home today. They
   b.

   _____ it here.
   c. (deliver)

3. **A:** Let's get in line. The rehearsal _____ in a few minutes.
   a. (start)

   B: We're bridesmaids. Where _____ we _____?
   b. (stand)

4. A: Gary! You _____ here!
  _{**a.** (be)}

  B: Why not?

  A: You _____ Netta until the ceremony. It's bad luck.
  _{**b.** (see)}

5. A: Sophie, could I borrow your handkerchief, please? I _____
  _{**a.** (wear)}

  something old, something new, something borrowed, and something blue. I don't

  have anything borrowed.

  B: It _____ today. Maybe I should lend you my
  _{**b.** (rain)}

  umbrella instead.

6. A: I hear Gary and Netta are going to Aruba on their honeymoon.

  B: Oh, that _____ a really nice island.
  _{**a.** (be)}

3

EDIT • *Read Sophie's letter to a friend. Find and correct six mistakes in the use of* **be supposed to**. *The first mistake is already corrected.*

Dear Kasha,

     I'm so sorry—I know I ~~am~~ ^{was} supposed to write to you last week about my plans

to visit. I've been awfully busy. My friend Netta is getting married soon, and she's

asked me to be her maid of honor. She and Gary want a big wedding. They're

supposed to have about two hundred guests. I have a lot of responsibilities. I will be

supposed to give Netta a shower before the wedding (that's a party where everyone

brings presents for the bride). I am also suppose to help her choose the bridesmaids'

dresses. The best man's name is Jim. He'll help Gary get ready. I haven't met him

yet, but he's supposes to be very nice.

     I'd better say goodbye now. I supposed to leave for rehearsal five minutes ago.

                                Love,
                                Sophie

P.S. About my visit—I'm supposing to get some time off in July. Would that

    be convenient?

Future Possibility:
May, Might, Could

EUROPE'S WEATHER

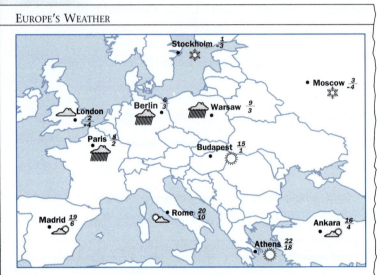

Temperatures in London **may drop** as much as eleven degrees by tomorrow morning. We **might** even **see** some snow flurries later on in the day. Winds **could reach** 40 mph.

CHECK *POINT*

Circle T (True) or F (False).

T F It's definitely going to snow in London tomorrow.

CHART CHECK 1

Circle T (True) or F (False).

T F *May*, *might*, and *could* have only one form for all subjects.

STATEMENTS			
SUBJECT	**MAY/MIGHT/COULD***	**BASE FORM OF VERB**	
I/He/She/It/We/You/They	**may (not)** **might (not)** **could (not)**	**get**	cold.

*These words are modals. They do not have -s in the third person singular.

CHART CHECK 2

Check the correct answer.

When do you use *may*, *might*, or *could* for future possibility?

❑ in questions
❑ in answers

YES/NO QUESTIONS
Are you going to fly to Paris?
Are you taking the train?

SHORT ANSWERS	
I/We	**may (not).** **might (not).** **could(n't).**

WH- QUESTIONS
When are you **going** to Paris?
How long will you **be** there?

ANSWERS			
I/We	**may** **might**	**go**	tomorrow.
	could	**be**	there a week.

EXPRESS CHECK

Complete this conversation with **might** *or* **might not**.

A: Are you going home after class?

B: I _____. It's very possible. Why?

A: I _____ call you about the homework assignment. I don't understand it.

B: Maybe you should call Jean instead. I _____ understand it either.

Grammar Explanations

Examples

---

1. Use *may*, *might*, and *could* to talk about <u>future possibility</u>.

▶ **BE CAREFUL!** Notice the difference between *may be* and *maybe*. Both express possibility.

   May be is a <u>modal + verb</u>. It is always two words.

   Maybe is not a modal. It is an <u>adverb</u>. It is always one word, and it comes at the beginning of the sentence.

- It **may be** windy later.
- It **might get** cold.
- It **could rain** tomorrow.

- He **may be** late today.

- **Maybe** he'll take the train.
  NOT <s>He'll maybe take the train.</s>

---

2. Use *may not* and *might not* to express the possibility that something <u>will not happen</u>.

   Use *couldn't* to say that something is <u>impossible</u>.

▶ **BE CAREFUL!** We usually <u>do not contract</u> *might not*, and we never contract *may not*.

- There are a lot of clouds, but it **might not rain**.

- **A:** Why don't you ask John for a ride?
- **B:** I **couldn't do** that. He's too busy.

- You **may not** need a coat.
  NOT <s>You mayn't need a coat.</s>

---

3. **Questions about possibility** usually are <u>not formed with *may, might,* or *could*</u>. Instead, they are formed with the future (*will, be going to,* the present progressive) or phrases such as *Do you think . . . ?* or *Is it possible that . . . ?* It's the **answers to these questions** that often have *may, might,* or *could*.

   In <u>short answers to *yes/no* questions</u>, use *may, might,* or *could* alone.

   USAGE NOTE: If a form of *be* is in the question, it is common to include *be* in the short answer.

- **A:** When *will* it *start* snowing?
- **B:** It **might start** around lunch time.

- **A:** *Are* you *going to drive* to work?
- **B:** I **might take** the bus instead.

- **A:** When *are* you *leaving*?
- **B:** I **may leave** now.

- **A:** Will your office close early?
- **B:** It **might**.

- **A:** *Is* our train arriving late?
- **B:** It **might be**.

1

IDENTIFY • *Alice is a college student who works part time; Bill is her boyfriend. Read their conversation. Underline the words that express future possibility or impossibility.*

ALICE: I just heard that it <u>may snow</u> today. Are you going to drive to work?

BILL: No. I'll take the 7:30 train instead.

ALICE: I'll take the train with you. I have some work to do in the library.

BILL: Great. Why don't you cut your afternoon class and have lunch with me too?

ALICE: Oh, I couldn't do that. But let's meet at the train station at 6:00, OK?

BILL: I might have to work until 8:00 tonight. I'll call you and let you know.

ANSWER • *What will Alice and Bill do <u>together</u>? Check the appropriate box for each activity.*

	Certain	**Possible**	**Impossible**
1. Take the train at 7:30 A.M.	❑	❑	❑
2. Have lunch.	❑	❑	❑
3. Meet at the train station at 6:00 P.M.	❑	❑	❑

2

COMPLETE • *Alice is graduating from college with a degree in Early Childhood Education. Complete this paragraph from her diary. Choose the appropriate words in parentheses.*

I just got the notice from my school. I _____**'m going to**_____
                 1. (might not / 'm going to)
graduate in June, but I still don't have any plans. Some day-care centers hire students
before they graduate, so I _____ apply for a job
            2. (could / couldn't)
now. Or I _____ apply to a graduate school and
     3. (might / might not)
get my master's degree. I'm just not sure though—these past two years have been
hard, and I _____ be ready to study for two more.
       4. (may / may not)
   At least I <u>am</u> sure about my career: I _____
               5. ('m going to / might)
work with children. That's certain. I made an appointment to discuss my plans with my
teacher, Mrs. Humphrey, tomorrow. I _____ talk
            6. (maybe / may)
this over with her. She _____ have an idea about
       7. (won't / might)
what to do.

3

DESCRIBE • *Look at Alice's schedule for Monday. She put a question mark (?) next to each item she wasn't sure about. Write sentences about Alice's plans for Monday. Use* **may** *or* **might** *for things that are possible and* **be going to** *for things that are certain.*

MONDAY

call Bill at 9:00   go to work at 1:00

buy some notebooks before class **?**   go shopping after work **?**

go to meeting with Mrs. Humphrey at 11:00   take 7:00 train **?**

have coffee with Sue after class **?**   pick up pizza
---

1. _Alice is going to call Bill at 9:00._

2. _She may buy some notebooks before class._

3. _____

4. _____

5. _____

6. _____

7. _____

8. _____

4

EDIT • *Read this student's report about El Niño. Find and correct eight mistakes in expressing future possibility. The first mistake is already corrected.*

Every few years, the ocean near Peru becomes warmer. Called El Niño, this

variation in temperature ~~maybe~~ ^{may} cause weather changes all over the world.

The west coasts of North and South America might to have heavy rains. On

the other side of the Pacific, New Guinea might becomes very dry. Northern

areas could have warmer, wetter winters, and southern areas could become

much colder. These weather changes affect plants and animals. Some fish

mayn't survive in warmer waters. Droughts could causing crops to die, and

food may get very expensive. El Niño may happen every two years, or it

could not come for seven years. Will El Niños get worse in the future? They

could be. Pollution holds heat in the air, and it will increase the effects of

El Niño, but no one is sure yet.

Assumptions:
May, Might, Could, Must, Have (got) to, Can't

The famous detective Sherlock Holmes is

☐ making a guess.

☐ talking about an obligation.

CHART CHECK 1

Circle T (True) or F (False).

T F The third-person singular modal does not end in **-s**.

STATEMENTS			
SUBJECT	**MODAL**	**BASE FORM OF VERB**	
I/He/She/It/We/You/They	**may (not)** **might (not)** **could (not)**	**be**	right.
	must (not) **can't**	**work**	there.

AFFIRMATIVE STATEMENTS: *HAVE (GOT) TO*			
SUBJECT	*HAVE (GOT) TO*	**BASE FORM**	
I/We/You/They	**have (got) to**	**be**	right.
He/She/It	**has (got) to**	**work**	there.

CHART CHECK 2

Circle T (True) or F (False).

T F All modals of assumptions are used in questions.

YES/NO QUESTIONS			
COULD	**SUBJECT**	**BASE FORM**	
Could	he	**work**	there?

NOTE: For contractions with *could not* and *cannot*, see Appendix 24 on page 346.

SHORT ANSWERS	
SUBJECT	**MODAL/** *HAVE (GOT) TO*
He	**must (not).** **may (not).** **might (not).** **could(n't).** **can't.** **has (got) to.**

EXPRESS CHECK

Circle the correct words to complete this conversation.

A: I heard a sound coming from the basement. What <u>could / might</u> it be?

B: I'm not sure. It <u>can / might</u> be the cat. It <u>can / can't</u> be the dog. The dog's upstairs.

Grammar Explanations

Examples

---

1. We often make **assumptions**, or "best guesses," based on information we have about a present situation. The <u>modal</u> that we choose depends on <u>how certain</u> we are about our assumption.

	100% certain	
AFFIRMATIVE		NEGATIVE
must		**can't, couldn't**
have (got) to		**must not**
may		**may not**
might, could		**might not**
	0% certain	

---

2. When you are <u>almost 100 percent certain</u> that something is **possible**, use *must*, *have to*, or *have got to*.

USAGE NOTE: We use *have got to* in <u>informal</u> speech and writing, and we usually contract it.

When you are <u>less certain</u>, use *may*, *might*, or *could*.

Holmes is a brilliant detective.
ASSUMPTION
■ He **must solve** a lot of crimes.

■ He**'s got to be** a genius!

Watson knows a lot about medicine.
ASSUMPTION
■ He **might be** a doctor.

---

3. When you are <u>almost 100 percent certain</u> that something is **impossible**, use *can't* or *couldn't*.

When you are <u>slightly less certain</u>, use *must not*.

Use *may not* or *might not* when you are <u>less certain</u>.

▶ **BE CAREFUL!** *Have to* and *have got to* are not used to make negative assumptions.

■ He **can't be** dead! I think he's still breathing!

■ She **must not feel** well. She looks pale.

■ He **may not know** about the plan. His boss doesn't tell him everything.

■ It **can't be** true!
NOT It doesn't have to be true!

---

4. Use *could* in **questions**.

USAGE NOTE: We rarely use *might* and we never use *may* in questions about possibility.

■ Someone's coming. Who **could** it be?

RARE: **Might** he be at home?
NOT May he be at home?

---

5. In **short answers**, use *have (got) to* or a modal alone.

Use *be* in short answers to questions that include a form of *be*.

A: *Could* Ann know Marie?
B: She **has to**. They're neighbors.

A: *Is* Ron still with City Bank?
B: I'm not sure. He **might not be**.

1 **MATCH** • *Each fact goes with an assumption. Match each fact with the correct assumption.*

Fact	Assumption
__f__ **1.** Her last name is Lemont. She	**a.** must not be at home.
_____ **2.** He's only thirteen. He	**b.** must be married.
_____ **3.** Her eyes are red. She	**c.** has to be older than twenty.
_____ **4.** She's wearing a wedding ring. She	**d.** can't be married.
_____ **5.** His initials are M.B. He	**e.** might have allergies.
_____ **6.** The house is completely dark. They	**f.** may be French.
_____ **7.** She has some gray hair. She	**g.** could be Marc Brunner.

2 **CHOOSE** • *Look at the picture and circle the correct words to complete this conversation.*

WATSON: Look! What's going on over there?

HOLMES: I don't know. It (could)/ couldn't be
                                    1.
some kind of delivery.

WATSON: At this hour? It can't / must be
                                2.
almost midnight! Nothing's

open now.

HOLMES: Hmm. 27 Carlisle Street. That

can't / 's got to be the bank.
   3.

WATSON: It *is* the bank.

HOLMES: Can you see what that man is taking out of the carriage?

WATSON: It looks like a box. What do you suppose is in it?

HOLMES: I don't know, but it seems heavy. It could / must not contain gold.
                                                              4.

WATSON: Look at that man in front of the bank. Could / Must he be the bank manager?
                                                        5.

HOLMES: He might / might be.
              6.

WATSON: But why are they making this delivery at this time? This could / couldn't
                                                                      7.

be normal.

HOLMES: The manager might not / must want people to know about it. He
                                  8.

couldn't / may be worried about robbers.
   9.

3   **COMPLETE** • *Read Sherlock Holmes's conversation with a murder suspect. Complete it with the words in parentheses and a modal that shows the degree of certainty. (There may be more than one correct answer.)*

HOLMES: <u>You must be Gina Lemont.</u>
                   1. Almost certain (You / be / Gina Lemont)

LEMONT: _____. Who wants to know?
              2. Possible (I / be)

HOLMES: Sherlock Holmes. I hear something in the next room.

LEMONT: _____. I'm alone.
           3. Possible (It / be / the cat)

HOLMES: Alone? _____. There are two
                 4. Almost certain (You / eat a lot)

     plates on the table. _____ that
                           5. Possible (it / be)

     you are mistaken?

LEMONT: No, _____. I was expecting
               6. Impossible (it / be)

     someone, but he never came.

HOLMES: Does your cat smoke? I smell pipe tobacco.

LEMONT: _____
              7. Almost certain (It / come / from your own pipe)

     _____
              8. Impossible (There / be / any other explanation)

HOLMES: Oh, _____. May we have
              9. Possible (there / be)

     a look at this "cat"?

4   **EDIT** • *Read this student's reading journal for a mystery novel. Find and correct six mistakes in expressing assumptions. The first mistake is already corrected.*

The main character, Molly Smith, is a college ESL teacher. She is trying to find her dead
grandparents' first home in the United States. It may ~~being~~ ^{be} in a nearby town. The
townspeople there seem scared. They could be have a secret, or they must just hate
strangers. Molly has some old letters that might lead her to the place. They are in
Armenian, but one of her students mights translate them for her. They hafta be
important because the author mentions them right away. The letter must contain
family secrets. Who is the bad guy? It couldn't be the student because he wants to help.
It might to be the newspaper editor in the town.

UNIT 38

Advisability in the Past

I could have become a doctor.

My parents **might** have **encouraged** me more.

I **ought to** have **applied** to college.

I **shouldn't have missed** that opportunity.

I **could have been** rich and famous.

CHECK *POINT*

Check the correct answer.

The man

☐ is planning his future.

☐ regrets things in his past.

CHART CHECK 1 ➡

Circle T (True) or F (False).

T F You can add **not** to all modals that express past advisability or obligation.

STATEMENTS

SUBJECT	MODAL	HAVE	PAST PARTICIPLE
I/He/She/We/You/They	should (not) ought (not) to could might	have	applied.

CHART CHECK 2 ➡

Circle T (True) or F (False).

T F In questions and short answers, we usually only use **should have**.

YES/NO QUESTIONS

SHOULD	SUBJECT	HAVE	PAST PARTICIPLE
Should	he	have	applied?

SHORT ANSWERS

AFFIRMATIVE	NEGATIVE
Yes, he should have.	No, he shouldn't have.

WH- QUESTIONS

WH- WORD	SHOULD	SUBJECT	HAVE	PAST PARTICIPLE
When	should	he	have	applied?

CHART CHECK 3

Check the correct answer.

Which words are NOT usually contracted?

❏ *should have*

❏ *could have*

❏ *ought to have*

CONTRACTIONS		
should have	=	**should've**
could have	=	**could've**
might have	=	**might've**
should not have	=	**shouldn't have**

EXPRESS CHECK

Complete this conversation.

A: Should I _____ called you yesterday?

B: Yes, you _____. I waited all day for your call.

Grammar Explanations

1. Use *should have, ought to have, could have,* and *might have* to talk about things that were <u>advisable in the past</u>. These modals often express regret or blame.

2. *Should not have* and *ought not to have* are the only forms used in <u>negative statements</u>. *Should not have* is more common.

Should have is the most common form used in <u>questions</u>.

Examples

■ I **should've applied** to college.
  (I didn't apply to college, and I'm sorry.)

■ I **ought to have taken** that job.
  (I didn't take the job. That was a mistake.)

■ She **could've gone** to a better school.
  (She didn't go to a good school. Now she regrets her choice.)

■ You **might've told** me.
  (You didn't tell me. That was wrong.)

■ He **shouldn't have missed** the exam.
■ He **ought not to have missed** the exam.

■ **Should he have called** the teacher?

PRONUNCIATION NOTE

In informal speech, *have* in <u>modal phrases</u> is often pronounced like the word *of* or *a*.

For example, *could have* sounds like "could of" or "coulda." Do not write *could of* or *coulda*.

Ought to is often pronounced like "oughta." Do not write *oughta*.

1   **TRUE OR FALSE** • *Read each numbered sentence. Write T (True) or F (False) for the statement that follows.*

1. I shouldn't have called him.

   __T__ I called him.

2. I should have told them what I thought.

   _____ I didn't tell them. Now I'm sorry.

3. He might have warned us about it.

   _____ He knew, but he didn't tell us.

4. Felicia could have been president.

   _____ Felicia is president.

5. I ought to have practiced more.

   _____ I didn't practice enough.

6. They shouldn't have lent him their car.

   _____ They lent him their car.

2   **COMPLETE** • *Read this excerpt from a magazine article. Complete it with the correct form of the words in parentheses and a short answer. Choose between affirmative and negative.*

Regrets . . .

It's not unusual to feel regret about things in the past that you think you

_____**should have done**_____ and did not do—or the opposite, about things
        1. (should / do)

you did do and feel you _____. In fact, we learn by
                              2. (should / do)

thinking about past mistakes. For example, a student who fails a test learns that

he or she _____ more and can improve on the
              3. (should / study)

next test. Often, however, people spend too much time thinking about what they

_____ differently. Many regrets are simply not based
        4. (could / do)

in fact. A mother regrets missing a football game in which her son's leg was

injured. "I _____," she keeps telling herself.
                  5. (ought to / go)

"I _____ home. I _____
        6. (should / stay)   **7.** (could / prevent)

the injury. The officials _____ at least

_____ me as soon as it happened." Did she *really*
        8. (might / call)

have the power to prevent her son's injury? _____ the

officials _____ her *before* looking at the injury? No, of
              9. (Should / contact)

course, they _____. There is an Italian proverb that says,
                  10.

"When the ship has sunk, everyone knows how they _____ it."
                                                        11. (could / save)

It's easy to second guess about the past: The real challenge is to solve the problems

you face right now.

---

3 **REWRITE •** *Read Greta's regrets. Rewrite them using the modals in parentheses and choose between affirmative and negative.*

1. I didn't go to college. Now I'm unhappy with my job.

(should) __I should have gone to college.__

2. I feel sick. I ate all the chocolate.

(should) _____

3. Christina didn't come over. She didn't even call.

(might) _____

4. I didn't have enough money to buy the shirt. Why didn't Ed offer to lend me some?

(could) _____

5. I jogged five miles yesterday, and now I'm exhausted.

(should) _____

6. The supermarket charged me for the plastic bags. They used to be free.

(should) _____

7. I didn't invite Cynthia to the party. Now she's angry at me.

(ought to) _____

8. Yesterday was my birthday, and my brother didn't send me a card. I'm hurt.

(might) _____

4 **EDIT •** *Read this journal entry. Find and correct six mistakes in the use of modals. The first mistake is already corrected.*

December 15

About a week ago, Jennifer was late for work again, and Doug, our boss, told me he wanted to get

                                                    have

rid of her. I was really upset. Of course, Jennifer shouldn't ~~had~~ been late so often, but he might has

talked to her about the problem before he decided to let her go. Then he told me to make her job

difficult for her so that she would quit. I just pretended I didn't hear him. What a mistake!

I oughta have confronted him right away. Or I could at least have warned Jennifer. Anyway,

Jennifer is still here, but now I'm worried about my own job. Should I of told Doug's boss? I wonder.

Maybe I should handle things differently last week. The company should never has hired this guy.

UNIT 39

Speculations
about the Past

EASTER ISLAND: **Could** visitors from another planet **have built** these giant statues?

CHECK **POINT**

Check the correct answer.

The question under the photograph asks

❑ if it was possible that something happened.

❑ if people had permission to do something.

CHART CHECK 1

Circle T (True) or F (False).

T F The form of the modal does not change for different subjects.

STATEMENTS				
SUBJECT	MODAL/ HAD TO	HAVE	PAST PARTICIPLE	
I/He/She/We/You/They	may (not) might (not) can't could (not) must (not) had to	have	seen	the statues.

CHART CHECK 2

Check the correct answer.

Which modal can be used in both questions and short answers for speculations about the past?

❑ *can*

❑ *could*

❑ *might*

YES/NO QUESTIONS: *COULD*			
COULD	SUBJECT	HAVE	PAST PARTICIPLE
Could	he	have	seen aliens?

SHORT ANSWERS		
SUBJECT	MODAL/ HAD TO	HAVE
He	may (not) might (not) can't could (not) must (not) had to	have.

EXPRESS **CHECK**

Circle the correct words to complete these sentences.

Could they <u>carved / have carved</u> the statues? They <u>might / might have</u>.

166

Grammar Explanations

Examples

1. We often **speculate**, or make "best guesses," about past situations based on the facts that we have. The <u>modal</u> that we choose depends on <u>how certain</u> we are about our speculations.

100% certain	
AFFIRMATIVE	NEGATIVE
must have	**can't have**
had to have	**couldn't have**
may have	**must not have**
might have	**may not have**
could have	**might not have**
0% certain	

2. When you are <u>almost 100 percent certain</u> that something was **possible**, use *must have* or *had to have*.

When you are <u>less certain</u>, use *may have*, *might have*, or *could have*.

The statues are very big.
SPECULATION
■ They **must have been** hard to move.

The islanders were able to carve the stone.
SPECULATION
■ The stone **may have been** quite soft.

3. When you are <u>almost 100 percent certain</u> that something was **impossible**, use *can't have* or *couldn't have*.

When you are <u>slightly less certain</u>, use *must not*.

Use *may not have* or *might not have* when you are <u>less certain</u>.

▶ **BE CAREFUL!** We do not usually use *had to have* for negative speculations.

■ The islanders **couldn't have moved** the stone! It was too heavy.

■ They **must not have moved** it without help.

■ The islanders **might not have moved** the statues over land. They could have used boats.

4. Use *could have* in **questions about possibility** or use questions without modals.

■ **Could** the islanders **have moved** the stone?
OR
■ Do you think they moved the stone?

5. Use *been* in **short answers** to questions that include a form of *be*.

Use only the **modal + *have*** in short answers to <u>questions with other verbs</u>.

A: Could von Däniken **have been** wrong?
OR
Was he wrong?
B: He certainly **could have been**.

A: Did the islanders *work* on their own?
B: They **could have**.

PRONUNCIATION NOTE
In informal speech, *have* in <u>modal phrases</u> is often pronounced like the word *of.*
For example, *must have* sounds like "must of." Do not write *must of.*

1 **MATCH** • *Each fact goes with a speculation. Match each fact with the correct speculation about author Erich von Däniken.*

Fact

_e_ **1.** The original title of *Chariots of the Gods?* was *Erinnerungen an die Zukunft.*

_____ **2.** Von Däniken visited every place he described in his book.

_____ **3.** In 1973, he wrote *In Search of Ancient Gods.*

_____ **4.** He doesn't have a degree in archaeology.

_____ **5.** Von Däniken's books sold millions of copies.

_____ **6.** As soon as von Däniken published his books, scientists attacked him.

Speculation

a. He must have traveled a lot.

b. They must not have believed his theories.

c. He could have learned about the subject on his own.

d. He must have made a lot of money.

e. He must have written it in German.

f. He might have written other books too.

2 **ANSWER** • *Some archaeology students are asking questions in class. Use the modals in parentheses to write short answers.*

1. A: Do you think the people on Easter Island built the giant statues themselves?

  B: _____They could have_____ . They had the knowledge and the tools.
            (could)

2. A: Were many people impressed by von Däniken's theories?

  B: _____ . His books were read all over the world.
            (must)

3. A: Von Däniken says that many ancient artifacts show pictures of astronauts. Could these pictures have illustrated anything closer to Earth?

  B: _____ . It's possible that the pictures show
            (may)
people dressed in local costumes.

4. A: Was von Däniken upset by all the criticism he received?

  B: _____ . After all, it helped his book sales.
            (might not)

5. A: Do you think von Däniken helped increase general interest in archaeology?

  B: _____ . Just look at the size of this class!
            (must)

3 **COMPLETE** • *Read part of a review of Erich von Däniken's book* Chariots of the Gods? *Complete it with the verbs in parentheses.*

Who ___could have made___ the Easter Island statues? According
    1. (could / make)

to Erich von Däniken, our ancestors _____ these
    2. (could not / build)

structures on their own because their cultures were too primitive. His solution:

They _____ help from space visitors. When he
    3. (had to / get)

wrote his popular book, von Däniken _____ about
    4. (must not / know)

the Easter Island experiments that proved that the ancient islanders

_____ and _____ these
  5 (could / carve)   **6** (transport)

statues without any help from alien visitors. Not only that, the island's population

_____ much larger than von Däniken believes. One
  7. (might / be)

scientist speculates that as many as 20,000 people _____
                           8. (may / live)

on Easter Island—enough people to have done the job. Visitors from another planet?

A more logical answer is to think that our ancestors _____
                            9. (must / have)

great skill, intelligence, and strength to create these wonderful things.

4 **EDIT** • *Read part of a student's essay. Find and correct six mistakes in the use of modals for speculations about the past. The first mistake is already corrected.*

                                     have been

In 1927, Toribio Mexta Xesspe of Peru must ~~be~~ very surprised to see lines in the

shapes of huge animals on the ground below his airplane. Created by the ancient

Nazca culture, these forms are too big to recognize from the ground. However, at

about 600 feet in the air the giant forms take

shape. Without airplanes, how could an ancient

culture had made them? What purpose could

they have had? Author Erich von Däniken

believes that the drawings might have mark a

landing strip for the spacecraft of astronauts

from another planet. Archaeologists, however,

now believe that the ancient Nazcan civilization might develop flight.

They could of built hot-air balloons and design the pictures from the air.

SelfTest

SECTION ONE

Circle the letter of the correct answer to complete each sentence.

EXAMPLE:

Jennifer never _____ coffee.   A **(B)** C D
(A) drink   (C) is drinking
(B) drinks   (D) was drinking

---

1. —Wasn't that Mehmet in class?   A B C D
   —It _____. Mehmet left school last week.
   (A) couldn't   (C) couldn't have been
   (B) could have been   (D) couldn't have

2. Frank watches all the Lakers games. He _____ to be one of   A B C D
   their biggest fans.
   (A) must   (C) couldn't
   (B) has got   (D) should have

3. Children under five years old _____ swim without an adult.   A B C D
   (A) don't have to   (C) have to
   (B) must not   (D) are supposed to

4. Where _____ we supposed to go for the test tomorrow?   A B C D
   (A) do   (C) will
   (B) are   (D) should

5. Bring your umbrella. It _____ later.   A B C D
   (A) might rain   (C) couldn't rain
   (B) rains   (D) might have rained

6. —Will your plane be late this afternoon?   A B C D
   —It _____. The airport was closed this morning.
   (A) couldn't be   (C) maybe
   (B) may be   (D) will

7. You _____ told Mark. You knew it was a secret.   A B C D
   (A) should have   (C) couldn't have
   (B) might have   (D) shouldn't have

8. They built this temple 3,000 years ago. This must _____   A B C D
   a great civilization.
   (A) has been   (C) was
   (B) have been   (D) not have been

9. Jan _____ to call Myra yesterday but he forgot.   A B C D
   (A) supposed   (C) supposes
   (B) is supposed   (D) was supposed

170

10. —Could Amy have been at home yesterday?
    —She _____. I really don't know.   **A B C D**
    (A) could have been   (C) had to have been
    (B) might be   (D) couldn't have

11. Chris _____ to clean up his room. It's a mess.   **A B C D**
    (A) have got   (C) must
    (B) has got   (D) got

12. I failed the test. I _____ studied harder.   **A B C D**
    (A) should have   (C) should
    (B) must have   (D) may

13. Lisa was in town recently. She might _____ me to say hello!   **A B C D**
    (A) call   (C) have called
    (B) has called   (D) be calling

SECTION TWO

Each sentence has four underlined words or phrases. The four underlined parts
of the sentence are marked A, B, C, and D. Circle the letter of the one underlined
word or phrase that is NOT CORRECT.

> **EXAMPLE:**
> Mike <u>usually</u> <u>drives</u> to school, but <u>today</u> he <u>walks</u>.   **A B C Ⓓ**
>   A   B   C   D

14. Tom <u>didn't</u> <u>wave</u> to me, so he <u>must have known</u> I <u>was</u> here.   **A B C D**
        A   B   C   D

15. We'd <u>better</u> <u>hurry</u>, or the train <u>might</u> <u>leaves</u> without us.   **A B C D**
         A   B   C   D

16. His English <u>is</u> excellent, so he <u>had to</u> <u>has</u> <u>studied</u> hard.   **A B C D**
                 A   B   C   D

17. We <u>ought to have</u> <u>look</u> at more cars <u>before</u> we <u>bought</u> ours.   **A B C D**
          A   B   C   D

18. You <u>gotta</u> <u>get</u> dressed <u>because</u> Sasha <u>may be</u> here soon.   **A B C D**
         A   B   C   D

19. You <u>have to</u> <u>buckle</u> your seat belt now or you <u>couldn't</u> <u>drive</u>. It's the law.   **A B C D**
         A   B   C   D

20. You <u>don't have to</u> <u>drive</u> faster <u>than</u> 65 mph or you <u>might</u> get a ticket.   **A B C D**
         A   B   C   D

21. Hardlie's <u>must</u> <u>has</u> <u>gone</u> out of business <u>recently</u>.   **A B C D**
              A   B   C   D

22. It <u>must</u> <u>rain</u> tonight, so <u>I'd better</u> <u>stay</u> home.   **A B C D**
        A   B   C   D

23. Jason <u>will be</u> <u>supposed</u> to be there <u>tomorrow</u>, but he <u>can't</u> attend.   **A B C D**
           A   B   C   D

24. It <u>must</u> <u>be</u> almost 11:00, so we really <u>hafta</u> <u>leave</u> now.   **A B C D**
        A   B   C   D

25. You <u>should of</u> <u>seen</u> that movie with us because it <u>may not</u> <u>be</u> here long.   **A B C D**
         A   B   C   D

Adjectives and Adverbs

The ad describes it **perfectly**.

Check the correct answer.

The owner thinks the apartment is:

☐ perfect

☐ warm and cozy

CHART CHECK	**ADJECTIVES**	**ADVERBS**
Circle T (True) or F (False).	They are **quiet** tenants.	They work **quietly**.
T F Adverbs often come before nouns.	It's a **fast** elevator.	It moves **very fast**.
	The building seems **nice**.	She described it **nicely**.
T F Adjectives often come after action verbs.	It's absolutely **perfect**.	It's **absolutely** perfect.
T F Adverbs often end in **-ly**.		

EXPRESS CHECK

Complete these sentences with the correct form of the word **slow**.

A: It's a _____ elevator. It moves very _____.

B: It's not _____. It just seems _____.

Grammar Explanations	**Examples**

1. Use **adjectives** to describe <u>nouns</u> or <u>pronouns</u> (for people, places, and things).

Adjectives usually come immediately <u>before the noun</u> they describe.

Adjectives can also come <u>after non-action verbs</u> such as *be, look,* or *seem.*

        noun   adjective   pron.   adjective
■ The **houses** are ***beautiful***. **They** are ***new***.

      adjective   noun
■ This is a ***small* apartment**.

        verb adjective
■ This apartment **seems** ***small***.

2. Use **adverbs** to describe <u>verbs</u>, <u>adjectives</u>, and other <u>adverbs</u>.

Adverbs that describe adjectives and other adverbs usually come immediately <u>before</u> the word they describe.

     verb   adverb
■ They **furnished** it ***nicely***.

    adverb adjective
■ It's an ***extremely* nice** house.

      adverb adverb
■ They found it ***very quickly***.

3. Use **adverbs of manner** to describe <u>action verbs</u>. These adverbs often answer *How?* questions. They come <u>after</u> the verb they describe.

▶ **BE CAREFUL!** Do not put an adverb of manner between the verb and its direct object.

■ It**'ll rent** ***quickly***.
(Quickly describes <u>how fast</u> it will rent.)

    verb   direct object
■ She**'ll rent** this apartment ***quickly***.
NOT ~~She'll rent quickly this apartment.~~

4. **Adverbs of manner** are often formed by <u>adding -*ly*</u> to <u>adjectives</u>.

▶ **BE CAREFUL!** Some adjectives also end in -*ly*— for example, *silly, friendly, lovely,* and *lonely.*

        adjective
■ We need a **quick** decision.

        adverb
■ You should decide **quickly**.

     adjective
■ It's a **lovely** apartment.

5. Some **common adverbs of manner** <u>do not end in -*ly*</u>.

  a. The adverb form of *good* is ***well***.

  b. Some adverbs have the <u>same form as their related adjectives</u>, for example, ***early***, ***fast***, ***wrong***, ***late***, and ***hard***.

▶ **BE CAREFUL!** ***Lately*** is not the adverb form of *late. Lately* means "recently." ***Hardly*** is not the adverb form of *hard. Hardly* means "almost not."

     adjective   adverb
■ She's a **good** writer. She writes **well**.

ADJECTIVE	ADVERB
Bob was **late**.	Bob came **late**.
She's a **hard** worker.	She works **hard**.

■ She hasn't met any new people ***lately***.

■ There's ***hardly*** enough time to prepare for her classes. Her part-time job takes up most of her time.

Check it out!

For a discussion of adverbs of frequency, see Unit 2, page 7.

1 **IDENTIFY** • *Read this notice about an apartment for rent. Underline the adjectives and circle the adverbs. Then draw an arrow from the adjective or adverb to the word it is describing.*

APT. FOR RENT

Students! Are you looking for a special place to live?
Come to 140 Grant Street, Apt. 4B. This apartment is
absolutely perfect for two serious students who are
looking for a quiet neighborhood, just 15 minutes from
campus. This lovely apartment is in a new building.
It is a short walk to the bus stop. The express bus goes
directly into town. At night the bus hardly makes any
stops at all. You can walk safely through the wonderful
parks on your way home. The rent is very affordable.
Call for an appointment: 555-5050.
Don't wait! This apartment will rent fast.

---

2 **COMPLETE** • *Many people went to see the apartment described in the notice above. Complete their comments about the apartment with the correct form of the words in parentheses.*

1. I'm very interested. I think the apartment is _____ extremely nice _____.
    (extreme / nice)

2. I was expecting much bigger rooms. I was _____.
    (terrible / disappointed)

3. I thought the apartment would be hard to find, but it was _____.
    (surprising / easy)

4. I was happy to hear that the park is _____.
    (extreme / safe)

5. It's a great place, and the price is reasonable. It will rent _____.
    (incredible / fast)

6. The owner seems nice, but she talks _____.
    (awful / slow)

7. The notice said it was quiet, but I heard the neighbors _____.
    (very / clear)

8. I heard them too. I thought their voices were _____.
    (unusual / loud)

9. All in all, it's an _____ place.
    (exceptional / pleasant)

3 **CHOOSE** • *Complete Maggie's letter with the correct word in parentheses.*

Dear Mom and Dad,

Life in New York is very _____exciting_____. Luis and I weren't sure we'd like
1. (exciting / excitingly)

such a _____ city, but it's so interesting! Yesterday we saw a street
2. (large / largely)

musician near school. He played the violin so _____ we couldn't believe he
3. (beautiful / beautifully)

wasn't in a big concert hall. You'd be surprised to see us. We walk _____
4. (happy / happily)

down the _____ streets, and the noise doesn't bother us at all! I'm sending
5. (busy / busily)

a photo of our apartment building. It looks _____, doesn't it? It's so
6. (nice / nicely)

_____ we can _____ believe it's in New York. Our next-
7. (quiet / quietly)   8. (hard / hardly)

door neighbor is very _____. At first she seemed _____,
9. (nice / nicely)   10. (shy / shyly)

but now we're _____ friends.
11. (good / well)

We hope you're both well. Please give our love to

everyone and write soon.

Love,
Maggie

4 **EDIT** • *Read this student's journal entry. Find and
correct seven mistakes in the use of adjectives
and adverbs. The first mistake is already corrected.*

>   funny
> Some apartment ads are so ~~funnily~~! One ad described a place as "warmly and cozy." It was
> really hot and crowded, but the owner insisted that it suited me perfect. I was trying very
> hardly not to laugh while he was describing it, so I had to leave quickly. Another place I saw
> was supposed to be "nice and cutely." What a mess!! I left that place very fastly too. I'm not
> asking for the moon! I only want a small place in a clean building with friendly neighbors.
> I'm looking at another place tomorrow. The ad says, "Clean and bright. Small but convenient
> apartment on lovely, quietly block." I wonder what that really means!

Participial Adjectives

New to the Area

Screen Name: newgal@XYZ.com
Age & Gender: 20 year old Female
Location: Miami, FL
Looking for: Friends

Tired of doing things alone? Me too! 20 year old college student, new to the area, is **interested** in meeting **interesting** people for friendship and fun.

> Send me e-mail!
> Send me an online greeting!
> Send this to a friend!

▶ print/save

CHECK *POINT*

Circle T (True) or F (False).

T F   The writer of the ad says that she is an interesting person.

CHART CHECK

Circle T (True) or F (False).

T F There are two types of participial adjectives.

PARTICIPIAL ADJECTIVES	
-ING ADJECTIVES	**-ED ADJECTIVES**
He is **boring**. They had a **boring** date.	She is **bored**. They had a **bored** look on their faces.
She is **amusing**. They had an **amusing** date.	He is **amused**. They had an **amused** look on their faces.
The movie was **frightening**. They saw a **frightening** movie.	They were **frightened**. They had a **frightened** look on their faces.
The job is **tiring**. She has a **tiring** job.	She's **tired**. She has a **tired** sound to her voice.
The weekend was **relaxing**. He had a **relaxing** weekend.	He felt **relaxed**. He had a **relaxed** manner.

EXPRESS CHECK

Complete the chart.

-ING Adjectives	-ED Adjectives
exciting	
	interested
frightening	
	amused
tiring	

Grammar Explanations

1. Participial adjectives are adjectives that end with *-ing* or *-ed*. They usually describe feelings or reactions. The two forms have different meanings.

2. Participial adjectives that end in *-ing* describe someone or something that <u>causes</u> a feeling or reaction.

3. Participial adjectives that end in *-ed* describe someone who <u>experiences</u> a feeling or reaction.

4. To the right are some <u>common participial adjective</u> pairs.

Examples

A: The last *Star Wars* movie was **amazing**!
B: I know. I was **amazed** by the special effects.

■ That actor is always **amusing**.
   (He causes amusement.)

■ These directions are **confusing**.
   (They cause confusion.)

■ We were **amused** by that actor.
   (We felt amusement.)

■ I'm really **confused** by these directions.
   (I feel confusion.)

annoying	annoyed
boring	bored
depressing	depressed
embarrassing	embarrassed
exciting	excited
frightening	frightened
relaxing	relaxed
shocking	shocked
surprising	surprised

Check it out!

For a list of common participial adjectives, see Appendix 11 on page 339.

1 **IDENTIFY •** *Read this article. Underline all the* **-ed** *participial adjectives. Circle all the* **-ing** *participial adjectives.*

14 • SECTION 4 • LIFESTYLES

Not Personal Enough?

INTERNATIONAL WIRE SERVICES

In some countries, people who are <u>interested</u> in meeting others turn for help to personal ads in newspapers and magazines, and online. A (surprising) number of busy people view these ads as a practical way of increasing their social circle. "I've tried hard to meet people on my own," said one <u>satisfied</u> customer. "I was new in town and wanted to make friends fast. The personals provided me with a quick way of meeting many <u>interesting</u> people in a short period of time." Others are not so <u>impressed</u>. "I think it's kind of <u>depressing</u> when people need to resort to placing ads to make friends," observed one man. "A friend of mine tried the ads several times and was really <u>disappointed</u> with the results. It's just not personal enough."

2 **CHOOSE •** *Read this conversation between Marta and Luis about their friend Alice. Circle the correct words to complete the conversation.*

MARTA: What's the matter with Alice?

LUIS: Who knows? She's always (annoyed)/ annoying about something.
<u>   1.</u>

MARTA: I know. I try to understand her, but this time I'm really <u>puzzled / puzzling</u>.
<u>   2.</u>

LUIS: Really? What's so <u>puzzled / puzzling</u> this time?
<u>   3.</u>

MARTA: I thought she was happy. She met an <u>interested / interesting</u> guy last week.
<u>   4.</u>

LUIS: That's nice. Was she <u>interested / interesting</u> in him?
<u>   5.</u>

MARTA: I thought she was. She said they saw a <u>fascinated / fascinating</u> movie together.
<u>   6.</u>

LUIS: Well, maybe she was <u>fascinated / fascinating</u> by the movie but
<u>   7.</u>
<u>disappointed / disappointing</u> with the guy.
<u>   8.</u>

MARTA: I don't know. It's hard to tell with Alice. Her moods are always very
<u>surprised / surprising</u>.
<u>   9.</u>

LUIS: I'm not <u>surprised / surprising</u> at all. That's just the way she is.
<u>   10.</u>

3

COMPLETE • *Read this conversation between Alice and her date, Jake. Complete it with the correct form of the words in parentheses. Choose between* **-ed** *and* **-ing** *participial adjectives.*

ALICE: That was a very _____interesting_____ movie. What did you think?
1. (interest)

JAKE: To be honest, I found it kind of _____. I'm not that
2. (bore)

_____ in science fiction.
3. (interest)

ALICE: Really? I find it _____. What kind of movies *do* you enjoy?
4. (fascinate)

JAKE: Mostly comedies. Have you seen *Home Again*?

ALICE: Yes, but I wasn't _____ at all. In fact, I thought it was
5. (amuse)

_____. The story line was _____, and I couldn't
6. (horrify)   7. (confuse)

find any humor in the characters' problems. When I left the theater, I felt

kind of _____.
8. (depress)

JAKE: I'm _____ that you felt that way! I thought it was very
9. (amaze)

_____.
10. (amuse)

ALICE: Well, I guess it's a matter of taste.

JAKE: Speaking of taste, would you like to get a bite to eat?

ALICE: Thanks, but it's late and I'm _____.
11. (exhaust)

4

EDIT • *Read Alice's journal entry. Find and correct six mistakes in the use of participial adjectives. The first mistake is already corrected.*

> disappointed
> Just got home. I'm ~~disappointing~~ with the evening. At first I thought Jake was an
>
> interested guy, but tonight I felt somewhat bored with his company. We saw a very
>
> entertained movie, but Jake didn't like it. In fact, it seems like we have completely
>
> different tastes in things. After the movie, I tried to make conversation, but all I
>
> really wanted was to go home. So, I told him I was exhausting and didn't want to
>
> get home late. If he asks me out again—I'm not interesting. Trying to meet people
>
> can be very frustrated.

Adjectives and Adverbs:
Equatives

She rides **as fast as** he does. She controls her bike just **as well**. But her shoulders aren't **as wide** and her arms aren't **as long as** his. Why should she ride a bike designed for him?

TRAX—sized to fit *you*.

CHECK POINT

Check the things the boy and girl have in common.

❑ riding speed

❑ width of shoulders

❑ control of bike

❑ length of arms

CHART CHECK

Check the correct answers.

Which words are always used in equatives?

❑ *not*

❑ *as*

❑ an adjective or an adverb

ADJECTIVES: EQUATIVES					
	VERB* (*NOT*)	**As**	**ADJECTIVE**	**As**	
The girl			**fast**		the boy.
She	is	**as**	**good**	**as**	he is.
Her bike	isn't		**big**		his.
The girl's bike			**heavy**		the boy's.

*Non-action verbs like *be, look, seem.*

ADVERBS: EQUATIVES					
	VERB* (*NOT*)	**As**	**ADVERB**	**As**	
The girl			**fast**		the boy.
She	rides	**as**	**well**	**as**	he does.
Her bike	doesn't ride		**smoothly**		his.
The girl's bike			**consistently**		the boy's.

*Action verbs

180

EXPRESS CHECK

Complete these sentences with the equative form of the words in parentheses.

A: My old bike wasn't _____ my new one. Of course, it
(expensive)

didn't perform _____ the new one.
(well)

B: And it didn't look _____ the new one either.
(good)

Grammar Explanations

Examples

1. You can use **equatives** (*as* + **adjective** + *as*) to compare <u>people, places, and things</u>.

- The Trax bike is **as expensive as** the Gordo. *(The Trax costs a lot of money. The Gordo costs the same amount of money.)*

- It's **not as light as** the Gordo, though. *(The two bikes are not the same weight.)*

Use *as* + **adjective** + *as* to compare people, places, and things that are <u>equal</u> in some way. Use *just* to emphasize the equality.

- This helmet is **as good as** yours.
- It's *just* **as expensive as** yours too.

Use *not as* + **adjective** + *as* to talk about people, places, and things that are <u>different</u> in some way.

- The new ad is **not as effective as** the old one.
- It isn**'t as funny as** the old one either.

2. You can also use **equatives** (*as* + **adverb** + *as*) to compare <u>actions</u>.

- He rides **as fast as** she does. *(They ride equally fast.)*

- He doesn**'t** ride **as safely as** she does, though. *(They don't ride the same way. He rides safely, but she rides more safely.)*

Use *as* + **adverb** + *as* to talk about actions that are the <u>same or equal</u>. Use *just* to emphasize the <u>equality</u>.

- Kleen brightens **as thoroughly as** Brite.
- It removes stains *just* **as effectively as** Brite.

Use *not as* + **adverb** + *as* to talk about <u>actions</u> that are <u>not the same or equal</u>.

- Kleen doesn**'t** clean **as well as** Brite.

3. You do not always have to mention both parts of a comparison. Sometimes the meaning is clear from the context.

- Trax and Gordo are both great bikes, but Trax is**n't as light** (as Gordo).

- Jake and Christopher both ride fast, but Christopher doesn**'t ride as skillfully** (as Jake).

1

IDENTIFY • *Read this article on laundry detergents. Underline all the equatives with adjectives. Circle the equatives with adverbs.*

PRODUCT REVIEWS ✦ LAUNDRY DETERGENTS

So you were riding the trails this weekend, and you hit the dirt. Now your clothes look as bad as your bike. Never mind. They'll look as good as new next weekend. We checked out three major brands of detergent, and we can tell you which ones clean best and which ones don't remove trail stains as effectively as others.

Overall, Brite and Kleen aren't as expensive as Trend, but they didn't perform as well either. However, they were almost as good in particular categories. Trend removed both mud and grass stains effectively. Brite removed mud just as effectively as Trend, but it didn't remove grass stains as well. Kleen was effective on grass stains, but not on mud. Brite cleaned clothes as thoroughly as Kleen, but again, Brite and Kleen weren't as good as Trend in this category. On the other hand, Brite came out on top in brightening. Colors washed in Kleen and Trend just didn't look as bright as the ones washed in Brite.

2

COMPLETE • *Read these conversations. Complete them with equatives using the correct form of the words in parentheses.*

1. **TOMÁS:** _____Does_____ your new bike _____ride as comfortably as_____ the old one?
   a. (ride / comfortable)

   DINA: It's great. The handlebars _____ and the handbrakes
   b. (not be / wide)

   _____ to reach. This bike was made for a small
   c. (not be / hard)

   person like me.

2. **HANS:** We need a name for this product. It should show that this detergent

   _____ the others but _____
   a. (clean / effective)   **b.** (not be / unfriendly)

   to the environment.

   EVA: I like "GreenKleen." It _____ other product names, and
   c. (sound / exciting)

   it _____ the message _____ theirs too.
   d. (express / clear)

3. **IN-SU:** The last group I rode with _____ a herd of
   a. (be / noisy)

   elephants. I prefer to ride alone, but I know it's dangerous.

   SUN-HI: Ride with me next weekend. I _____ a mouse.
   b. (pedal / quiet)

   I promise.

3 **COMPARE & COMPLETE** • *Read the chart comparing several models of bicycles. Complete the sentences with equatives using the correct form of the words in parentheses. Choose between affirmative and negative.*

MODEL	PRICE	COMFORT	BRAKING SPEED, DRY GROUND	BRAKING SPEED, WET GROUND	SHIFTING EASE	ON-ROAD HANDLING	OFF-ROAD HANDLING
PRODUCT RATINGS ✦ BICYCLES						KEY: BETTER ● → ◐ → ○ WORSE	
Trax	$999	◒	●	◐	●	◒	●
Huff	$550	●	◒	●	◐	●	◐
Gordo	$225	◒	○	○	◒	◒	○

1. The Gordo __doesn't stop as quickly as__ the Trax and the Huff.
   (stop / quick)
2. On wet ground, the Huff _____ the Trax.
   (stop / slow)
3. The Gordo _____ the Trax and the Huff.
   (be / expensive)
4. The Trax _____ the Huff.
   (feel / comfortable)
5. The Trax _____ either.
   (be / cheap)
6. Even the Gordo _____ the Trax.
   (ride / comfortable)
7. On the road, the Gordo _____ the Trax.
   (handle / good)
8. Off the road, the Gordo and the Huff _____ the Trax.
   (handle / good)
9. The Gordo _____ the Huff.
   (shift / easy)

4 **EDIT** • *Read these bulletin board postings. Find and correct six mistakes in the use of equatives. The first mistake is already corrected.*

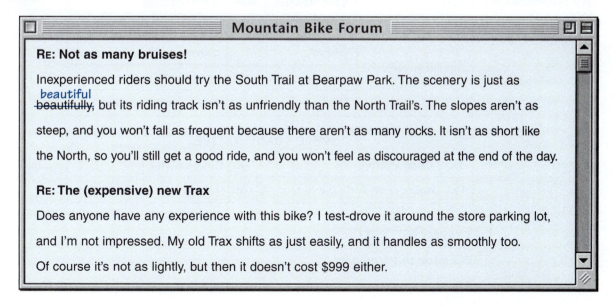

Mountain Bike Forum

RE: Not as many bruises!

Inexperienced riders should try the South Trail at Bearpaw Park. The scenery is just as
~~beautifully~~ *beautiful*, but its riding track isn't as unfriendly than the North Trail's. The slopes aren't as
steep, and you won't fall as frequent because there aren't as many rocks. It isn't as short like
the North, so you'll still get a good ride, and you won't feel as discouraged at the end of the day.

RE: The (expensive) new Trax

Does anyone have any experience with this bike? I test-drove it around the store parking lot,
and I'm not impressed. My old Trax shifts as just easily, and it handles as smoothly too.

Of course it's not as lightly, but then it doesn't cost $999 either.

Adjectives: Comparatives

CHECK POINT

Check the correct answer.

The new restaurant will be

☐ different from the old restaurant.

☐ the same as the old restaurant.

CHART CHECK

Circle T (True) or F (False).

T F The comparative adjective form always ends in *-er*.

T F You can use the same comparative adjective twice in a statement to show a change in a situation.

COMPARATIVES

	COMPARATIVE		**THAN**	
The new restaurant is	brighter better		than	the old one.
	more less	comfortable beautiful		

REPEATED COMPARATIVES

	COMPARATIVE	**AND**	**COMPARATIVE**	
The food is getting	better	and	better.	
	worse		worse.	
	more		more	delicious.
	less		less	interesting.

DOUBLE COMPARATIVES

THE	**COMPARATIVE**		**THE**	**COMPARATIVE**	
The	more crowded	the restaurant,	the	slower	the service.

EXPRESS CHECK

Complete this sentence.

Mo's is bigger and _____ popular _____ Val's.

Grammar Explanations	**Examples**
1. Use the **comparative** form of adjectives to focus on a <u>difference</u> between people, places, and things.	■ The new menu is **bigger than** the old menu. ■ The new waiters are **more experienced than** the old waiters.

2. There is more than one way to **form the comparative of adjectives**.

   a. For one-syllable adjectives and two-syllable adjectives ending in -*y*, use **adjective + -*er***.

   ▶ **BE CAREFUL!** There are often <u>spelling changes</u> when you add -*er*.

   ▶ **BE CAREFUL!** Some adjectives have <u>irregular comparative</u> forms.

   b. For most other adjectives of two or more syllables, use **more/less + adjective**.

   c. For some adjectives, use either -*er* or **more/less**.

ADJECTIVE	COMPARATIVE
bright	**brighter**
friendly	**friendlier**
nice	**nicer**
big	**bigger**
pretty	**prettier**
good	**better**
bad	**worse**
comfortable	**more comfortable** **less comfortable**

■ The Inn is **quieter** than Joe's.
■ The Inn is **more quiet** than Joe's.

3. Use the comparative **with *than*** when you mention the things you are comparing.

■ The apple pie is **better *than*** the cake.

Use the comparative **without *than*** when it is clear which things you are comparing.

■ The new desserts are **better**.
  (The new desserts are better than the old desserts.)

4. Repeat the same comparative to talk about change—<u>an increase or a decrease</u>:
comparative adjective + ***and*** + **comparative adjective**
        OR
***more/less* + *and* + *more/less* + adjective**

■ It's getting **harder and harder** to find an inexpensive restaurant.

■ It's getting **more and more difficult**.
  (The difficulty is increasing.)

5. Use a double comparative to show <u>cause and effect</u>:
***the* + comparative adjective + *the* + comparative adjective**

■ **The shorter** the line, **the faster** the service.
  (When the line is shorter, the service is faster.)

Check it out!

For spelling rules for the comparative form of adjectives, see Appendix 22 on page 344.

For a list of irregular comparative adjectives, see Appendix 10 on page 339.

For a list of some adjectives that form the comparative in two ways, see Appendix 12 on page 339.

1 **TRUE OR FALSE •** *Look at these two restaurant ads. Then read the statements below, and decide if they are True (T) or False (F).*

Luigi's Italian Restaurant	Antonio's Ristorante Italiano
Family-style eating since 1990	*Established in 1990*
Open Tuesday–Sunday, 12:00–9:00	*Relaxed dining in a romantic atmosphere*
EARLY-BIRD SPECIAL	open seven days a week—dinner only
(full dinner for $10.95 if ordered before 6:00)	reservations suggested
No reservations necessary	**all credit cards accepted**
No credit cards	1273 Orange Street 453-3285
875 Orange St.	*one free beverage with this ad*

____F____ **1.** Luigi's is older than Antonio's.

_____ **2.** Antonio's is more romantic than Luigi's.

_____ **3.** Luigi's is probably less crowded.

_____ **4.** Antonio's seems cheaper than Luigi's.

_____ **5.** On Tuesdays, Luigi's has shorter business hours.

2 **COMPARE & COMPLETE •** *Look at part of Luigi's menu. Then complete the comparisons. Use the comparative form of the words in parentheses.*

> ♥ **Spaghetti Primavera** *(with lightly sautéed vegetables)* $6.95
> 🌶 **Spaghetti Arrabbiata** *(with hot chili peppers and tomatoes)* $7.85
> **Fettuccini Alfredo** *(with butter and heavy cream)* $8.29
> **Linguine Aglio e Olio** *(with garlic and oil)*....................................$5.67
> ♥ low fat, low salt 🌶 hot and spicy

1. The spaghetti primavera is _____cheaper than_____ the spaghetti arrabbiata.
(cheap)

2. The linguine aglio e olio is _____ the fettuccini Alfredo.
(expensive)

3. The spaghetti arrabbiata is _____ and
(hot)
_____ the linguine aglio e olio.
(spicy)

4. The fettuccini Alfredo is _____ the spaghetti primavera.
(fattening)

5. The spaghetti primavera is _____ the fettuccini Alfredo.
(healthy)

3 **COMPLETE** • *Read these comments about a restaurant. Complete them with the comparative form of the words in parentheses to show cause and effect or a change.*

1. **A:** I can't believe the size of this menu. It's going to take me forever to choose.

   B: ___The longer___ the menu, ___the more difficult___ the choice.
   (long)   (difficult)

2. **A:** They say the food here is getting _____ and _____.
   (good)

   B: And _____ the food, _____ it is.
   (good)   (expensive)

3. **A:** The service seems a little slow tonight.

   B: Yes, _____ the restaurant, _____ the service.
   (popular)   (slow)

4. **A:** The cigarette smoke here is getting _____ and _____.
   (bad)

   B: _____ the room, _____ my cough gets.
   (smoky)   (bad)

5. **A:** It's pretty loud in here.

   B: _____ the restaurant, _____ it is.
   (crowded)   (noisy)

6. **A:** They certainly give you a lot of food. I can't eat another bite.

   B: _____ the portions, _____ it is to finish.
   (big)   (hard)

7. **A:** Their desserts keep getting _____ and _____.
   (delicious)

   B: And I keep getting _____ and _____!
   (heavy)

4 **EDIT** • *Read this restaurant review. Find and correct eight mistakes in the use of the comparative of adjectives. The first mistake is already corrected.*

Dining Out

BY BRUCE NEWHART

Pete's Place has just reopened under new management. The dining room
                      brighter
looks bigger, ~~more bright~~, and prettier as the old one. Although the food isn't better, it *is* just as good. The menu is more varied and less expensiver. Try one of their pasta dishes. You won't find a more fresher tomato sauce in town. And leave room for dessert. They just keep getting good and better.

The wait staff is friendly but not able to handle large numbers of people—the crowded the restaurant, the slower the service. At dinnertime the lines outside this popular eatery are getting longer and more long. Try lunchtime for a quieter and relaxeder meal.

Adjectives: Superlatives

To the **loveliest**
Most original
Most vibrant
Most exciting
Woman I know...

Who just
happens to be
my wife!
HAPPY
VALENTINE'S
DAY!

NOTE: Valentine's Day (February 14) is a holiday in the United States and Canada.
Many people send cards to special people in their lives to tell them their feelings.

CHART CHECK

*Check the correct
answers.*

Which word always
goes before the
superlative form
of the adjective?

❑ *a* or *an*

❑ *the*   ❑ *most*

Which letters do you
add to the end of a
short adjective to
form the superlative?

❑ *-er*   ❑ *-est*

Which words do you
add before a long
adjective to form the
superlative?

❑ *more* or *less*

❑ *most* or *least*

SUPERLATIVES		
	SUPERLATIVE ADJECTIVE FORM	
You are	**the sweetest** **the funniest** **the best** **the most wonderful** **the least selfish**	person in the world.
That's	**the nicest** **the loveliest** **the worst** **the most amusing** **the least original**	card I've ever received.

EXPRESS CHECK

Complete the chart.

ADJECTIVE	SUPERLATIVE
nice	
beautiful	
warm	
happy	

Grammar Explanations

Examples

1. Use the **superlative** form of adjectives to <u>single out people, places, and things</u> from other people, places, and things.	■ You are **the best** parents in the world. ■ You are **the most wonderful** friend I've ever had.

2. There is more than one way to **form the superlative of adjectives**.

a. For one-syllable or two-syllable adjectives ending in -y, use *the* + **adjective** + *-est*.

▶ **BE CAREFUL!** There are often <u>spelling changes</u> when you add *-est*.

▶ **BE CAREFUL!** Some adjectives have <u>irregular superlative</u> forms.

b. For most other adjectives of two or more syllables, use *the most/the least* + **adjective**.

c. For some adjectives use either *the . . . -est* or *the most/the least*.

ADJECTIVE	SUPERLATIVE
bright	**the brightest**
friendly	**the friendliest**
nice	**the nicest**
big	**the biggest**
pretty	**the prettiest**
good	**the best**
bad	**the worst**
comfortable	**the most comfortable** **the least comfortable**

■ My third hotel was **the quietest**.
■ My third hotel was **the most quiet**.

3. The superlative is often used **with expressions beginning with** *in* or *of*, such as *in the world* and *of all*.	■ You're **the best** mother *in the world*. ■ He's **the smartest** one *of us all*.

4. The superlative is sometimes **followed by a clause**. Often the clause uses the present perfect with *ever*.	■ That's **the nicest** card *I've ever received*. ■ You have **the loveliest** smile *I've ever seen*.

Check it out!

For spelling rules for the superlative form of adjectives, see Appendix 22 on page 344.

For a list of irregular superlative adjectives, see Appendix 10 on page 339.

For a list of some adjectives that form the superlative in two ways, see Appendix 12 on page 339.

1

IDENTIFY • *Read this Mother's Day card written by a young child. Underline all the superlative adjectives.*

You are the best mother
in the whole wide world.
You are the smartest, the brightest, and
the funniest of all moms I've ever known.
You are the nicest mom I've ever had.
You are the most wonderful and definitely
the least mean.
No mom in the whole wide world is
better than you.
You are the greatest mother of all.
I love you very, very much!
Happy Mother's Day!

Love,
Erin

2

COMPLETE & CHOOSE • *Read these sentences from Valentine's Day cards. Complete them with the superlative form of the adjectives in parentheses and the expressions in the box.*

| of all | in the school | of my life | in our family | ~~in the world~~ | of the year |

1. You are so good to me. I am __the luckiest__ person __in the world__ .
   (lucky)

2. The day we were married was _____ day _____.
   (happy)

3. You are a terrific teacher. You are _____ teacher _____.
   (good)

4. You make me feel warm even in _____ months _____.
   (cold)

5. You are _____ cousin _____.
   (nice)

6. Grandma, you are _____ person _____. Maybe that's
   (wise)
   why I love you the most.

3 **DESCRIBE** • *Look at these gift items. Write sentences about them. Use the superlative form of the words in parentheses.*

$34.99

$11.00

$4.95

$27.99

1. The book ___is the least expensive gift._____
   (expensive)

2. The painting _____
   (unusual)

3. The painting _____
   (practical)

4. The book _____
   (small)

5. The painting _____
   (big)

6. The scarf _____
   (expensive)

7. The toy _____
   (funny)

4 **EDIT** • *Read this paragraph from a student's essay. Find and correct five mistakes in the use of superlative adjectives. The first mistake is already corrected.*

               most serious

Ramadan is the ~~seriousest~~ time in Muslim culture. During Ramadan, we do not eat from

sunup to sunset. This is difficult for everyone, but teenagers have the hardest time.

Right after Ramadan is the Eid al-Fitr. This holiday lasts three days, and it's the most

happiest time of the year. The morning of Eid, my family gets up early and goes to the

mosque. After we greet our neighbors by saying "Eid Mubarek" (Happy Eid), we go

home. We eat the big breakfast you have ever seen. Our parents give us gifts, usually

new clothes and money. One year, Eid came around the time I graduated from high

school. That year, I got the most beautiful clothes and the fatter envelope of money of all

the children in my family. Eid Mela is part of Eid al-Fitr. On that day, we all go to

a big park. Last year at Eid Mela, I had the better time of my life. I met my old high

school friends, and we all ate junk food and showed off our new clothes.

UNIT 45

Adverbs: Comparatives and Superlatives

Watch Jordan. **The more** he plays, **the better** he looks.

Come on, Bryant, try **harder**, man!

CHECK *POINT*

Circle T (True) or F (False).

T   F   Jordan improves every time he plays.

CHART CHECK

Check the correct answer.

What do you add to long adverbs to form the comparative?

❏ *more* or *less*

❏ *-er* or *-est*

Which word do you always add to form the superlative?

❏ *most*

❏ *the*

COMPARATIVES			
	COMPARATIVE ADVERB FORM	***THAN***	
Jordan played	**harder** **better**	**than**	Bryant.
	more **less**	**aggressively** **consistently**	

SUPERLATIVES		
	SUPERLATIVE ADVERB FORM	
He threw	**the fastest** **the best**	of anyone in the game.
	the most **the least**	**accurately** **frequently**

EXPRESS CHECK

Circle the correct words to complete these sentences.

Sims threw faster <u>than / of</u> Jones. He played <u>better / the best</u> of all.

Grammar Explanations	**Examples**
1. Use the **comparative form of adverbs** to focus on <u>differences</u> between actions.	■ The Bulls played **better than** the Lakers. ■ Jordan played **more skillfully than** O'Neal.
Use the comparative **without** *than* when it is clear which things you are comparing.	■ He played **less aggressively**, though.
2. Use the **superlative form of adverbs** to <u>single out something about an action</u>.	■ Bryant worked **the hardest**.
We often use the superlative **with expressions beginning with** *of*, such as *of any player*.	■ He scored **the most frequently** *of any player* on the team.

3. There is more than one way to **form the comparative and superlative of adverbs**.

    a. For one-syllable adverbs, use **adverb + -er** or *the* + adverb + *-est*.

    ▶ **BE CAREFUL!** Some adverbs have <u>irregular comparative and superlative</u> forms.

    b. For most adverbs of two or more syllables, use *more/less* + adverb or *the most/the least* + adverb.

    c. Some adverbs use either *more/less* or *-er* and *the most/the least* or *the . . . -est*.

ADVERB	COMPARATIVE	SUPERLATIVE
fast	**faster**	**the fastest**
hard	**harder**	**the hardest**
well	**better**	**the best**
badly	**worse**	**the worst**
skillfully	**more/less skillfully**	**the most/the least skillfully**
quickly	**more quickly quicker**	**the most quickly the quickest**

4. Repeat the same comparative to talk about change—<u>an increase or a decrease</u>:

    comparative adverb + *and* + **comparative adverb**

    OR

    more/less + *and* + *more/less* + **adverb**

■ Bryant is playing **better and better** as the season continues.
(His performance keeps improving.)

■ He is shooting **more and more accurately**.
(His shooting keeps getting more accurate).

5. Use a double comparative to show <u>cause and effect</u>:

    the + **comparative adverb** + *the* + **comparative adverb**

■ **The harder** he played, **the better** he performed.
(When he played harder, his performance improved.)

Check it out!
For a list of irregular comparisons of adverbs, see Appendix 10 on page 339.

IDENTIFY • *Read this feature story from the sports section of the newspaper. Underline all the comparative forms once. Underline all the superlative forms twice.*

Section 3   **Sports**

Golds Beat Silvers!

In the first soccer game of the season, the Golds beat the Silvers, 6 to 3. The Silver team played a truly fantastic game, but its defense is still weak. The Golds defended the ball much more aggressively than the Silver team did. Of course, Ace Jackson certainly helped win the game for the Golds. The Golds' star player was back on the field today to the delight of his many fans. He was hurt badly at the end of last season, but he has recovered quickly. Although he didn't play as well as people expected, he still handled the ball like the old Ace. He certainly handled it the most skillfully of anyone on the team. He controlled the ball the best, kicked the ball the farthest, and ran the fastest of any of the players on either team. He played hard and helped the Golds look good. In fact, the harder he played, the better the Golds performed. Watch Ace this season.

And watch the Silvers. They have a new coach, and they're training more seriously this year. I think we'll see them play better and better as the season progresses.

 COMPLETE • *Read this conversation between friends. Complete it with the comparative or superlative forms of the words in parentheses. Add **the** and **than** where necessary.*

BILLY: Did you hear about that new speed-reading course? It helps you read

_____ faster _____ and _____ .
      1. (fast)   **2.** (well)

MIGUEL: I don't believe it! The _____ you read, the _____
          3. (fast)   **4.** (little)
you understand.

BILLY: The ad says that after the course you'll read ten times _____
                                                 5. (rapidly)
and understand five times more. And the best thing is that you won't have

to work any _____ .
         6. (hard)

MIGUEL: I'd like to see that. All through high school, I read _____ of
                                                 7. (slowly)
any student in my class, but I also remembered details _____
                                                 8. (clearly)
and _____ of any of my classmates.
     9. (long)

BILLY: Maybe you could read even _____ that and still remember
                                     10. (quickly)
details. That way, you'd have more time to go to the gym.

MIGUEL: Did you read the course description completely?

BILLY: I read it _____ I read most things.
         11. (completely)

3 **CHOOSE & COMPLETE** • *Look at the chart. Then complete the sentences with the comparative or superlative form of the words in the box. You will use some words more than once.*

far	good	fast	bad	slow	high

ATHLETE	BROAD JUMP	POLE VAULTING	5-MILE RUN
Cruz	14.3 feet	7 feet 3 inches	24 minutes
Smith	14.1 feet	7 feet 2 inches	28 minutes
Lin	15.2 feet	7 feet 8 inches	30 minutes
Storm	15.4 feet	8 feet 2 inches	22 minutes

1. Cruz jumped _____*farther than*_____ Smith.

2. Storm vaulted _____*the highest*_____ of all.

3. Lin ran _____.

4. Smith ran _____ Storm.

5. Storm jumped _____.

6. Cruz ran _____ Smith.

7. Storm vaulted _____ Smith.

8. All in all, Storm did _____.

9. All in all, Smith did _____.

4 **EDIT** • *Read this student's report about a basketball game. Find and correct seven mistakes in the use of adverbs. The first mistake is already corrected.*

Last night I watched the Lakers and the Bulls. Both teams played more
aggressively ᴀ I've ever seen them. In fact, they played the better of any game
          than
I've watched this season. In the first half, Michael Jordan sprained his left ankle,
and Shaquille O'Neal was out of the game because of fouls. But they still didn't
start the second half any slower that the first. With Jordan out, Kukoc scored the
most frequenter of any player. He's been playing more and more better as the
season goes on. In fact, more he plays, the better he looks. The Bulls won 97 to
88. The Lakers seemed to get tired at the end. They played little and less
consistently as the game went on.

SelfTest

Circle the letter of the correct answer to complete each sentence.

EXAMPLE:
Jennifer never _____ coffee.   A (B) C D
(A) drink   (C) is drinking
(B) drinks   (D) was drinking

---

1. I have _____ job in the world.   A B C D
   (A) a good   (C) the best
   (B) best   (D) the better

2. The apple pie smells _____!   A B C D
   (A) wonderful   (C) more wonderfully
   (B) wonderfully   (D) the most wonderfully

3. Our team didn't play _____ I expected. I was disappointed.   A B C D
   (A) as well as   (C) as badly as
   (B) well   (D) better

4. I passed my driver's test. It seemed much _____ this time.   A B C D
   (A) easy   (C) easiest
   (B) easier   (D) easily

5. The faster Tranh walks, _____.   A B C D
   (A) more tired   (C) the more tired he gets
   (B) he gets tired   (D) he gets more tired

6. Could you talk _____? I'm trying to work.   A B C D
   (A) more quietly   (C) more quiet
   (B) quieter than   (D) quiet

7. Lisa is staying home. Her cold is a lot _____ today.   A B C D
   (A) bad   (C) worst
   (B) worse   (D) the worst

8. Sorry we're late. Your house is much _____ than we thought. A B C D
   (A) far   (C) farther
   (B) the farthest   (D) the farther

9. The movie was so _____ that we couldn't sleep last night.   A B C D
   (A) excitingly   (C) excite
   (B) excited   (D) exciting

10. Chris is working very _____ these days.   A B C D
    (A) hardly   (C) harder
    (B) hard   (D) hardest

196

11. Write the report first. It's more important _____ your other work.   **A B C D**
    (A) than   (C) from
    (B) as   (D) then

12. The lunch menu is very short. It's _____ than the dinner menu.   **A B C D**
    (A) varied   (C) less varied
    (B) more varied   (D) the least varied

13. Thank you! That's _____ I've ever received.   **A B C D**
    (A) the nicer gift   (C) nicest gift
    (B) a nice gift   (D) the nicest gift

14. It's getting more _____ to find a cheap apartment.   **A B C D**
    (A) hardly   (C) the most difficult
    (B) and more difficult   (D) and very difficult

SECTION TWO

Each sentence has four underlined words or phrases. The four underlined parts of the sentence are marked A, B, C, and D. Circle the letter of the one underlined word or phrase that is NOT CORRECT.

> **EXAMPLE:**
>
> Mike <u>usually</u> <u>drives</u> to school, but <u>today</u> he <u>walks</u>.   **A B C (D)**
>   A   B   C   D

15. <u>The harder</u> Sylvia <u>tries</u>, <u>less</u> she <u>succeeds</u>.   **A B C D**
     A   B C   D

16. This has been <u>the</u> <u>best</u> day <u>than</u> my <u>whole</u> life!   **A B C D**
                   A B   C   D

17. We're <u>always</u> <u>amazing</u> <u>by</u> John's <u>incredible</u> travel stories.   **A B C D**
         A   B C   D

18. We took <u>a lot of</u> photos because she was <u>such</u> a <u>cutely</u> <u>little</u> baby.   **A B C D**
         A   B   C D

19. Our <u>new</u> car is <u>hard</u> to drive <u>than</u> our <u>old</u> one.   **A B C D**
      A   B   C   D

20. Patrick doesn't <u>run quickly</u> <u>as</u> Lee, <u>but</u> he can run <u>farther</u>.   **A B C D**
           A   B   C   D

21. You did <u>much</u> <u>more</u> <u>better</u> in the last test <u>than</u> in this one.   **A B C D**
         A   B   C   D

22. What's <u>the</u> <u>more</u> <u>popular</u> of all the <u>new</u> TV shows?   **A B C D**
         A B   C   D

23. <u>The more</u> I practice the piano, the <u>most</u> <u>skilled</u> I get.   **A B C D**
     A B   C   D

24. The garbage in the street <u>is</u> <u>more</u> <u>disgusted</u> <u>than</u> the potholes.   **A B C D**
                       A B   C   D

25. Today seems <u>as</u> <u>hotter</u> <u>as</u> yesterday, but the humidity is <u>lower</u>.   **A B C D**
             A   B   C   D

Gerunds:
Subject and Object

I'm all out of breath again. I really need to quit **jogging**!

CHECK *POINT*

Check the correct answer.

What does the woman want to give up?

☐ cigarettes

☐ exercise

CHART CHECK

Check the correct answer.

What does the gerund end with?

☐ *-ed*

☐ *-ing*

What goes before the gerund to make it negative?

☐ *not*

☐ *don't* or *doesn't*

GERUND AS SUBJECT		
GERUND (SUBJECT)	**VERB**	**OBJECT**
Smoking	harms	your health.
Not smoking	makes	you healthier.

GERUND AS OBJECT		
SUBJECT	**VERB**	**GERUND (OBJECT)**
You	should quit	**smoking**.
My doctor	suggests	**not smoking**.

EXPRESS CHECK

Complete this conversation with the correct form of the verb **drink**.
Use the affirmative or negative.

A: _____ too much coffee isn't good for you.

B: I know. I quit _____ coffee last year.

A: My doctor suggested _____ soda either.

Grammar Explanations

Examples

1. A **gerund** (base form of verb + **-ing**) is a <u>verb that functions like a noun</u>.

A gerund can be the **subject** of a sentence.

▶ **BE CAREFUL!** There are often <u>spelling changes</u> when you add **-ing** to the base form of the verb.

Notice that a gerund is always <u>singular</u> and is followed by the third-person-singular form of the verb.

▶ **BE CAREFUL!** Don't confuse a gerund with the progressive form of the verb.

- **Drinking** too much coffee is bad for your health.

- **Smoking** is also unhealthy.

smoke	**smoking**
jog	**jogging**

- **Eating** junk food *makes* me sick.
- **Inhaling** smoke *gives* me bronchitis.

  gerund
- **Drinking** coffee isn't healthy.

  progressive form
- He **is drinking** coffee right now.

2. A **gerund** can also be the **object** of certain verbs.

To the right is a short list of <u>verbs that can be followed by a gerund</u>.

- I **enjoy** *exercising*.
- I've **considered** *joining* a gym.

admit	**miss**
avoid	**practice**
consider	**quit**
deny	**resent**
enjoy	**suggest**
finish	**understand**

3. There are many common expressions with **go + gerund**. These expressions usually describe <u>activities</u>, such as *shopping, fishing, skiing, swimming,* and *camping.*

- We often **go** *swimming* in the lake.
- Yesterday I **went** *shopping* for a new pair of running shoes.

Check it out!

For more complete lists of common verbs that can be followed by the gerund, see Appendix 3 on page 337 and Appendix 6 on page 338.

1 **IDENTIFY** • *Read part of an article from a health newsletter. Underline the words ending in* **-ing** *that are gerunds.*

YOUR HEALTH

<u>SWIMMING</u> is great exercise. It's healthy, fun, and relaxing. Because swimming is a "low-impact" sport, most people enjoy participating in this activity without fear of injury to their bones or muscles. Jogging, which is a "high-impact" activity, can at times be harmful. I know this from personal experience. Last year while I was jogging, I injured my right knee. I don't go jogging anymore. After a painful month of recovery, I stopped running and switched to water sports. I'm now considering joining a swimming team and competing in races.

2 **CHOOSE & COMPLETE** • *Read these statements about health issues. Complete them with the gerund form of the verbs in the box. Choose between affirmative and negative.*

increase	eat	do	walk	drink	~~smoke~~	swim	run	go

1. _____Smoking_____ is bad for your heart and lungs.

2. _____ too much fat and sugar is also unhealthy.

3. _____ enough water is bad for your general health.

4. Doctors suggest _____ the amount of fruits and vegetables in your diet.

5. Avoid _____ too many high-impact sports such as jogging and jumping rope.

6. Instead, consider _____ in a pool every day. It's an excellent low-impact activity.

7. Many health experts think that _____ is better than _____ because there is less stress on your body when your feet come into contact with the ground.

8. Some people are afraid of the doctor, but _____ for regular checkups is a mistake.

3 **SUMMARIZE** • *Read each numbered statement. Complete the following summary using the appropriate verb from the box and the gerund form of the verb in parentheses.*

| acknowledge | avoid | consider | deny | ~~enjoy~~ | go | quit |

1.   **TOM:** Ann jogs, but I don't really like that kind of exercise.

SUMMARY: Tom doesn't _____enjoy jogging._____
                                    (jog)

2.   **MARTA:** Oh, no thanks. I don't smoke anymore.

SUMMARY: Marta _____
                                    (smoke)

3.   **CHEN:** I'm going to that new swimming pool. Would you like to go with me?

SUMMARY: Chen is going to _____
                                    (swim)

4.   **JIM:** I smell smoke too. But don't look at me! I didn't have a cigarette!

SUMMARY: Jim _____
                                    (smoke)

5.   **INA:** I know I should exercise, but I don't want to. I guess you're right. I *am* lazy.

SUMMARY: Ina _____ lazy.
                                    (be)

6.   **PHIL:** No, thanks. The cake looks great, but I'm trying to stay away from sweets.

SUMMARY: Phil _____ sweets.
                                    (eat)

7.   **VILMA:** I'm not sure, but I *may* go on a vacation.

SUMMARY: Vilma _____ a vacation.
                                    (take)

4 **EDIT** • *Read Jim's notes. Find and correct nine mistakes in the use of the gerund. The first mistake is already corrected.*

> SMOKING
> <u>WAYS I CAN QUIT ~~SMOKE~~ CIGARETTES</u>
>
> Pick an exact date to quit smoke.
>
> Stop smoking completely. (Cut down is harder than stopping all at once.)
>
> Avoid to be around other smokers (at least at the beginning).
>
> Start exercising daily. To exercise can reduce stress.
>
> No drinking coffee may help too.
>
> Imagine been a non-smoker. Positive mental images can help.
>
> Consider to join a support group.
>
> Don't delay to ask for help. Call Dr. Burns right away!
>
> Keep trying and don't give up!

UNIT 47 — **Gerunds** after Prepositions

GET INVOLVED!

Interested **in improving** life on campus?

Tired **of hearing** complaints and not **finding** solutions?

Join the Student Council!

Next Meeting: Mon., March 25, 8:00 P.M., Main Auditorium

We look forward **to seeing** you there.

You CAN make a difference!

 CHECK POINT

Circle T (True) or F (False).

The Student Council is looking for students who

T F   want to make new friends.

T F   want to improve life on campus.

T F   like to complain.

CHART CHECK

Check the correct answers.

What part of speech is the word ***to*** in ***look forward to***?

☐ part of the infinitive

☐ a preposition

What form of the verb follows a preposition?

☐ the base form

☐ the gerund

☐ the infinitive

GERUNDS AFTER PREPOSITIONS				
	PREPOSITION	**(NOT)**	**GERUND**	
Do you have ideas	**for**		**improving**	life on campus?
We're good	**at**		**planning**	ahead.
You can help	**by**		**taking**	notes.
She believes	**in**	(not)	**compromising**.	
Are you tired	**of**		**hearing**	complaints?
Let's work	**instead of**		**complaining**.	
They insist	**on**	(not)	**coming**	to the meeting.
I look forward	**to**	(not)	**having to**	study next summer.

EXPRESS CHECK

Complete this conversation with the correct form of the verb **join**.

A: Are you happy about _____ the Student Council?

B: Sure. I'd been looking forward to _____ a group for a while.

Grammar Explanations

Examples

1. A **preposition** is a word such as *about*, *against*, *at*, *by*, *for*, *in*, *instead of*, *of*, *on*, *to*, *with*, and *without*. A preposition can be followed by a noun or a pronoun.

Because a **gerund** (base form of verb + *-ing*) acts as a noun, it <u>can follow a preposition</u> too.

- The council insists **on *elections***.
  noun
- The council insists **on *them***.
  pronoun
- The council insists **on *voting***.
  gerund

2. Many **common expressions** are made up of a verb or an adjective followed by a preposition.

These expressions can be <u>followed by a gerund</u>.

VERB + PREPOSITION	ADJECTIVE + PREPOSITION
advise **against**	afraid **of**
believe **in**	bored **with**
count **on**	excited **about**

- She **counts on *going*** to college.
- He **is bored with *working*** in a store.

3. **BE CAREFUL!**

a. In the **expressions** to the right, *to* is a <u>preposition</u>, not part of an infinitive form. For this reason it can be <u>followed by the gerund</u>.

VERB + PREPOSITION	ADJECTIVE + PREPOSITION
look forward **to**	accustomed **to**
object **to**	opposed **to**
resort **to**	used **to**

- I'm looking forward **to *seeing*** you.
  NOT I'm looking forward ~~to see you~~.

b. Do not confuse *used to* + **base form** of verb (for habits in the past) with *be/get used to* + **gerund** (meaning "be/get accustomed to").

- I **used to take** the train.
  (It was my habit to take the train, but I no longer take the train.)
- I**'m used to *taking*** the train.
  (I'm accustomed to taking the train.)
- I**'m getting used to *taking*** the train.
  (I'm getting accustomed to taking the train.)

Check it out!

For a list of common verb plus preposition combinations, see Appendix 7 on page 338.
For a list of common adjective plus preposition combinations, see Appendix 8 on page 338.

IDENTIFY • *The Student Council wrote a letter to the college president. Read it and underline all the preposition + gerund combinations.*

> We, the members of the Student Council, would like to share with you the thoughts and concerns of the general student body. As you probably know, many students are complaining about life on campus. We are interested <u>in meeting</u> with you to discuss our ideas for dealing with these complaints.
>
> We know that you are tired of hearing students complain and that you are not used to working with the Student Council. However, if you really believe in giving new ideas a try, we hope you will think about speaking with our representatives soon. We look forward to hearing from you soon.

CHOOSE & COMPLETE • *Read these comments from the school newspaper. Complete the students' statements with the appropriate preposition from the box (you will use one of them several times) and the gerund form of the verb in parentheses.*

at	on	in	to	about	for

1. I don't have any plans for spring break, but I'm not concerned _____ **about getting** _____ (get)

   bored. I can always take a walk or something.—*Jim Hsu*

2. What are my plans for spring break? I'm very interested _____ (listen)

   to jazz. I'm going to attend the Spring Jazz Festival.—*Lisa Suarez*

3. My friends and I are driving to New Orleans. I'm excited _____, (go)

   but I'm nervous _____ at night.—*Emilia Leale* (drive)

4. I'm really looking forward _____ at home and just (stay)

   _____.—*Don Pitt* (relax)

5. I'm driving to Quebec. It's famous _____ great food. —*Eun Ko* (have)

6. I love languages, but I'm not good _____ them, so I'm studying for (learn)

   my Japanese class over the break. —*Claire Kaplan*

7. My friends and I are going camping, but my little brother insists _____ (come)

   with us. A lot of fun that'll be!—*Omar Sisane*

8. My girlfriend plans _____ and _____ to the (read) (go)

   movies, so I guess I'll read a lot and see a lot of movies.—*Tim Riley*

3 **COMBINE •** *Read these pairs of sentences about school life. Combine them with the prepositions in parentheses.*

1. You can't walk on campus late at night. You have to worry about your safety.

   You can't walk on campus late at night without worrying about your safety.
   (without)

2. We can make changes. We can tell the administration about our concerns.

   _____
   (by)

3. The administration can help. It can listen to our concerns.

   _____
   (by)

4. In some cases, students just complain. They don't make suggestions for improvements.

   _____
   (instead of)

5. Students get annoyed with some teachers. Some teachers come late to class.

   _____
   (for)

6. You can improve your grades. Study regularly.

   _____
   (by)

4 **EDIT •** *Read this student's letter. Find and correct seven mistakes in the use of gerunds after prepositions. The first mistake is already corrected.*

> Dear Brian,
>
>   I have been attending Longtree College for a year. I'm very happy
> about ~~study~~ **studying** here. At first, it was a little hard getting used to speak English
> all the time, but now I feel very comfortable about communicate in my
> second language.
>
>   I just joined an international student group, and I'm excited with
> meeting new people. Summer break is coming, and a few of us are planning
> on do some traveling together. Before to join this group, I used to spend
> holidays alone.
>
>   Please write. I look forward to hear from you!
>
>   K.

Infinitives
after Certain Verbs

Lifestyles Section 4

ASK ANNIE

Dear Annie,

A month ago I met this great woman, Megan, and I **asked her to marry** me right away. She says things are "moving too fast," and she **wants me to think** about my proposal some more. I told her I **can't afford to wait** forever. Am I right? —*Impatient*

CHECK *POINT*

Check the correct answer.

❑ Megan wants more time to consider the marriage proposal.

❑ Megan thinks "Impatient" should consider his proposal more.

CHART CHECK

Circle T (True) or F (False).

T F The infinitive = base form + **to**.

T F The negative infinitive = **not** + infinitive.

T F All verbs need an object before the infinitive.

STATEMENTS: WITHOUT AN OBJECT

SUBJECT	VERB	(NOT)	INFINITIVE	
They	decided agreed	(not)	to call to ask	Annie.

STATEMENTS: WITH AN OBJECT

SUBJECT	VERB	OBJECT	(NOT)	INFINITIVE	
They	urged advised	John him	(not)	to call to ask	her.

STATEMENTS: WITH AN OPTIONAL OBJECT

SUBJECT	VERB	(OBJECT)	INFINITIVE	
They	wanted needed	(John) (him)	to call to ask	her.

EXPRESS CHECK

Unscramble these words to form a sentence.

to • want • Annie • write • to • I _____

Grammar Explanations

Examples

1. Certain **verbs** can be followed by an **infinitive** (*to* + base form of the verb).
- I **want** *to get* married.
- I **asked** Annie *to help* me.

2. Some of these verbs are followed **directly by an infinitive**.

The verbs to the right can be followed directly by an infinitive.
- He **decided** *to write* to Annie.
- He **hoped** *to get* a quick reply.

agree	plan
begin	refuse
fail	seem

3. Some verbs need an **object** (noun or pronoun) **before the infinitive**.

The verbs to the right need an object before the infinitive.
- I **invited** *Mary* to celebrate with us. *(object)*
- I **reminded** *her* to come. *(object)*

advise	tell
encourage	urge
order	warn

4. Some verbs can be followed by either:
- **an infinitive**
  OR
- **an object + infinitive**

The verbs to the right can be followed either directly by an infinitive or by an object + infinitive.
- He **wants** *to leave*. He's tired.
  OR
- He **wants** *you to leave*. You're tired.

ask	need
expect	want
help	would like

5. Form a **negative infinitive** by placing *not* before the infinitive.

▶ **BE CAREFUL!** A sentence with a negative infinitive can have a very different meaning from a sentence with a negative main verb.
- Lee remembered **not** *to call* after 5:00.
  (Lee didn't call after 5:00.)
- Ana told me **not** *to go* to class.
  (Ana: "Don't go. The teacher is sick.")
- Van told me **not** *to give up*.
  (Van: "Don't give up.")
- Van **didn't tell** me to give up.
  (Van didn't say anything.)

Check it out!

For a list of common verbs followed directly by the infinitive, see Appendix 4 on page 338.

For a list of verbs followed by objects and the infinitive, see Appendix 5 on page 338.

For a list of verbs that can be followed either directly by an infinitive or by an object + infinitive, see Appendix 5 on page 338.

1 **IDENTIFY** • *Read Annie's response to "Impatient." Underline all the verb + infinitive and verb + object + infinitive combinations.*

Lifestyles 17

Dear Impatient,

Slow down! You <u>appear to be</u> in too much of a hurry. You've only known this person for a month and yet you asked her to marry you! What's the big rush? *Why* can't you afford to wait? Are you afraid that if she gets to know you better, she may decide not to tie the knot? I agree with your girlfriend. You need to consider things more carefully. You can't expect her (or yourself) to make such an important decision so quickly. If you don't want to regret a hasty decision, I advise you both to get to know each other better before you hurry to the altar.   —Annie

2 **COMPLETE** • *Read this article. Complete it with the correct form of the verbs in parentheses. Use the simple present or the imperative form of the first verb.*

Planning for Love

Most people make careful plans when they _____ *decide to take* _____ a vacation.
1. (decide / take)
Yet when they _____ a mate, they depend on luck.
2. (attempt / find)
Edward A. Dreyfus, Ph.D., _____ love to chance.
3. (warn / single people / not / leave)
He _____ his four-step plan when they search for a life partner.
4. (urge / them / use)
Remember: When you _____ you _____.
5. (fail / plan)   **6.** (plan / fail)

STEP ONE: Make a list. What kind of person do you _____?
7. (wish / meet)
Someone intelligent? Someone who loves sports? List everything.

STEP TWO: Make another list. What kind of person are you? _____
8. (Ask / two friends / read)
your list and comment on it. The two lists should match.

STEP THREE: Increase your chances. _____ in activities you like.
9. (Choose / participate)

STEP FOUR: Ask for introductions. Dr. Dreyfus _____
10. (advise / people / not / feel)
embarrassed to ask. Everyone _____ a matchmaker!
11. (want / be)

3 **SUMMARIZE** • *Read each numbered statement. Complete the summary using the appropriate verb from the box followed by an infinitive or an object + infinitive.*

| agree | remind | would like | ~~urge~~ | invite | need | forget | encourage |

1. **ANNIE:** I really think you should take things more slowly, Chet.

   SUMMARY: Annie _____urged Chet to take things more slowly._____

2. **CARYN:** Tom, could you call me at 10:00?

   SUMMARY: Caryn _____

3. **KURT:** Emily, please remember to buy gas today.

   SUMMARY: Kurt _____

4. **JOHN:** We're going out for coffee, Marta. Would you like to join us?

   SUMMARY: John _____

5. **JASON:** OK, OK, Dad. I'll be home by 10:30 if that's what you want.

   SUMMARY: Jason _____

6. **JEFF:** Oh, no! It's 4:15. I didn't go to the 2:00 staff meeting!

   SUMMARY: Jeff _____

7. **MOM:** Come on, Lisa, don't be scared. Just try again.

   SUMMARY: Lisa's mother _____

8. **TERRY:** I'm using the car tonight. I'm taking Sue to the mall.

   SUMMARY: Terry _____

4 **EDIT** • *Read this entry in a personal diary. Find and correct seven mistakes in the use of infinitives after certain verbs. The first mistake is already corrected.*

>   to join
> Annie advised me ~~joining~~ a club or take a class, and I finally did it! I decided become
> a member of the school's Outdoor Adventure Club, and I went to my first meeting last night.
> I'm really excited about this. The club is planning a hiking trip next weekend. I definitely want
> to go rafting in the spring. At first I didn't want signing up, but the leader was so nice.
> He urged me to not miss this trip, so I put my name on the list. After the meeting, a group
> of people asked me to go out with them. We went to a coffee shop and talked for hours.
> Well, I hoped make some friends when I joined this club, but I didn't expect everyone being
> so friendly. I'm glad Annie persuaded me no to give up.

UNIT 49

Infinitives
after Certain Adjectives and Certain Nouns

It's **hard to find** good fries these days.

CHECK POINT

Check the correct answer.

☐ Finding good fries is difficult.
☐ The man hardly eats anything but fries.

CHART CHECK

Check the correct answers.

The infinitive is formed with:

☐ *to* + base form of verb

☐ *to* + base form of verb + *-ing*

The infinitive follows:

☐ certain nouns and adjectives

☐ certain prepositions

INFINITIVES AFTER CERTAIN ADJECTIVES

	ADJECTIVE	INFINITIVE	
It's	**hard**	**to find**	nutritious fast food.
We're	**eager**	**to hear**	about the new restaurant.
He seemed	**surprised**	**to learn**	the amount of fat in a burger.

INFINITIVES AFTER CERTAIN NOUNS

	NOUN	INFINITIVE	
It's	**time**	**to go**.	
That's a high	**price**	**to pay**.	
Does he have	**permission**	**to stay**	out late?

210

EXPRESS CHECK

Unscramble these words to form two sentences.

convenient • It's • eat • fast • food • to _____ .

pay • a • price • low • That's • to _____ .

Grammar Explanations

Examples

---

1. Certain **adjectives** can be followed by an **infinitive** (*to* + base form of the verb).

adjective infinitive

■ They were **eager** *to try* the new taco.

Many of these adjectives describe a <u>feeling</u> about the action in the infinitive.

■ She was **glad** *to hear* that it was low in calories.

Adjectives that express <u>praise or blame</u> are often followed by an infinitive.

■ I was **wrong** *to leave*.
■ They were **brave** *to tell* him.

Adjectives that show <u>the order of actions</u> are often followed by an infinitive.

■ We were **last** *to order*.
■ When the check came, she was **first** *to leave* the restaurant.

---

2. We often use *It's* + **adjective** + **infinitive**.

adjective infinitive

■ **It's great** *to see* you again.

When the action in the infinitive is done by a person, we often use *of* or *for* + **noun/pronoun**.

■ It was **silly** *of Tom* to leave.
■ It's **hard** *for us* to get here on time.

It's + **adjective** + **infinitive** is often used to make <u>general observations</u>.

■ **It's convenient** *to eat* fast food.
■ **It's difficult** for students *to work* full time.

---

3. Certain **nouns** can be followed by an **infinitive**.

noun infinitive

■ It's **time** *to take* a break.
■ I have the **right** *to eat* what I want.
■ They made a **decision** *to lose* weight.
■ It's a high **price** *to pay*.
■ He has **permission** *to stay* out late.

The **noun** + **infinitive** combination often expresses <u>advisability or necessity</u>.

■ Robin is the **person** *to ask* about that.
(You should ask Robin about that.)

■ I have a **test** *to study* for right now.
(I must study for my test.)

Check it out!

For a list of common adjectives that can be followed by the infinitive, see Appendix 9 on page 338.

1 **IDENTIFY •** *Read this questionnaire. Underline all the adjective + infinitive and noun + infinitive combinations. Write **A** over the adjectives and **N** over the nouns.*

FAST-FOOD QUESTIONNAIRE

Please take a few <u>minutes to complete</u> this questionnaire about fast-food restaurants.
(N over "minutes to complete")

Check (✓) all the answers that are appropriate for you.

1. How often are you <u>likely to eat</u> at a fast-food restaurant?
(A over "likely to eat")

☐ 1–3 times a week ☐ 4–6 times a week

☐ more than 6 times a week ☐ never

2. In your opinion, fast food is:

☐ good to eat ☐ a way to save time

☐ fun to order occasionally ☐ unhealthy to have every day

3. Which statement best describes your feelings about the cost of fast food?

☐ It's a high price to pay for convenience. ☐ You get a lot for just a little money.

4. Is it a good idea to include healthy choices in fast-food menus?

☐ Yes ☐ No

2 **COMPLETE •** *Read these excerpts from letters to the editor of a college newspaper. Complete them with the correct form of the words in parentheses.*

Last year I stopped eating in the school cafeteria because the food was so bad and it

was such a grim ____place to have____ a meal. Yesterday I went back for
                1. (place / have)

the first time. I was _____ Taco Bell there. Fast foods are
                        2. (delighted / find)

the _____! They're _____, and the
        3. (way / go)   4. (fun / eat)

cheerful atmosphere has made the cafeteria a _____ in. I'll be
                                              5. (pleasure / eat)

eating lunch there every day from now on.—*L. Brenner*

It was a _____ fast-food chains to the campus. It's
          6. (mistake / bring)

_____ the exact same restaurants everywhere you go. The
7. (outrageous / see)

food they serve isn't _____. It contains much too much sugar,
                      8. (good / eat)

salt, and fat. For commuter students, it's _____ a healthy
                                          9. (essential / have)

meal before evening class, and it's _____ off campus for
                                    10. (difficult / go)

dinner. We just don't have the time.—*B. Chen*

3 **CHOOSE & COMPLETE** • *Read these conversations between co-workers. Complete them with the words in parentheses and the infinitive form of a verb from the box.*

| get | cry | hear | keep | work | find | decide | wake up | show | ~~take~~ |

CHRIS: Hey, Dana. I've got to talk to you. Do you have ____time to take____
1. (time)
a break?

DANA: Sure, Chris. What's wrong? You look like you're _____.
2. (ready)

CHRIS: Mr. Kay just asked me if I'd be _____ from 4:00 P.M.
3. (willing)
to midnight.

DANA: You have an early class. It's _____ early after
4. (hard)
working late.

CHRIS: Right. When I told him that he said, "I'm _____ that,
5. (suprised)
Chris. I thought you were _____ a promotion to
6. (eager)
shift manager."

DANA: It's _____ your grades up too. Did he give you
7. (important)
_____?
8. (time)

CHRIS: He just said, "OK. I'll ask Steve. We'll give *him* the _____
9. (chance)
his loyalty to the company."

DANA: Fast-food jobs are _____. Just concentrate on school.
10. (easy)

4 **EDIT** • *Read Mr. Kay's journal. Find and correct seven mistakes in the use of infinitives. The first mistake is already corrected.*

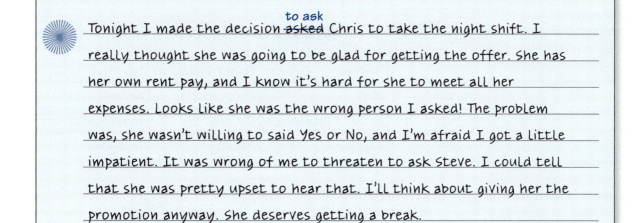

> to ask
> Tonight I made the decision ~~asked~~ Chris to take the night shift. I
> really thought she was going to be glad for getting the offer. She has
> her own rent pay, and I know it's hard for she to meet all her
> expenses. Looks like she was the wrong person I asked! The problem
> was, she wasn't willing to said yes or No, and I'm afraid I got a little
> impatient. It was wrong of me to threaten to ask Steve. I could tell
> that she was pretty upset to hear that. I'll think about giving her the
> promotion anyway. She deserves getting a break.

Infinitives
with *Too* and *Enough*

"Son, your mother and I think that you are now old enough to get your own drink of water."

CHECK POINT

Circle T (True) or F (False).

T F The man's parents want the man to get them a drink of water.

T F The man wants his parents to get him a drink of water.

CHART CHECK

Check the correct answer.

Which word comes before the adjective or adverb?

☐ *too*

☐ *enough*

INFINITIVES WITH *TOO*					
	TOO	**ADJECTIVE/ ADVERB**	**(*FOR* + NOUN/ OBJECT PRONOUN)**	**INFINITIVE**	
We're (not)		**young**	(for people)	**to trust**.	
The teacher talked	**too**	**quickly**	(for me)	**to take**	notes.
It's (not)		**hard**	(for us)	**to decide**.	

INFINITIVES WITH *ENOUGH*					
	ADJECTIVE/ ADVERB	*ENOUGH*	**(*FOR* + NOUN/ OBJECT PRONOUN)**	**INFINITIVE**	
They're (not)	**old**		(for people)	**to trust**.	
She hasn't come	**often**	**enough**	(for me)	**to recognize**	her.
It's (not)	**easy**		(for us)	**to decide**.	

EXPRESS CHECK

Unscramble these words to form two sentences.

vote • She's • to • young • too _____

to • enough • old • We're • work _____

Grammar Explanations

Examples

1. Use *too* + **adjective/adverb** + **infinitive** to give a <u>reason</u>.

■ I'm **too young *to drive***.
(I'm not sixteen yet, so I can't drive.)

■ She is**n't too young *to drive***.
(She's over sixteen, so she can drive.)

■ She arrived **too late *to take*** the test.
(She arrived twenty minutes after the test started, so she couldn't take the test.)

■ She did**n't** arrive **too late *to take*** the test.
(She arrived only two minutes after the test started, so she could take the test.)

2. You can also use **adjective/adverb** + ***enough*** + **infinitive** to give a <u>reason</u>.

■ I'm **old enough *to go*** into the army.
(I'm over eighteen, so I can go into the army.)

■ He is**n't old enough *to go*** into the army.
(He isn't eighteen yet, so he can't go into the army.)

■ I ran **fast enough *to pass*** the physical.
(I ran very fast, so I passed the physical.)

■ She did**n't** run **fast enough *to pass*** the physical.
(She didn't run very fast, so she didn't pass the physical.)

3. Notice that you don't need to use the infinitive when the meaning is clear from the context.

▶ **BE CAREFUL!** Note the <u>placement</u> of ***too*** and ***enough***.

Too comes <u>before</u> the adjective or adverb.

Enough comes <u>after</u> the adjective or adverb.

■ I'm seventeen years old, and I can't vote yet. I'm **too young**. I'm not **old enough**.

■ She's ***too old***.

■ I'm not **old *enough***. NOT I'm not ~~enough old~~.

4. Sometimes we use ***for*** + **noun** or ***for*** + **object pronoun** before the infinitive.

■ We are too young **for people *to trust*** us.
(People don't trust us.)

■ We are too young **for them *to trust*** us.
(They don't trust us.)

1 **CHOOSE** • *People have different opinions about public issues. Read each numbered statement of opinion. Then circle the letter of the sentence (a) or (b) that best summarizes that opinion.*

1. Teenagers are responsible enough to stay out past 10:00 P.M.
   - **(a.)** Teenagers should have permission to stay out past 10:00 P.M.
   - **b.** Teenagers shouldn't have permission to stay out past 10:00 P.M.

2. Teenagers are too immature to vote.
   - **a.** Teenagers should be able to vote.
   - **b.** Teenagers shouldn't be able to vote.

3. Teenagers are responsible enough to use the Internet without censorship.
   - **a.** Teenagers can use the Internet without censorship.
   - **b.** Teenagers can't use the Internet without censorship.

4. Adults are too afraid of change to listen to children's ideas.
   - **a.** Adults listen to children's ideas.
   - **b.** Adults don't listen to children's ideas.

5. At age seventy, people are not too old to work.
   - **a.** At age seventy, people can work.
   - **b.** At age seventy, people can't work.

6. Sixteen-year-olds are not experienced enough to drive at night.
   - **a.** Sixteen-year-olds can drive at night.
   - **b.** Sixteen-year-olds can't drive at night.

2 **UNSCRAMBLE** • *Gina wants to drive to another city for a concert, but her mother thinks she's too young. Make sentences with the words in parentheses. Then write* **G (Gina)** *or* **M (Mother)** *to show whose opinion each sentence represents.*

1. You're too young to be out so late.   M
   (too / You're / young / to / out / be / so / late)

2. _____
   (get / It's / to / by ten / us / too / home / far / for)

3. _____
   (take care of / mature / myself / I'm / to / enough)

4. _____
   (dangerous / too / night / It's / to / drive / at)

5. _____
   (too / give / worry / I / much / to / permission / you)

6. _____
   (that / experienced / drive / aren't / far / enough / to / You)

3 **COMPLETE** • *Some teenagers are leaving a concert. Complete the sentences. Use the words in parentheses with the infinitive and* **too** *or* **enough**.

1. I couldn't hear that last song. The guitar was ___*too loud for me to hear*___ the words.

(loud / me / hear)

2. Let's get tickets for the concert in Hampton. They're _____.

(cheap / us / afford)

3. I hope the concert hall is _____ all the fans!

(large / hold)

4. I hope my mother lets me go. This concert is going to be _____.

(good / me / miss)

5. Let's get a pizza at Sal's. The large ones are _____.

(big / share)

6. It's 9:30 already. It's _____ for pizza.

(late / stop)

7. I hate this curfew! I think we're _____ out past 10:00!

(old / stay)

8. Kyle didn't get out of work _____ tonight.

(early / come)

9. Van, I'm playing basketball tomorrow. Are you still _____ me?

(slow / beat)

10. Let's find out. But I want to walk. Your car isn't _____.

(safe / drive)

4 **EDIT** • *Read this student's journal entry. Find and correct eight mistakes in the use of infinitives with* **too** *or* **enough**. *The first mistake is already corrected.*

                                                                   to sleep

The Phish concert was awesome! Now I'm too excited ~~for sleeping~~. That Mike Gordon can really sing. My voice isn't enough good to sing in the shower! After the concert we were really hungry, but it was to late to go for pizza. I HATE this stupid curfew! It's too weird understand. My friend Todd works and has to pay taxes, but the law says he's too young for staying out past 10:00! That's crazy enough to make me want to scream. That reminds me. I sure hope my mother changes her mind soon enough for I to buy a ticket to the Hampton concert. They sell out very quickly. Why doesn't she think I'm mature to drive fifty miles? I'll have to do it sometime! Well, I'd better try to get some sleep or I'll be too tired too get up in the morning.

Infinitives of Purpose

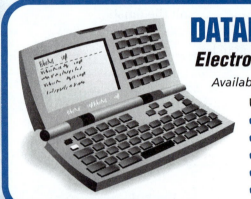

DATALATOR 534 F
Electronic Organizer $89.95

Available at all Lacy's Department Stores.

Use me
- ✔ **to look up** words
- ✔ **to store** names and phone numbers
- ✔ **to add** and **subtract**
- ✔ **to write down** ideas
- ✔ **to look** cool!

CHECK *POINT*

Check all the correct answers.

What can you use the Datalator as?

☐ an address book ☐ a telephone ☐ a dictionary ☐ a note pad ☐ a radio

---

CHART CHECK	**AFFIRMATIVE**	**NEGATIVE**
Circle T (True) or F (False).	I put his number in my organizer **(in order) to save** it.	I put his number in my organizer **in order not to lose** it.
T F There are two ways to form the affirmative infinitive of purpose.	I made a note **(in order) to remember** our date.	I made a note **in order not to forget** our date.
	I left at 9:00 **(in order) to arrive** early.	I left at 9:00 **in order not to arrive** late.
T F There are two ways to form the negative infinitive of purpose.	I ran **(in order) to catch** the bus.	I ran **in order not to miss** the bus.

EXPRESS CHECK

Unscramble these words to form two sentences.

store • addresses • use • I • an • organizer • to

_____

in order • I • not • set • oversleep • my • alarm clock • to

_____

Grammar Explanations	Examples
1. Use an **infinitive** (*to* + **base form** of the verb) to explain the <u>purpose of an action</u>. It often answers the question *Why?*	**A:** *Why* did you go to Lacy's? **B:** I went there **to buy** one of those Datalators I saw in an ad.
USAGE NOTE: In spoken English, you can answer the question *Why?* with an <u>incomplete sentence</u> beginning with *To*.	**A:** *Why* did you go to Lacy's? **B:** **To buy** an electronic organizer.
2. You can also use the longer form *in order to* + **base form** of the verb to explain a purpose.	■ I bought an organizer **in order to store** names and phone numbers.
USAGE NOTE: *To* + **base form** of the verb is more common in <u>informal</u> speech and writing.	■ I bought an organizer **to store** names and phone numbers.
3. Use *in order not to* + **base form** of the verb to express a <u>negative purpose</u>.	■ I use my Datalator **in order not to make** mistakes in pronunciation. *(I don't want to make mistakes.)*
4. You can also use **noun/pronoun + infinitive** to express the <u>purpose of an object</u>.	■ I need an **organizer to help** me remember my schedule. ■ I need **it to help** me remember my schedule.

1 **IDENTIFY** • *Read this conversation. Underline all the infinitives that express a purpose.*

YOKO: It's 5:00. Aren't you going home?

LEE: No. I'm staying late <u>to finish</u> this report. What about you? Are you going straight home?

YOKO: No. I'm going to stop at the bank to get some cash. Then I'm going to Lacy's Department Store to take advantage of the sale they're having.

LEE: Oh, what are you going to get?

YOKO: One of those new electronic organizers they're advertising. I've been looking for something to help me with my work.

LEE: What's wrong with just a regular calculator?

YOKO: Nothing. But sometimes I have to convert other currencies to dollars.

LEE: What else are you going to use it for?

YOKO: Oh, to store important names and phone numbers and to balance my checkbook.

LEE: What did we do before they invented all these electronic gadgets?

YOKO: We made a lot of mistakes!

 2 **ANSWER** • *Look at Yoko's list of things to do. Then write a phrase to answer each question.*

> **To Do**
> —Get gas
> —Make dental appointment
> —Buy batteries
> —Withdraw $100
> —Invite Rika and Taro to dinner
> —Buy milk and eggs

1. Why did she call Dr. Towbin's office? *To make a dental appointment.*

2. Why did she go to the bank? _____

3. Why did she call Mrs. Watanabe? _____

4. Why did she go to the supermarket? _____

5. Why did she go to the electronics store? _____

6. Why did she go to the service station? _____

3 **MATCH •** *For each action, find the correct purpose.*

Action	Purpose
_g_ 1. He enrolled in Chinese 101 because he	**a.** didn't want to get any phone calls.
_b_ 2. She took a bus because she	**b.** didn't want to be late.
___ 3. She went to the store because she	**c.** wanted to store information.
___ 4. We disconnected our phone because we	**d.** wanted to listen to the news.
___ 5. He turned on the radio because he	**e.** didn't want to worry me.
___ 6. He didn't tell me he was sick because he	**f.** needed to buy some dishes.
___ 7. She bought a Datalator because she	**g.** wanted to learn the language.

REWRITE • *Combine the sentence parts above. Use the infinitive of purpose.*

1.   He enrolled in Chinese 101 to learn the language. _____

2.   She took a bus in order not to be late. _____

3. _____

4. _____

5. _____

6. _____

7. _____

EDIT • *Read Yoko's journal entry. Find and correct six mistakes in the use of the infinitive of purpose. The first mistake is already corrected.*

>   to get
> I went to Dr. Towbin ~~for getting~~ my teeth cleaned today. While I was waiting, I used my
> Datalator to study for the TOEFL. Then I used it to helps me pronounce "novocaine" and
> "dental floss" for my appointment. After the dentist, I checked my schedule and saw
> "Rika and Taro, dinner, 7:30." I should use it in order to not forget appointments! Luckily,
> my recipes are already on the Datalator, so I used them for making a quick shopping
> list. When I got home, there was a note on my door—"Call bldg. super." I checked the
> Datalator dictionary to find "bldg. super." The "building superintendent" wanted to come
> up in order fix the doorbell! Rika, Taro, and I played with the Datalator all evening.
> You can program it for to play computer games too. I don't know how I lived without it!

Gerunds and Infinitives

I'm so embarrassed. I didn't **remember meeting** Bob.

How could you forget?

Hi! I'm Bob

CHECK *POINT*

Circle T (True) or F (False).

T F The woman had an appointment with Bob, but she forgot to go.

T F The woman forgot that she had met Bob once before.

CHART CHECK

Circle T (True) or F (False).

T F Some verbs can be followed by either the gerund or the infinitive.

T F The infinitive sometimes follows a preposition.

T F A gerund can be the subject of a sentence.

GERUNDS
Marta **enjoys going** to parties.
She **loves meeting** new people.
She **stopped buying** ice cream.
She's worried **about forgetting** people's names.
Meeting new people is fun.

INFINITIVES
Marta **wants to go** to parties.
She **loves to meet** new people.
She **stopped to buy** ice cream.
It's fun **to meet** new people.

EXPRESS CHECK

*Complete these sentences with the correct form of the verbs **go** or **talk**.*

• Phil wants _____ to the party.

• _____ to parties is exciting.

• Phil enjoys _____ about a lot of different things.

• It's fun _____ to new people.

Grammar Explanations	**Examples**
1. Some **verbs** are **followed by a gerund**.	■ Marta **enjoys** *meeting* people. ■ She **misses** *going* to parties.
2. Some **verbs** are **followed by an infinitive**.	■ Marta **wants** *to meet* people. ■ She**'d like** *to go* to parties.
3. Some **verbs** can be followed by either **a gerund or an infinitive**.	■ Marta **loves** *meeting* new people. OR ■ Marta **loves** *to meet* new people.
4. **BE CAREFUL!** A few verbs can be followed by either a gerund or an infinitive, but the **meanings are very different**.	■ Marta **stopped eating** ice cream. *(She doesn't eat ice cream anymore.)* ■ Marta **stopped to eat** ice cream. *(She stopped another activity in order to eat some ice cream.)* ■ Richard **remembered mailing** the invitation. *(First he mailed the invitation. Then he remembered that he did it.)* ■ Richard **remembered to mail** the invitation. *(First he remembered. Then he mailed the invitation. He didn't forget.)* ■ Marta **forgot meeting** Richard. *(Marta met Richard, but afterwards she didn't remember the event.)* ■ Marta **forgot to meet** Richard. *(Marta had plans to meet Richard, but she didn't meet him because she forgot about the plans.)*
5. A **gerund** is the only verb form that **can follow a preposition**.	preposition ■ Marta's worried **about** *forgetting* names.
6. To make **general statements**, you can use: • **gerund as subject** OR • *It's* + **adjective/noun + infinitive**	■ **Meeting** new people is fun. OR ■ **It's** fun **to meet** new people

Check it out!

For a list of common verbs followed by the gerund, see Appendix 3 on page 337.

For a list of common verbs followed by the infinitive, see Appendix 4 on page 338.

For a list of verbs that can be followed by the gerund or the infinitive, see Appendix 6 on page 338.

TRUE OR FALSE • *Read each numbered sentence. Write T (True) or F (False) for the statement that follows.*

1. Marta remembered meeting Mr. Jackson.

   __T__ Marta has already met Mr. Jackson.

2. Richard stopped smoking.

   _____ Richard doesn't smoke anymore.

3. She didn't remember to buy a cake for the party.

   _____ She bought a cake.

4. She stopped eating desserts.

   _____ She used to eat desserts.

5. Richard forgot to invite his boss to the party.

   _____ Richard invited his boss.

6. Richard forgot inviting his neighbor to the party.

   _____ Richard invited his neighbor.

7. Richard thinks giving a party is fun.

   _____ Richard thinks it's fun to give a party.

8. Marta likes going to parties.

   _____ Marta likes to go to parties.

2 **CHOOSE** • *Circle the correct words to complete these ideas from a book called Super Memory.**

1. Get into the habit of repeating / to repeat things aloud.

2. Never rely on someone else's memory. Learn trusting / to trust your own.

3. It's easy forgetting / to forget what you don't want remembering / to remember.

4. Study immediately before going / to go to sleep. You'll remember a lot more.

5. Our memories are filled with things we never meant remembering / to remember.

6. Make it a habit to pass in front of your car every time you get out, and you'll never forget turning off / to turn off your headlights.

7. Playing / To play games is a fun way of improving / to improve your memory skills.

*SOURCE: Douglas J. Hermann, Super Memory: A Quick Action Program for Memory Improvement (Avenel, NJ: Wings Books, 1991).

3

SUMMARIZE • *Read each numbered statement or conversation. Complete the summary statement using a gerund or an infinitive.*

1.　**ROGER:** Hi, Richard. I brought the soda. Where do you want me to put it?

　　SUMMARY: Roger remembered ___*to bring the soda.*___

2.　**MARTA:** You're Natalya! We met last year at Richard's party! How have you been?

　　SUMMARY: Marta remembers _____

3.　**ROGER:** Don't look at *me*! I didn't spill grape juice on the couch!

　　SUMMARY: Roger denied _____

4.　**NATALYA:** I'm so glad Richard plays jazz at his parties. I listen to it a lot at home too.

　　SUMMARY: Natalya enjoys _____

5.　　　**LEV:** Would you like to go dancing some time?

　　MARTA: Sure. I'd like that very much.

　　SUMMARY: Lev suggested _____

　　　　　　Marta agreed _____

6.　**NATALYA:** Marta, can we give you a ride home?

　　MARTA: Thanks, but I think I'll stay a little longer.

　　SUMMARY: Natalya offered _____

　　　　　　Marta decided _____

 4

EDIT • *Read Marta's journal entry about Richard's party. Find and correct seven mistakes in the use of the gerund and infinitive. The first mistake is already corrected.*

> 　　　　　　　　　　　　　　　　*going*
> What a great party! I usually avoid ~~to go~~ to parties because it's such a problem for me to
> remember people's names. I'm so glad I read that book about improve your memory. The
> author suggested to do exercises, and they really helped. I stopped to worry about what
> people would think of me, and I tried to pay attention to what people were saying. As a
> result, I had a great time! I'm even planning going dancing with this guy Lev.
> 　　　　I have an English test tomorrow, so I should stop writing now and start studying.
> The book even had some good tips about study for an exam. I hope I remember using some
> of them tonight!

Make, Have, Let, Help, and *Get*

He'll never **let me take** that quiz again.

Oh, no! He's going to **make us stay** after class.

Jaime Escalante with two of his students.

CHART CHECK

Circle T (True) or F (False).

T   F   *Make*, *have*, and *let* are always followed by the base form of the verb.

T   F   *Get* can be followed by either the base form of the verb or the infinitive.

T   F   *Help* can be followed by either the base form of the verb or the infinitive.

MAKE, HAVE, LET, HELP				
SUBJECT	**MAKE/HAVE/ LET/HELP**		**OBJECT**	**BASE FORM OF VERB**	
The teachers	**(don't)**	**make** **have** **let** **help**	us students	**do**	homework.

GET, HELP				
SUBJECT	**GET/HELP**		**OBJECT**	**INFINITIVE**	
The teachers	**(don't)**	**get** **help**	us students	**to do**	homework.

EXPRESS CHECK

Complete these sentences with the correct form of the verbs **correct** *or* **stay**.

A: Did the teacher get the students _____ their essays?

B: Yes. He had them _____ their essays in groups.

A: Do you think he'll make them _____ late again today?

B: I don't think so. But he'll let them _____ late if they need help.

Grammar Explanations

Examples

1. Use *make*, *have*, and *let* followed by **object + base form** of the verb to talk about things that someone can require, cause, or permit another person to do.

- The teacher **makes** *his students do* homework every night.
  (He requires them to do homework.)

- He **has** *them take* responsibility for their own learning.
  (He causes them to take responsibility.)

- He **lets** *them choose* their own essay topics.
  (He permits them to choose their own essay topics.)

You can also use *make* to mean "cause to."

- This will **make** *you become* a better student.
  (This will cause you to become a better student.)

2. *Help* can be followed by either:

- **object + base form** of the verb
  OR
- **object + infinitive**.

The meaning is the same.

- She **helped** *me understand* the homework.
  OR
- She **helped** *me to understand* the homework.

USAGE NOTE: *help* + base form of the verb is more common.

3. *Get* has a similar meaning to *make* and *have*, but it is followed by **object + infinitive**, not the base form of the verb.

- The teacher **got** *us to stay* a little later.
  NOT ~~The teacher got us stay a little later.~~
  (The teacher persuaded us to stay a little later.)

- She always **gets** *me to do* my best.
  (She always persuades me to do my best.)

1 **TRUE OR FALSE** • *Read each numbered sentence. Write T (True) or F (False) for the statement that follows.*

1. My teacher made me rewrite the report.

   __T__ I wrote the report again.

2. Ms. Trager let us use our dictionaries during the test.

   _____ We had to use our dictionaries.

3. Mr. Goldberg had us translate a short story.

   _____ We translated a short story.

4. Paulo helped Meng do her homework.

   _____ Paulo did Meng's homework for her.

5. Ms. Bates got the director to arrange a class trip.

   _____ The director arranged a class trip.

6. Professor Washington let us choose our own topic for our term paper.

   _____ We didn't choose our own topic.

2 **CHOOSE** • *Circle the correct words to complete this article about Jaime Escalante.*

Miracle Teacher

When Jaime Escalante first arrived at Garfield High, the administration of this East L.A.* high school (let)/ made gangs of
1.
students roam the halls and spray the walls with graffiti. However, this math teacher from Bolivia believed in his U.S. students too much to help / let them run wild. He made / let them
2.   **3.**
do massive amounts of homework, had / got
4.
them take daily quizzes, and even got / let
5.
them to fill out daily time cards. To develop team spirit, he got / made his students do
6.
football-like cheers before class. He knew

they could succeed and would never let / get
7.
them drop out of class. Then he did the impossible. He had / let his students take
8.
the Advanced Placement Exam, a very difficult national test. When his students passed, the testing company suspected them of cheating. To prove their innocence, Escalante had / got them take the test again.
9.

Again, everyone passed. How did Escalante work these miracles? In the words of a student, Escalante "let / made us feel
10.
powerful, that we could do anything."

*L.A. = Los Angeles

3 **SUMMARIZE •** *Read each numbered statement. Complete the summary with the correct form of the verbs in parentheses. Choose between affirmative and negative forms.*

1. **Ms. Allen:** Pablo, you can rewrite this composition, but only if you want to.

   Summary: She _____ didn't make Pablo rewrite _____ his composition.
   (make / rewrite)

2. **Ms. Allen:** I know you prefer working alone, Ana, but you really need to work in a group today.

   Summary: She _____ in a group.
   (make / work)

3. **Ms. Allen:** Listen, everyone! No dictionaries during the test, please. You should be able to guess the meaning from context.

   Summary: She _____ dictionaries.
   (let / use)

4. **Ms. Allen:** Fernando, could you do me a favor and clean the board before you leave?

   Summary: She _____ the board.
   (have / clean)

5. **Ms. Allen:** Jean-Paul, put the tip of your tongue between your teeth and say "th–, thorn." Yes! That's it!

   Summary: She _____ an English *th.*
   (get / pronounce)

6. **Ms. Allen:** Greta, please use English in class!

   Summary: She _____ in German.
   (let / speak)

7. **Ms. Allen:** Olga, you can take the test in the classroom. Just move your desk to a corner.

   Summary: She _____ the room.
   (make / leave)

4 **EDIT •** *Read this student's journal entry. Find and correct seven mistakes in the use of* **make**, **have**, **let**, **help**, *and* **get**. *The first mistake is already corrected.*

When I was a teenager, my parents never let me ~~to play~~ ^{play} until I had finished all my homework. They even made me helping my brothers with their homework before I could have any fun. On the one hand, they certainly got me learn a lot. On the other hand, they made me became too serious. I wish they had let me to have a little more fun. When I become a parent, I want to have my child learns responsibility, but also I would want to let he or she have fun. As Ben Franklin said, "All work and no play makes Jack become a dull boy." I want to avoid that mistake.

SelfTest

Circle the letter of the correct answer to complete each sentence.

> **EXAMPLE:**
> Jennifer never _____ coffee.   A (B) C D
> (A) drink   (C) is drinking
> (B) drinks   (D) was drinking

1. Maria's going to stop _____ dinner, so she may be late.   A B C D
   (A) eating   (C) to eat
   (B) for eating   (D) eat

2. My glasses are in my book bag, but I don't remember _____   A B C D
   them there.
   (A) putting   (C) I put
   (B) to put   (D) put

3. I asked him _____, but he went anyway.   A B C D
   (A) not to go   (C) not going
   (B) to not go   (D) he doesn't go

4. _____ in a foreign country is sometimes difficult.   A B C D
   (A) I live   (C) Live
   (B) Living   (D) Lives

5. He's not used to _____ up so early.   A B C D
   (A) wake   (C) wakes
   (B) waken   (D) waking

6. We're eighteen, so we're _____ vote.   A B C D
   (A) too old to   (C) old enough to
   (B) young enough to   (D) old enough for

7. I don't think Tom enjoyed _____ me study for the test.   A B C D
   (A) helping   (C) helped
   (B) to help   (D) helps

8. I bought this new software _____ Chinese.   A B C D
   (A) for learning   (C) to learn
   (B) learning   (D) learned

9. We got a new card holder _____ lose our credit cards.   A B C D
   (A) in order not to   (C) not to
   (B) not   (D) for not

10. It isn't difficult _____ this textbook.   A B C D
    (A) understand   (C) for understanding
    (B) in order to understand (D) to understand

11. Are you ready? It's time _____.   **A B C D**
    (A) for going   (C) going
    (B) to go   (D) go

12. I resented _____ that. He could have been more polite.   **A B C D**
    (A) he said   (C) his saying
    (B) he saying   (D) him to say

13. I talked to the students about working harder, but I couldn't _____   **A B C D**
them to study.
    (A) make   (C) got
    (B) get   (D) let

14. My mother _____ do my homework or I can't go out.   **A B C D**
    (A) makes me   (C) gets me
    (B) helps me   (D) lets me

SECTION TWO

Each sentence has four underlined words or phrases. The four underlined parts of the sentence are marked A, B, C, and D. Circle the letter of the one underlined word or phrase that is NOT CORRECT.

> **EXAMPLE:**
> Mike <u>usually</u> <u>drives</u> to school, but <u>today</u> he <u>walks</u>.   **A B C (D)**
>   A   B   C   D

15. I <u>decided</u> <u>changing</u> jobs because my boss <u>makes</u> <u>me work</u> overtime.   **A B C D**
      A   B   C   D

16. Most students <u>appreciate</u> their <u>principal's</u> <u>try</u> to <u>improve</u> school conditions.   **A B C D**
               A   B C   D

17. I <u>succeeded in</u> <u>to find</u> a job, so my parents <u>didn't make</u> me <u>go</u> to college.   **A B C D**
      A   B   C   D

18. <u>Get</u> more exercise <u>appears</u> <u>to be</u> the best way <u>to lose</u> weight.   **A B C D**
    A   B   C   D

19. <u>In order</u> <u>to not</u> <u>forget</u> things, I <u>put</u> a string around my finger.   **A B C D**
    A   B   C   D

20. Hans <u>is</u> only fourteen, but he <u>seems</u> <u>enough old</u> <u>to stay</u> out until ten.   **A B C D**
       A   B   C   D

21. I know you're <u>too busy</u> <u>to stay</u>, but I <u>look forward</u> <u>to see</u> you again.   **A B C D**
             A   B   C   D

22. I forgot <u>buying</u> gas, but I <u>got</u> to a gas station <u>before</u> I <u>ran out</u>.   **A B C D**
          A   B   C   D

23. <u>Getting</u> enough sleep <u>is</u> important <u>in order</u> <u>not fall</u> asleep in class.   **A B C D**
    A   B   C   D

24. <u>Let's stop</u> <u>to watch</u> so much TV so that we can <u>read</u> or <u>go out</u> instead.   **A B C D**
    A   B   C   D

25. I'm <u>trying</u> <u>to persuade</u> my sister <u>to drive</u>, but I can't get her <u>do</u> it.   **A B C D**
      A   B   C   D

Phrasal Verbs:
Inseparable

CHECK *POINT*

Check the correct answer.

Where does the woman suggest eating?

☐ at home

☐ in a restaurant

☐ in a park

CHART CHECK

Check the correct answer.

Where does the particle go?

☐ before the direct object

☐ after the direct object

INSEPARABLE PHRASAL VERBS			
SUBJECT	**VERB**	**PARTICLE**	**DIRECT OBJECT**
They	came	back.	
	gave	up.	
	ate	out.	
	ran	into	his teacher.
	stuck	to	their decision.

EXPRESS CHECK

Unscramble these words to form two sentences.

into • We • Bob • ran

_____

out • was • He • eating

_____

Grammar Explanations	**Examples**
1. A **phrasal verb** (also called a <u>two-part</u> or <u>two-word verb</u>) consists of a **verb + particle**.	verb + particle ■ We often **eat out**.
2. **Particles** and prepositions look the same. However, particles are <u>part of the verb phrase</u>, and they often <u>change the meaning of the verb</u>.	verb + preposition ■ She **ran into** another runner because she wasn't paying attention. *(She collided with another runner.)* verb + particle ■ I **ran into** John at the supermarket. *(I met John by accident.)*
3. The verb and particle are usually common words, but their separate meanings may not help you guess the **meaning of the phrasal verb**. **USAGE NOTE:** Phrasal verbs are <u>very common</u> in everyday speech.	■ Please **go on**. I didn't mean to interrupt. *(Please continue.)* ■ We **got back** after dark. *(We returned after dark.)* ■ They **called off** the meeting. *(They canceled the meeting.)*
4. Most phrasal verbs are **transitive**. (They take direct objects). Some transitive phrasal verbs are **inseparable**. This means that both <u>noun and pronoun objects</u> always go <u>after the particle</u>. You cannot separate the verb from its particle.	direct object ■ You should **go after** *your goals*. direct object ■ She **ran into** *her friend* at the library. NOT She ~~ran her friend into~~ at the library. direct object ■ She **ran into** *her*. NOT She ~~ran her into~~.
5. Some phrasal verbs are used <u>in combination with certain prepositions</u>. These combinations are usually **inseparable**.	■ She **came up** *with* a brilliant idea. ■ I **dropped out** *of* school and got a job.

Check it out!

For a list of some common inseparable phrasal verbs, see Appendix 17 on pages 341–342.

To learn about separable phrasal verbs, see Unit 55, pages 236–237.

1 **IDENTIFY** • *Read this article. Circle all the phrasal verbs.*

The Art of Feng Shui

Ho Da-ming's new restaurant was failing. His customers rarely (came back). Why? Mr. Ho contacted a feng shui consultant to find out. Feng shui (meaning "wind and water") is the ancient Chinese art of placing things in the environment. According to this art, the arrangement of furniture, doors, and windows affects our health, wealth, and happiness. Mr. Ho was concerned about his business, but he didn't give up. Following the consultant's advice, he remodeled and redecorated his restaurant. His actions paid off. Soon business picked up and Mr. Ho became rich. "It was the best decision I ever made," he glows. And he isn't alone in his enthusiasm. Feng shui has caught on with modern architects and homeowners everywhere.

MATCH • *Write each phrasal verb from the article next to its meaning.*

Phrasal Verb	Meaning	Phrasal Verb	Meaning
1. _____	has become popular	**4.** _____	learn information
2. _____came back_____	returned	**5.** _____	quit
3. _____	were worthwhile	**6.** _____	improved

 2 **CHOOSE** • *Complete this student's journal entry by circling the correct particles.*

 I just finished an article about feng shui. At the end, the author suggests sitting (down) / up in your home and thinking about how your environment makes you feel.
1.
So today when I got up / back from school, I tried it. I noticed that my apartment is
2.
really quite dark and it makes me feel down. I think with the addition of some lights,
I'd cheer away / up considerably. I've come out / up with a few other ideas too.
3.   **4.**
My apartment is small, but I think it will look more spacious if I just straighten out / up
5.
more frequently. Hanging some more shelves for my books might work in / out well too.
6.
With just a few small changes, I could end out / up feeling happier in my own home.
7.
It's certainly worth trying on / out!
8.

3 **CHOOSE & COMPLETE** • *Read this article about the architect I. M. Pei. Complete it using the correct form of the phrasal verbs in the box.*

| come up with | give up | go back | go up | ~~grow up~~ | keep on | pay off | turn out |

Born in 1917, Ieoh Ming Pei (better known as I. M. Pei)

_____ grew up _____ in Canton, China. When he was
                1.

seventeen, he went to the United States to learn about building.

As it _____, Pei became one of the most
                2.

famous architects of the twentieth century.

Pei is famous for his strong geometric forms. One of his

most controversial projects was his glass pyramid at the Louvre in Paris. The old museum

had a lot of problems, but no one wanted to destroy it. Pei had to _____
                                                                                    3.

a solution. Many Parisians were shocked with his proposal for a 71-foot-high glass

pyramid. It _____ anyway, blending with the environment. Today
                    4.

many people say that it is a good example of the principles of feng shui.

Pei _____ despite criticism. He strongly believed that "you have
              5.

to identify the important things and press for them, and not _____."
                                                                                    6.

His determination _____. He continued to build structures that
                              7.

reflected the environment. Pei received many prizes for his work. He used some of the

prize money to start a scholarship fund for Chinese students to study architecture in

the United States and then to _____ to China to work as architects.
                                              8.

4 **EDIT** • *Read Bob's note to his roommate. Find and correct eight mistakes in the use of inseparable phrasal verbs. The first mistake is already corrected.*

> up
> Sorry the apartment is such a mess. I got ~~down~~ late this morning and didn't have time to
>
> straighten out. I'm going to the gym now to work off for an hour. I should get across before
>
> you, and I'll clean up then. How about eating tonight out? Afterward, we can get together with
>
> some of the guys and maybe see a movie. Or maybe we'll come over with a better idea. —Bob
>
> Oh, —I ran Tom into at school. He'll drop off to see you later.

Phrasal Verbs:
Separable

Burr

CHECK *POINT*

Check the correct answer.

The dog thinks that

❏ George is dreaming.

❏ George is getting an idea for an invention.

SEPARABLE PHRASAL VERBS

CHART CHECK

Check the correct answer.

❏ Direct objects that are nouns can go before or after the particle.

❏ Direct objects that are pronouns always go after the particle.

NOT SEPARATED			
SUBJECT	**VERB**	**PARTICLE**	**DIRECT OBJECT**
He	**dreamed**	**up**	the idea.
	worked	**out**	the details.

SEPARATED			
SUBJECT	**VERB**	**DIRECT OBJECT**	**PARTICLE**
He	**dreamed**	the idea it	**up**.
	worked	the details them	**out**.

EXPRESS CHECK

Complete these sentences with the correct form of the words in parentheses.

Who _____? Did *you* _____?
       (dream up / that idea)   (dream up / it)

Grammar Explanations

Examples

---

1. A **phrasal verb** consists of a **verb + particle**.

Particles look the same as prepositions, but they are <u>part of the verb phrase</u>. They often <u>change the meaning of the verb</u>.

The separate meanings of the verb and particle may be very different from the **meaning of the phrasal verb**.

verb + particle
■ She **set up** an experiment.

verb + preposition
■ He **looked up** at the sky.
(He looked in the direction of the sky.)

verb + particle
■ He **looked up** the information on the Internet.
(He found the information on the Internet.)

■ They **turned down** my application.
(They rejected my application.)

---

2. Most phrasal verbs are transitive (they take direct objects). Most transitive phrasal verbs are **separable**.
This means the **direct object** can go:

  a. <u>after</u> the particle
    (verb and particle are <u>not separated</u>)
            OR
  b. <u>between</u> the verb and the particle
    (verb and particle are <u>separated</u>)

    Notice that when the direct object is **in a long phrase**, it comes <u>after the particle</u>.

▶ **BE CAREFUL!** When the direct object is a <u>pronoun</u>, it **must** go <u>between the verb and the particle</u>.

verb + particle + direct object
■ I just **dreamed up** *a new idea*.
          OR
verb + direct object + particle
■ I just **dreamed** *a new idea* **up**.

direct object
■ She **dreamed up** *an unusually complicated new device*.
NOT She ~~dreamed an unusually complicated new device up.~~

■ She **dreamed** *it* **up**.
NOT She ~~dreamed up it.~~

---

3. With a small group of phrasal verbs, the verb and particle **must be separated**.

keep something *on*

talk someone *into*

■ **Keep** *your hat* **on**.
NOT ~~Keep on your hat.~~

■ She **talked** *her boss* **into** a raise.
NOT She ~~talked into her boss~~ a raise.

Check it out!
For a list of common separable phrasal verbs, see Appendix 17 on pages 341–342.
For a list of common phrasal verbs that must be separated, see Appendix 17 on pages 341–342.
For information about inseparable phrasal verbs, see Unit 54, pages 232–233.

1 **IDENTIFY •** *Read this article. Underline the phrasal verbs. Circle the direct objects.*

Eureka!

Did you know that two college dropouts thought up the idea of the first personal computer? What's more, they put it together in a garage. Inventions don't have to come out of fancy laboratories. Average people in classrooms, kitchens, and home workshops often dream up new and useful ideas.

The ability to think of something new seems like magic to many people, but in fact anyone can develop the qualities of an inventor. First, inventors follow their curiosity. The Swiss inventor George de Mestral wanted to find out the reason it was so hard to remove burrs from his dog's coat. His answer led to the idea for Velcro®, now used to fasten everything from sneakers to space suits. Second, inventors use imagination to put things together in new ways. Walter Morrison watched two men tossing a pie pan to each other and thought up the Frisbee®, one of the most popular toys in the world. Perhaps most important, successful inventors don't quit. They continuously look up information about their ideas and try new designs out until they succeed.

2 **CHOOSE & COMPLETE •** *Read about one of history's greatest inventors. Complete the information with the correct form of the appropriate phrasal verbs from the box.*

| fill up | keep away | bring about | ~~try out~~ | set up | carry out | pay back | pick up |

As a child, Thomas Alva Edison (1847–1931) _____tried out_____
1.
almost anything he heard about—he even tried to hatch goose eggs

by sitting on them! Before he was twelve, he _____
2.
his first laboratory using money he had earned himself.

He had hundreds of bottles, and he _____ them

_____ with chemicals for his experiments. He
3.
labeled the bottles "poison" to _____ his family

_____. When he was fifteen, Edison _____ a new skill. He
4. **5.**
had saved a child's life, and the grateful father, a telegraph operator, _____

Edison _____ by teaching him telegraphy. After that, Edison was able to
6.
work nights and _____ his experiments during the day.
7.

In 1869, Edison fixed a piece of equipment for a company that supplied prices to gold brokers. This _____ his first useful invention—the stock ticker—
    8.
for which he received $40,000. He was then able to spend all his time working on his new inventions. During his lifetime, Edison was issued 1,093 patents!

3 **COMPLETE •** *Read these conversations that take place in a school laboratory. Complete them with phrasal verbs and pronouns.*

1. **A:** Please **put on** your lab coats.

   B: Do we really have to _____ put them on _____? It's hot in here.

2. **A:** I can't **figure out** this problem.

   B: I know what you mean. I can't _____ either.

3. **A:** Remember to **fill out** these forms.

   B: Can we _____ at home, or do we have to do it now?

4. **A:** Are you going to **hand out** the next assignment today?

   B: I _____ a few minutes ago. Weren't you here?

5. **A:** I can't get this to work. We'd better **do** the whole procedure **over**.

   B: We don't have time to _____. Class is over in ten minutes.

6. **A:** Are we supposed to **turn in** our lab reports today?

   B: No. Please _____ next week.

 EDIT • *Read an inventor's notes. Find and correct seven mistakes in the use of phrasal verbs. The first mistake is already corrected.*

> <u>May 3</u>   I dreamed ~~over~~ ^{up} a really good idea—a jar of paint with an applicator like the kind used for shoe
>   polish. It can be used to touch on spots on a wall, when people don't want to paint a whole
>   room. I know a manufacturer. I'll call up him and order several types so I can try them in.
>
> <u>July 3</u>   I filled down an application for a patent and mailed it yesterday. I'll be able to set a strong and
>   convincing demonstration of the product up soon.
>
> <u>August 30</u> I demonstrated the product at an exhibition for decorators. I wanted to point out that it's very
>   neat to use, so I put white gloves for the demonstration. It went over very well.

SelfTest

Circle the letter of the correct answer to complete each sentence.

> **EXAMPLE:**
> Jennifer never _____ coffee.   A **Ⓑ** C D
> (A) drink   (C) is drinking
> (B) drinks   (D) was drinking

1. Come in. Please sit _____.   A B C D
   (A) down   (C) it down
   (B) down it   (D) up

2. Your mother called. She wants you to call her _____ tonight.   A B C D
   (A) in   (C) back
   (B) off   (D) over

3. Could you turn _____ the music so we can sleep?   A B C D
   (A) down   (C) over
   (B) away   (D) up

4. Please put _____ your lab coats before you leave the laboratory.   A B C D
   (A) off   (C) up
   (B) away   (D) in

5. Mark works so hard that he's sure to _____.   A B C D
   (A) give up   (C) turn over
   (B) work off   (D) get ahead

6. Kevin is going to _____ from vacation tomorrow.   A B C D
   (A) call back   (C) get back
   (B) give back   (D) get along

7. A lamp will _____ this corner nicely.   A B C D
   (A) turn on   (C) put up
   (B) blow up   (D) light up

8. Instead of arguing about the problem, let's _____.   A B C D
   (A) look it over   (C) take it away
   (B) charge it up   (D) talk it over

9. That's very original. How did you dream _____ that idea?   A B C D
   (A) about   (C) of
   (B) down   (D) up

10. That pot is hot. Don't pick _____!   A B C D
    (A) it up   (C) up
    (B) up it   (D) it

11. —It's cold outside. You need your jacket.
—OK. I'll put _____.
(A) it on   (C) on it
(B) it over   (D) over it

A B C D

12. She ran _____ on the way home.
(A) him into   (C) into Jason
(B) into   (D) Jason into

A B C D

13. Slow down. I can't keep up _____ you!
(A) of   (C) after
(B) with   (D) to

A B C D

SECTION TWO

Each sentence has four underlined words or phrases. The four underlined parts of the sentence are marked A, B, C, and D. Circle the letter of the one underlined word or phrase that is NOT CORRECT.

> **EXAMPLE:**
> Mike <u>usually</u> <u>drives</u> to school, but <u>today</u> he <u>walks</u>.
>   A   B   C   D
>   A B C (D)

14. Could we talk <u>over it</u> before you <u>turn</u> the whole <u>idea</u> <u>down</u>?
                A   B   C   D

A B C D

15. I know I <u>let</u> <u>Andy</u> <u>down</u> when I forgot to pick his suit <u>out</u> from
          A   B   C   D
the dry cleaner's.

A B C D

16. I <u>ran into</u> <u>him</u> while I was <u>getting</u> <u>the bus off</u>.
    A   B   C   D

A B C D

17. As soon as I <u>hand</u> <u>in</u> <u>my report</u>, I'm going to take all these books
               A B   C
<u>on</u> to the library.
D

A B C D

18. <u>We'd better</u> <u>get the bus on</u> now, or <u>we're</u> going to <u>miss it</u>.
    A   B   C   D

A B C D

19. Instead of <u>calling</u> <u>off</u> the meeting, maybe we can just <u>put it</u> <u>over</u>
            A   B   C   D
until next week.

A B C D

20. If you don't use <u>out</u> the milk by Monday, please <u>throw</u> <u>it</u> <u>away</u>.
              A   B C D

A B C D

21. Chet had to <u>cheer</u> <u>up her</u> after the company <u>turned down</u> <u>her application</u>.
          A   B   C   D

A B C D

22. Do you want to <u>get up</u> by yourself, or would you <u>like</u> <u>me</u> to <u>wake up you</u>?
            A   B C   D

A B C D

23. Tom <u>asked</u> me to <u>pick</u> some stamps for <u>him</u> at the post office <u>up</u>.
     A   B   C   D

A B C D

24. Did you <u>find</u> <u>out</u> how Jane <u>talked</u> <u>into Meg</u> working on Saturday?
        A   B   C   D

A B C D

25. We <u>got</u> <u>over</u> well after we <u>found</u> <u>out</u> we were both from Chicago.
   A   B   C   D

A B C D

UNIT 56

Nouns

ACROSS THE ATLANTIC ON A REED BOAT

BARBADOS—**May** 17, 1970. Norwegian **explorer Thor Heyerdahl**, along with an international **crew**, has crossed the **Atlantic Ocean** on **Ra II**. The **reed boat**, modeled after those of the ancient **Egyptians**, made the **journey** in 57 **days**.

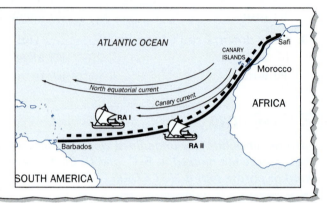

CHECK POINT

Check the correct answer.

The name of Heyerdahl's boat was: ☐ Ra II   ☐ Reed Boat

CHART CHECK 1

Circle T (True) or F (False).

T F Common nouns are written with capital letters.

PROPER NOUNS
Heyerdahl sailed **Ra II** across the **Atlantic**.

COMMON NOUNS
The **explorer** sailed his **boat** across the **ocean**.

CHART CHECK 2

Circle T (True) or F (False).

T F Count nouns can be plural.

T F Non-count nouns can be plural.

COUNT NOUNS				NON-COUNT NOUNS		
ARTICLE/ NUMBER	**NOUN**	**VERB**		**NOUN**	**VERB**	
A One	**sailor**	is	brave.	**Fire**	is	dangerous.
(The) Two	**sailors**	are		**Sailing**		

EXPRESS CHECK

Circle the correct words to complete these sentences.

The boats <u>was / were</u> made of reed. Crossing the ocean <u>was / were</u> hard.

Grammar Explanations

Examples

1. Proper nouns are the names of <u>particular people, places, and things</u>. To the right are some categories and examples of proper nouns.

<u>Capitalize</u> the first letter of most proper nouns. We <u>do not usually use an article</u> (*a/an* or *the*) with proper nouns.

Note that ***the*** is used with some nouns of places.

People	Heyerdahl, Egyptians
Places	Africa, Morocco, the Atlantic Ocean
Months	September, October
Days	Monday, Tuesday
Holidays	Easter, Passover, Ramadan
Languages	Arabic, Spanish

■ Heyerdal sailed across ***the* Atlantic Ocean**.

2. Common nouns refer to people, places, and things, but <u>not by their individual names</u>. For example, *explorer* is a common noun, but *Heyerdahl* is a proper noun.

People	explorer, sailor, builder
Places	continent, country, city
Things	pots, eggs, fish, honey

3. Common nouns are either count or non-count. **Count nouns** are things that you can <u>count separately</u>. They can be singular or plural. For example, you can say *a ship* or *three ships.* You can <u>use *a/an* or *the* before count nouns</u>.

Form the **plural** of most nouns by adding *-s* or *-es* to the noun. There are sometimes <u>spelling changes</u> when you form the plural.

▶ **BE CAREFUL!** Some nouns are <u>irregular</u>. They do not form the plural by adding *-s* or *-es.*

■ **a** sailor, **the** sailor, **two** sailors
■ **an** island, **the** island, **three** islands
■ **a** ship, **the** ship, **four** ships

ship	ship**s**		potato	potato**es**
watch	watch**es**		country	countr**ies**

foot	**feet**		man	**men**
child	**children**		mouse	**mice**

4. Non-count nouns are things that you <u>cannot count separately</u>. For example, in English you can say *gold*, but you cannot say *a gold* or *two golds.* Non-count nouns usually have no plural forms. We usually <u>do not use *a/an*</u> with non-count nouns. To the right are some categories and examples of non-count nouns.

Abstract words	courage, education, time
Activities	exploring, sailing, farming
Fields of study	geography, history
Food	corn, chocolate, fish
Gases	air, oxygen, steam
Liquids	water, milk, coffee, gasoline
Materials	cotton, plastic, silk
Natural forces	cold, electricity, weather
Particles	dust, sand, sugar, salt, rice

Some common non-count nouns do not fit into these categories. You must memorize nouns such as the ones to the right.

advice	furniture	jewelry	money
clothing	garbage	luggage	news
equipment	homework	mail	work
food	information		

▶ **BE CAREFUL!** Non-count nouns take <u>singular</u> verbs and pronouns.

■ ***Reed* is** a good material for boats.
■ ***It* floats** in the heaviest storm.

Check it out!

For a list of some common irregular plural nouns, see Appendix 18 on page 343.

1   **IDENTIFY** • *Read this article about Thor Heyerdahl. Circle all the proper nouns. Underline once all the common count nouns. Underline twice the common non-count nouns.*

Who Really Discovered America?

Was (Columbus) really the first explorer to discover the Americas? Thor Heyerdahl didn't think so. He believed that ancient people were able to build boats that could cross oceans. To test his ideas, he decided to build a copy of the reed boats that were pictured in ancient paintings and sail across the Atlantic from North Africa to Barbados. Heyerdahl's team also copied ancient Middle Eastern pots and filled them with food for their journey—dried fish, honey, oil, eggs, nuts, and fresh fruit. Ra, the expedition's boat, carried an international group including a Norwegian, an Egyptian, an Italian, a Mexican, and a Chadian.

The first trip failed, but everyone survived and wanted to try again. Departing on May 17, 1970, under the flag of the United Nations, Ra II crossed the Atlantic in 57 days. The expedition proved that ancient civilizations had the skill to reach the Americas long before Columbus.

---

2   **COMPLETE** • *Megan and Jason McKay are planning a hiking trip. Complete their conversation with the correct form of the words in parentheses.*

JASON: There ____'s____ still a lot of
                   1. (be)
____work____ to do this evening.
    2. (work)
We have to plan the food for the trip.

MEGAN: You're right. _____ certainly
                          3. (Food)
_____ important. I've been
    4. (be)
reading this book about camping. There _____ some good
                                          5. (be)
_____ in it.
    6. (idea)

JASON: Oh? What does it say?

MEGAN: We should bring a lot of _____ and _____.
                                    7. (bean)   **8.** (rice)

JASON: _____ _____ good on camping
           9. (Potato)   **10.** (be)
_____ too.
    11. (trip)

MEGAN: No, fresh _____ _____ too heavy to carry. Maybe we
                     12. (vegetable) **13.** (be)
can get some when we pass through a town.

JASON: _____ the _____ ready? We should go over
        14. (Be)   **15.** (equipment)
the checklist.

MEGAN: I did that. We need _____ for the radio.
        16. (battery)

JASON: Why do we need a radio? I thought we were running away from civilization.

MEGAN: But the _____ never _____. I still want to know
        17. (news)   **18.** (stop)
what's happening.

JASON: That's OK with me. By the way, do we have enough warm _____?
        19. (clothing)
It gets chilly in the mountains.

MEGAN: That's true. And the _____ really _____ me at night.
        20. (cold)   **21.** (bother)

JASON: But we have warm sleeping _____.
        22. (bag)

MEGAN: And we have each other!

EDIT • *Tina Arbeit sailed around the world alone on a small boat. Read her diary entries. There are fifteen mistakes in the use of nouns and subject–verb agreement. Find and correct them. The first two mistakes are already corrected.*

>   Canary
> October 27. I've been on the ~~canary~~ Islands for three days now. I'll start home when
>   weather is
> the ~~weathers are~~ better. I was so surprised when I picked up my mails today.
> My family sent me some birthday presents. My Birthday is the 31st. I won't open
> the gifts until then.
>
> october 29. I think the weather is getting worse. I heard thunders today, but there
> wasn't any rain. I stayed in bed with my cat, Typhoon. Every time it thundered,
> typhoon and I snuggled up closer under the covers. I started reading a Novel,
> Brave New World.
>
> October 30. I left the Canary Islands today—just like columbus. There's a strong wind
> and plenty of sunshine now. I went 250 Miles.
>
> October 31. I'm 21 today! To celebrate, I drank some coffees for breakfast and I
> opened my presents. I got some perfume and pretty silver jewelries.
>
> November 1. The electricities are very low. I'd better not use much until I get near
> new York. I'll need the radio then. It rained today, so I collected waters for cooking.

UNIT 57 Quantifiers

CHECK *POINT*

Check the correct answer.

The child wants to know if they have

☐ chocolate.

☐ a good supply of chocolate.

CHART CHECK

Circle T (True) or F (False).

T F *A lot of* is used with both count and non-count nouns.

T F *Several* is used with non-count nouns.

T F *A few* is used with count nouns.

T F *Any* is used in negative sentences.

QUANTIFIERS AND COUNT NOUNS

	QUANTIFIER	NOUN
I have	some enough a lot of	batteries. cookies.
	a few several many	
I don't have	any enough a lot of many	

QUANTIFIERS AND NON-COUNT NOUNS

	QUANTIFIER	NOUN
I have	some enough a lot of	candy. water.
	a little a great deal of much	
I don't have	any enough a lot of much	

EXPRESS CHECK

Complete this conversation with **much** *or* **many**.

A: We didn't buy _____ batteries.

B: Well, we didn't have _____ time before the storm.

A: That's true. We had _____ things to do.

Grammar Explanations | ## Examples

---

1. **Quantifiers** are expressions of quantity such as *a lot of* and *many*. They are used <u>before a noun</u>.

Quantifiers can also be <u>used alone</u>, when it is clear what they refer to. Note that in **a lot of**, *of* is dropped.

- We used **a lot of water** last summer.
- There were **many storms**.

A: How many **eggs** do we have?
B: Not **a lot**, just **a few**.

---

2. Use **some**, **enough**, **a lot of**, and **any** with both <u>count and non-count nouns</u>.

Use **any** in <u>questions</u> and in <u>negative sentences</u>.

Use **some** when you make an <u>offer</u>.

              count   non-count
- We have **some batteries** and **some gasoline**.

          non-count   count
- We have **enough water** and **eggs** for a week.

            count   non-count
- We have **a lot of beans** and **rice** left.

        non-count   count
A: Do we have **any milk** or **teabags**?
B: No, and we don't have **any coffee** or **paper plates** either.

- Would you like **some coffee**?

---

3. Use **a few**, **several**, and **many** with <u>plural count nouns</u> in <u>affirmative sentences</u>.

Use **a little**, **a great deal of**, and **much** with <u>non-count nouns</u> in <u>affirmative sentences</u>.

USAGE NOTE: In <u>affirmative sentences</u>, **many** is more formal than *a lot of*; **much** is very formal.

► **BE CAREFUL!** Don't confuse **a few** and **a little** with *few* and *little*. **Few** and **little** usually mean "not enough."

- **A few people** got sick.
- **Several children** went to the hospital.
- **Many rescue workers** arrived.

- They had **a little trouble** with the radio.
- They threw away **a great deal of food**.
- **Much planning** went into the rescue.

MORE FORMAL: **Many people** agreed.
LESS FORMAL: **A lot of people** agreed.
VERY FORMAL: He showed **much courage**.
LESS FORMAL: He showed **a lot of courage**.

- They received **a little news** last night.
  (not a lot, but probably enough)

- They received **little news** last night.
  (probably not enough news)

---

4. Use **many** with count nouns and **much** with non-count nouns in <u>questions</u> and <u>negative sentences</u>.

USAGE NOTE: In <u>questions</u> and <u>negative sentences</u>, **many** and **much** are used in both formal and informal English.

A: **How many people** did you see?
B: We **didn't** see **many**.

A: **How much food** did they carry?
B: **Not much**.

1 **IDENTIFY** • *Read this article about preparing for natural disasters. Underline the quantifiers + count nouns. Circle the quantifiers + non-count nouns.*

BE PREPARED

Are you ready? <u>Many people</u> don't realize that some natural disasters such as earthquakes can strike with (little warning). It may take several days for assistance to reach you. Prepare your disaster kit in advance! Here are a few tips.

 Water may be unsafe to drink. Store enough water for several days. Each person needs a gallon per day for cooking and washing.

 You will also need food for several days. It's a good idea to store a lot of of canned meat, fruit, vegetables, and milk. However, also include several kinds of high-energy food, such as peanut butter and jelly. And don't forget some "comfort food" like cookies and chocolate!

 If you don't have any electricity, you might not have any heat either. Keep some blankets, sleeping bags, and extra clothes for everyone.

 Prepare a first aid kit with some pain relievers, several sizes of bandages, and an antiseptic.

 The ATMs might not be working. Do you have any cash? You shouldn't keep much money in the house, but you should have a lot of small bills, and a few larger bills too.

2 **CHOOSE** • *Circle the correct words to complete this radio interview between* **This Morning (TM)** *and food psychologist Angie Welnitz* (AW).

TM: Dr. Welnitz, in a crisis, (a lot of)/ much people crave chocolate. Does comfort food
1.
have <u>any / many</u> real benefit?
2.
AW: Yes. <u>Several / A little</u> types of food help give emotional balance. Chocolate gives an
3.
emotional lift because it contains a <u>great deal of / many</u> sugar, for example.
4.
TM: What about mashed potatoes? When I'm sad, I cook <u>a lot of / much</u> potatoes.
5.
AW: They remind you of childhood, when you felt safe. <u>Much / Many</u> traditional foods
6.
comfort us like this.
TM: I have <u>a few / a little</u> friends who eat comfort food to celebrate. Why?
7.
AW: We have <u>much / many</u> change in our lives today and <u>a few / few</u> ways to calm down.
8.   **9.**
Comfort food tells us, "Don't worry. <u>Some / A little</u> things are still the same."
10.
TM: We only have <u>a few / a little</u> time left. Tell us—what is *your* favorite comfort food?
11.
AW: Pistachio ice cream. I always feel better after I eat <u>a few / few</u> spoonfuls.
12.

3   **COMPLETE** • *Read these conversations. Complete them with the correct words.*

1. **much, many, a few, a little**

   A: Hi, Barb. Did you and Jim lose _____*many*_____ trees in the storm?

a.

   B: Just one. And the house is OK. We only lost _____ windows.

b.
   How about you?

   A: We didn't have _____ problems either. We didn't have

c.

   _____ time to shop before the storm, but thanks to the disaster kit,

d.

   we had _____ candles and _____ food on hand.

e.   f.

2. **little, a little, a few, few**

   A: It's interesting to see what we used up from the disaster kit. I noticed we have

   only _____ hot chocolate left.

a.

   B: That's because _____ things taste better in a crisis. I bet there are

b.

   more than _____ cans of spinach, though.

c.

   A: Six cans. I guess there's _____ reason to buy more of that.

d.

   B: We learned _____ things about comfort foods during the storm,

e.

   didn't we?

4   **EDIT** • *Read this child's diary entry. Find and correct seven mistakes in the use of quantifiers. The first mistake is already corrected.*

>   *a*
> We had a big storm last week, and we lost the electricity for ‸few days. Once I got
> over being scared, it was a lot of fun—a little like camping out. We have an electric
> furnace, so we didn't have some heat. We slept in our sleeping bags around the
> fireplace. We sure used up many wood! Mom baked some bread in an iron pan in the
> fireplace. She had to try several times, but it was really good when it worked. We ate
> it with little peanut butter. The first night we had much problems figuring out what
> to do. It got dark early, and we only had a little candles—and no TV! Cindy is five,
> and she was really freaked out until we made hot chocolate over the fire. Finally,
> everybody took turns telling stories. I found out that Dad knows a lot good stories.

Articles:
Indefinite and Definite

An evil magician from **a** universe beyond ours is trying to conquer **the** Earth.

The magician is Zado. He has four helpers— and only YOU can destroy him!

SPACE DEFENDER

A NEW GAME FROM CEREBRO

CHECK *POINT*

Check the correct answer.

According to the ad for the video game:

☐ There is only one universe beyond ours.　　☐ There is only one Earth.

INDEFINITE　　　　　　　　DEFINITE

CHART CHECK

Circle T (True) or F (False).

T F *A/An* can be used with non-count nouns.

T F *The* can be used with singular and plural nouns.

T F Use *the* when you mention a noun for the second time.

SINGULAR COUNT NOUNS		
	A/An	NOUN
Let's rent	**a**	**video game**.
It's	**an**	**adventure**.

SINGULAR COUNT NOUNS			
	THE	NOUN	
Let's rent	**the**	**game**	by Cerebro.
It's		**adventure**	of Zado.

PLURAL COUNT NOUNS/ NON-COUNT NOUNS		
	(SOME)	NOUN
Let's play	**(some)**	**video games**.
I won		**gold**.

PLURAL COUNT NOUNS/ NON-COUNT NOUNS			
	THE	NOUN	
Let's play	**the**	**games**	we rented.
It's		**gold**	Zado lost.

EXPRESS **CHECK**

Circle the correct articles to complete these sentences.

Cerebro has <u>a / the</u> new video game. <u>A / The</u> game is called *Space Defender*.

Grammar Explanations

Examples

1. We can use **nouns** in two ways:

a. A noun is **indefinite** (not specific) when either you or your listener <u>do not have a particular person, place, or thing in mind</u>.

A: Let's buy **a video game**.
B: Good idea. Which one should we buy?
(A and B are not talking about a specific game.)

b. A noun is **definite** (specific) when you and your listener <u>both know which person, place, or thing you mean</u>.

A: I bought **the new game** from Cerebro!
B: Great! Is it fun?
(A and B are both talking about a specific game.)

2. The **article** you use before a noun depends on <u>the kind of noun</u> (count or non-count) it is and on <u>how you are using the noun</u> (indefinite or definite).

a. Use the **indefinite article** *a/an* with <u>singular count nouns</u> that are **indefinite**.

Also use *a/an* for singular count nouns when you <u>classify</u> (say what something is).

Use *a* before <u>consonant sounds</u>.
Use *an* before <u>vowel sounds</u>.

▶ **BE CAREFUL!** It is the <u>sound</u>, not the letter, that determines whether you use *a* or *an*.

A: I'm reading about **a magician**.
B: Oh, really? Which one?

A: What do you do for a living?
B: I'm **a pilot**. And you?

■ *a* **m**agician, *a* **g**reat adventure
■ *an* **e**vil magician, *an* **a**dventure

■ *a* **u**niverse (pronounced "yuniverse")
■ *a* **h**ostile army (pronounced "hostile")
■ *an* **h**onest warrior (pronounced—"ahnest")

b. Use **no article** or *some* with <u>plural count nouns</u> and with <u>non-count nouns</u> that are **indefinite**.

■ There are *(some)* **games** on the shelf.
■ I had to buy *(some)* **medicine**.

3. Use the **definite article** *the* with most nouns <u>(count and non-count, singular and plural)</u> that are **definite**.

Use *the* when:

A: *The* **magician** I told you about is on TV tonight.
B: Let's watch him!

a. a person, place, or thing is <u>unique</u>—there is only one.

■ *The* **moon** is 250,000 miles away.
(The Earth has only one moon.)

b. the <u>context</u> makes it clear which person, place, or thing you mean.

A: *The* **music** was great.
B: I enjoyed it too.
(A and B are coming out of a concert.)

c. the noun is mentioned for the <u>second time</u> (it has already been identified).

■ *A* **magician** is trying to conquer the Earth. *The* **magician** is very powerful.

d. <u>a phrase or an adjective</u> such as *first*, *best*, *right*, *wrong*, or *only* identifies which one.

■ Donkey Kong was **the first** video game with a story.

CHOOSE & DESCRIBE • *Read these conversations. Circle the letter of the statement that best describes each conversation.*

1. **CORA:** I'm bored. Let's rent a video game.
   FRED: OK.

   a. Fred knows which game Cora is going to rent.

   ⓑ Fred and Cora aren't talking about a particular game.

2. **CORA:** Mom, where's the new video game?
   MOM: Sorry, I haven't seen it.

   a. Mom knows that Cora rented a new game.

   b. Mom doesn't know that Cora rented a new game.

3. **FRED:** I'll bet it's in the hall. You always drop your things there.
   CORA: I'll go look.

   a. There are several halls in Fred and Cora's house.

   b. There is only one hall in Fred and Cora's house.

4. **FRED:** Was I right?
   CORA: You weren't even close. It was on a chair in the kitchen.

   a. There is only one chair in the kitchen.

   b. There are several chairs in the kitchen.

5. **FRED:** Wow! Look at that! The graphics are awesome.
   CORA: So is the music.

   a. All video games have good graphics and music.

   b. The game Cora rented has good graphics and music.

6. **CORA:** This was fun. But why don't we rent a sports game next time?
   FRED: Good idea. I love sports games.

   a. Fred is talking about sports games in general.

   b. Fred is talking about a particular sports game.

CHOOSE & COMPLETE • *Circle the correct articles to complete this paragraph.*

Board games are popular all over a / the world. Mah Jong is an / the example of
                1.   **2.**

a / an very old one. I had an / a uncle who had an / the old set from Singapore.
  3.   **4.**   **5.**

He kept a / the set in the / a beautiful box in a / the living room. He used to open
         6.   **7.**   **8.**

the / a box and tell me about the / a pieces. They were made of bamboo, and each
  9.   **10.**

one had a / the Chinese character on it. To me, they were the / a most fascinating
       11.   **12.**

things in a / the world.
          13.

COMPLETE • *Read each conversation. Complete it with the appropriate article* (*a, an,* or *the*).

1. **A:** _____A_____ car just pulled up. Are you expecting someone?

   B: No, I'm not. I wonder who it is.

2. **A:** Can we use _____ car?

   B: OK, but bring it back by 11:00 o'clock.

3. **A:** Let's turn off _____ game system before we leave.

   B: We don't have to. We can just leave it on *Pause*.

4. **A:** Do you have _____ game system?

   B: Yes, I do. I just bought a Sega Genesis.

5. **A:** Do you see the video store? I was sure it was on Main Street.

   B: I think it's on _____ side street, but I'm not sure which one.

6. **A:** There it is.

   B: Good. You can park right across _____ street from the store.

7. **A:** Excuse me, do you have any new games?

   B: _____ newest games are in the front of the store.

8. **A:** We'd better go. We've been here for _____ hour.

   B: That was _____ fastest hour I've ever spent.

9. **A:** Excuse me. I'd like to rent this game.

   B: Just take it to _____ cashier. She's right over there.

EDIT • *Read this magazine article about video games. Find and correct nine mistakes in the use of articles. The first mistake is already corrected.*

The plumber

Once there was a plumber named Mario. ~~Plumber~~ had beautiful girlfriend. One day, a ape fell in love with the girlfriend and kidnapped her. The plumber chased ape to rescue his girlfriend.

This simple tale became *Donkey Kong*, a first video game with a story. It was invented by Sigeru Matsimoto, a artist with Nintendo, Inc. Matsimoto loved the video games, but he wanted to make them more interesting. He liked fairy tales, so he invented story similar to a famous fairy tale. Story was an immediate success, and Nintendo followed it with *The Mario Brothers.* The rest is video game history.

Ø (No Article) and *The*

Roller coaster **rides** are a lot like **life**. You just have to relax and enjoy yourself.

So how are you enjoying **the ride**?

CHECK POINT

Check the correct answer.

Who is talking about roller coaster rides in general?

☐ the little girl   ☐ the little boy

CHART CHECK

Check the correct answer.

You can use Ø (no article) for a noun that is:

☐ indefinite

☐ definite

You can use Ø for a count noun that is:

☐ singular

☐ plural

NO ARTICLE (INDEFINITE)	*THE* (DEFINITE)
Ø + NON-COUNT NOUN	***THE* + NON-COUNT NOUN**
Do you like **cotton candy**?	**The cotton candy** in this park is great.
Ø + PLURAL COUNT NOUN	***THE* + PLURAL COUNT NOUN**
Rides can be very exciting.	**The rides** in this park are exciting.
	***THE* + SINGULAR COUNT NOUN**
	The ride near the entrance is exciting.

EXPRESS CHECK

Circle **the** *or* **Ø** *(no article) to complete these sentences.*

A: Did you enjoy Ø / the roller coaster ride?

B: Yes, I love Ø / the roller coaster rides.

A: And did you try Ø / the cotton candy?

B: No. I don't like Ø / the cotton candy. It's always too sweet.

Grammar Explanations

Examples

1. We often use **Ø (no article)** before <u>non-count nouns</u> and <u>plural count nouns</u> that are **indefinite** (not specific).

Use **Ø** when you:

a. have **no specific** person, place, or thing in mind.

A: What do you want to do tonight?
B: Let's stay home. We can listen to **music** or watch **videos**.

b. **classify** (say what something or someone is).

A: What's that?
B: It's **cotton candy**.
A: And what are those?
B: They're **tickets** for the roller coaster. I bought them while you were on the phone.

c. make **general statements**.

■ **Cotton candy** is very sweet.
(cotton candy in general)

■ **Roller coasters** are popular.
(roller coasters in general)

2. Use *the* with <u>non-count nouns</u> and <u>count nouns</u> (singular and plural) that are **definite**—when you are talking about a **specific or unique** person, place, or thing that you and your listener know about.

A: Can I taste *the* **cotton candy**?
B: Sure. Have as much as you'd like.

A: Where are *the* **tickets** for *the* **roller coaster**?
B: I put them in my pocket.

A: This is *the* **best roller coaster** in *the* **world**.

3. BE CAREFUL! <u>Singular count nouns cannot stand alone.</u> You must always use either an article, a pronoun, *one*, or a word such as *this, that, each,* or *every* before a singular count noun.

■ This is *a* delicious **candy bar**.
NOT This is ~~delicious candy bar~~.

■ It's hard to eat just *one* **candy bar**, isn't it?
■ Give me *that* **candy bar**! You've had enough.
■ It's *my* **candy bar**.

1 IDENTIFY • *Read this announcement for a new amusement park. Underline all the common nouns that have no articles. Circle all the nouns with **the**.*

Grand Opening!

Do you enjoy <u>amusement parks</u>? Tomorrow, Blare Gardens will open to (the public) for the first time. The park features a wide variety of rides and games that will appeal to both adults and children. And of course an amusement park would not be complete without cotton candy and hot dogs. The food at Blare Gardens promises to be very good. Come early, bring the whole family, and be sure to stay for the fireworks display that takes place right after the sun sets. So check it out! You won't be disappointed.

2 CHOOSE • *Circle the correct words to complete this magazine article.*

Thrills and Chills

Why do people around (the)/ Ø world flock to
1.
the / Ø amusement parks? The / Ø places like
2.   **3.**
Disney World and Coney Island offer the / Ø fun, relaxation, and escape from the / Ø
4.   **5.**
problems and boredom of everyday life. They offer the / Ø adults and children alike a
6.
chance to take the / Ø risks without the / Ø consequences. Thanks to advances in
7.   **8.**
the / Ø technology, the / Ø accidents in the / Ø amusement parks are now rare. You can
9.   **10.**   **11.**
go on the / Ø rides that look scary but are actually safe. You can scream and laugh as
12.
the / Ø roller coaster races down toward the / Ø ground and loops up to the / Ø sky
13.   **14.**   **15.**
again, leaving your cares and troubles behind.

Even though the / Ø roller coasters are the / Ø most
16.   **17.**
popular of all the / Ø rides, they are not for everyone. But
18.
don't worry. Today's amusement parks offer a lot more
than the / Ø thrills and chills. There are train rides
19.
through a replica of the / Ø rain forest. And there are
20.
the / Ø games with the / Ø prizes too. The / Ø hot dogs,
21.   **22.**   **23.**
ice cream, and cotton candy complete the / Ø picture of
24.
this perfect getaway for the / Ø whole family.
25.

3 **COMPLETE** • *Read this conversation about an amusement park. Complete the sentences with **the** where necessary. Use Ø if you don't need an article.*

A: I'm going to Blare Gardens next weekend. You work there. What's it like?

B: That depends. Do you like _____Ø_____ scary rides? If you do, then you're going
    1.

to love _____ rides at Blare Gardens.
        2.

A: What's _____ most exciting ride there?
          3.

B: The Python. I've seen people actually shaking with fear before they got on it.

A: Sounds like _____ fun. By the way, how's _____ food there? I
                4.   **5.**

hate _____ hot dogs.
      6.

B: Then you might have a little problem. They sell _____ hot dogs and
                                                      7.

_____ pizza, and that's about it. But do you like _____ music?
      8.   **9.**

A: I love it. I listen to _____ country music all the time. Why?
                        10.

B: _____ music at Blare Gardens is great. They have _____ best
      11.   **12.**

country music groups in _____ entire state.
                        13.

A: What exactly do you do there? Maybe we'll see you.

B: I dress like a cartoon character and guide people around _____ park.
                                                                14.

4 **EDIT** • *Read this postcard from Blare Gardens. Find and correct eight mistakes in the use of **the** and Ø (no article). The first mistake is already corrected.*

Blare Gardens Amusement Park

Hi! Blare Gardens is awesome! This
                   the
is ⌃best vacation we've ever gone on!

I love the rides here. I mean, I've been on the roller

coasters before, but nothing is like the one they've got

here! And food is great too. I usually don't eat the hot

dogs, but hot dogs here are great. So is pizza. Do you

like the amusement parks? If so, you've got to get your

family to come. The only problem is crowds here. People

have to wait to get into *everything*—even the

restrooms! See you soon.   *Nicky*

USA
24¢

To: *Ryan Turner*

31 Barcelona Dr.

Boulder, CO 80303

Reflexive Pronouns and Reciprocal Pronouns

"I will not talk to myself, I will not talk to myself."

Circle T (True) or F (False).

T F The man is talking to another person.

CHART CHECK

Circle T (True) or F (False).

T F Singular reflexive pronouns end in *-selves*.

T F Reciprocal pronouns always refer to more than one person.

REFLEXIVE PRONOUNS		
SUBJECT PRONOUN		REFLEXIVE PRONOUN
I		**myself**.
You		**yourself**.
He		**himself**.
She	looked at	**herself**.
It		**itself**.
We		**ourselves**.
You		**yourselves**.
They		**themselves**.

RECIPROCAL PRONOUNS		
SUBJECT PRONOUN		RECIPROCAL PRONOUN
We You They	looked at	**each other**. **one another**.

EXPRESS CHECK

Circle the correct words to complete this conversation.

A: Is someone in there with you, or are you talking to

yourself / themselves?

B: No one's here. I'm just talking to one another / myself.

Grammar Explanations	**Examples**
1. Use a **reflexive pronoun** when the <u>subject and object</u> of a sentence refer to the <u>same people or things</u>. In **imperative sentences** use: —*yourself* when the <u>subject is singular</u> —*yourselves* when the <u>subject is plural</u>	subject = object ■ **Sara** looked at ***herself*** in the mirror. *(Sara looked at her own face.)* ■ "Don't push ***yourself*** so hard, **Tom**," Sara said. ■ "Don't push ***yourselves*** so hard, **guys**," Sara said.
2. Use a **reflexive pronoun** to <u>emphasize a noun</u>. In this case, the reflexive pronoun usually follows the noun directly.	■ Tom was upset when he lost his job. The **job** ***itself*** wasn't important to him, but he needed the money.
3. *By* + **a reflexive pronoun** means *alone* or *without any help.* *Be* + **a reflexive pronoun** means *act in the usual way.*	■ Sara lives **by herself**. *(Sara lives alone.)* ■ We painted the house **by ourselves**. *(No one helped us.)* ■ Just **be yourself** at your interview. *(Act like you usually act.)* ■ He **wasn't himself** after he lost his job. *(He seemed different.)*
4. Use a **reciprocal pronoun** when the subject and the object of a sentence refer to the <u>same people</u> and these people have a <u>two-way relationship</u>. Use *each other* when the subject is <u>two people</u>. Use either *one another* or *each other* when the subject is <u>more than two people</u>. ▶ **BE CAREFUL!** Reciprocal pronouns and plural reflexive pronouns have <u>different meanings</u>.	subject = object ■ **Tom and Sara** met ***each other*** at work. *(Tom met Sara, and Sara met Tom.)* subject = object ■ **We all** told ***one another*** about our jobs. OR subject = object ■ **We all** told ***each other*** about our jobs. *(Each person exchanged information with every other person.)* ■ Fred and Jane talked to ***each other***. *(Fred talked to Jane, and Jane talked to Fred.)* ■ Fred and Jane talked to ***themselves***. *(Fred talked to himself, and Jane talked to herself.)*
5. **Reciprocal pronouns** have <u>possessive forms</u>: *each other's*, *one another's*.	■ Tom and Sara took ***each other's*** numbers. *(Tom took Sara's number. Sara took Tom's number.)*

Check it out!

For a list of verbs and expressions commonly used reflexively, see Appendix 16 on page 340.

1 **IDENTIFY** • *Read this article about self-talk. Underline the reflexive pronouns once and the reciprocal pronouns twice. Draw an arrow to the word that each pronoun refers to.*

SELF-TALK

Self-talk is the way we explain a problem to <u>ourselves</u>. It can affect the way we feel and how we act. Tom and Sara, for example, both lost their jobs when their company laid off a lot of people. Sara kept herself fit and spent time with friends. Tom gained ten pounds and spent all his time by himself. They were both unemployed, so the situation itself can't explain why they acted so differently from <u>each other</u>. The main difference was the way Tom and Sara explained the problem to themselves. Sara believed that she herself could change her situation. Tom saw himself as helpless. Later, everyone got their jobs back. When they all talked to one another back at the office, Tom grumbled, "They must have been desperate." Sara replied, "They finally realized they need us!"

2 **CHOOSE** • *Tom and Sara's company held an office party. Choose the correct reflexive or reciprocal pronouns to complete the conversations.*

1. A: Do you mind if we pour _____*ourselves*_____ something to drink?
   (myself / ourselves)

   B: Of course not. And there's food too. Please help _____.
   (yourselves / themselves)

2. A: That's the new head of Marketing. She's standing by _____.
   (herself / himself)

   B: Let's go and introduce _____.
   (himself / ourselves)

3. A: I'm nervous about my date with Niki. I cut _____ twice shaving.
   (myself / herself)

   B: You'll be fine. Just relax and be _____.
   (yourselves / yourself)

4. A: My boss and I always give _____ the same holiday gifts. Every year
   (ourselves / each other)
   I give him a book and he gives me a scarf.

   B: Funny. I always thought you bought _____ a lot of scarves.
   (yourself / himself)

5. A: The new software is so easy, it just seems to run by _____.
   (itself / myself)

   B: Really? In our department, we're still teaching _____ how to use it.
   (themselves / ourselves)

6. A: Did you and Armina go to Japan by _____ or with a tour group?
   (yourself / yourselves)

   B: With a group. We've all kept in touch with _____ since the trip.
   (one another / ourselves)

3 **COMPLETE** • *George Prudeau is a high school French teacher. Complete his talk to a group of new teachers. Use reflexive and reciprocal pronouns.*

I teach French, but the subject _____**itself**_____ isn't that important. I think my
                                        1.

experience applies to all subjects. Your first year may be hard, so teach

_____ to use positive self-talk and keep things simple. Remember that
        2.

a good teacher helps students learn by _____. Recently, John, one of my
                                              3.

students, was having trouble teaching _____ how to bake French bread.
                                              4.

I encouraged him to keep trying, and in the end he succeeded. As far as discipline

goes, I have just a few rules. I tell my students, "Keep _____ busy.
                                                               5.

Discuss the lessons, but don't interfere with _____'s work." Keep
                                                      6.

teaching materials simple too. I pride _____ on being able to teach
                                              7.

anywhere, even on a street corner. Finally, the salary for teachers is not great, but

you have a lot of freedom. I run my class by _____—just the way I want to.
                                                    8.

You will all have to decide for _____ if it's worth it. I can't afford to
                                      9.

travel to France, but I satisfy _____ with trips to Quebec!
                                      10.

4 **EDIT** • *Read this woman's diary. Find and correct seven mistakes in the use of reflexive and reciprocal pronouns. The first mistake is already corrected.*

>   *myself*
> I forgot to call Jan on his birthday. I reminded ~~me~~ all day, and then I forgot
> anyway! I felt terrible. My sister Anna said, "Don't be so hard on yourselves,"
> but I didn't believe her. She prides her on remembering everything. Then
> I read an article on self-talk. It said that people can change the way they
> explain problems to theirselves. I realized that the way I talk to me is
> insulting—like the way our high school math teacher used to talk to us.
> I thought, Jan and I treat each other well. He forgave myself for my mistake
> right away, and I forgave him for forgetting our dinner date two weeks ago.
> Jan and I could forgive themselves, so I guess I can forgive myself.

SelfTest

SECTION ONE

Circle the letter of the correct answer to complete each sentence. Choose Ø when no article is needed.

> **EXAMPLE:**
> Jennifer never _____ coffee.   A Ⓑ C D
> (A) drink   (C) is drinking
> (B) drinks   (D) was drinking

1. I introduced _____ to Bill as soon as I saw him.   A B C D
   (A) himself   (C) myself
   (B) me   (D) each other

2. The job _____ isn't a problem. It's my boss.   A B C D
   (A) myself   (C) himself
   (B) itself   (D) it

3. The students exchange cards with _____ during the holidays.   A B C D
   (A) themselves   (C) each other's
   (B) ourselves   (D) one another

4. What a beautiful bracelet! Is it made of _____ gold?   A B C D
   (A) the   (C) Ø
   (B) some   (D) a

5. I bought _____ bottled water before the hurricane.   A B C D
   (A) a lot of   (C) twelve
   (B) a few   (D) many

6. How _____ eggs do you need for the cake?   A B C D
   (A) many   (C) Ø
   (B) much   (D) more

7. She was lonely because she had _____ friends at first.   A B C D
   (A) little   (C) few
   (B) a little   (D) a few

8. That's _____ best movie I've ever seen.   A B C D
   (A) a   (C) the
   (B) an   (D) Ø

9. Di's in _____ Europe on vacation.   A B C D
   (A) a   (C) Ø
   (B) an   (D) the

10. Freda's _____ astronaut. There are six of them on this mission.   A B C D
    (A) Ø   (C) an
    (B) a   (D) the

11. —I just rented _____ video.   **A B C D**
    —Great! Which one?
    (A) the   (C) a
    (B) some   (D) any

12. We don't have _____ fruit left. Could you buy some apples?   **A B C D**
    (A) much   (C) little
    (B) some   (D) many

SECTION TWO

Each sentence has four underlined words or phrases. The four underlined parts of the sentence are marked A, B, C, and D. Circle the letter of the one underlined word or phrase that is NOT CORRECT.

> **EXAMPLE:**
> Mike <u>usually</u> <u>drives</u> to school, but <u>today</u> he <u>walks</u>.   **A B C (D)**
>   A   B   C   D

13. There <u>are</u> <u>a lot of</u> <u>food</u> in the fridge, so help <u>yourself</u>.   **A B C D**
          A   B   C   D

14. Do <u>your</u> families <u>come</u> for <u>thanksgiving</u> or do you celebrate   **A B C D**
          A   B   C
    by <u>yourselves</u>?
       D

15. The <u>news</u> <u>are starting</u>, so let's watch <u>TV</u> in <u>the</u> living room.   **A B C D**
         A   B   C   D

16. Lee wants to open <u>his</u> business in <u>may</u> and <u>start</u> working   **A B C D**
                    A   B   C
    for <u>himself</u>.
       D

17. I <u>myself</u> don't eat chili, but it's <u>the most</u> popular <u>spice</u> in <u>a</u> world.   **A B C D**
      A   B   C   D

18. <u>A money</u> <u>isn't</u> everything—the job <u>itself</u> <u>has to</u> be interesting.   **A B C D**
     A   B   C   D

19. <u>Mathematics</u> <u>isn't</u> Todd's <u>best</u> subject, but he succeeds with <u>the</u>   **A B C D**
     A   B   C   D
    hard work.

20. <u>How</u> <u>many times</u> do <u>we</u> have before <u>the</u> movie starts?   **A B C D**
     A   B   C   D

21. <u>Smith</u> was <u>an</u> unpopular mayor, so he had <u>a few</u> friends in <u>politics</u>.   **A B C D**
     A   B   C   D

22. <u>We</u> have only <u>a few</u> milk left, so could you pick <u>some</u> up for <u>us</u>?   **A B C D**
     A   B   C   D

23. <u>We</u> didn't know <u>one another</u> names before <u>Maria</u> introduced <u>us</u>.   **A B C D**
     A   B   C   D

24. <u>Ben</u> has to save <u>a few</u> money so that he can go to <u>school</u> in <u>the</u> fall.   **A B C D**
     A   B   C   D

25. I met <u>an accountant</u> and <u>a lawyer</u> at <u>your party</u>, and <u>an accountant</u>   **A B C D**
          A   B   C   D
    said he'd help me.

The Passive: Overview

The World Keeps Informed With Reader's Digest

Reader's Digest **was founded** in 1922.
Today it **is read** by people in every country in the world.
Shouldn't you be one of them? Subscribe today.

CHECK POINT

Check the information you can get from the ad.

☐ the name of the founder

☐ the number of years the magazine has existed

☐ the price of the magazine

CHART CHECK

Circle T (True) or F (False).

T F The object of an active sentence becomes the subject of the passive sentence.

T F Passive statements always have a form of the verb *be*.

T F Passive statements always have an object.

ACTIVE	PASSIVE
OBJECT →	**SUBJECT**
Millions of people **buy** *it*.	*It* **is bought** by millions of people.
OBJECT →	**SUBJECT**
Someone **published** *it* in 1922.	*It* **was published** in 1922.

PASSIVE STATEMENTS

SUBJECT	BE (NOT)	PAST PARTICIPLE	(BY + OBJECT)	
It	**is (not)**	**bought**	by millions of people.	
It	**was (not)**	**published**		in 1922.

YES/NO QUESTIONS

BE	SUBJECT	PAST PARTICIPLE	
Is	it	**sold**	in China?
Was			

SHORT ANSWERS

AFFIRMATIVE		NEGATIVE	
Yes, it	**is.**	**No**, it	**isn't.**
	was.		**wasn't.**

WH- QUESTIONS

WH- WORD	BE	SUBJECT	PAST PARTICIPLE
Where	**is**	it	**sold?**

EXPRESS CHECK

Complete this sentence with the passive form of the verb **print**.

How many copies of *Reader's Digest* _____ last year?

Grammar Notes	Examples
1. **Active** and **passive sentences** often have similar meanings but <u>different focuses</u>.	ACTIVE ■ Millions of people **read** the magazine. *(The focus is on the people.)* PASSIVE ■ The magazine **is read** by millions of people. *(The focus is on the magazine.)*
2. Form the **passive** with a form of *be* + **past participle**.	■ It **is written** in nineteen languages. ■ It **was published** in 1922. ■ It **has** just **been printed**.
3. Use the **passive** when: **a.** the <u>agent</u> (the person or thing doing the action) is <u>unknown or not important</u>. **b.** the identity of the <u>agent is clear from the context</u>. **c.** you want to <u>avoid mentioning the agent</u>.	 ■ The magazine **was founded** in 1922. *(I don't know who founded it.)* ■ The magazine **is sold** at newsstands. *(We can assume that the newsstand owners and employees sell it. We don't need to mention them.)* ■ Some mistakes **were made** in that article. *(I know who made the mistakes, but I don't want to blame the person who made them.)*
4. Use the **passive with** *by* if you mention <u>the agent</u>. Mention the **agent** when: **a.** you introduce <u>necessary new information</u> about the agent. **b.** you want to give credit to someone who <u>created something</u>. **c.** the agent is <u>surprising</u>. ▶ **BE CAREFUL!** In most cases, you do not need to mention an agent in passive sentences. Do not include an agent unnecessarily.	■ The article **was written** *by a psychologist*. ■ John Delgado is a famous sports writer. He **has** just **been hired** *by National Sports* to write a monthly column. *(The name of John's employer is necessary new information.)* ■ The article **was written** *by John Delgado*. ■ Our windows **are washed** *by a robot*. ■ The magazine **is published** once a week. NOT The magazine is published ~~by the publisher~~ once a week.

1 **CHOOSE** • *Read these sentences and decide if they are* **Active (A)** *or* **Passive (P).**

__P__ 1. *Reader's Digest* was founded in 1922.

_____ 2. Millions of people read it.

_____ 3. A large-type edition is also printed.

_____ 4. They also record it.

_____ 5. *Reader's Digest* is published once a month.

_____ 6. It has been translated into many languages.

_____ 7. Many readers subscribe to the magazine.

_____ 8. It is sold at newsstands everywhere.

_____ 9. I read an interesting article in it.

_____ 10. The article was written by a famous scientist.

2 **READ & COMPLETE** • *Look at the chart. Then complete the sentences. Use the verb* **speak** *in the active or the passive form.*

LANGUAGE	NUMBER OF SPEAKERS (IN MILLIONS)
Arabic	246
Cantonese (China)	71
English	508
Ho (Bihar and Orissa States, India)	1
Japanese	126
Spanish	417
Swahili (Kenya, Tanzania, Uganda, Democratic Republic of Congo)	49
Tagalog (Philippines)	57

1. Japanese __is spoken by 126 million people_____.

2. One million people __speak Ho_____.

3. _____ by 57 million people.

4. Spanish _____.

5. _____ Cantonese.

6. _____ 246 million people.

7. More than 500 million people _____.

8. _____ in Uganda.

3   **COMPLETE** • *Use the passive form of the verbs in the first set of parentheses to complete this report. Include the agent (from the second set of parentheses) only if absolutely necessary.*

Modern Reader Newsletter   TENTH ANNIVERSARY ISSUE

DID YOU KNOW . . . ?

▶ *Modern Reader* __was founded by A. J. Thompson__ ten years ago.
   1. (found) (A. J. Thompson)

▶ At first it __was printed__ only in English.
   2. (print) ~~(the printer)~~

▶ Today it _____ in three foreign-language editions.
   3. (publish) (the publisher)

▶ It _____ in more than ten countries.
   4. (read) (readers)

▶ Since 2000, twenty new employees _____.
   5. (hire) (our international offices)

▶ Back at home, ten new computers _____ last month.
   6. (purchase) (the company)

▶ They _____ to write our award-winning articles.
   7. (use) (our writers)

▶ *Modern Reader* _____ all over the world.
   8. (advertise) (advertisers)

▶ Our editorial staff _____ last month.
   9. (interview) (*Live at Ten TV*)

▶ The interview _____.
   10. (see) (millions of viewers)

---

4   **EDIT** • *Read an editor's notes for a story for* **Modern Reader**. *Find and correct eight mistakes in the use of the passive. The first mistake is already corrected.*

>   **are located**
> Two-thirds of Bolivia's five million people ~~locate~~ in the cool western highlands known as the Altiplano.
>
> For centuries, the grain quinoa has been grew in the mountains. Llamas raised for fur, meat, and
>
> transportation. And tin, Bolivia's richest natural resource, is mining by miners in the high Andes.
>
>   The Oriente, another name for the eastern lowlands, is mostly tropical. Rice is the major food
>
> crop, and cows are raised for milk. Oil is also find there.
>
>   Although Spanish is the official language, Native American languages are still spoken by
>
> people. Traditional textiles are woven by hand, and music played on reed pipes whose tone
>
> resembles the sound of the wind blowing over high plains in the Andes.

The Passive with Modals

Bill, something **has to be done** about Ed. He snores so loud he's going to knock us out of orbit!

zZzZzZ

I know, Carla. He **can be heard** back on Earth!

CHECK POINT

Check the correct answer.

According to Carla,

☐ Ed has to do something about his snoring.

☐ somebody has to do something about Ed's snoring.

CHART CHECK 1

Circle T (True) or F (False).

T F Passives with modals always use **be**.

T F You cannot talk about the future using the passive with modals.

STATEMENTS

SUBJECT	MODAL*	BE	PAST PARTICIPLE	
The crew	will (not) should (not)	be	replaced	next month.

SUBJECT	HAVE (GOT) TO/ BE GOING TO	BE	PAST PARTICIPLE	
The crew	has (got) to doesn't have to is (not) going to	be	replaced	next month.

*Modals have only one form. They do not have -*s* in the third person singular.

CHART CHECK 2

Check the correct answer.

What comes before the subject in questions?

☐ **be**

☐ a modal or an auxiliary verb

YES/NO QUESTIONS

MODAL	SUBJECT	BE	PAST PARTICIPLE
Will	it	be	replaced?
Should			

SHORT ANSWERS

AFFIRMATIVE		NEGATIVE	
Yes, it	will. should.	No, it	won't. shouldn't.

YES/NO QUESTIONS				
AUXILIARY VERB	**SUBJECT**	**HAVE TO/ GOING TO**	**BE**	**PAST PARTICIPLE**
Does	it	**have to**	**be**	**replaced?**
Is		**going to**		

SHORT ANSWERS			
AFFIRMATIVE		**NEGATIVE**	
Yes, it	**does.**	**No,** it	**doesn't.**
	is.		**isn't.**

EXPRESS CHECK

Complete this conversation with the passive form of **will prepare**.

A: _____ food _____ on board?

B: No, it _____ . It _____ on Earth.

Grammar Explanations

Examples

1. To form the passive with a modal, use **modal + *be* + past participle**.

- The Space Shuttle ***will be launched*** soon.
- The launch ***won't be postponed***.
- The crew ***must be given*** time off.
- Decisions ***shouldn't be made*** too quickly.

2. Use ***will*** or ***be going to*** with the passive to talk about the **future**.

- It ***will be launched*** very soon.
  OR
- It***'s going to be launched*** very soon.

3. Use ***can*** with the passive to express **present ability**.

Use ***could*** with the passive to express **past ability**.

- The blastoff ***can be seen*** for miles.

- It ***could be seen*** very clearly last year.

4. Use ***could***, ***may***, ***might***, and ***can't*** with the passive to express **future possibility** or **impossibility**.

- It ***could be launched*** very soon.
- French scientists ***may be invited*** to participate.
- Plants ***might be grown*** on board.
- It ***can't be done***.

5. Use ***should***, ***ought to***, ***had better***, ***have (got) to***, and ***must*** with the passive to express:

   a. advisability

- The crew ***should be prepared*** to work hard.
- Crew members ***ought to be given*** a day off.
- Privacy ***had better be respected***.

   b. necessity

- Reports ***have to be filed***.
- Everyone ***must be consulted***.

1 **IDENTIFY** • *Read this article about the International Space Station* Unity. *Underline all the passives with modals.*

Living in Outer Space

Space Station *Unity* <u>will be completed</u> within the next decade, and international teams of astronauts will then be sharing close quarters for long periods of time. What can be done to improve living conditions in space? Here's what former astronauts suggest:

✳ FOOD It doesn't taste as good in zero gravity. Food should be made spicier to overcome those effects. International tastes must also be considered.

✳ CLOTHING Layered clothing could help astronauts stay comfortable. The top layer could be removed or added as temperatures vary.

✳ SLEEPING Because of weightlessness, sleep is often interrupted in space. Comfortable restraints must be provided to give a sense of stability.

✳ EMOTIONAL NEEDS People need "down time" in space just as they do on Earth. Time ought to be provided for relaxation and privacy.

2 **COMPLETE** • Comet Magazine (CM) *is interviewing aerospace engineer Dr. Bernard Kay (BK). Complete the interview with the passive form of the verbs in parentheses.*

CM: Dr. Kay, I'd like to ask how meals _____will be handled_____ in the Space Station.
  1. (will / handle)

_____ food _____ on board or
  2. (Be going to / prepare)

_____ from tubes?
3. (squeeze)

BK: Neither. Gourmet meals _____ on Earth and then they
  4. (will / prepackage)

_____ on board.
5. (can / warm up)

CM: The Space Station will have an international crew. How _____

food _____ to suit everyone's taste?
  6. (should / choose)

BK: An international menu _____. Food _____
  7. (have to / offer) **8.** (could / select)

from food preference forms that the crew members complete.

CM: _____ dishes _____ on board?
  9. (Will / use)

BK: Probably. But utensils _____ to the plates so they won't fly
  10. (had better / attach)

around! Meals _____ as pleasant as possible.
  11. (ought to / make)

3 **CHOOSE & COMPLETE** • *Some scientists just completed a simulation of life on the Station. Complete their conversations with the modals in parentheses and the correct verbs from the box.*

design	improve	keep	remove	~~solve~~

KENT: These simulations showed that there are still some problems. I hope they

_____can be solved_____ before the real thing. For example, the temperature
1. (can)

_____ at 68°, but I was uncomfortably warm most of the time.
2. (should)

LYLE: The material for our clothing _____. Maybe clothing
3. (ought to)

_____ in layers. A layer _____ if
4. (could)   **5.** (can)

it's too warm.

do	deliver	give	store

HANS: I didn't like the food very much. We _____ more fresh food.
6. (ought to)

HISA: Well, fresh fruits and vegetables _____ by the Shuttle regularly.
7. (be going to)

HANS: What _____ with the trash? Space litter is already a problem.
8. (will)

HISA: I'm sure it _____ on board and carried to Earth by the Shuttle.
9. (will)

4 **EDIT** • *Read an astronaut's journal notes. Find and correct seven mistakes in the use of the passive with modals. The first mistake is already corrected.*

>   be made
> I used the sleeping restraints last night and slept a lot better. They ought to ~~make~~ more comfortable,
> though. I felt trapped. I just looked in the mirror. My face is puffy and my eyes are red. I'd better be
> gotten on the exercise bike right away. I can be misunderstanding when I look like this. Last night
> Max thought I was angry at him for turning on "Star Trek." Actually, I love that show. I might be given
> early lunch shift today. I hope they have more teriyaki. It's nice and spicy, and the sauce can actually
> been tasted, even at zero gravity. Some of it had better be fly in on the Shuttle pretty soon, or there
> might be some unhappy astronauts! Speaking of unhappy, last night Kristen called and told me she
> was planning to quit school. I think she could be talk out of it, but I'm afraid I'll get angry and yell if
> we discuss it. I might overheard by others. We need some privacy here!

UNIT

63

The Passive Causative

Bye, Emily, see you next week.

One week later . . .

Hi, Emily! . . . Hmm . . . Something's different. Did you **get your hair cut?**

CHECK *POINT*

Check the correct answer.

The guy wants to know if his girlfriend

❏ cut her own hair.

❏ went to a hair salon.

CHART CHECK

Circle T (True) or F (False).

T   F The passive causative always has a form of the verb **be**.

T   F You can form the passive causative with **have** or **get**.

T   F The passive causative always needs an agent.

STATEMENTS					
SUBJECT	*HAVE/GET*	**OBJECT**	**PAST PARTICIPLE**	**(BY + AGENT)**	
She	**has**	*her hair*	**cut**	by André	every month.
He	**has had**	*his beard*	**trimmed**		before.
I	**got**	*my nails*	**done**		at André's.
She	**is going to get**	*her ears*	**pierced**.		

YES/NO QUESTIONS					
AUXILIARY VERB	**SUBJECT**	*HAVE/GET*	**OBJECT**	**PAST PARTICIPLE**	**(BY + AGENT)**
Does	she	**have**	*her hair*	**cut**	by André?
Has	he	**had**	*his beard*	**trimmed**?	
Did	you	**get**	*your nails*	**done**?	
Is	she	**going to get**	*her ears*	**pierced**?	

EXPRESS CHECK

Complete this conversation with the correct form of the verb **do**.

A: Where do you get your hair _____?

B: I don't get it _____. I _____ it myself.

Grammar Explanations

Examples

---

1. Use the **passive causative** to talk about <u>services that you arrange for someone to do for you</u>.

■ I used to color my own hair, but now I **have** *it* **colored**.

■ I **get** *my nails* **done** by Marie.

▶ **BE CAREFUL!** Do not confuse the simple past causative (*had something done*) with the past perfect in active sentences (*had done something*).

SIMPLE PAST CAUSATIVE
■ I **had** *it* **done** last week.
(*Someone did it for me.*)

PAST PERFECT
■ I **had done** *it* before.
(*I did it myself.*)

---

2. Form the **passive causative** with the appropriate form of *have* or *get* + **object** + **past participle**.

The passive causative can be used in <u>all tenses</u> and with <u>modals</u>.

■ I always **have** *my hair* **cut** by André.

■ I **haven't had** *it* **done** since June.

■ Last year I **got** *my coat* **cleaned** once.

■ Next week I**'m going to have** *my windows* **washed**.

■ I**'m getting** *them* **done** by Spotless.

■ I **had** *them* **washed** a long time ago.

■ You **should get** *the car* **checked**.

■ You **ought to have** *it* **done** soon.

---

3. Use *by* when it is necessary to mention the <u>person doing the service</u> (the agent).

Do not mention the agent unnecessarily.

■ Lynne gets her hair done *by André*.

■ Where does Lynne **get her hair done**?
NOT Where does Lynne get her hair done ~~by a hair stylist~~?

Check it out!

For more information about when to use an agent, see Unit 61, page 265.

1 **TRUE OR FALSE** • *Read each person's statement. Write T (True) or F (False) for the sentence that follows.*

1. **JAKE:** I'm going to get my hair cut tomorrow after work.

    __F__ Jake cuts his own hair.

2. **DEBRA:** I'm coloring my hair this afternoon.

    _____ Debra colors her own hair.

3. **AMBER:** I didn't pack any nail polish, because I had done my nails before the trip.

    _____ Amber did her own nails.

4. **JAKE:** I'm thinking of getting the floors waxed before the party.

    _____ Jake might hire someone to wax the floors.

5. **MARIE:** I had my apartment painted two months ago.

    _____ Marie painted her own apartment.

6. **TONY:** I'll wash the car this weekend.

    _____ Tony is going to wash the car himself.

2 **FIND OUT & REPORT** • *It's February 15. Look at the Santanas' calendar and write sentences about things they **had done** and things they **are going to have done**.*

FEBRUARY						
SUNDAY	**MONDAY**	**TUESDAY**	**WEDNESDAY**	**THURSDAY**	**FRIDAY**	**SATURDAY**
1	2	3	4	5	6	7 Deb–hairdresser
8	9	10	11	Jake– 12 barber	13 carpets	Amber– 14 dog groomer
Today's 15 date	windows 16	17	18	19	20 food and drinks	21 party!!
22	23	24	Amber– 25 ears pierced	26	27	28 family pictures

1. They / have / pictures / take ___They are going to have pictures taken.___

2. Debra / get / her hair / perm ___Debra got her hair permed.___

3. Amber / have / the dog / groom _____

4. They / get / the windows / wash _____

5. They / have / the carpets / clean _____

6. Amber / have / her ears / pierce _____

7. Jake / get / his hair / cut _____

8. They / have / food and drinks / deliver _____

3

CHOOSE & COMPLETE • *Debra and Jake are going to have a party. Complete the conversations with the passive causative of the appropriate verbs in the box.*

> dry clean   color   cut   paint   ~~shorten~~   wash

1. **DEBRA:** Your new dress is a little long. Why don't you __get it shortened__?

   AMBER: OK. They do alterations at the cleaners. I'll take it in tomorrow.

2. **DEBRA:** My blue dress has a small stain. I have to _____.

   AMBER: I can drop it off at the cleaners with my dress.

3. **JAKE:** The house is ready, except for the windows. They look pretty dirty.

   DEBRA: Don't worry. We _____ tomorrow.

4. **DEBRA:** Your hair is getting really long. I thought you were going to cut it.

   AMBER: I decided not to do it myself this time. I _____ by André.

5. **DEBRA:** My hair's getting a lot of gray in it. Should I _____?

   JAKE: It looks fine to me, but it's up to you.

6. **GUEST:** The house looks beautiful. _____ you _____?

   JAKE: No, actually we did it ourselves last summer.

4

EDIT • *Read Amber's diary entry. Find and correct seven mistakes in the use of the passive causative. The first mistake is already corrected.*

February 21

The party was tonight. It went really well! The house looked great. Mom and Dad had the floors

waxed and all the windows ~~clean~~ ^{cleaned} professionally so everything sparkled. And of course we had the

whole house painted ourselves last summer. (I'll never forget *that*. It took us two weeks!) I wore my

new black dress that I have shortened by Bo, and I got cut my hair by André. He did a great job. There

were a lot of guests at the party. We had almost fifty people invited, and they almost all showed

up! The food was great too. Mom made most of the main dishes herself, but she had the rest of

the food prepare by a caterer. Mom and Dad hired a professional photographer, so at the end of the

party we all took our pictures. Dad's getting them back next week. I can't wait to see them!

SelfTest

SECTION ONE

Circle the letter of the correct answer to complete each sentence.

> **EXAMPLE:**
> Jennifer never _____ coffee.   A Ⓑ C D
> (A) drink   (C) is drinking
> (B) drinks   (D) was drinking

1. This book _____ written in 1999.   A B C D
   (A) is   (C) was
   (B) has   (D) were

2. Coffee is _____ in Colombia.   A B C D
   (A) grow   (C) been growing
   (B) grew   (D) grown

3. Millions of people _____ the movie.   A B C D
   (A) saw   (C) will be seen
   (B) were seen   (D) must be seen

4. The meeting won't _____.   A B C D
   (A) cancel   (C) been cancelled
   (B) be cancelled   (D) cancelled

5. Sally doesn't cut her own hair. She _____ at the salon.   A B C D
   (A) cuts it   (C) has it cut
   (B) has cut it   (D) gets it

6. That book was written _____ Maya Angelou.   A B C D
   (A) at   (C) from
   (B) by   (D) of

7. The report _____ soon.   A B C D
   (A) publishes   (C) will be published
   (B) is published   (D) will publish

8. —When will the work be completed?   A B C D
   —It _____ be by June, but I'm not really sure.
   (A) has   (C) will
   (B) might   (D) won't

9. How often _____ your car serviced since you bought it?   A B C D
   (A) do you get   (C) had you gotten
   (B) did you get   (D) have you gotten

10. I have to get my picture _____ for my Web site.   A B C D
    (A) take   (C) taking
    (B) taken   (D) took

SECTION TWO

Each sentence has four underlined words or phrases. The four underlined parts of the sentence are marked A, B, C, and D. Circle the letter of the one underlined word or phrase that is NOT CORRECT.

EXAMPLE:

Mike <u>usually</u> <u>drives</u> to school, but <u>today</u> he <u>walks</u>.
A B C **Ⓓ**
_A _B _C _D

11. Tomorrow <u>I'm getting</u> my car <u>serviced</u> <u>from</u> the mechanic that
Jake <u>uses</u>.
A B C D

12. The reports <u>were</u> <u>arrived</u> late, so I <u>had</u> <u>them sent</u> to you this morning.
A B C D

13. Some mistakes <u>were</u> <u>made</u> in the brochure, but they might <u>corrected</u>
before you <u>get</u> back.
A B C D

14. You<u>'ll see</u> a copy before they<u>'re</u> <u>printed</u> <u>by the printer</u>.
A B C D

15. A funny thing <u>was</u> happened when your <u>office</u> <u>was</u> <u>painted</u> yesterday.
A B C D

16. <u>Will</u> your stay <u>be</u> <u>extended</u>, or will you <u>be returned</u> next week?
A B C D

17. I used to <u>do</u> my own taxes, but now I <u>have</u> <u>done</u> <u>them</u> <u>by</u> an accountant.
A B C D

18. Before a final decision <u>is reached</u>, the various possibilities <u>should</u>
probably <u>discussed</u> <u>by</u> the whole team.
A B C D

19. The house <u>painted</u> more than three years ago, but I'm not <u>going to</u>
<u>have</u> <u>it done</u> again for a while.
A B C D

20. We <u>didn't</u> <u>know</u> about the problem, so it <u>shouldn't</u> <u>be handled</u> in time.
A B C D

21. A lot of crops <u>can't</u> be <u>grew</u> in the mountains because <u>it</u> <u>gets</u> too cold.
A B C D

22. That pottery <u>was</u> <u>found</u> <u>by</u> an archaeologist while she <u>was worked</u> in
this area.
A B C D

23. <u>Does</u> the lightbulb <u>have to replaced</u> or is <u>it</u> still <u>working</u>?
A B C D

24. <u>Have</u> you <u>had</u> your teeth <u>clean</u> yet <u>by</u> Dr. Ellin's new oral hygienist?
A B C D

25. The last payment shouldn't <u>make</u> until all the work <u>has been</u>
<u>completed</u> and carefully <u>checked</u>.
A B C D

Factual Conditionals:
Present

Sorry, Sir.
If you **don't fit,**
you **can't board.**

CHECK *POINT*

Circle T (True) or F (False).

T F   The man may not be able to board the plane.

CHART CHECK

Circle T (True) or F (False).

T F   The verbs in both clauses are in the present tense.

T F   The *if* clause always comes first.

T F   There is always a comma between the two clauses.

STATEMENTS		
IF CLAUSE		**RESULT CLAUSE**
If	it **snows,**	the airport **closes.**
	it**'s** foggy,	planes **can't leave.**

STATEMENTS		
RESULT CLAUSE		**IF CLAUSE**
The airport **closes**	**if**	it **snows.**
Planes **can't leave**		it**'s** foggy.

YES/NO QUESTIONS		
RESULT CLAUSE		**IF CLAUSE**
Does the airport **close**	**if**	it **snows?**
Can planes **leave**		it**'s** foggy?

SHORT ANSWERS			
AFFIRMATIVE		**NEGATIVE**	
Yes,	it **does.**	**No,**	it **doesn't.**
	they **can.**		they **can't.**

WH- QUESTIONS	
RESULT CLAUSE	**IF CLAUSE**
Why **does** air **get** lighter	**if** it **expands?**

EXPRESS CHECK

Match the if *clauses with the result clauses.*

_____ **1.** If you hate airplane food,

_____ **2.** You might not be able to board

_____ **3.** If people travel a long distance,

a. they often feel jet lag.

b. you can order a special meal.

c. if you don't check in at the gate.

Grammar Explanations

Examples

1. Use **present factual conditional** sentences to talk about <u>general truths</u> and <u>scientific facts</u>.

The *if* clause talks about the condition, and the result clause talks about what happens if the condition occurs.

Use the **simple present tense** in <u>both clauses</u>.

■ *if clause*   *result clause*
   ***If** it's* noon in Lima, it's 6:00 P.M. in Rome.

■ *if clause*   *result clause*
   ***If** air* **expands**, it **becomes** lighter.

2. You can also use **present factual conditional** sentences to talk about <u>habits</u> and <u>recurring events</u> (things that happen again and again).

Use the <u>simple present tense</u> or <u>present progressive</u> in the *if* clause. Use the <u>simple present tense</u> in the result clause.

■ *if clause*   *result clause*
   ***If** Bill* **flies**, he **orders** a special meal.

■ *if clause*   *result clause*
   ***If** I'm* **traveling** far, I always **fly**.

3. You can also use **modals** in the result clause.

■ If you practice your Chinese everyday, you ***can* improve** quickly.

■ You ***might* learn** more if you listen to Chinese tapes.

4. Use the **imperative** in the result clause to give <u>instructions</u>, <u>commands</u>, and <u>invitations</u> that depend on a certain condition.

■ If you want the seat to recline, **press** the button.

■ If the seat belt light is on, **don't leave** your seat.

■ If you come to Tokyo, **stay** with us.

5. You can **begin conditional sentences** with <u>the *if* clause or the result clause</u>. The meaning is the same.

Use a **comma** between the two clauses only when the *if* clause comes first.

■ **If the light goes on,** buckle your seat belt.
   OR
■ Buckle your seat belt **if the light goes on**.

1 **IDENTIFY** • *Read this article. In each factual conditional sentence, underline the result clause once. Underline the clause that expresses the condition twice.*

═══════════════════ **PASSENGERS' RIGHTS** ═══════════════════

<u>I</u><u>f you run into problems on your journey</u>, <u>know your rights as a passenger</u>. Often the airline company is required to compensate you for delays or damages. For example, the airline provides meals and hotel rooms if a flight is unduly delayed. However, the airline owes you a lot more if it caused the delay by overbooking. This can occur especially during holidays if airlines sell more tickets than there are seats. If all the passengers actually show up, then the flight is overbooked. Airlines usually award upgrades or additional free travel to passengers who volunteer to take a later flight. However, if no one volunteers, your flight may be delayed. In that case, the airline must repay you 100 percent of the cost of your ticket for a delay of up to four hours on an international flight. If the delay is more than four hours, you receive 200 percent of the cost of your ticket.

2 **SUMMARIZE** • *Read these conversations about Hong Kong. Summarize the advice with conditional sentences.*

1. A: I hate hot weather.
   B: The best time to go to Hong Kong is November or December.

   If you hate hot weather, the best time to go to Hong Kong is November or December.

2. A: I'm traveling with my children.
   B: Take them to Lai Chi Kok Amusement Park in Kowloon.

   _____

3. A: We need a moderately priced hotel.
   B: I suggest the Harbour View International House.

   _____

4. A: We like seafood.
   B: There are wonderful seafood restaurants on Lamma Island.

   _____

5. A: I'm fascinated by Chinese opera.
   B: You might like the street opera in the Shanghai Street Night Market.

   _____

6. A: I'd like to get a good view of Hong Kong.
   B: You should take the funicular to the Peak.

   _____

3 **COMBINE** • *Complete this interview between* **Careers Magazine (CM)** *and flight attendant May Simka (MS). Combine the sentences in parentheses to make a factual conditional sentence. Use the same order. Make necessary changes in capitalization and punctuation.*

CM: How long are you usually away?

MS: ___If I go to the Bahamas, I have a two-day layover.___
    1. (I go to the Bahamas. I have a two-day layover.)

CM: What do you do for two days?

MS: _____
    2. (I spend a lot of time at the pool. I stay at a hotel.)

_____
    3. (I stay with friends. I spend time with them.)

CM: Sounds nice.

MS: _____
    4. (It's not so nice. I get a "Dracula.")

That's when you fly somewhere at midnight, spend four hours, and then fly back.

CM: Sounds like a tough job. Is it worth it?

MS: _____
    5. (It's very rewarding. You don't mind hard work.)

CM: Who walks the dog and waters the plants when you're away?

MS: _____
    6. (You have three roommates. You don't have trouble finding dogwalkers.)

CM: What's the best thing about this job?

MS: Free trips. _____
    7. (A flight has an empty seat. I ride for free!)

4 **EDIT** • *Read May's journal entry. Find and correct seven mistakes in the use of present factual conditionals. The first mistake is already corrected. Don't forget to check punctuation!*

> *don't*
> What a great weekend! If Lou and Teri aren't the best hosts in the world, I ~~won't~~ know who is.
> I've invited them to New York, but if you live in the Bahamas, you rarely want to leave. Tomorrow at
> midnight I fly round trip from New York to Pittsburgh. There's always a price to pay. If I get a free
> weekend in the islands I always get a "Dracula" afterwards. Oh, well. If I won't fall asleep, I can usually
> get a lot of reading done. Pat and Kim both flew to London yesterday. I hope someone can walk Frisky
> for me. Usually, if I'll be working, one of them is off. If Frisky is alone for a long time, he barked a lot.
> That disturbs the neighbors. Maybe I should just leave the TV on for him. He's always very calm, if
> the TV is on. Or maybe I'd better call Pat and ask her about her schedule. If it was 6:00 p.m. here in
> New York, it's 11:00 p.m. in London. That's not too late to call.

UNIT
65

Factual Conditionals:
Future

If Baker **raises** taxes, small businesses **will leave**.

CHECK *POINT*

Circle T (True) or F (False).

T F   Baker is definitely going
to raise taxes.

T F   Small businesses are
definitely going to leave.

CHART CHECK

Check the correct answer.

Use the simple present tense in

☐ the **if** clause.

☐ the result clause.

Use a comma between the two clauses

☐ when the **if** clause comes first.

☐ when the result clause comes first.

AFFIRMATIVE STATEMENTS	
IF CLAUSE: PRESENT	**RESULT CLAUSE: FUTURE**
If Baker **wins,**	he**'ll raise** taxes. he**'s going to fight** crime.

NEGATIVE STATEMENTS	
IF CLAUSE: PRESENT	**RESULT CLAUSE: FUTURE**
If he **doesn't lower** taxes,	businesses **won't return**.

YES/NO QUESTIONS	
RESULT CLAUSE: FUTURE	**IF CLAUSE: PRESENT**
Will he **lower** taxes **Is** he **going to fight** crime	**if** he **wins?**

SHORT ANSWERS			
AFFIRMATIVE		**NEGATIVE**	
Yes, he	**will**.	**No**, he	**won't**.
	is.		**isn't**.

282

WH- QUESTIONS		
RESULT CLAUSE: FUTURE		**IF CLAUSE: PRESENT**
What	**will** he **do** **is** he **going to do**	**if** he **wins**?

EXPRESS CHECK

Unscramble these words to form a sentence. Add a comma if necessary.

fight • she • crime • she'll • If • wins

_____

Grammar Explanations

Examples

1. Use **future factual conditional** sentences to talk about what <u>will happen under certain conditions</u>. The *if* clause states the condition. The result clause states the result.

Use the **simple present tense** in the *if* clause. Use the **future** with ***will*** or ***be going to*** in the result clause.

You can also use a **modal** in the result clause.

▶ **BE CAREFUL!** Even though the *if* clause refers to the future, use the <u>simple present tense</u>.

if clause   result clause
- ***If*** Baker **wins**, he'**ll raise** taxes.
  (It's a real possibility that Baker will win.)

- ***If*** Soto **wins**, she'**ll improve** housing.
- ***If*** Soto **wins**, she'**s going to improve** housing.

- If you want to vote, you ***must register***.
- If you don't vote, you ***might regret*** it.

- ***If*** she **wins**, she'll fight crime.
  NOT ~~If she will win . . .~~

2. You can **begin conditional sentences** with <u>the *if* clause or the result clause</u>. The meaning is the same.

Use a **comma** between the two clauses only when the *if* clause comes first

- **If you vote for Soto,** you won't regret it.
  OR
- You won't regret it **if you vote for Soto**.

3. ***If*** and ***unless*** can both be used in conditional sentences, but their meanings are very different.

Use ***unless*** to state a <u>negative condition</u>.

Unless often has the same meaning as ***if . . . not***.

- ***If*** you vote, you'll have a say in the future of our city.

- ***Unless*** you vote, you won't have a say in the future of our city.
  OR
- ***If*** you do**n't** vote, you won't have a say in the future of our city.

1

MATCH • *Each condition will have a result. Match the condition with the appropriate result.*

Condition

___f___ **1.** If Soto wins, she

_____ **2.** If she lowers taxes, business people

_____ **3.** If the education system improves, we

_____ **4.** Unless young people have hope for the future, they

_____ **5.** If crime decreases, this

_____ **6.** Unless you register, you

_____ **7.** If you don't vote, you

Result

a. won't stay out of trouble.

b. won't have a say in the government.

c. will have an educated work force.

d. won't be able to vote.

e. will move their companies back to the city.

f. will lower taxes.

g. will be a safer place to live.

2

COMPLETE • *Read this interview between* Politics Today (PT) *and mayoral candidate Daniel Baker* (DB). *Complete it with the correct form of the verbs in parentheses and* **if** *or* **unless**.

PT: What's the first thing you __'ll do__ __if__ you
          1. (do)   **2.** (if / unless)

_____ elected?
3. (get)

DB: Well, it's been a long, hard campaign. _____ I _____,
                                              4. (If / Unless)   **5.** (win)

I _____ a short vacation before I begin my new job.
  6. (take)

PT: Sounds good. Where to?

DB: Sorry, but I'd rather not say. _____ I _____ mayor,
                                      7. (If / Unless)   **8.** (become)

I _____ to keep my personal life private. Even mayors need privacy.
  9. (try)

PT: I can understand that. Now, every election has a winner and a loser.

What _____ you _____ _____
                          10. (do)   **11.** (if / unless)

you _____?
    12. (lose)

DB: _____ I _____ this election, I _____ to be
        13. (If / Unless)   **14.** (lose)   **15.** (continue)

active in politics as a private citizen. _____ *both* parties
                                          16. (If / Unless)

_____, this city _____ as great as it can be.
17. (cooperate)   **18.** (not be)

Finally, _____ the people _____ me to office this time,
          19. (if / unless)   **20.** (not elect)

I _____ back in four years to try again!
  21. (be)

3 **COMBINE •** *Yuko Tamari is trying to decide whether to go to law school. She made a decision tree to help her decide. In the tree, arrows connect the conditions and the results. Write sentences about her decisions. Use future factual sentences.*

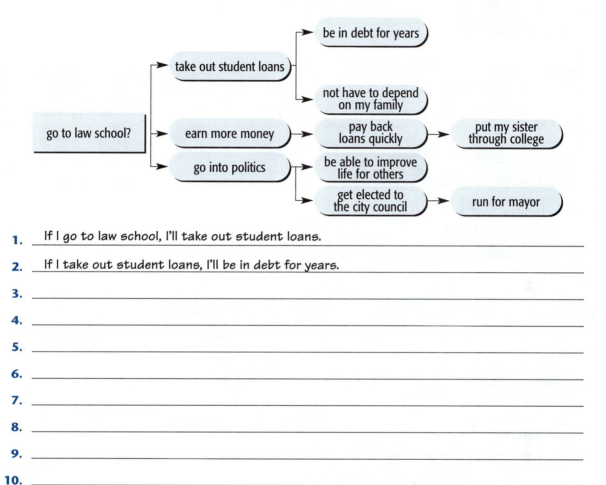

1. If I go to law school, I'll take out student loans.

2. If I take out student loans, I'll be in debt for years.

3. _____

4. _____

5. _____

6. _____

7. _____

8. _____

9. _____

10. _____

4 **EDIT •** *Read this journal entry. Find and correct six mistakes in the use of future factual conditionals. The first mistake is already corrected. Don't forget to check punctuation!*

> Should I campaign for student council president? I'll have to decide soon if I ~~wanted~~ ^{want} to run. If I'll be
>
> busy campaigning, I won't have much time to study. That's a problem, because I'm not going to get into
>
> a good college if I get good grades this year. On the other hand, there's so much to do in this school,
>
> and nothing is getting done if Todd Laker becomes president again. A lot of people know that. But
>
> will I know what to do if I'll get the job? Never mind. I'll deal with that problem, if I win.

UNIT 66

Unreal Conditionals:
Present

CHECK POINT

Circle T (True) or F (False).

T   F   Schroeder, the piano player, wants to marry Lucy.

CHART CHECK

Circle T (True) or F (False).

T   F   Use the simple present tense in the *if* clause.

T   F   Use *were* for all subjects.

T   F   Use a comma between the two clauses when the result clause comes first.

AFFIRMATIVE STATEMENTS

IF CLAUSE: SIMPLE PAST		RESULT CLAUSE: *WOULD* + BASE FORM OF VERB
If	he **loved** her, he **were*** in love,	he **would get** married.

*Note that *were* is used for all subjects with *be*.

NEGATIVE STATEMENTS

IF CLAUSE: SIMPLE PAST		RESULT CLAUSE: *WOULD* + BASE FORM OF VERB
If	he **didn't love** her, he **weren't** in love,	he **would not get** married.

YES/NO QUESTIONS

RESULT CLAUSE	IF CLAUSE	
Would I **get** married	*if*	I **loved** her? I **were** in love?

SHORT ANSWERS

AFFIRMATIVE	NEGATIVE
Yes, I **would**.	**No**, I **wouldn't**.

WH- QUESTIONS

RESULT CLAUSE	IF CLAUSE	
What **would** you **do**	*if*	you **loved** her? you **were** in love?

NOTE: For contractions with *would,* see Appendix 24 on page 346.

EXPRESS CHECK

Circle the correct words to complete this question.

What <u>will / would</u> he do <u>if / when</u> he <u>was / were</u> a millionaire?

Grammar Explanations

Examples

1. Use **present unreal conditional** sentences to talk about <u>unreal, untrue, imagined, or impossible</u> conditions and their results.

The *if* clause presents the unreal condition. The result clause presents the unreal result of that condition.

- *if* clause   result clause
- ■ *If* I **loved** him, I **would marry** him.
  (But I don't love him, so I won't marry him.)

- *if* clause   result clause
- ■ *If* I **had** more time, I **would travel**.
  (But I don't have time, so I don't travel.)

2. Use the **simple past tense** in the *if* clause. Use *would* + **base form** of the verb in the result clause.

▶ **BE CAREFUL!**

  a. The *if* clause uses the simple past tense form, but the <u>meaning is not past</u>.

  b. <u>Don't use *would* in the *if* clause</u> in present unreal conditional sentences.

  c. Use *were* for <u>all subjects</u> when the verb in the *if* clause is a form of *be*.

  USAGE NOTE: You will sometimes hear native speakers use *was* in the *if* clause. However, many people think that this is <u>not correct</u>.

- If clause   result clause
- ■ *If* they **had** money, they **wouldn't live** there.

- ■ *If* I **had** more money *now*, I would take a trip around the world.

- ■ *If* she **knew** the answer, she would tell you. NOT ~~If she would know the answer . . .~~

- ■ *If* I **were** rich, I would travel around the world. NOT ~~If I was rich . . .~~

3. You can also use a **modal** in the result clause.

- ■ If I had time, I *could read* more.

4. You can **begin conditional sentences** with <u>the *if* clause or the result clause</u>. The meaning is the same.

Use a **comma** between the two clauses only when the *if* clause comes first.

- ■ **If I had more money,** I would move.
                    OR
- ■ I would move **if I had more money**.

5. Statements beginning with *If I were you, . . .* are often used to <u>give advice</u>.

- ■ *If I were you*, I'd read "Peanuts." It's really funny.

1 **TRUE OR FALSE** • *Read each quotation from these "Peanuts" characters. Write T (True)
or F (False) for the statement that follows.*

1. **SNOOPY:** If I were a human being, I wouldn't even *own* a dog!

   ___F___ Snoopy is a human being.

2. **LUCY to SNOOPY:** You wouldn't be so happy if you knew what was going to happen.

   _____ Snoopy is happy.

3. **LUCY to LINUS:** If I were you, I'd sleep underneath that tree.

   _____ Lucy is giving Linus advice.

4. **SNOOPY to WOODSTOCK:** What would you do if you had forty dollars?

   _____ Woodstock has forty dollars.

5. **SNOOPY:** If I ate one more snowflake, I'd turn into a blizzard.

   _____ Snoopy plans to eat another snowflake.

6. **LUCY:** If we were married, Schroeder, I'd come in every morning and dust your piano.

   _____ Lucy dusts Schroeder's piano.

2 **COMPLETE** • *Read part of an article about the comic strip "Peanuts." Complete it with
the correct form of the verbs in parentheses.*

Peanuts

What makes "Peanuts" so popular? Of course, if it ___**weren't**___
1. (not be)

funny, people _____ it so much. But "Peanuts" provides
2. (not like)

more than just laughs. It addresses such universal themes as love, jealousy, loneliness, and

hope. If the characters _____ so real, we _____ with them.
3. (not be)   **4.** (couldn't / identify)

Take Lucy, for example. In love with the piano-playing Schroeder, Lucy complains, "If we

_____ married, and you _____ golf, I _____
5. (be)   **6.** (love)   **7.** (hate)

your golf clubs! If you _____ a sports car, I _____ your sports
8. (drive)   **9.** (hate)

car! If you _____ a bowler, I _____ your bowling ball." Without
10. (be)   **11.** (hate)

looking up from his piano or missing a beat, Schroeder asks, "So?" "I hate your piano!" shouts

Lucy as she kicks it out from under him. Recognizable behavior? In "Peanuts" we see ourselves

along with our weaknesses and hopes. But we don't have to analyze "Peanuts" to enjoy it.

If it _____ for comic strips like "Peanuts," our lives _____
12. (not be)   **13.** (might / be)

a little less fun.

3

COMBINE • *Read about these "Peanuts" characters. What would happen if their situations were different? Combine the two sentences into one, using the unreal present conditional.*

1. Schroeder ignores Lucy. She gets angry at him.

   If Schroeder didn't ignore Lucy, she wouldn't get angry at him.

2. Schroeder loves Beethoven. He plays his sonatas all the time.

   _____

3. Charlie Brown doesn't have enough friends. He feels lonely.

   _____

4. Sally doesn't know her teacher's name. She can't send her a card.

   _____

5. Linus is smart. He finds clever solutions to life's problems.

   _____

6. Woodstock and Snoopy have a close relationship. Woodstock confides in Snoopy.

   _____

7. Rerun's parents refuse to let him have a dog. He tries to borrow Charlie's dog.

   _____

8. Pig Pen doesn't take enough baths. He's filthy.

   _____

4

EDIT • *Read this boy's journal entry. Find and correct six mistakes in the use of the present unreal conditional. The first mistake is already corrected.*

I've got to stop staying up late reading "Peanuts"! If I weren't always so tired, I ~~will~~ *would* be able to stay awake in class. Whenever the teacher calls on me, I don't know what to say. Then I get really embarrassed because of that cute red-haired girl that I like. I would talk to her if I wouldn't be so shy. My friend Jason says, "If I was you, I'd ask her to a party," but I'm too afraid that if I asked her, she would have said no. After class, I played baseball. Nobody wanted me on their team. If I play better, I would get chosen sometimes. Life is hard! I can really understand that Charlie Brown character in "Peanuts." In fact, if I didn't laugh so hard while reading "Peanuts," I would cried!

UNIT 67

Unreal Conditionals:
Past

 Best Bets for Holiday Viewing

*George (seated)
with his guardian angel*

It's a Wonderful Life

Rating: ★★★★ out of ★★★★

What would have happened if you had never been born? George Bailey's guardian angel, Clarence, shows George that **life in Bedford Falls would have been a lot different if George hadn't been there**. In the process, Clarence teaches us all how our lives touch those of others. Highly recommended for the whole family.

CHECK POINT

Circle T (True) or F (False).

T   F   George Bailey was never in Bedford Falls.

CHART CHECK ➞

Check the correct answers.

Use the past perfect in

☐ the *if* clause.

☐ the result clause.

Use a comma between the two clauses when

☐ the *if* clause comes first.

☐ the result clause comes first.

STATEMENTS	
IF CLAUSE: **PAST PERFECT**	**RESULT CLAUSE:** **WOULD (NOT) HAVE + PAST PARTICIPLE**
If I **had (not) had** money,	I **would (not) have moved** away.

YES/NO QUESTIONS	
RESULT CLAUSE	**IF CLAUSE**
Would you **have left**	**if** you **had had** money?

SHORT ANSWERS	
AFFIRMATIVE	**NEGATIVE**
Yes, I **would have**.	**No**, I **wouldn't have**.

290

WH- QUESTIONS	
RESULT CLAUSE	**IF CLAUSE**
What **would** you **have done**	*if* you **had had** money?

CONTRACTIONS
would have = **would've** would not have = **wouldn't have**

EXPRESS CHECK

Complete this sentence with the correct form of the verb **study**. *Add a comma if necessary.*

I _____ if I had known about the quiz today.

Grammar Explanations	**Examples**
1. Use **past unreal conditional** sentences to talk about past conditions and results that <u>never happened</u>. The *if* clause presents the unreal condition. The result clause presents the imagined result of that condition.	*if* clause result clause ■ *If* George **had died** young, he **wouldn't have had** children. *(But he didn't die young, so he had children.)* ■ *If* George **hadn't been born**, many people's lives **would have been** worse. *(But George was born, so their lives were better.)*
2. Use the **past perfect** in the *if* clause. Use *would have* + **past participle** in the result clause.	*if* clause result clause ■ *If* the film **had won** an Oscar, it **would have become** famous right away.
3. You can also use **modals** in the result clause.	■ If George had gone to college, he *might have* **become** an architect. ■ If George had become an architect, he *could have* **designed** bridges.
4. You can **begin conditional sentences** with <u>the *if* clause or the result clause</u>. The meaning is the same. Use a **comma** between the two clauses only when the *if* clause comes first.	■ **If he had won a million dollars,** he would have traveled to China. OR ■ He would have traveled to China **if he had won a million dollars**.
5. **Past unreal conditionals** are often used to <u>express regret</u> about what happened in the past.	■ *If* I **had known** Mary was in town, I **would have invited** her to the party. *(I regret that I didn't invite her.)*

1

TRUE OR FALSE • *Read each numbered sentence. Write T (True) or F (False) for the statement that follows.*

1. If I had had time, I would have watched *It's a Wonderful Life*.

_____T_____ I didn't have time to watch *It's a Wonderful Life*.

2. I would have taped the movie if my VCR hadn't broken.

_____ I taped the movie.

3. If Clarence hadn't been there, George might have killed himself.

_____ Clarence was there.

4. George wouldn't have met Mary if he hadn't gone to his brother's graduation party.

_____ George didn't go to the party.

5. George would have been happier if he had become an architect.

_____ George became an architect.

6. The movie wouldn't have been so good if James Stewart hadn't played the part of George Bailey.

_____ James Stewart played the part of George Bailey.

2

COMPLETE • *George is thinking about the past. Complete his thoughts with the correct form of the words in parentheses.*

1. I didn't go into business with my friend Sam. If I _____**had gone**_____ into
                                                              (go)
business with him, I _____**would have become**_____ a success.
                              (become)

2. I couldn't go into the army because I was deaf in one ear. I _____
                                                                          (go)
into the army if I _____ my hearing in that ear.
                         (not lose)

3. Mary and I weren't able to go on a honeymoon. We _____ away if
                                                              (can / go)
my father _____ sick.
                (not get)

4. Clarence showed me how the world would look without me. I _____
                                                                          (not know)
that I was so important if Clarence _____ me.
                                          (not show)

5. My old boss once made a terrible mistake. If I _____ him, he
                                                          (not help)
_____ to jail.
        (can / go)

6. Mary _____ a happy life if she _____ me.
              (may / not lead)   (not marry)

7. Life here _____ really different if I _____.
                      (be)   (not live)

3 **REWRITE •** *Read each true situation. Then write a past unreal conditional sentence to express how things could have been different.*

1. Clarence wasn't a first-class angel, so he didn't have much self-confidence.

   If Clarence had been a first-class angel, he would have had more self-confidence.

2. George was unhappy about his business. He yelled at his daughter on Christmas Eve.

   _____

3. Poor people could buy houses because George's business loaned them money.

   _____

4. Mr. Potter wasn't able to trick George, so George didn't sell Potter the business.

   _____

5. George's Uncle Billy lost $8,000. George got into trouble with the law.

   _____

6. George's friends didn't know about his troubles. They didn't help him right away.

   _____

7. George's friends collected money for him, so he didn't go to jail.

   _____

4 **EDIT •** *Read Clarence's diary entry. Find and correct six mistakes in the use of the unreal conditional. The first mistake is already corrected. Remember to check punctuation!*

Dear Diary,

It's funny how things work out sometimes. If George ~~hasn't~~ **hadn't** wanted to jump off that bridge on Christmas Eve, I might never have getting an important job like saving him. And if he hadn't been so stubborn, I would never had thought of the idea of showing him life in Bedford Falls without him. One of the saddest things was seeing all those people who didn't have homes. If George gave up and sold his business to Mr. Potter, then Potter would have rented run-down apartments to all those people. But because of George, they now have good homes. By the time we were finished, George realized he really had a wonderful life. In fact, he will have gone to jail happily, if his friends hadn't given him the money he needed. Well, luckily they helped him out, and he didn't go to jail. And I got my wings and became a first-class angel!

Wish: Present and Past

Tiny Fairy Tales   THE THREE WISHES

The Three Wishes

One day a poor woodcutter was given three wishes by a tree elf. When his hungry wife heard the news, she said, "I **wish** I **had** some sausages."
At once five sausages appeared on a plate.
The woodcutter was furious about wasting a wish. "I **wish** those sausages **were hanging** from your nose," he shouted. At once the sausages hung from her nose. The two struggled to get them loose, but they could not. "I **wish** I **hadn't made** that wish," the woodcutter sighed. At once the sausages were on the plate again. The couple happily ate the sausages and wished for nothing more. ❀

49

CHECK POINT

Check the correct answer.

The woman wanted sausages

☐ that day.

☐ the day before.

CHART CHECK 1

Check the correct answer.

In wishes about the present, what verb tense follows *wish*?

☐ the simple present

☐ the simple past

WISHES ABOUT THE PRESENT			
MAIN CLAUSE	**WISH CLAUSE**		
She **wishes**	she	**had**	some food right now.
		were*	rich.

*Note that *were* is used for all subjects with *be*.

CHART CHECK 2

Check the correct answer.

In wishes about the past, what verb tense follows *wish*?

❑ the simple past

❑ the past perfect

WISHES ABOUT THE PAST			
MAIN CLAUSE	**WISH CLAUSE**		
He **wishes**	he	**had had**	food last night.
		had been	rich as a child.

EXPRESS CHECK

Complete these sentences with the correct forms of the verb **know**.

- I wish I _____ a good story to tell in my next class.

- I wish I _____ more stories as a child.

Grammar Explanations

Examples

1. Use *wish* followed by a verb in the **simple past** tense to talk about <u>things that you want to be true now but that are not true</u>.

After *wish*, use *were* instead of *was*.

- He **wishes** he *had* a yacht.
  (He doesn't have a yacht, but he wants one.)

- Sometimes I **wish** I *were* a child again.
  NOT Sometimes I wish I was a child again.

2. Use *wish* followed by the **past perfect** to express <u>regrets about events in the past</u>.

- They **wish** they *had moved* to the city.
  (They didn't move to the city, and now they think that was a mistake.)

3. Use *would* after *wish* to express a desire for someone or something to act in a different way. This often communicates <u>a complaint or a regret</u>.

Do not use *will* after *wish*.

- I **wish** you *would* **cook** breakfast. You have more time than I do.

- I **wish** she *would* **visit** more often. I really miss her.

  NOT I wish she will visit more often.

4. Use *could* or *could have* after *wish* to express <u>ability</u>.

Do not use *can* after *wish*.

- He **wishes** he *could* **earn** more money now.

- He **wishes** he *could have* **found** a better job when he was younger.

  NOT He wishes he can earn more money.

1 **TRUE OR FALSE** • *Read each numbered sentence. Write T (True) or F (False) for the statement that follows.*

1. I wish I were a princess.

___T___ I'm not a princess.

2. I hated living in a big house as a child.

_____ I wish I had lived in a small house.

3. He wishes he could find a better job.

_____ He likes his job.

4. They couldn't take computer classes in college, so they are taking them now.

_____ They wish they could take computer classes.

5. Hal's wife plays computer games a lot. He wants her to stop.

_____ He wishes she wouldn't play computer games.

6. He wishes he had a lot of money.

_____ He doesn't have a lot of money.

2 **COMPLETE** • *Read this article from a psychology magazine. Complete it with the correct form of the verbs in parentheses.*

PSYCHOLOGY FOR YOU   April 2000

WISHES AND SOLUTIONS

The old saying goes, "If wishes were horses, then beggars would ride." "I wish it ___*were*___ that easy," says therapist Joel Grimes. "But we can't just wish
1. (be)

problems _____. We have to make our own solutions." According to him,
2. (will / go away)

complainers are really saying, "I wish I _____ a magical solution. I wish
3. (have)

I _____ with this myself." One client, for example, kept complaining,
4. (not have to / deal)

"I wish I _____ people, but my apartment is too small." Grimes urged her
5. (can / entertain)

to solve the problem. This year, she hosted a holiday open house, with people coming at

different times. She still wishes she _____ her whole family last year, but
6. (can / invite)

she learned she could solve her own problems. "At first clients get angry at me for not

handing them solutions," says Grimes. "But when they experience their own power, they

wish they _____ about it sooner."
7. (know)

3

REWRITE • *Joel Grimes's clients complain about things in the past and in the present. Rewrite their complaints as wishes.*

1. I didn't have time to read bedtime stories to my children.

   I wish I had had time to read bedtime stories to my children.

2. My husband won't ask for a raise.

   _____

3. My wife couldn't balance the checkbook last month.

   _____

4. My boyfriend is out of shape.

   _____

5. I'm too old to go back to school.

   _____

6. I can't stop smoking.

   _____

7. My son doesn't call me.

   _____

8. My parents didn't understand me.

   _____

 4

EDIT • *Read this journal entry. Find and correct five mistakes in the use of* **wish.** *The first mistake is already corrected.*

> were
> Today I told Dr. Grimes, "I wish there ~~was~~ a way to spend more time with my boyfriend,
> but we're both too busy." He just said, "If wishes were horses, beggars would ride." That's
> cute, but I wish I understand its meaning. Maybe it means that wishing won't solve
> problems. Well, that's why I went to see him!!! I wish he will tell me what to do right
> then and there, but he refused. Speaking of wishful thinking, I wish Todd and I could have
> spent the weekend together next week. My exams are over, but he has to fly to Denver to
> his job. If wishes were horses, I'd ride one to Denver. Hey! Todd is always saying, "I wish
> you would come with me sometimes." I guess I <u>can</u> go with him to Denver. Dr. Grimes must
> have meant that I can solve my own problems. Now I wish I haven't been so rude to him.

SelfTest

Circle the letter of the correct answer to complete each sentence.

> **EXAMPLE:**
> Jennifer never _____ coffee.   **A Ⓑ C D**
> (A) drink   (C) is drinking
> (B) drinks   (D) was drinking

1. If you _____ a headache, you should take an aspirin.   **A B C D**
   (A) 'll have   (C) have
   (B) had   (D) are having

2. I wish we _____ a bigger house. This one is too small.   **A B C D**
   (A) have   (C) would have
   (B) had   (D) had had

3. _____ it rains very hard, the streets flood.   **A B C D**
   (A) If   (C) During
   (B) Always   (D) Unless

4. We'll be late unless we _____ now.   **A B C D**
   (A) leave   (C) had left
   (B) don't leave   (D) have left

5. What would Tom do if he _____ the truth?   **A B C D**
   (A) would know   (C) knows
   (B) has known   (D) knew

6. If I _____ you, I'd call and apologize.   **A B C D**
   (A) am   (C) were
   (B) would be   (D) was

7. If I _____ you were sick, I would have called sooner.   **A B C D**
   (A) have known   (C) would have known
   (B) had known   (D) know

8. If you want to go skiing in the South, _____ to Black Mountain.   **A B C D**
   (A) you go   (C) go
   (B) you'll go   (D) went

9. Jennifer has trouble with college math. She wishes she _____   **A B C D**
   more in high school.
   (A) studies   (C) had studied
   (B) has studied   (D) studied

10. —If we invited you, would you come?
    —Of course I _____ .   **A B C D**
    (A) do   (C) would have
    (B) am   (D) would

11. Jake will win the election if he _____ harder.   **A B C D**
    (A) campaigns   (C) will campaign
    (B) would campaign   (D) campaigned

12. If you _____ told us about the bad service, we would have   **A B C D**
    eaten there.
    (A) didn't   (C) haven't
    (B) wouldn't have   (D) hadn't

SECTION TWO

Each sentence has four underlined words or phrases. The four underlined parts of the sentence are marked A, B, C, and D. Circle the letter of the one underlined word or phrase that is NOT CORRECT.

> **EXAMPLE:**
> Mike <u>usually</u> <u>drives</u> to school, but <u>today</u> he <u>walks</u>.   **A B C (D)**
>   A   B   C   D

13. <u>If</u> you <u>had been</u> here yesterday, you <u>would have</u> <u>see</u> Jean.   **A B C D**
     A   B   C   D

14. I <u>wish</u> our family <u>could of</u> <u>taken</u> vacations when we <u>were</u> younger.   **A B C D**
       A   B   C   D

15. Unless <u>we</u> work harder, we <u>will</u> <u>finish</u> on <u>time</u>.   **A B C D**
           A   B   C   D

16. <u>If</u> I <u>will have</u> to make a difficult decision, I always <u>discuss</u> it with   **A B C D**
    A   B   C   D
    my friends.

17. <u>If</u> Lara <u>is</u> older, she <u>would try</u> <u>to get</u> a job in California.   **A B C D**
    A   B   C   D

18. We <u>could had</u> <u>done</u> more <u>if</u> we <u>had had</u> more time.   **A B C D**
         A   B   C   D

19. We <u>ate</u> outside <u>tomorrow</u> <u>unless</u> it <u>rains</u>.   **A B C D**
        A   B   C   D

20. I <u>would</u> <u>take</u> the job <u>if</u> I <u>am</u> you.   **A B C D**
       A   B   C   D

21. What <u>would</u> you <u>do</u> if you <u>will</u> <u>won</u> the lottery?   **A B C D**
           A   B   C   D

22. It<u>'s</u> hot, so you <u>will feel</u> better, if you <u>drink</u> more water.   **A B C D**
       A   B   C   D

23. If I <u>had</u> <u>set</u> my alarm clock, I <u>woulda</u> <u>gotten</u> up on time.   **A B C D**
          A   B   C   D

24. <u>If</u> I have to <u>fly</u>, I <u>would get</u> very nervous, so I usually <u>drive</u>.   **A B C D**
    A   B   C   D

25. Lynn <u>wishes</u> she <u>had</u> a bigger apartment and <u>can</u> <u>buy</u> a car.   **A B C D**
          A   B   C   D

Adjective Clauses with Subject Relative Pronouns

> Bill, come meet the woman **who has changed my life**.

Circle T (True) or F (False).

T F   The man is talking about the woman holding a report.

ADJECTIVE CLAUSE AFTER THE MAIN CLAUSE

CHART CHECK

Check the correct answers.

Adjective clauses describe:

❑ nouns

❑ verbs

Adjective clauses can go:

❑ before the main clause

❑ in the middle of the main clause

❑ after the main clause

MAIN CLAUSE	ADJECTIVE CLAUSE		
	SUBJECT RELATIVE PRONOUN	VERB	
That's my friend	*who*	lives	in Rome.

ADJECTIVE CLAUSE INSIDE THE MAIN CLAUSE

MAIN CLAUSE	ADJECTIVE CLAUSE			MAIN CLAUSE (CONT.)
	SUBJECT RELATIVE PRONOUN	VERB		
My friend	*who*	lives	in Rome	is a dancer.

EXPRESS CHECK

Unscramble these words to form a sentence.

the man • works • who • in the cafeteria • That's

_____

Grammar Explanations	**Examples**

1. Use **adjective clauses** to identify or give additional information about <u>nouns</u> or <u>indefinite pronouns</u> such as ***someone***, ***somebody***, ***something***, ***another***, and ***other(s)***.

- I know the woman **who lives there**.
  (The adjective clause identifies the woman we are talking about.)

- Rome is a city **which attracts tourists**.
  (The adjective clause gives additional information about the city.)

The adjective clause <u>directly follows the noun (or pronoun)</u> it is identifying or describing.

- Someone **who has a lot of friends** is lucky.
  Not ~~Someone is lucky who has a lot of friends.~~

---

2. **Sentences with adjective clauses** can be seen as a combination of two sentences.

- *I have a friend. + He loves to shop. =*
- I have a friend **who loves to shop**.

- *My friend lives in Rome. + She paints. =*
- My friend **who lives in Rome** paints.

---

3. Adjective clauses are introduced by **relative pronouns**.

Subject relative pronouns are:

a. *who* or *that* for <u>people</u>
USAGE NOTE: *That* is less formal than *who*.

b. *which* or *that* for <u>places or things</u>
USAGE NOTE: *That* is less formal than *which*.

c. *whose* + **noun** for <u>people's possessions</u>

▶ BE CAREFUL! Do not use both a subject relative pronoun and a subject pronoun (*I, you, he, she, it, we, they*) in the same adjective clause.

- I have a **friend** *who* lives in Mexico.
- I have a **friend** *that* lives in Mexico.

- New York is a **city** *which* never sleeps.
- New York is a **city** *that* never sleeps.

- He's the **man** *whose* **dog** barks all day.

- Scott is someone *who* **loves sports**.
  Not Scott is someone ~~who he loves sports.~~

---

4. Subject relative pronouns have the **same form** whether they refer to singular or plural nouns or to masculine or feminine nouns.

- That's the **man** *who* lives next door.
- That's the **woman** *who* lives next door.
- Those are the **people** *who* live next door.

---

5. The **verb in the adjective clause** is singular if the subject relative pronoun refers to a singular noun. It is plural if it refers to a plural noun.

▶ BE CAREFUL! When *whose* + **noun** is the subject of an adjective clause, the verb agrees in number with the subject of the adjective clause.

- Ben is my **friend** *who* **lives** in Boston.
- Al and Ed are my **friends** *who* **live** in Boston.

- Meg is a person *whose* **friends depend** on her.
  Not Meg is a person ~~whose friends depends~~ on her.

1 **IDENTIFY** • *Read this paragraph about friendship. First circle the relative pronouns and underline the adjective clauses. Then draw an arrow from the relative pronoun to the noun or pronoun it describes.*

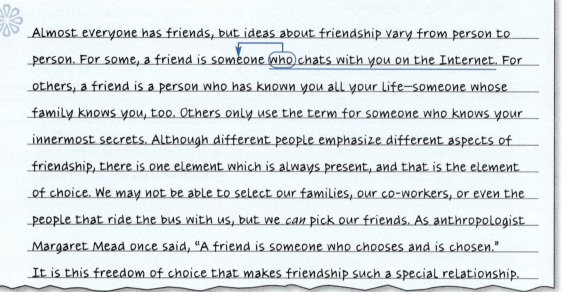

Almost everyone has friends, but ideas about friendship vary from person to person. For some, a friend is someone who chats with you on the Internet. For others, a friend is a person who has known you all your life—someone whose family knows you, too. Others only use the term for someone who knows your innermost secrets. Although different people emphasize different aspects of friendship, there is one element which is always present, and that is the element of choice. We may not be able to select our families, our co-workers, or even the people that ride the bus with us, but we *can* pick our friends. As anthropologist Margaret Mead once said, "A friend is someone who chooses and is chosen." It is this freedom of choice that makes friendship such a special relationship.

2 **COMPLETE** • *A U.S. magazine,* Psychology Today, *conducted a national survey on friendship. Here are some of the results. Complete each sentence with an appropriate relative pronoun and the correct form of the verb in parentheses.*

1. People ___who___ ___have___ moved a lot have fewer friends.
   (have)

2. People _____ _____ lived in the same place have more friends.
   (have)

3. The qualities _____ _____ most important in a friend are loyalty,
   (be)
   warmth, and the ability to keep secrets.

4. Someone _____ _____ a crisis turns to friends before family.
   (face)

5. Betrayal is the cause _____ _____ most often responsible for
   (be)
   ending a friendship.

6. Many people have friends _____ social or religious backgrounds _____
   (be)
   different from theirs.

7. Most people _____ friends _____ members of the opposite sex say
   (include)
   that these relationships are different from relationships with people of the same sex.

8. A survey _____ _____ in a magazine may not represent everyone.
   (appear)

9. Someone _____ _____ the magazine might have other ideas.
   (not read)

3 | **COMBINE • *Read each pair of sentences. Use a relative pronoun to combine them into one sentence.***

1. I have a friend. My friend lives in Mexico City.

   I have a friend who lives in Mexico City.

2. Mexico City is an exciting city. The city attracts a lot of tourists.

3. Marta has a brother. Her brother's name is Manuel.

4. He works for a magazine. The magazine is very popular in Mexico.

5. Manuel writes a column. The column deals with relationships.

6. An article won a prize. The article discussed friendships.

7. A person is lucky. That person has a lot of friends.

 4 | **EDIT • *Read part of a student's essay. Find and correct six mistakes in the use of adjective clauses. The first mistake is already corrected.***

> A writer once said that friends are born, not made. This means that we automatically become friends with people who ~~they~~ are compatible with us. I don't agree with this writer. Last summer, I made friends with some people who's completely different from me.
>
> In July, I went to Mexico City to study Spanish for a month. In our group, there was a teacher which was much older than I am. We became really good friends. In my first week, I had a problem which was getting me down. Mexico City is a city who has a lot of distractions. As a result, I went out all the time, and I stopped going to my classes. Bob helped me get back into my studies. After the trip, I kept writing to Bob. He always writes stories that is interesting and encouraging. Next summer, he's leading another trip what sounds interesting. I hope I can go.

Adjective Clauses with
Object Relative Pronouns
or *When* and *Where*

Minna,

Cracow is wonderful! Here's a picture of the main square with the café **where I spend all my time**. Can you find me with the new friend **that I made yesterday?** He's a writer, with gorgeous green eyes! I'm in love!

Vana

CHECK *POINT*

Circle T (True) or F (False).

T F   Vana is pointing out her favorite café.

ADJECTIVE CLAUSE AFTER THE MAIN CLAUSE

CHART CHECK

Check the correct answer.

The verb in the adjective clause agrees with

☐ the noun in the main clause.

☐ the subject of the adjective clause.

Circle T (True) or F (False).

T F   The adjective clause always follows the main clause.

MAIN CLAUSE	ADJECTIVE CLAUSE		
	OBJECT RELATIVE PRONOUN	SUBJECT	VERB
He reads all the books	*that*	**she**	**writes**.

ADJECTIVE CLAUSE INSIDE THE MAIN CLAUSE

MAIN CLAUSE	ADJECTIVE CLAUSE			MAIN CLAUSE (CONT.)
	OBJECT RELATIVE PRONOUN	SUBJECT	VERB	
The book	*that*	**they**	**borrowed**	seems very interesting.

EXPRESS **CHECK**

Unscramble these words to form a sentence.

I • the • movies • all • he • directs • see • that

_____

Grammar Explanations

Examples

1. A **relative pronoun** can be the **object** of an adjective clause. Notice that:

obj.
Eva is a writer. + *I saw **her** on TV.* =

obj.
■ Eva, ***who(m)** I saw on TV*, is a writer.

a. The **object relative pronoun** comes at the beginning of the adjective clause.

b. Object relative pronouns have the **same form** whether they refer to singular or plural nouns or to masculine or feminine nouns.

■ That's the **man *who(m)*** I met.
■ That's the **woman *who(m)*** I met.
■ Those are the **people *who(m)*** I met.

subj. verb
c. The **verb in the adjective clause** <u>agrees with the subject</u> of the adjective clause.

■ I like the columns *which* **he writes**.
■ I like the column *which* **they write**.

▶ **Be careful!** Do not use both an object relative pronoun and an object pronoun (*me, you, him, her, it, us, them*) in the same adjective clause.

■ She is the writer *who* **I saw on TV**.
Not She is the writer ~~who I saw her on TV.~~

Note: Object relative pronouns are often <u>left out</u>.

■ She is the writer **I saw on TV**.

2. Object relative pronouns are:

a. *whom*, *who*, or *that* for <u>people</u>
Usage Note: *Whom* is very formal. *That* is less formal than *who*. <u>Leaving out the pronoun</u> is the least formal.

■ She's the writer *whom* **I met**.
■ She's the writer *who* **I met**.
■ She's the writer *that* **I met**.
■ She's the writer **I met**.

FORMAL

INFORMAL
FORMAL

b. *which* or *that* for <u>things</u>
Usage Note: *That* is less formal than *which*.

■ I read the book *which* **she wrote**.
■ I read the book *that* **she wrote**.
■ I read the book **she wrote**.

INFORMAL

c. *whose* + noun for <u>people's possessions</u>

■ That's the author *whose* **book I read**.

3. A relative pronoun can be the **object of a preposition**.

Usage Note: In **informal** speaking and writing, we put the <u>preposition at the end</u> of the clause, and we often leave out the relative pronoun. In **formal** English, we put the <u>preposition at the beginning</u> of the clause. In this case, we use only *whom* and *which* (not *who* or *that*).

He's the writer. + *I work **for him**.* =
■ He's the writer *that* **I work *for***.
■ He's the writer **I work *for***.

■ He's the writer ***for whom*** I work.
■ That's the book ***about which*** I told you.

4. *Where* and *when* can also be used to introduce adjective clauses:

a. *Where* refers to a <u>place</u>.

That's the library. + *She works **there**.* =
■ That's the library ***where* she works**.

b. *When* or *that* refers to a <u>time</u>.

I remember the day. + *I met him **then**.* =
■ I remember the day ***when* I met him**.
■ I remember the day ***that* I met him**.

1 **IDENTIFY** • *Read this part of a book review. Underline all the adjective clauses with object relative pronouns. Circle the object relative pronouns, **when**, or **where**. Then draw a line from the circled word to the noun it refers to.*

Section 4   **BOOKS**

Lost in Translation: A Life in a New Language

At the age of nine, Eva Hoffman left Poland with her family. She was old enough to know what she was losing: Cracow, a city that she loved as one loves a person, the sun-baked villages where they had taken summer vacations, and the conversations and escapades with her friends. Disconnected from a city where life was lived intensely, her father would become overwhelmed by the transition to Canada. Eva would lose the parent whom she had watched in lively conversation with friends in Cracow cafés.

Eva Hoffman

And nothing could replace her friendship with the boy whose home she visited daily and whom she assumed she would someday marry. Worst of all, however, she would miss her language. For years, she would feel no connection to the English name of anything that she felt was important. *Lost in Translation: A Life in a New Language* (New York: Penguin, 1989) tells how Eva came to terms with her new identity and language. It's a story that readers will find fascinating and moving.

---

2 **COMPLETE** • *A school newspaper, the* Grover Bugle *(GB), interviewed a student, Maniya Suarez (MS). Complete the interview with relative pronouns, **when**, or **where**, and the correct form of the verbs in parentheses.*

📢 ## The Grover Bugle   VOLUME IX, ISSUE 20

GB: Maniya Suarez is a student _____who_____ many of you already
　　　　　　　　　　　　　　　　　　　　　1.

_____know_____. Maniya, why did your family settle in Atlanta?
　　2. (know)

MS: The cousin _____ we _____ with at first
　　　　　　　　　　3.　　　　　　**4. (stay)**

　　lives here. That's the reason we chose Atlanta.

Maniya Suarez

GB: What was the most difficult thing about going to school in the U.S.?

MS: The class in _____ I _____ the biggest problems at first
　　　　　　　　　5.　　　**6. (have)**

　　was English. It was hard to say the things _____ I _____ to.
　　　　　　　　　　　　　　　　　　　　　　　7.　　　**8. (want)**

GB: What is the biggest change _____ you _____ so far?
　　　　　　　　　　　　　　　　　9.　　　**10. (experience)**

MS: We used to live in a house _____ there _____ always
　　　　　　　　　　　　　　　11.　　　　**12. (be)**

　　a lot of people. Here I live with my parents and two younger sisters _____
　　　　　　　　　　　　　　　　　　　　　　　　　　　　　　13.

　　I _____ after school. I get a little lonely sometimes.
　　14. (take care of)

Grammar Explanations	**Examples**

1. Adjective clauses can be **identifying** or **non-identifying**.

  a. Use an **identifying adjective clause** to <u>identify which member of a group</u> the sentence talks about.

■ I have three phones. The phone **which is in the kitchen** is broken.
  (The adjective clause is necessary to identify which phone is meant.)

  b. Use a **non-identifying adjective clause** to <u>give additional information</u> about the noun it refers to. The information is not necessary to identify the noun.

■ I have only one phone. The phone, **which is in the kitchen,** is broken.
  (The adjective clause gives additional information, but it isn't needed to identify the phone.)

  ▶ **BE CAREFUL!** Do not use *that* to introduce a non-identifying adjective clause. Use *who* for <u>people</u> and *which* for <u>places and things</u>.

■ **Marie**, *who* introduced us at the party, called me last night.
  NOT Marie, ~~that introduced us at the party~~, . . .

2. In <u>writing</u>, a **non-identifying adjective clause** is separated from the rest of the sentence by **commas**.

In <u>speaking</u>, a non-identifying adjective clause is separated from the rest of the sentence by brief **pauses**.

Without commas or pauses, the clause is an **identifying adjective clause**, and the sentence has a very <u>different meaning</u>.

■ The switch, **which is on the back,** is off.
  (The machine has only one switch. It's on the back.)

■ The switch *(pause)* **which is on the back** *(pause)* is off.
  (The machine has only one switch. It's on the back.)

■ The switch **which is on the back** is off.
  (The machine has more than one switch. This one is off.)

3. You **can leave out**:

  a. **object relative pronouns** in <u>identifying adjective clauses</u>

■ That's the computer *that I bought*.
■ That's the computer **I bought**.

  b. *when*

■ I remember the day *when I met him*.
■ I remember the day **I met him**.

  USAGE NOTE: The most common spoken form is the one with no relative pronoun.

4. You **cannot leave out**:

  a. **relative pronouns** in a <u>non-identifying adjective clause</u>

■ She remembers Marc, *who she visited often*.
  NOT She remembers Marc, ~~she visited often~~.

  b. *whose*

■ That's the author *whose book I read*.
  NOT That's the author ~~book I read~~.

  c. *where*

■ That's the library *where I work*.
  NOT That's the library ~~I work~~.

1 **TRUE OR FALSE** • *Read each numbered sentence. Write T (True) or F (False) for the statement that follows.*

1. Use the computer which is in the living room.

____F____ There is only one computer.

2. Press the red button, which is on the right.

_____ There is probably only one red button.

3. My sister who fixes computers lives in Texas.

_____ I have more than one sister.

4. My stereo, which worked yesterday, doesn't work today.

_____ It's likely that I have another stereo I can use.

5. A cell phone which remembers numbers is very convenient.

_____ All cell phones can remember numbers.

6. My roommate, who is afraid of computers, has never been on the Internet.

_____ I probably have more than one roommate.

2 **ADD & CROSS OUT** • *Read this article about technophobia. Add commas where necessary. Cross out the relative pronouns that can be left out.*

,tech · no ·'pho · bia   *(noun)* a fear ~~that~~ some people have about using technology

If you have it, you're one of the 85 percent of people that this new "disease" has struck. Maybe you bought a phone on which you can program 25 numbers—then couldn't turn it on. Or perhaps you have just read that your new CD player, which you have finally learned how to use, will soon be replaced by DVD which you have never even heard of.

Some experts say that things have just gotten too complex. William Staples who authored a book on the electronic age tried to help a friend who had just bought a new stereo. The stereo which worked before wasn't working anymore. "On the front of the stereo receiver it literally had a couple of dozen buttons," says Staples. Donald Norman who has written about the effects of technology on people blames the designers of these devices, not the people who use them. "The best way to cure technophobia is to cure the reasons that cause it—that is, to design things that people can use and design things that won't break," claims Norman. Michael Dyrenfurth who teaches at the University of Missouri–Columbia believes we cause our own problems by buying technology that we just don't need. "Do we really need an electric toothbrush?" he asks. According to Dyrenfurth, important technology that we can't afford to run away from actually exists. To prosper, we have to overcome our technophobia and learn to use it.

3 **COMBINE •** *Read these pairs of sentences. Combine them by changing the second sentence into an adjective clause. Use a relative pronoun only when necessary. Use commas for non-identifying adjective clauses.*

1. I bought a cell phone. I can use it to send and receive e-mail.

   I bought a cell phone I can use to send and receive e-mail.

2. My new cell phone has become a necessary part of life. I only bought it a month ago.

   _____

3. I remember the day. I was afraid to use my new computer then.

   _____

4. Now, there are psychologists. They help technophobes use technology.

   _____

5. Dr. Michelle Weil wrote a book about "technostress." She is a psychologist.

   _____

6. I work in an office. In my office, the software changes frequently.

   _____

7. A lot of people suffer from technostress. Those people work in my office.

   _____

8. Some people dream of a job. They can do the job without technology.

   _____

 4 **EDIT •** *Read this student's book report. Find and correct six mistakes in the use of identifying and non-identifying adjective clauses. The first mistake is already corrected.*

I just read a book called *Technostress,* which was written by Dr. Michelle Weil.
Her co-author was Dr. Larry Rosen, that is her husband and also a psychologist.
According to the authors, everybody feels stress about technology. Our cell phones
and beepers, that we buy for emergencies, soon invade our privacy. Just because
they can, people contact us at places, where we are relaxing. Another problem is
having to learn too much too fast. Technological changes, used to come one at a
time, now overwhelm us. Dr. Weil suggests dealing with technostress using tips from
her latest book which can be purchased from her web site.

SelfTest

Circle the letter of the correct answer to complete each sentence. Choose Ø when no word is needed.

> **EXAMPLE:**
> Jennifer never _____ coffee.   A **(B)** C D
> (A) drink   (C) is drinking
> (B) drinks   (D) was drinking

1. That's my friend _____ lives in Rio.   A B C D
   (A) which   (C) whom
   (B) who   (D) where

2. The plants which _____ in the living room need a lot of water.   A B C D
   (A) are   (C) is
   (B) be   (D) am

3. She's the woman _____ sister babysits for us.   A B C D
   (A) who   (C) that's
   (B) which   (D) whose

4. That's the doctor for _____ Cliff works.   A B C D
   (A) that   (C) whom
   (B) which   (D) whose

5. Marie, _____ I met at the party, called me last night.   A B C D
   (A) that   (C) which
   (B) who   (D) whose

6. I remember Al, _____ rode the bus to school with.   A B C D
   (A) I   (C) which I
   (B) who I   (D) who

7. I used to enjoy the summer, _____ we had a big family picnic.   A B C D
   (A) where   (C) which
   (B) when   (D) that

8. Take in the roll of film _____ Uncle Pete took at the reunion.   A B C D
   (A) what   (C) Ø
   (B) with which   (D) whom

9. Please pay all the bills _____ are due this week.   A B C D
   (A) Ø   (C) when
   (B) that   (D) they

10. Let's try to agree on a time _____ we can all get together.   A B C D
    (A) which   (C) Ø
    (B) where   (D) at

11. Tell me about the city _____ you grew up.   **A B C D**
    (A) that   (C) which
    (B) where   (D) Ø

12. Annie found the souvenirs that _____ wanted at the gift shop.   **A B C D**
    (A) Ø   (C) she
    (B) where   (D) which

SECTION TWO

Each sentence has four underlined words or phrases. The four underlined parts of the sentence are marked A, B, C, and D. Circle the letter of the one underlined word or phrase that is NOT CORRECT.

> **EXAMPLE:**
> Mike <u>usually</u> <u>drives</u> to school, but <u>today</u> he <u>walks</u>.   **A B C Ⓓ**
>   A   B   C   D

13. After a week, <u>we</u> finally got to <u>Miami</u>, <u>that</u> my aunt <u>lives</u>.   **A B C D**
                    A   B   C   D

14. My favorite uncle, <u>which</u> <u>lives</u> in Texas<u>,</u> <u>arrived</u> last night.   **A B C D**
                        A   B   C D

15. Paulo is <u>someone</u> <u>who</u> <u>he</u> really <u>loves</u> soccer.   **A B C D**
               A   B C   D

16. One <u>singer</u> <u>who's</u> voice <u>I</u> like a lot <u>is</u> Madonna.   **A B C D**
          A   B   C   D

17. The <u>stories</u> <u>what</u> <u>I've told</u> you <u>are</u> all true.   **A B C D**
        A   B   C   D

18. I <u>enjoyed</u> reading the article <u>that</u> you <u>told</u> me about <u>it</u>.   **A B C D**
     A   B   C   D

19. She's read some <u>books</u> <u>that</u> <u>discusses</u> the time <u>when</u> this area   **A B C D**
                        A   B   C   D
was undeveloped.

20. <u>San Francisco</u>, <u>that</u> <u>is</u> a beautiful city, <u>has</u> a population of six million.   **A B C D**
     A   B C   D

21. Do you know <u>whom</u> <u>wrote</u> the song <u>that</u> Al <u>was</u> singing last night?   **A B C D**
                    A   B   C   D

22. My aunt's new <u>house</u> <u>is</u> next to a beautiful canal <u>in where</u> we <u>go</u>   **A B C D**
                      A B   C   D
swimming every day.

23. Van<u>,</u> <u>who with</u> I <u>went</u> to school, <u>has become</u> a famous writer.   **A B C D**
        A   B   C   D

24. Do you remember <u>the</u> <u>night</u> <u>which</u> we ate at the restaurant <u>that</u>   **A B C D**
                       A B   C   D
Bill owned?

25. Our neighbors, <u>who their</u> daughter <u>babysits</u> for us<u>,</u> <u>have</u> moved.   **A B C D**
               A   B   C D

Direct and Indirect Speech: Imperatives

Dara! What are you doing?!

*I've been having trouble sleeping. The doctor told me **not to eat a heavy meal before bed**, so I'm having it now.*

CHECK POINT

*Check the doctor's **exact** words.*

☐ "Eat a heavy meal before bed."

☐ "Don't eat a heavy meal before bed."

☐ "Not to eat a heavy meal before bed."

CHART CHECK

Check the correct answer.

Which type of speech uses quotation marks?

☐ direct speech

☐ indirect speech

Circle T (True) or F (False).

T F Indirect imperatives always use the infinitive form of the verb (**to** + base form).

DIRECT SPEECH		
SUBJECT	**REPORTING VERB**	**DIRECT SPEECH**
He	said,	**"Drink** milk." **"Don't drink** coffee."

INDIRECT SPEECH			
SUBJECT	**REPORTING VERB**	**NOUN/ PRONOUN**	**INDIRECT SPEECH**
He	told	her	**to drink** milk.
	said		**not to drink** coffee.

EXPRESS CHECK

Circle the correct words to complete these sentences.

• The doctor told me <u>go / to go</u> to bed at the same time every night.

• She told me, "<u>Don't work / Not to work</u> in bed."

Grammar Explanations	**Examples**

1. Direct speech states <u>the exact words</u> a speaker used. In writing, use <u>quotation marks</u>.

- **"Come early and bring your insurance card,"** said the doctor.

Indirect speech reports what a speaker said <u>without using the exact words</u>. There are <u>no quotation marks</u>.

- The doctor told her **to come early and bring her insurance card**.

---

2. The **reporting verb** (such as **say** or **tell**) is usually in the <u>simple past tense</u> for both direct and indirect speech.

DIRECT SPEECH
- "Drink warm milk," he **said**.

INDIRECT SPEECH
- He **told** her to drink warm milk.

▶ **BE CAREFUL!** Use **say** when the <u>listener is not mentioned</u>. Do not use **tell**.

- He **said** to call him in the morning.
  NOT He ~~told to call him~~ in the morning.

---

3. Direct speech imperatives use the base form of the verb. **Indirect speech imperatives** use the **infinitive** to report:

	DIRECT SPEECH	INDIRECT SPEECH
a. instructions	"**Come** early," he said.	He said **to come** early.
b. commands	"**Wait**."	He told me **to wait**.
c. requests	"Could you please **arrive** by 8:00?"	She asked him **to arrive** by 8:00.
d. invitations	"Could you **join** us for lunch?"	She invited me **to join** them for lunch.

---

4. Use a **negative infinitive** (**not** + infinitive) to report negative imperatives.

DIRECT SPEECH	INDIRECT SPEECH
"**Don't go**."	He told her **not to go**.

---

5. In **indirect speech**, make <u>changes to keep the speaker's original meaning</u>.

a. Change **pronouns** and **possessives**.

- He said to Ann, "Tell **me your** problem."
- He told Ann to tell **him her** problem.

b. Change **time phrases**.

- "Call me **tomorrow**."
- She said to call her **the next day**.

c. Change **this** and **here**.

- "Sign **this** form **here**."
- She told him to sign **that** form **there**.

Check it out!

For punctuation rules for direct speech, see Appendix 25 on page 347.

For a list of common reporting verbs, see Appendix 13 on page 340.

For a list of common time word changes in indirect speech, see Appendix 14 on page 340.

IDENTIFY • Read this article about sleep disorders. Circle all the reporting verbs. Underline once all the direct imperatives. Underline twice all the indirect imperatives.

Tossing and Turning
BY CONNIE SUNG

Can't sleep? You're not alone. Millions of people are up tossing and turning instead of getting their zzzz's. Dr. Ray Thorpe, Director of the Sleep Disorders Clinic, says, "Don't think that loss of sleep is just a minor inconvenience." During an interview he told me to think about what can happen if people drive when they're tired. Every year up to 200,000 car accidents are caused by drowsy drivers. Then he asked me to think about a recent industrial disaster. Chances are that it was caused at least in part by sleep deprivation.

Being an insomniac myself, I asked Dr. Thorpe for some suggestions. He told me to stop drinking coffee. He said to have a warm glass of milk instead. "A lot of old-fashioned remedies work. Have a high-carbohydrate snack like a banana before you go to bed," he said. But he advises patients not to eat a heavy meal before turning in for the night. What about exercise? "Regular exercise helps, but don't exercise too close to bedtime," he suggested. Finally, he told me not to despair. "Don't worry about not sleeping. It's the worst thing to do," he said. I don't know. After thinking about those industrial accidents, I doubt I'll be able to sleep at all!

CHOOSE • Connie Sung visited Dr. Thorpe's sleep clinic. Complete her notes with the correct words in parentheses.

Last week I visited the sleep clinic. Dr. Thorpe called and asked me _____to arrive_____
                                                    1. (arrive / to arrive)

at 8:30 _____. He _____ me to bring _____
      2. (tonight / that night)   **3.** (said / told)   **4.** (my / your)

nightshirt and toothbrush. I arrived on schedule. The technician, Juan Estrada,

invited me _____ TV in the lounge. He _____ to relax
        5. (watch / to watch)   **6.** (said / told)

_____ while they got my room ready. An hour later, Juan came back and
7. (here / there)

got me ready to sleep. He attached electrodes to my body and hooked me up to a

machine. "Could you please _____?" I asked. The machine records brain
            8. (explain / to explain)

activity. Juan instructed me _____ leave the bed until _____
          9. (don't / not to)   **10.** (tomorrow / the next)

morning. To my surprise, I fell asleep right away. In the morning, Dr. Thorpe told me

that except for some leg movements during the night, I have healthy sleep patterns. He

advised me _____ some more exercise.
      11. (get / to get)

3

REWRITE • *Read the advice that TV news commentator John Stossel gave viewers about the common and very dangerous problem of feeling sleepy when driving. Rewrite his advice in indirect speech.*

1. "Pull over and take a brief nap." He told them to pull over and take a brief nap.

2. "Don't take a long nap." He said not to take a long nap.

3. "Sing to yourselves." _____

4. "Turn your radio to an annoying station." _____

5. "Don't drink coffee." _____

6. "Open your window." _____

7. "Let cold air in." _____

8. "Be careful when you stop your car." _____

9. "Don't stop on a deserted roadside." _____

10. "Don't drink and drive." _____

 4

EDIT • *Read this student's journal entry. Find and correct fourteen mistakes in the use of indirect imperatives. The first mistake is already corrected. Remember to check punctuation!*

> In writing class today, Juan read one of his stories. It was wonderful. After class,
> the teacher invited me ^to read a story in class next week. However, I asked her no to call on
> me next week because I'm having trouble getting ideas. She said me not to worry, and
> she said to wait for two weeks. Then I talked to Juan, and I asked him tell me the source
> for your ideas. He said that they came from his dreams, and he told me keep a dream
> journal for ideas. He invited me "to read some of his journal." It was very interesting, so
> I asked him to give me some tips on remembering dreams. He said getting a good
> night's sleep because the longer dreams come after a long period of sleep. He also tell
> me to keep my journal by the bed and to write as soon as I wake up. He said to no move
> from the sleeping position. He also told me to don't think about the day at first. (If you
> think about your day, you might forget your dreams.) Most important—every night he
> tells himself that to remember his dreams tomorrow morning.

Indirect Speech:
Statements (1)

*It **looks** great on you!*

*He said it **looked** great on me. I'll take them all!*

CHECK POINT

Check the man's exact words.

☐ "It looks great on you!"   ☐ "It looked great on me!"

CHART CHECK

Check the correct answers.

What can change when you go from a direct to an indirect statement?

☐ the punctuation

☐ the word order in the statement

☐ the verb tense in the statement

☐ pronouns in the statement

DIRECT SPEECH		
SUBJECT	**REPORTING VERB**	**DIRECT STATEMENT**
She	said,	"I **like** the dress." "I **bought** it on sale." "I**'ve worn** it twice."

INDIRECT SPEECH				
SUBJECT	**REPORTING VERB**	**NOUN/ PRONOUN**		**INDIRECT STATEMENT**
She	told	Jim me	*(that)*	she **liked** the dress. she **had bought** it on sale.
	said			she **had worn** it twice.

EXPRESS CHECK

Circle the correct words to complete this sentence.

She <u>said / told</u> the salesperson that she <u>is / was</u> going to buy the dress.

Grammar Explanations

Examples

1. An **indirect speech statement** reports what a speaker said <u>without using the exact words</u>. The word **_that_** can introduce the indirect statement.

DIRECT SPEECH
■ **"It's a great dress,"** he said.
INDIRECT SPEECH
■ He told her **_that_ it was a great dress**.
■ He told her **it was a great dress**.

▶ **BE CAREFUL!** Use **_say_** as the reporting verb when the <u>listener is not mentioned</u>. Do not use **_tell_**.

■ He **said** that it was a great dress.
NOT He ~~told that~~ it was a great dress.

2. When the **reporting verb** is in the **simple past tense**, the <u>verb in the indirect speech statement is often in a different tense</u> from the verb in the direct speech statement.

DIRECT SPEECH		INDIRECT SPEECH
Simple present	→	**Simple past**
Present progressive	→	**Past progressive**
Simple past	→	**Past perfect**
Present perfect	→	**Past perfect**

DIRECT SPEECH	INDIRECT SPEECH
He said, "It**'s** great."	He said it **_was_** great.
"I**'m leaving**."	She said she **_was leaving_**.
"I **made** it."	He said that he **_had made_** it.
He said to her, "I**'ve** never **lied**."	He told her that he **_had_** never **_lied_**.

3. In indirect speech the **verb tense change** is **optional** when reporting:

   a. something someone has **just said**

A: What did you just say?
B: I said I**'m** tired. OR I said I **was** tired.

   b. something that is **still true**

■ Rick said the bank **_wants_** a check.
■ Rick said the bank **_wanted_** a check.

   c. a **general truth** or **scientific law**

■ She said that everyone **_lies_** sometime.
■ She said that everyone **_lied_** sometime.

4. When the **reporting verb** is in the **present tense**, <u>do not change the verb tense</u> in indirect speech.

■ "I **run** a mile every day."

■ She **says** that she **runs** a mile every day.

5. **REMEMBER!** <u>Change</u> pronouns, time expressions, **_this_**, and **_here_** in indirect speech to <u>keep the speaker's original meaning</u>.

■ Ann told Rick, "**I** bought **this** dress **here**."
■ Ann told Rick that **_she_** had bought **_that_** dress **_there_**.

Check it out!

For a list of common reporting verbs, see Appendix 13 on page 340.

For a list of common time word changes in indirect speech, see Appendix 14 on page 340.

1   *IDENTIFY • Read this article about lying. Circle all the reporting verbs. Underline once all the direct statements. Underline twice all the indirect statements.*

THE TRUTH ABOUT LYING ——

BY JENNIFER MORALES

At 9:00 Rick Spivak's bank phoned and (said) that his credit card payment was late. "The check is in the mail," Rick (replied) quickly. At 11:45 Rick left for a 12:00 meeting across town. Arriving late, Rick told his client that traffic had been bad. That evening, Rick's fiancée wore a new dress. Rick hated it. "It looks just great on you," he said.

Three lies in one day! Yet Rick is just an ordinary guy. Each time, he told himself that sometimes the truth causes too many problems. He told himself that his fiancée was feeling good about her purchase. Why should he hurt her feelings?

Is telling lies a new trend? The majority of people in a recent survey said that people were more honest ten years ago. Nevertheless, lying wasn't really born yesterday. In the eighteenth century, the French philosopher Vauvenargues told the truth about lying when he wrote, "All men are born truthful and die liars."

2   *COMPLETE • Read this magazine article. Complete it with the correct words in parentheses.*

"Lying during a job interview is risky business," _____**said**_____ Marta Toledo,
                                                    1. (said / told)

director of a management consulting firm. "The truth always _____ a funny
                                                               2. (has / had)

way of coming out." Toledo tells the story of one woman applying for a job as an office

manager. The woman _____ the interviewer _____ she
                    3. (said / told)   **4.** (that / what)

_____ a B.A. degree. Actually, she was eight credits short. She also said
5. (has / had)

_____ _____ $30,000 at her last job. The truth was $5,000
6. (I / she)   **7.** (made / had made)

less. When the interviewer called to check the information, the applicant's former boss

told her that the applicant _____. Another applicant, Gloria, reported that
                            8. (has lied / had lied)

she _____ her current job to advance her career. She got the new job.
    9. (is quitting / was quitting)

All went well until the company hired Pete, who had worked at Gloria's old company.

Pete eventually told his boss that his old company _____ Gloria.
                                                    10. (fired / had fired)

The new company fired her too, proving, once again, that it doesn't pay to lie.

3

REPORT • *Lisa and Ben are talking about Ben's job search. Use the verbs in parentheses to report their conversation. Make necessary changes in verbs and pronouns.*

1. **BEN:** I'm still looking for a job.

(tell) ___He told her he was still looking for a job.___

2. **LISA:** I just heard about a job at a scientific research company.

(say) _____

3. **BEN:** I majored in science at Florida State.

(say) _____

4. **LISA:** They want someone with some experience as a programmer.

(tell) _____

5. **BEN:** I work as a programmer for Data Systems.

(tell) _____

6. **LISA:** They don't want a recent college graduate.

(say) _____

7. **BEN:** I got my degree four years ago.

(tell) _____

8. **LISA:** It sounds like the right job for you.

(say) _____

 4

EDIT • *Read this student's essay. Find and correct ten mistakes in the use of indirect statements. The first mistake is already corrected.*

Once when I was a teenager, I went to my Aunt Leah's house. Aunt Leah collected

      told
pottery, and when I got there, she ~~said~~ me that she wants to show me her new bowl.

She told she has just bought it. It was beautiful. When Aunt Leah went to answer the

door, I picked up the bowl. It slipped from my hands and smashed to pieces on the floor.

When Aunt Leah came back, I screamed and said what the cat had just broken your

new bowl. Aunt Leah got this funny look on her face and told me that it isn't important.

I didn't sleep at all that night, and the next morning, I called my aunt and confessed

that I have broken her bowl. She said I had known that all along. I promised that

I am going to buy her a new one someday. We still laugh about the story today.

Indirect Speech:
Statements (2)

They said **it would be windy**, but this is ridiculous!

Check the weather forecaster's exact words.

☐ "It would be windy."

☐ "It will be windy."

CHART CHECK

Check the modals that <u>do not change</u> when you go from direct to indirect speech.

☐ will

☐ ought to

☐ might

☐ must

☐ may

☐ should have

	DIRECT SPEECH	
SUBJECT	**REPORTING VERB**	**DIRECT STATEMENT**
He	said,	"I'**ll leave** now." "I'**m going to drive**." "Traffic **may be** bad." "She **might move**." "He **can help**." "They **have to stay**." "You **must be** careful." "They **ought to buy** batteries." "We **should have left** sooner."

	INDIRECT SPEECH		
SUBJECT	**REPORTING VERB**	**NOUN/ PRONOUN**	**INDIRECT STATEMENT**
He	told	Jim me them	*(that)* he **would leave** then. he **was going to drive**. traffic **might be** bad. she **might move**. he **could help**. they **had to stay**. I/we **had to be** careful. they **ought to buy** batteries.
	said		they **should have left** sooner.

EXPRESS CHECK

Read Jim's words. Check the sentence that correctly reports what he said.

JIM: "I may move soon."

❏ Jim said that I may move soon.   ❏ Jim said that he might move soon.

Grammar Explanations

Examples

---

1. As you learned in Unit 73, when the **reporting verb** is in the **simple past tense**, in the indirect speech statement the <u>verb tense often changes</u>.

Modals often change in indirect speech too.

DIRECT SPEECH		INDIRECT SPEECH
will	→	**would**
can	→	**could**
may	→	**might**
must	→	**had to**

DIRECT SPEECH	INDIRECT SPEECH
She said, "It'**s** windy."	She said it **was** windy.

DIRECT SPEECH	INDIRECT SPEECH
I said, "The winds **will be** strong."	I said the winds **would be** strong.
They told us, "You **can stay** with us."	They told us we **could stay** with them.
He said, "The storm **may last** all night."	He said that the storm **might last** all night.
She told us, "You **must leave**."	She told us we **had to leave**.

---

2. Some verbs do not change in indirect speech.

   a. Do not change *should*, *could*, *might*, and *ought to* in indirect speech.

   b. Do not change the **past perfect** in indirect speech.

   c. Do not change verbs in **present and past unreal conditional** sentences in indirect speech.

   d. Do not change **past modals** in indirect speech.

DIRECT SPEECH	INDIRECT SPEECH
"You **should listen** to the weather report," he told us.	He told us that we **should listen** to the weather report.
"I **had** just **moved** here a week before," she said.	She said she **had** just **moved** there a week before.
"If I **knew**, I **would tell** you."	Jim said if he **knew**, he **would tell** me.
"If I **had known**, I **would have told** you," said Jim.	He said if he **had known**, he **would have told** me.
"I **should have left**."	He said that he **should have left**.

---

3. REMEMBER! <u>Change</u> pronouns, time phrases, *here*, and *this* in indirect speech to <u>keep the speaker's original meaning</u>.

- "I just got **here yesterday**."
- Sam told me **he** had just gotten **there the day before**.

CHOOSE • *Read what someone reported about the weather forecast. Then check the sentence that shows the weather forecaster's exact words.*

1. She said it was going to be a terrible storm.
   - ☐ "It was a terrible storm."
   - ☑ "It's going to be a terrible storm."

2. She said the winds might reach 170 miles per hour.
   - ☐ "The winds may reach 170 miles per hour."
   - ☐ "The winds would reach 170 miles per hour."

3. She said there would be more rain the next day.
   - ☐ "There will be more rain the next day."
   - ☐ "There will be more rain tomorrow."

4. She told people that they should try to leave the area.
   - ☐ "You should have tried to leave the area."
   - ☐ "You should try to leave the area."

5. She said that they could expect a lot of damage.
   - ☐ "We can expect a lot of damage."
   - ☐ "We could expect a lot of damage."

"The Weather Watch" on Channel 5

REPORT • *You are in New York. Imagine you heard these rumors about a hurricane in Florida yesterday, and you are reporting them today. Use **They said** to report the rumors.*

1. "The hurricane will change direction tonight."

   They said that the hurricane would change direction last night.

2. "It's going to pass north of here."

   _____

3. "It may become a tropical storm when it lands here."

   _____

4. "They had to close some bridges yesterday because of high tides."

   _____

5. "They won't restore electricity until tomorrow."

   _____

6. "The schools here may be closed for a while."

   _____

7. "We ought to use bottled water for a few days."

   _____

3 **REWRITE •** *Read this interview with a meteorologist. Rewrite his answers as indirect speech. Change verb tenses when possible.*

1. **Q: A hurricane is just a bad storm, right?**
   A: To be a hurricane, a storm has to have winds of at least 74 miles per hour.

   He said that to be a hurricane, a storm had to have winds of at least 74 miles per hour.

2. **Q: We seem to be having more of these big storms.**
   A: It's true, and they will probably become more frequent.

   _____

3. **Q: Why is that?**
   A: The planet may be getting warmer, and that can cause more severe storms.

   _____

4. **Q: What went wrong after the last storm?**
   A: Emergency workers should have arrived much more quickly.

   _____

5. **Q: Is there an upside to all this?**
   A: The new satellites will help. If we didn't have them, we wouldn't be able to warn people.

   _____

4 **EDIT •** *Read Rita's e-mail to her friend Emily. Find and correct twelve mistakes in the use of indirect speech. The first mistake is already corrected.*

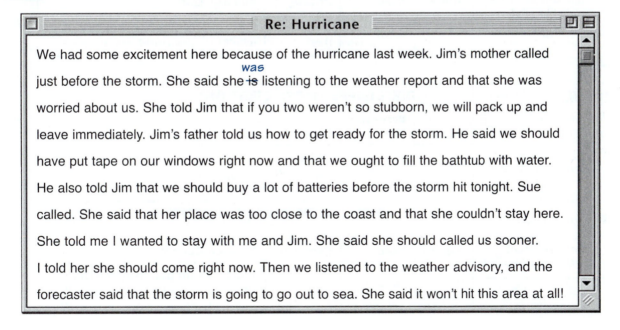

Re: Hurricane

We had some excitement here because of the hurricane last week. Jim's mother called
                                             was
just before the storm. She said she ~~is~~ listening to the weather report and that she was

worried about us. She told Jim that if you two weren't so stubborn, we will pack up and

leave immediately. Jim's father told us how to get ready for the storm. He said we should

have put tape on our windows right now and that we ought to fill the bathtub with water.

He also told Jim that we should buy a lot of batteries before the storm hit tonight. Sue

called. She said that her place was too close to the coast and that she couldn't stay here.

She told me I wanted to stay with me and Jim. She said she should called us sooner.

I told her she should come right now. Then we listened to the weather advisory, and the

forecaster said that the storm is going to go out to sea. She said it won't hit this area at all!

Indirect Questions

The Stress Interview

Perhaps you didn't hear the question. Ms. Bentley asked **why you were still single.**

CHECK *POINT*

Check Ms. Bentley's exact words.

☐ "Why were you still single?"

☐ "Why are you still single?"

CHART CHECK 1

Circle T (True) or F (False).

T F   You can leave out *if* or *whether* in indirect *yes/no* questions.

T F   You do not use *do* to form indirect *yes/no* questions.

DIRECT SPEECH: *YES/NO* QUESTIONS		
SUBJECT	**REPORTING VERB**	**DIRECT QUESTION**
He	asked,	"**Do you have** any experience**?**" "**Can you use** a computer**?**"

INDIRECT SPEECH: *YES/NO* QUESTIONS			
SUBJECT	**REPORTING VERB**	**(NOUN/ PRONOUN)**	**INDIRECT QUESTION**
He	asked	(Melissa) (her)	*if* — **she had** any experience. *whether* — **she could use** a computer.

CHART CHECK 2

Circle T (True) or F (False).

T F   An indirect question always ends in a question mark.

T F   You do not use *do* to form indirect *wh-* questions.

DIRECT SPEECH: *WH-* QUESTIONS		
SUBJECT	**REPORTING VERB**	**DIRECT QUESTION**
He	asked,	"**Who told you** about the job**?**" "**When do you want** to start**?**"

INDIRECT SPEECH: *WH-* QUESTIONS			
SUBJECT	**REPORTING VERB**	**(NOUN/ PRONOUN)**	**INDIRECT QUESTION**
He	asked	(Melissa) (her)	*who* **had told her** about the job. *when* **she wanted** to start.

EXPRESS CHECK

Unscramble these words to complete the indirect question.

why • he • job • his • quit • had

He asked him _____

Grammar Explanations

Examples

---

1. Use *if*, *whether*, or *whether or not* to form **indirect *yes/no* questions**.

USAGE NOTE: *Whether* is more formal than *if*.

DIRECT SPEECH
■ *"Can you type?"* she asked.
INDIRECT SPEECH
■ She asked *if I could type*.
■ She asked *whether (or not) I could type*.

---

2. In **indirect *yes/no* questions**, the subject comes before the verb, the same as in <u>statement word order</u>.

Because of the statement word order, <u>do not use *do*, *does*, or *did*</u> to form indirect questions.

DIRECT SPEECH
■ *"Can I start* tomorrow?"
INDIRECT SPEECH
■ He asked *if he could start* tomorrow.
   NOT He asked ~~could he start~~ tomorrow.

DIRECT SPEECH
■ *"Does the job provide* benefits?"
INDIRECT SPEECH
■ He asked *if the job provided* benefits.
   NOT He asked ~~does the job provide~~ benefits.

---

3. Use **question words** to form **indirect *wh-* questions**.

DIRECT SPEECH
■ *"Where is your office*?" I asked.
INDIRECT SPEECH
■ I asked *where his office was*.

---

4. In **indirect *wh-* questions**, the subject also comes before the verb <u>as in statements</u>, and you <u>do not use *do*, *does*, or *did*</u>.

In **indirect *wh-* questions about the subject**, the <u>question word is the subject</u> and the verb follows as in <u>statement word order</u>.

DIRECT SPEECH
"*Why did you leave* your job?"
INDIRECT SPEECH
■ She asked me *why I had left* my job.
   NOT She asked me ~~why did I leave my job~~.

DIRECT SPEECH
■ Bob asked, "*Who got* the job?"
INDIRECT SPEECH
■ Bob asked *who had gotten* the job.

---

5. **Indirect questions** often end in a **period**, <u>not a question mark</u>.

■ I asked *why I didn't get the job*.
   NOT I asked ~~why didn't I get the job?~~

Check it out! For a list of common verbs used to report questions, see Appendix 13 on page 340.

1 IDENTIFY • *Read this article about stress interviews. Underline all the indirect questions.*

The Stress Interview

A few weeks ago, Melissa Morrow had a stress interview, one which featured tough, tricky questions and negative evaluations. First, the interviewer asked <u>why she couldn't work under pressure</u>. Before she could answer, he asked who had written her application letter for her. Melissa was shocked, but she handled herself very well. She asked the interviewer whether he was going to ask her any serious questions. Then she left.

Companies give stress interviews in order to watch how candidates handle pressure.

Suppose, for example, that there is an accident in a nuclear power plant. The plant's public relations officer must remain calm when reporters ask how the accident could have happened. Be aware, however, that in some countries, like the United States, certain questions are not allowed unless they are directly related to the job. If your interviewer asks how old you are, you can refuse to answer. The interviewer also should not ask whether you are married or how much money you owe. If you think a question is improper, ask how the question relates to the job. If it doesn't, you don't have to answer.

MATCH • *Check the direct questions that match the indirect questions in the article.*

☐ **1.** Can you work under pressure?

☑ **2.** Who wrote your application letter for you?

☐ **3.** Are you going to ask me any serious questions?

☐ **4.** Was there an accident in a nuclear power plant?

☐ **5.** How old are you?

☐ **6.** When were you married?

☐ **7.** Is the question improper?

2 REPORT • *Claire's friend Jaime wants to know all about her interview. Report his questions.*

1. "What kind of job is it?" __He asked what kind of job it was._____

2. "When is the interview?" _____

3. "Where's the company?" _____

4. "Do you need directions?" _____

5. "How long does it take to get there?" _____

6. "Are you going to drive?" _____

7. "Who's going to interview you?" _____

8. "When will they let you know?" _____

3

REWRITE • *These questions were asked at Claire's interview. Decide which ones Claire asked and which ones Pete, the manager, asked. Rewrite each question as indirect speech.*

1. "What type of training is available for the job?"

   Claire asked what type of training was available for the job.
   _____

2. "What kind of experience do you have?"

   Pete asked what kind of experience she had.
   _____

3. "Are you interviewing with other companies?"

   _____

4. "What will my responsibilities be?"

   _____

5. "How is job performance rewarded?"

   _____

6. "What was your starting salary at your last job?"

   _____

7. "Did you get along well with your last employer?"

   _____

8. "Do you hire many women?"

   _____

 4

EDIT • *Read part of a memo an interviewer wrote. Find and correct eight mistakes in the use of indirect questions. The first mistake is already corrected. Check punctuation!*

Inter-Office Memo

I did some stress questioning in my interview with Carl Treng this morning. I asked
                    he couldn't
Mr. Treng why ~~couldn't he~~ work under pressure. I also asked him why did his

supervisor dislike him. Finally, I inquired when he would quit the job with our

company? Mr. Treng answered my questions calmly, and he had some excellent

questions of his own. He asked "if we expected changes on the job." He also wanted

to know how often do we evaluate employees. I was impressed when he asked why

did I decide to join this company. I think we should hire him.

Embedded Questions

CHART CHECK

Circle T (True) or F (False).

T F Embedded questions always end with a period.

T F You can use the infinitive after **whether** or a question word.

MAIN CLAUSE	EMBEDDED QUESTION
I'm not sure	*if I left* the right tip. *whether it was* enough.
Can you remember	*how much it was?* *where we ate?*
I don't know	*whether to tip.*
Do you know	*how much to tip?* *where to leave* the tip?

EXPRESS CHECK

Punctuate these sentences.

A: Do you know how much to tip____

B: About 15%. But I'm not sure where to leave the tip____

Grammar Explanations

Examples

1. In Unit 75 you learned to use **indirect questions** to report another person's words.

Indirect questions are a kind of **embedded question**—one that is <u>included in another sentence</u>. This unit discusses embedded questions <u>that do not report another person's words</u>.

DIRECT QUESTION	INDIRECT QUESTION
Should I tip?	He asked **if he should tip.**

EMBEDDED QUESTION
Do you know **whether I should tip?**

---

2. If the embedded question is **in a statement**, use a <u>period</u> at the end of the sentence. If the embedded question is **in a question**, use a <u>question mark</u> at the end of the sentence.

MAIN SENTENCE = STATEMENT
■ *I don't know* who our server is**.**
MAIN SENTENCE = QUESTION
■ *Do you know* who our server is**?**

---

3. We often **use embedded questions** to

a. <u>express something we do not know</u>.

b. <u>ask politely for information</u>.

USAGE NOTE: With strangers or in a formal situation, an embedded question is considered <u>more polite</u> than a direct question.

■ I wonder **why he didn't tip the mechanic.**

■ Can you tell me **if the tip is included?**

LESS FORMAL
■ Does our bill include a tip?
MORE POLITE
■ Can you tell me **if our bill includes a tip?**

---

4. Introduce **embedded yes/no questions** with *if*, *whether*, or *whether or not*.
USAGE NOTE: *Whether* is more <u>formal</u> than *if*.

Introduce **embedded wh- questions** with a <u>question word</u>.

You can also use the **infinitive** <u>after a question word or *whether*</u>.

▶ **BE CAREFUL!** Do not use the infinitive after *if* or *why*.

■ Do you know *if he tips?*
■ Do you know *whether (or not) he tips?*

■ Many tourists wonder *how much* **they should tip their restaurant server**.

■ Many tourists wonder *how much* **to tip**.
■ Some wonder *whether* **to tip** at all.

■ We wondered *why* **we should leave a tip**.
NOT We wondered ~~why to leave a tip~~.

---

5. **BE CAREFUL!** Use **statement word order** in all embedded questions.

<u>Do not leave out</u> *if* or *whether* in embedded *yes/no* questions.

<u>Do not use</u> *do*, *does*, or *did* in embedded questions.

■ Could you tell me *where* **they are**?
NOT Could you tell me ~~where are they~~?

■ Could you tell me *if it is* 6:00 yet?
NOT Could you tell me ~~is it 6:00 yet~~?

■ I don't know *when* **the pizza came**.
NOT I don't know ~~when did the pizza come~~.

Check it out!

For a list of common phrases introducing embedded questions, see Appendix 15 on page 340.

1 **IDENTIFY** • *Read this online ad for the book* Tips on Tipping. *Underline the embedded questions.*

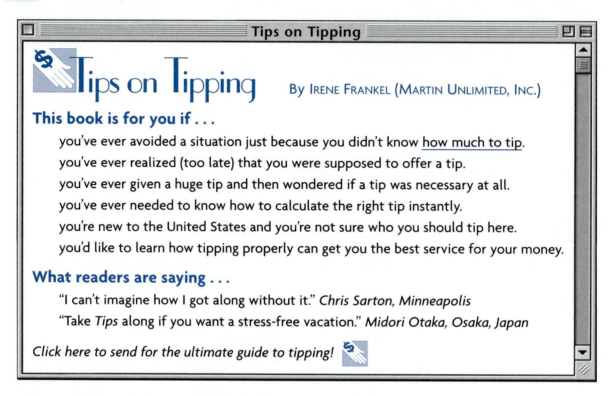

Tips on Tipping

Tips on Tipping

BY IRENE FRANKEL (MARTIN UNLIMITED, INC.)

This book is for you if . . .

you've ever avoided a situation just because you didn't know <u>how much to tip</u>.

you've ever realized (too late) that you were supposed to offer a tip.

you've ever given a huge tip and then wondered if a tip was necessary at all.

you've ever needed to know how to calculate the right tip instantly.

you're new to the United States and you're not sure who you should tip here.

you'd like to learn how tipping properly can get you the best service for your money.

What readers are saying . . .

"I can't imagine how I got along without it." *Chris Sarton, Minneapolis*

"Take *Tips* along if you want a stress-free vacation." *Midori Otaka, Osaka, Japan*

Click here to send for the ultimate guide to tipping!

---

2 **REWRITE** • *Complete these questions about tipping customs. Change the direct questions in parentheses to embedded questions. Use the infinitive whenever possible. Use correct punctuation.*

1. Can you tell me whether ___to tip in Canada?_____
   (Should I tip in Canada?)

2. I'm going to France. Please explain _____
   (How can I tell if the tip is included in the bill?)

3. Can you tell me _____
   (Why did service people in Iceland refuse my tips?)

4. I'm moving to Japan. I'd like to know _____
   (How much should I tip airport porters?)

5. We're visiting Australia. Please tell us _____
   (Who expects a tip and who doesn't?)

6. I'm vacationing in Norway. I'd like to know if _____
   (Should I tip my ski instructor?)

7. I took a job in China. I need to know whether _____
   (Is tipping still illegal there?)

8. In Germany the tip is included. I don't know whether _____
   (Should I tip anyway?)

3   **CHOOSE & REWRITE** • *Two foreign exchange students are visiting Washington, D.C. Complete their conversations. Choose the appropriate questions from the box and change them to embedded questions. Remember to punctuate the sentences correctly.*

How much should we tip the taxi driver?	Where is the Smithsonian Museum?
Could we rent a car and drive?	What did they put in the sauce?
Where can we buy metro tickets?	~~Where is It?~~

1.   **MARTA:** We're going to the Hotel Edison. Do you know ___where it is?___

   DRIVER: Sure. Get in and I'll take you there.

2.   **MIUKI:** *(whispering)* Do you know _____

   MARTA: According to the book, we're supposed to leave 10 to 15 percent. I've got it.

3.   **MARTA:** Excuse me. Can you tell me _____

   OFFICER: Sure. Just turn right at the corner. You'll see it right away.

4.   **MIUKI:** I'd like to take the metro to the zoo, but I don't know _____

   MARTA: Probably right in the station.

5.   **MARTA:** I want to visit Williamsburg. Do you think _____

   MIUKI: Let's find out. That sounds like fun.

6.   **MARTA:** This is delicious. Let's try to find out _____

   MIUKI: It tastes like ginger and garlic to me.

4   **EDIT** • *Read this entry from Marta's journal. Find and correct seven mistakes in the use of embedded questions. The first mistake is already corrected. Remember to check punctuation!*

When you live in a foreign country even a small occasion can be an adventure! Before my date
with Janek tonight, I didn't even know what ~~should I~~ **I should** wear! Jeans? A dress? John's Grill isn't a
fancy restaurant, but it was Janek's birthday and I wanted to make it a big occasion. Miuki was
very helpful, as always. I knew how to get to John's Grill, but I didn't know how long it was going
to take to get there? I left at 6:00, which should have given me plenty of time, but when I got
off the bus, I wasn't sure if to turn left or right. I asked a police officer where was John's, and
I was only a few minutes late. I had planned to take Janek out for a special dessert afterward,
but I couldn't remember how I to find the place Miuki had suggested, and Janek has been here
even less time than me. (Anyway, the desserts at John's turned out to be very good.) Then,
when we got the bill, I was wondering whether to tip or no. I had to ask Janek did he know.
Fortunately, he had read *Tips on Tipping*, so he told me to leave about 15%.

SelfTest  XV

Circle the letter of the correct answer to complete each sentence.

EXAMPLE:
Jennifer never _____ coffee.   **A** Ⓑ **C D**
(A) drink   (C) is drinking
(B) drinks   (D) was drinking

---

1. "You look beautiful in that dress."   **A B C D**
   Last night she told me _____ beautiful in that dress.
   (A) you look   (C) I'll look
   (B) you looked   (D) I looked

2. We'd better find out _____ the train left.   **A B C D**
   (A) if   (C) has
   (B) does   (D) did

3. —Should we turn left or go straight?   **A B C D**
   —Hmm. I'm not sure which way _____.
   (A) do we turn   (C) should we turn
   (B) to turn   (D) it turned

4. "Why don't you join us for coffee, Don?"   **A B C D**
   After the movie, we asked Don _____ us for coffee.
   (A) would he join   (C) to join
   (B) why he didn't join   (D) for joining

5. "We must leave immediately!"   **A B C D**
   When the fire alarm rang, our teacher said _____ leave immediately.
   (A) we had to   (C) not to
   (B) we have to   (D) he must

6. "Today is the happiest day of my life."   **A B C D**
   At the reception last night, the groom said _____ the happiest day
   of his life.
   (A) today was   (C) yesterday was
   (B) that day is   (D) today is

7. I wonder who _____   **A B C D**
   (A) our waiter is?   (C) our waiter is.
   (B) is our waiter.   (D) is our waiter?

8. "Please don't leave your boots in the hall."   **A B C D**
   My mother is always telling me _____ boots in the hall.
   (A) not to leave my   (C) to not leave my
   (B) not to leave your   (D) don't leave my

9. "Hi, Bob. Did you take the job?"　　　　　　　　　　　　**A　B　C　D**
　　Bob's friend asked him _____ the job.
　　(A) did he take　　　　(C) if he had taken
　　(B) did you take　　　　(D) had he taken

10. "Weather patterns change."　　　　　　　　　　　　**A　B　C　D**
　　Experts now say that weather patterns _____.
　　(A) changed　　　　　(C) had changed
　　(B) are changing　　　(D) change

SECTION TWO

Each sentence has four underlined words or phrases. The four underlined parts of the sentence are marked A, B, C, and D. Circle the letter of the one underlined word or phrase that is NOT CORRECT.

> **EXAMPLE:**
> Mike <u>usually</u> <u>drives</u> to school, but <u>today</u> he <u>walks</u>.　　**A　B　C　Ⓓ**
> 　　　A　　　　B　　　　　　　C　　　D

11. The teacher <u>said</u> the class <u>that</u> hot air <u>rises</u> and cold air <u>sinks</u>.　**A　B　C　D**
　　　　　　A　　　　　B　　　　　C　　　　　　　D

12. I <u>asked</u> Sean <u>how</u> <u>to pronounce</u> his name<u>?</u>　　　　**A　B　C　D**
　　　　A　　　　B　　　C　　　　　　D

13. Gerry <u>called</u> last week and <u>said</u> <u>that</u> he needed the report right <u>now</u>.　**A　B　C　D**
　　　　　A　　　　　　　　　B　　C　　　　　　　　　　D

14. Two days ago, the weather forecaster <u>warned</u> <u>us</u> <u>that</u> a tornado <u>is coming</u>.　**A　B　C　D**
　　　　　　　　　　　　　　　A　　B　　C　　　　　　D

15. Sandy <u>called</u> from Miami during the storm and <u>said</u> <u>she</u> was swimming <u>here</u>.　**A　B　C　D**
　　　　　A　　　　　　　　　　　　　　　B　　C　　　　　　D

16. <u>Do you know</u> <u>if</u> or not <u>we</u> <u>need</u> to bring our passports?　**A　B　C　D**
　　A　　　　　B　　　　C　D

17. She didn't know <u>if</u> to tip, so she <u>asked</u> me <u>what</u> <u>to do</u>.　　**A　B　C　D**
　　　　　　　A　　　　　　B　　　　C　　D

18. Ron <u>said</u> <u>that</u> he <u>wasn't</u> sure, but the storm <u>might stop</u> already.　**A　B　C　D**
　　　A　　B　　C　　　　　　　　D

19. <u>I'd like</u> lobster, but the menu <u>doesn't say</u> <u>how much</u> <u>does it cost</u>.　**A　B　C　D**
　　A　　　　　　　　B　　　　C　　　D

20. Lin <u>always</u> says <u>that</u> he <u>ran</u> a mile <u>every day</u> these days.　**A　B　C　D**
　　　　A　　　　B　　　C　　　　D

21. Could you tell me <u>when</u> the next train <u>leaves</u> and where <u>to buy</u> tickets<u>.</u>　**A　B　C　D**
　　　　　　A　　　　　　　B　　　　　　C　　　D

22. "<u>If</u> you can wait a few minutes<u>,</u> I <u>will give</u> you a ride<u>.</u> Rhoda said.　**A　B　C　D**
　　A　　　　　　　　　　B　　C　　　　D

23. Jim <u>wants</u> to know <u>could you</u> call him and <u>tell</u> him where <u>to meet</u> you.　**A　B　C　D**
　　　A　　　　B　　　　　C　　　　　D

24. The dentist <u>said</u> <u>to brush</u> three times a day and <u>don't</u> <u>eat</u> candy.　**A　B　C　D**
　　　　A　　B　　　　　　　　C　　D

25. At the interview they <u>asked</u> me when <u>can you</u> <u>start</u> work<u>.</u>　**A　B　C　D**
　　　　　　　A　　　　B　　C　　D

Appendices

 Irregular Verbs

BASE FORM	SIMPLE PAST	PAST PARTICIPLE
arise	arose	arisen
awake	awoke	awoken
be	was/were	been
beat	beat	beaten
become	became	become
begin	began	begun
bend	bent	bent
bet	bet	bet
bite	bit	bitten
bleed	bled	bled
blow	blew	blown
break	broke	broken
bring	brought	brought
build	built	built
burn	burned/burnt	burned/burnt
burst	burst	burst
buy	bought	bought
catch	caught	caught
choose	chose	chosen
cling	clung	clung
come	came	come
cost	cost	cost
creep	crept	crept
cut	cut	cut
deal	dealt	dealt
dig	dug	dug
dive	dived/dove	dived
do	did	done
draw	drew	drawn
dream	dreamed/dreamt	dreamed/dreamt
drink	drank	drunk
drive	drove	driven
eat	ate	eaten
fall	fell	fallen
feed	fed	fed
feel	felt	felt
fight	fought	fought
find	found	found
fit	fit	fit
flee	fled	fled
fling	flung	flung
fly	flew	flown
forbid	forbade/forbad	forbidden
forget	forgot	forgotten
forgive	forgave	forgiven
freeze	froze	frozen
get	got	gotten/got
give	gave	given
go	went	gone

BASE FORM	SIMPLE PAST	PAST PARTICIPLE
grind	ground	ground
grow	grew	grown
hang	hung	hung
have	had	had
hear	heard	heard
hide	hid	hidden
hit	hit	hit
hold	held	held
hurt	hurt	hurt
keep	kept	kept
kneel	knelt	knelt
knit	knit/knitted	knit/knitted
know	knew	known
lay	laid	laid
lead	led	led
leap	leapt	leapt
leave	left	left
lend	lent	lent
let	let	let
lie (lie down)	lay	lain
light	lit/lighted	lit/lighted
lose	lost	lost
make	made	made
mean	meant	meant
meet	met	met
pay	paid	paid
prove	proved	proved/proven
put	put	put
quit	quit	quit
read /rid/	read /rɛd/	read /rɛd/
ride	rode	ridden
ring	rang	rung
rise	rose	risen
run	ran	run
say	said	said
see	saw	seen
seek	sought	sought
sell	sold	sold
send	sent	sent
set	set	set
sew	sewed	sewn/sewed
shake	shook	shaken
shave	shaved	shaved/shaven
shine	shone	shone
shoot	shot	shot
show	showed	shown
shrink	shrank/shrunk	shrunk/shrunken
shut	shut	shut
sing	sang	sung

BASE FORM	SIMPLE PAST	PAST PARTICIPLE	BASE FORM	SIMPLE PAST	PAST PARTICIPLE
sink	sank	sunk	sweep	swept	swept
sit	sat	sat	swim	swam	swum
sleep	slept	slept	swing	swung	swung
slide	slid	slid	take	took	taken
speak	spoke	spoken	teach	taught	taught
speed	sped	sped	tear	tore	torn
spend	spent	spent	tell	told	told
spill	spilled/spilt	spilled/spilt	think	thought	thought
spin	spun	spun	throw	threw	thrown
spit	spit/spat	spat	understand	understood	understood
split	split	split	upset	upset	upset
spread	spread	spread	wake	woke	woken
spring	sprang	sprung	wear	wore	worn
stand	stood	stood	weave	wove	woven
steal	stole	stolen	weep	wept	wept
stick	stuck	stuck	win	won	won
sting	stung	stung	wind	wound	wound
stink	stank/stunk	stunk	withdraw	withdrew	withdrawn
strike	struck	struck	wring	wrung	wrung
swear	swore	sworn	write	wrote	written

2 Common Non-action (Stative) Verbs

EMOTIONS	MENTAL STATES		WANTS AND PREFERENCES	APPEARANCE AND VALUE	POSSESSION AND RELATIONSHIP
admire	agree	know	hope	appear	belong
adore	assume	mean	need	be	contain
appreciate	believe	mind	prefer	cost	have
care	consider	presume	want	equal	own
detest	disagree	realize	wish	feel	possess
dislike	disbelieve	recognize		look	
doubt	estimate	remember	**PERCEPTION AND THE SENSES**	matter	
envy	expect	see *(understand)*	feel	represent	
fear	feel *(believe)*	suppose	hear	resemble	
hate	find	suspect	notice	seem	
like	guess	think *(believe)*	observe	signify	
love	hesitate	understand	perceive	smell	
regret	imagine	wonder	see	sound	
respect			smell	taste	
trust			taste	weigh	

3 Common Verbs Followed by the Gerund (Base Form of Verb + *-ing*)

acknowledge	consider	endure	give up *(stop)*	miss	quit	resist
admit	delay	enjoy	imagine	postpone	recall	risk
advise	deny	escape	justify	practice	recommend	suggest
appreciate	detest	explain	keep *(continue)*	prevent	regret	support
avoid	discontinue	feel like	mention	prohibit	report	tolerate
can't help	discuss	finish	mind *(object to)*	propose	resent	understand
celebrate	dislike	forgive				

Common Verbs Followed by the Infinitive (*To* + Base Form of Verb)

afford	can('t) afford	expect	hurry	neglect	promise	volunteer
agree	can('t) wait	fail	intend	offer	refuse	wait
appear	choose	grow	learn	pay	request	want
arrange	consent	help	manage	plan	seem	wish
ask	decide	hesitate	mean	prepare	struggle	would like
attempt	deserve	hope	need	pretend	swear	yearn

 ## Verbs Followed by Objects and the Infinitive

advise	challenge	encourage	get	need*	persuade	require	want*
allow	choose*	expect*	help*	order	promise*	teach	warn
ask*	convince	forbid	hire	pay*	remind	tell	wish*
cause	enable	force	invite	permit	request*	urge	would like*

*These verbs can also be followed by the infinitive without an object (example: *ask to leave* or *ask someone to leave*).

 ## Common Verbs Followed by the Gerund or the Infinitive

begin	continue	hate	love	remember*	stop*
can't stand	forget*	like	prefer	start	try

*These verbs can be followed by either the gerund or the infinitive but there is a big difference in meaning.

 ## Common Verb + Preposition Combinations

admit to	believe in	count on	insist on	plan on	talk about
advise against	choose between/	deal with	look forward to	rely on	think about
apologize for	among	dream about/of	object to	resort to	wonder about
approve of	complain about	feel like/about	pay for	succeed in	worry about

 ## Common Adjective + Preposition Combinations

accustomed to	bored with/by	famous for	opposed to	sick of
afraid of	capable of	fed up with	pleased about	slow at
amazed at/by	careful of	fond of	ready for	sorry for/about
angry at	concerned about	glad about	responsible for	surprised at/about/by
ashamed of	content with	good at	sad about	terrible at
aware of	curious about	happy about	safe from	tired of
awful at	different from	interested in	satisfied with	used to
bad at	excited about	nervous about	shocked at/by	worried about

 ## Common Adjectives that Can Be Followed by the Infinitive*

afraid	anxious	depressed	disturbed	encouraged	happy	pleased	reluctant	surprised
alarmed	ashamed	determined	eager	excited	hesitant	proud	sad	touched
amazed	curious	disappointed	easy	fortunate	likely	ready	shocked	upset
angry	delighted	distressed	embarrassed	glad	lucky	relieved	sorry	willing

*Example: *I'm happy to hear that.*

Irregular Comparisons of Adjectives, Adverbs, and Quantifiers

ADJECTIVE	ADVERB	COMPARATIVE	SUPERLATIVE
bad	badly	worse	worst
far	far	farther/further	farthest/furthest
good	well	better	best
little	little	less	least
many/a lot of	—	more	most
much*/a lot of	much*/a lot	more	most

Much is usually only used in questions and negative statements.

 Common Participial Adjectives

-ed	-ing	-ed	-ing	-ed	-ing
alarmed	alarming	disturbed	disturbing	moved	moving
amazed	amazing	embarrassed	embarrassing	paralyzed	paralyzing
amused	amusing	entertained	entertaining	pleased	pleasing
annoyed	annoying	excited	exciting	relaxed	relaxing
astonished	astonishing	exhausted	exhausting	satisfied	satisfying
bored	boring	fascinated	fascinating	shocked	shocking
confused	confusing	frightened	frightening	surprised	surprising
depressed	depressing	horrified	horrifying	terrified	terrifying
disappointed	disappointing	inspired	inspiring	tired	tiring
disgusted	disgusting	interested	interesting	touched	touching
distressed	distressing	irritated	irritating	troubled	troubling

 Some Adjectives that Form the Comparative and Superlative in Two Ways

ADJECTIVE	COMPARATIVE	SUPERLATIVE
common	commoner / more common	commonest / most common
cruel	crueler / more cruel	cruelest / most cruel
deadly	deadlier / more deadly	deadliest / most deadly
friendly	friendlier / more friendly	friendliest / most friendly
handsome	handsomer / more handsome	handsomest / most handsome
happy	happier / more happy	happiest / most happy
likely	likelier / more likely	likeliest / most likely
lively	livelier / more lively	liveliest / most lively
lonely	lonelier / more lonely	loneliest / most lonely
lovely	lovelier / more lovely	loveliest / most lovely
narrow	narrower / more narrow	narrowest / most narrow
pleasant	pleasanter / more pleasant	pleasantest / most pleasant
polite	politer / more polite	politest / most polite
quiet	quieter / more quiet	quietest / most quiet
shallow	shallower / more shallow	shallowest / most shallow
sincere	sincerer / more sincere	sincerest / most sincere
stupid	stupider / more stupid	stupidest / most stupid
true	truer / more true	truest / most true

Common Reporting Verbs

STATEMENTS				INSTRUCTIONS, COMMANDS REQUESTS, AND INVITATIONS		QUESTIONS
acknowledge	claim	indicate	reply	advise	invite	ask
add	complain	maintain	report	ask	order	inquire
admit	conclude	mean	say	caution	say	question
announce	confess	note	state	command	tell	want to know
answer	declare	observe	suggest	demand	urge	wonder
argue	deny	promise	tell	instruct	warn	
assert	exclaim	remark	warn			
believe	explain	repeat	write			

 ## Common Time Word Changes in Indirect Speech

DIRECT SPEECH		INDIRECT SPEECH
now	→	then
today	→	that day
tomorrow	→	the next day OR the following day OR the day after
yesterday	→	the day before OR the previous day
this week/month/year	→	that week/month/year
last week/month/year	→	the week/month/year before
next week/month/year	→	the following week/month/year

 ## Common Phrases Introducing Embedded Questions

I don't know . . .	I'd like to know . . .	Do you know . . . ?
I don't understand . . .	I want to understand . . .	Do you understand . . . ?
I wonder . . .	I'd like to find out . . .	Can you tell me . . . ?
I'm not sure . . .	We need to find out . . .	Could you explain . . . ?
I can't remember . . .	Let's ask . . .	Can you remember . . . ?
I can't imagine . . .		Would you show me . . . ?
It doesn't say . . .		Who knows . . . ?

 ## Verbs and Expressions Commonly Used Reflexively

amuse oneself	behave oneself	feel sorry for oneself	keep oneself	see oneself
ask oneself	believe in oneself	forgive oneself	kill oneself	take care of oneself
avail oneself of	blame oneself	give oneself	look after oneself	talk to oneself
be hard on oneself	cut oneself	help oneself	look at oneself	teach oneself
be oneself	deprive oneself of	hurt oneself	pride oneself on	tell oneself
be pleased with oneself	dry oneself	imagine oneself	push oneself	treat oneself
be proud of oneself	enjoy oneself	introduce oneself	remind oneself	wash oneself

17 Some Common Phrasal Verbs

(s.o. = someone s.t. = something)

NOTE 1: **Inseparable phrasal verbs** are shown with the object after the particle (**go after** s.t.).
Separable phrasal verbs are shown with the object between the verb and the particle (**call** s.o. **up**).
Verbs which <u>must be separated</u> are shown with an asterisk (*) (**do** s.t. **over**).

NOTE 2: **Separable phrasal verbs** can have the noun object either between the verb and the particle
or after the particle (**call** Jan **up** OR **call up** Jan). These verbs must, however, be separated when there
is a pronoun object (**call** her **up** NOT ~~call up her~~).

PHRASAL VERB	MEANING	PHRASAL VERB	MEANING
ask s.o. **over**	*invite to one's home*	**drop** s.o. or s.t. **off**	*take someone/something someplace*
block s.t. **out**	*stop from passing through (light, noise)*	**drop out (of** s.t.)	*quit*
blow s.t. **out**	*stop burning by blowing*	**eat out**	*eat in a restaurant*
blow s.t. **up**	*fill something with air (a balloon, a water toy)*	**empty** (s.t.) **out**	*empty completely*
blow (s.t.) **up**	*(make s.t.) explode*	**end up**	*1. do something unexpected or unintended*
break down	*stop functioning*		*2. reach a final place or condition*
break out	*occur suddenly*	**fall off**	*become detached*
bring s.t. **about**	*make something happen*	**figure** s.o. or s.t. **out**	*understand (after thinking about)*
bring s.o. or s.t. **back**	*return someone or something*	**fill** s.t. **in**	*complete with information*
bring s.o. **down**	*depress*	**fill** s.t. **out**	*complete (a form, an application)*
bring s.t. **out**	*introduce (a new product, a book)*	**fill** (s.t.) **up**	*fill completely*
bring s.o. **up**	*raise (children)*	**find** (s.t.) **out**	*learn information*
burn (s.t.) **down**	*burn completely*	**follow** (s.t.) **through**	*complete*
call (s.o.) **back**	*return a phone call*	**fool around**	*be playful*
call s.t. **off**	*cancel*	**get** s.t. **across**	*get people to understand an idea*
call s.o. **up**	*telephone someone*	**get ahead**	*make progress, succeed*
carry on s.t.	*continue*	**get along**	*relate well*
carry s.t. **out**	*conduct*	**get back**	*return*
catch on	*become popular*	**get by**	*survive*
cheer (s.o.) **up**	*(make someone) feel happier*	**get out (of** s.t.)	*leave (a car, a taxi)*
clean (s.o. or s.t.) **up**	*clean completely*	**get** s.t. **out of** s.t.*	*benefit from*
clear (s.t.) **up**	*make or become clear*	**get together**	*meet*
come about	*happen*	**get up**	*rise from bed*
come along	*accompany*	**give** s.t. **away**	*give without charging money*
come back	*return*	**give** s.t. **back**	*return something*
come in	*enter*	**give** s.t. **out**	*distribute*
come off s.t.	*become unattached*	**give** (s.t.) **up**	*quit, abandon*
come out	*appear*	**go after** s.o. or s.t.	*pursue*
come up	*arise*	**go along with** s.t.	*1. support*
come up with s.t.	*invent*		*2. be part of*
cover s.t. **up**	*cover completely*	**go back**	*return*
cross s.t. **out**	*draw a line through*	**go off**	*explode (a gun, fireworks, a rocket)*
cut s.t. **down**	*bring down by cutting*	**go on**	*continue*
cut s.t. **off**	*1. stop the supply of something*	**go out**	*leave*
	2. remove by cutting	**go over**	*succeed with an audience*
cut s.t. **out**	*remove by cutting*	**go up**	*be built*
do s.t. **over**	*do again*	**grow up**	*become an adult*
dream s.t. **up**	*invent*	**hand** s.t. **in**	*give some work to a boss or teacher*
dress up	*put on special or formal clothes*	**hand** s.t. **out**	*distribute*
drink s.t. **up**	*drink completely*	**hang up**	*end a phone conversation*
drop by/in	*visit unexpectedly*	**hang** s.t. **up**	*put on a hook or hanger*

(continued on next page)

PHRASAL VERB	MEANING
help (s.o.) **out**	*assist*
hold **on**	*wait, not hang up the phone*
keep (s.o. or s.t.) **away**	*(cause to) stay at a distance*
keep **on**	*continue*
keep s.t. **on***	*not remove (a piece of clothing or jewelry)*
keep **up** (**with** s.o. or s.t.)	*go as fast as*
lay s.o. **off**	*end someone's employment*
leave s.t. **on***	*1. not turn off (a light, a radio)*
	2. not remove (a piece of clothing or jewelry)
leave s.t. **out**	*omit*
let s.o. **down**	*disappoint*
let s.o. or s.t. **in**	*allow to enter*
let s.o. **off**	*allow to leave (a bus, a train, a car)*
let s.o. or s.t. **out**	*allow to leave*
lie **down**	*recline*
light (s.t.) **up**	*illuminate*
look **out**	*be careful*
look s.o. or s.t. **over**	*examine*
look s.t. **up**	*try to find in a book or on the Internet*
make s.t. **up**	*create*
pass s.t. **out**	*distribute*
pay s.o. or s.t. **back**	*repay*
pay **off**	*be worthwhile*
pick s.o. or s.t. **out**	*1. select*
	2. identify
pick **up**	*improve*
pick s.o. or s.t. **up**	*1. lift*
	2. get (an idea, a new book, an interest)
play **around**	*have fun*
point s.o. or s.t. **out**	*indicate*
put s.t. **away**	*put something in an appropriate place*
put s.t. **back**	*return something to its original place*
put s.o. or s.t. **down**	*stop holding*
put s.t. **off**	*postpone*
put s.t. **on**	*cover the body with a piece of clothing or jewelry*
put s.t. **together**	*assemble*
put s.t. **up**	*erect*
run **into** s.o.	*meet accidentally*
run **out** (of s.t.)	*not have enough of a supply*
see s.t. **through***	*complete*
set s.t. **off**	*cause to explode*
set s.t. **up**	*1. establish (a business, an organization)*
	2. prepare for use

PHRASAL VERB	MEANING
show s.o. or s.t. **off**	*display the best qualities*
show **up**	*appear*
shut s.t. **off**	*stop a machine or light*
sign **up**	*register*
sit **down**	*take a seat*
stand **up**	*rise*
start (s.t.) **over***	*start again*
stay **up**	*remain awake*
stick **with**/**to** s.o. or s.t.	*not quit, not leave*
straighten (s.t.) **up**	*make neat*
switch s.t. **on**	*start a machine or a light*
take s.t. **away**/**off**	*remove*
take s.t. **back**	*return*
take **off**	*depart (a plane)*
take s.o. **on**	*hire*
take s.t. **out**	*borrow from a library*
talk s.o. **into***	*persuade*
talk s.t. **over**	*discuss*
team **up with** s.o.	*start to work with*
tear s.t. **down**	*destroy*
tear s.t. **up**	*tear into small pieces*
think **back on** s.o. or s.t.	*remember*
think s.t. **over**	*consider*
think s.t. **up**	*invent*
throw s.t. **away**/**out**	*discard*
touch s.t. **up**	*improve by making small changes*
try s.t. **on**	*put clothing on to see if it fits*
try s.t. **out**	*find out if something works*
turn s.o. or s.t. **down**	*1. reject*
	2. decrease the volume (a radio, a TV)
turn s.t. **in**	*submit*
turn s.o. or s.t. **into**	*change from one form to another*
turn s.o. **off**	*(slang) destroy interest*
turn s.t. **off**	*stop a machine or light*
turn s.t. **on**	*start a machine or light*
turn **out**	*have a particular result*
turn **up**	*appear*
turn s.t. **up**	*raise the volume*
use s.t. **up**	*use completely, consume*
wake **up**	*arise after sleeping*
wake (s.o.) **up**	*awaken*
watch **out**	*be careful*
work s.t. **off**	*remove by work or activity*
work **out**	*1. be resolved*
	2. exercise
work s.t. **out**	*solve*
write s.t. **down**	*write on a piece of paper*
write s.t. **up**	*write in a finished form*

18 Some Common Irregular Plural Nouns

SINGULAR	PLURAL	SINGULAR	PLURAL	SINGULAR	PLURAL	SINGULAR	PLURAL
analysis	analyses	half	halves	man	men	mouse	mice
basis	bases	knife	knives	woman	women		
crisis	crises	leaf	leaves	child	children	deer	deer
hypothesis	hypotheses	life	lives			fish	fish
		loaf	loaves	foot	feet	sheep	sheep
		shelf	shelves	goose	geese		
		wife	wives	tooth	teeth	person	people

19 Spelling Rules for the Present Progressive

1. Add -ing to the base form of the verb.

read	reading
stand	standing

2. If a verb ends in a silent -e, drop the final -e and add -ing.

leave	leaving
take	taking

3. In a one-syllable word, if the last three letters are a consonant-vowel-consonant combination (CVC), double the last consonant before adding -ing.

   C V C
   ↓ ↓ ↓
   s i t   sitting

   C V C
   ↓ ↓ ↓
   r u n   running

   However, do not double the last consonant in words that end in w, x, or y.

sew	sewing
fix	fixing
enjoy	enjoying

4. In words of two or more syllables that end in a consonant-vowel-consonant combination, double the last consonant only if the last syllable is stressed.

admit	admitting	(The last syllable is stressed, so you double the -t.)
whisper	whispering	(The last syllable is not stressed, so you don't double the -r.)

5. If a verb ends in -ie, change the ie to y before adding -ing.

die	dying

20 Spelling Rules for the Simple Present Tense: Third-Person Singular (he, she, it)

1. Add -s for most verbs.

work	works
buy	buys
ride	rides
return	returns

2. Add -es for words that end in -ch, -s, -sh, -x, or -z.

watch	watches
pass	passes
rush	rushes
relax	relaxes
buzz	buzzes

3. Change the y to i and add -es when the base form ends in a consonant + y.

study	studies
hurry	hurries
dry	dries

   Do not change the y when the base form ends in a vowel + y. Add -s.

play	plays
enjoy	enjoys

4. A few verbs have irregular forms.

be	is
do	does
go	goes
have	has

21 Spelling Rules for the Simple Past Tense of Regular Verbs

1. If the verb ends in a consonant, add *-ed*.
return	return*ed*
help	help*ed*

2. If the verb ends in *-e*, add *-d*.
live	live*d*
create	create*d*
die	die*d*

3. In one-syllable words, if the verb ends in a consonant-vowel-consonant combination (CVC), double the final consonant and add *-ed*.

   C V C
   ↓ ↓ ↓
h o p	hop*ped*

   C V C
   ↓ ↓ ↓
r u b	rub*bed*

   However, do not double one-syllable words ending in *-w, -x,* or *-y*.
bow	bow*ed*
mix	mix*ed*
play	play*ed*

4. In words of two or more syllables that end in a consonant-vowel-consonant combination, double the last consonant only if the last syllable is stressed.
prefér	prefer*red*	(The last syllable is stressed, so you double the *-r*.)
vísit	visit*ed*	(The last syllable is not stressed, so you don't double the *t*.)

5. If the verb ends in a consonant + *y*, change the *y* to *i* and add *-ed*.
worry	worr*ied*
carry	carr*ied*

6. If the verb ends in a vowel + *y*, add *-ed*. (Do not change the *y* to *i*.)
play	play*ed*
annoy	annoy*ed*

   Exceptions: pay—paid, lay—laid, say—said

22 Spelling Rules for the Comparative *(-er)* and Superlative *(-est)* of Adjectives

1. Add *-er* to one-syllable adjectives to form the comparative. Add *-est* to one-syllable adjectives to form the superlative.
cheap	cheap*er*	cheap*est*
bright	bright*er*	bright*est*

2. If the adjective ends in *-e*, add *-r* or *-st*.
nice	nice*r*	nice*st*

3. If the adjective ends in a consonant + *y*, change *y* to *i* before you add *-er* or *-est*.
pretty	prett*ier*	prett*iest*

   Exception: shy shyer shyest

4. If the adjective ends in a consonant-vowel-consonant combination (CVC), double the final consonant before adding *-er* or *-est*.

   C V C
   ↓ ↓ ↓
b i g	big*ger*	big*gest*

   However, do not double the consonant in words ending in *-w* or *-y*.
slow	slow*er*	slow*est*
coy	coy*er*	coy*est*

23 Spelling Rules for Adverbs Ending in *-ly*

1. Add *-ly* to the corresponding adjective.
nice	nice*ly*
quiet	quiet*ly*
beautiful	beautiful*ly*

2. If the adjective ends in a consonant + *y*, change the *y* to *i* before adding *-ly*.
easy	eas*ily*

3. If the adjective ends in *-le*, drop the *e* and add *-y*.
possible	possib*ly*

   However, do not drop the *e* for other adjectives ending in *-e*.
extreme	extreme*ly*

   Exception: true tru*ly*

4. If the adjective ends in *-ic*, add *-ally*.
basic	basic*ally*
fantastic	fantastic*ally*

Contractions with Verb Forms

1. SIMPLE PRESENT TENSE, PRESENT PROGRESSIVE, AND IMPERATIVE

Contractions with *Be*

I am	=	I'm
you are	=	you're
he is	=	he's
she is	=	she's
it is	=	it's
we are	=	we're
you are	=	you're
they are	=	they're

I am not	=	I'm not		
you are not	=	you're not	or	you aren't
he is not	=	he's not	or	he isn't
she is not	=	she's not	or	she isn't
it is not	=	it's not	or	it isn't
we are not	=	we're not	or	we aren't
you are not	=	you're not	or	you aren't
they are not	=	they're not	or	they aren't

Contractions with *Do*

do not	=	don't
does not	=	doesn't

SIMPLE PRESENT	PRESENT PROGRESSIVE
I'm a student.	I'm studying here.
He's my teacher.	He's teaching verbs.
We're from Canada.	We're living here.

SIMPLE PRESENT	PRESENT PROGRESSIVE
She's not sick.	She's not reading.
He isn't late.	He isn't coming.
We aren't twins.	We aren't leaving.
They're not here.	They're not playing.

SIMPLE PRESENT	IMPERATIVE
They don't live here.	Don't run!
It doesn't snow much.	

2. SIMPLE PAST TENSE AND PAST PROGRESSIVE

Contractions with *Be*

was not	=	wasn't
were not	=	weren't

Contractions with *Do*

did not	=	didn't

SIMPLE PAST	PAST PROGRESSIVE
He wasn't a poet.	He wasn't singing.
They weren't twins.	They weren't sleeping.
We didn't see her.	

3. FUTURE

Contractions with *Will*

I will	=	I'll
you will	=	you'll
he will	=	he'll
she will	=	she'll
it will	=	it'll
we will	=	we'll
you will	=	you'll
they will	=	they'll

will not	=	won't

FUTURE WITH *WILL*
I'll take the train.
It'll be faster that way.
We'll go together.
He won't come with us.
They won't miss the train.

(continued on next page)

Contractions with *Be going to*

I am going to	=	**I'm going to**
you are going to	=	**you're going to**
he is going to	=	**he's going to**
she is going to	=	**she's going to**
it is going to	=	**it's going to**
we are going to	=	**we're going to**
you are going to	=	**you're going to**
they are going to	=	**they're going to**

FUTURE WITH *BE GOING TO*
I'm going to buy tickets tomorrow.
She's going to call you.
It's going to rain soon.
We're going to drive to Boston.
They're going to crash!

4. PRESENT PERFECT AND PRESENT PERFECT PROGRESSIVE

Contractions with *Have*

I have	=	**I've**
you have	=	**you've**
he has	=	**he's**
she has	=	**she's**
it has	=	**it's**
we have	=	**we've**
you have	=	**you've**
they have	=	**they've**
have not	=	**haven't**
has not	=	**hasn't**

You've already read that page.
We've been writing for an hour.
She's been to Africa three times.
It's been raining since yesterday.
We haven't seen any elephants yet.
They haven't been living here long.
She hasn't taken any photos today.

5. MODALS AND MODAL-LIKE EXPRESSIONS

cannot or can not	=	**can't**
could not	=	**couldn't**
should not	=	**shouldn't**
had better	=	**'d better**
would prefer	=	**'d prefer**
would not	=	**wouldn't**
would rather	=	**'d rather**

She can't dance.
We shouldn't go.
They'd better decide.
I'd prefer coffee.
She wouldn't.
I'd rather take the bus.

could have	=	**could've**
should have	=	**should've**
would have	=	**would've**
must have	=	**must've**
might have	=	**might've**

We could've walked.
We might've arrived late.

6. CONDITIONALS WITH *WOULD*

I would	=	**I'd**
you would	=	**you'd**
he would	=	**he'd**
she would	=	**she'd**
we would	=	**we'd**
you would	=	**you'd**
they would	=	**they'd**
would have	=	**would've**
would not	=	**wouldn't**

If I had time, I'd travel.
If you moved here, you'd be happy.
If she knew the answer, she'd tell you.
We'd buy a new car if we had the money.
If you invited them, they'd come.
If I had known, I would've told you.
I wouldn't do that if I were you.

25 Punctuation Rules for Direct Speech

Direct speech may either follow or come before the reporting verb. When direct speech follows the reporting verb,

a. Put a comma after the reporting verb.

b. Use opening quotation marks (") before the first word of the direct speech.

c. Begin the quotation with a capital letter.

d. Use the appropriate end punctuation for the direct speech. It may be a period (.), a question mark (?), or an exclamation point (!).

e. Put closing quotation marks (") after the end punctuation of the quotation.

Examples: He said, "I had a good time."
She asked, "Where's the party?"
They shouted, "Be careful!"

When direct speech comes before the reporting verb,

a. Begin the sentence with opening quotation marks (").

b. Use the appropriate end punctuation for the direct speech.
If the direct speech is a statement, use a comma (,).
If the direct speech is a question, use a question mark (?).
If the direct speech is an exclamation, use an exclamation point (!).

c. Use closing quotation marks after the end punctuation for the direct speech (").

d. Begin the reporting clause with a lower-case letter.

e. Use a period at the end of the main sentence (.).

Examples: "I had a good time," he said.
"Where's the party?" she asked.
"Be careful!" they shouted.

26 Pronunciation Table

VOWELS				CONSONANTS			
Symbol	**Key Word**	**Symbol**	**Key Word**	**Symbol**	**Key Word**	**Symbol**	**Key Word**
i	beat, feed	ə	banana, among	p	pack, happy	ʃ	ship, machine, station, special, discussion
ɪ	bit, did	ɚ	shirt, murder	b	back, rubber		
eɪ	date, paid	aɪ	bite, cry, buy, eye	t	tie	ʒ	measure, vision
ɛ	bet, bed			d	die	h	hot, who
æ	bat, bad	aʊ	about, how	k	came, key, quick	m	men
ɑ	box, odd, father	ɔɪ	voice, boy	g	game, guest	n	sun, know, pneumonia
ɔ	bought, dog	ɪr	beer	tʃ	church, nature, watch	ŋ	sung, ringing
oʊ	boat, road	ɛr	bare	dʒ	judge, general, major	w	wet, white
ʊ	book, good	ɑr	bar	f	fan, photograph	l	light, long
u	boot, food, student	ɔr	door	v	van	r	right, wrong
ʌ	but, mud, mother	ʊr	tour	θ	thing, breath	y	yes, use, music
				ð	then, breathe	t̬	butter, bottle
		STRESS		s	sip, city, psychology		
		' shows main stress.		z	zip, please, goes		

Pronunciation Rules for the Simple Present Tense:
27 Third-Person Singular *(he, she, it)*

1. The third person singular in the simple present tense always ends in the letter -*s*. There are, however, three different pronunciations for the final sound of the third person singular.

/s/	/z/	/ɪz/
talks	loves	dances

2. The final sound is pronounced /s/ after the voiceless sounds /p/, /t/, /k/, and /f/.

top	tops
get	gets
take	takes
laugh	laughs

3. The final sound is pronounced /z/ after the voiced sounds /b/, /d/, /g/, /v/, /ð/, /m/, /n/, /ŋ/, /l/, and /r/.

describe	describes
spend	spends
hug	hugs
live	lives
bathe	bathes
seem	seems
remain	remains
sing	sings
tell	tells
lower	lowers

4. The final sound is pronounced /z/ after all vowel sounds.

agree	agrees
try	tries
stay	stays
know	knows

5. The final sound is pronounced /ɪz/ after the sounds /s/, /z/, /ʃ/, /ʒ/, /tʃ/, and /dʒ/. /ɪz/ adds a syllable to the verb.

relax	relaxes
freeze	freezes
rush	rushes
massage	massages
watch	watches
judge	judges

6. *Do* and *say* have a change in vowel sound.

say	/seɪ/	says	/sɛz/
do	/du/	does	/dʌz/

28 Pronunciation Rules for the Simple Past Tense of Regular Verbs

1. The regular simple past always ends in the letter -*d*. There are, however, three different pronunciations for the final sound of the regular simple past.

/t/	/d/	/ɪd/
raced	lived	attended

2. The final sound is pronounced /t/ after the voiceless sounds /p/, /k/, /f/, /s/, /ʃ/, and /tʃ/.

hop	hopped
work	worked
laugh	laughed
address	addressed
publish	published
watch	watched

3. The final sound is pronounced /d/ after the voiced sounds /b/, /g/, /v/, /z/, /ʒ/, /dʒ/, /m/, /n/, /ŋ/, /l/, /r/, and /ð/.

rub	rubbed
hug	hugged
live	lived
surprise	surprised

massage	massaged
change	changed
rhyme	rhymed
return	returned
bang	banged
enroll	enrolled
appear	appeared
bathe	bathed

4. The final sound is pronounced /d/ after all vowel sounds.

agree	agreed
play	played
die	died
enjoy	enjoyed
row	rowed

5. The final sound is pronounced /ɪd/ after /t/ and /d/. /ɪd/ adds a syllable to the verb.

start	started
decide	decided

Index

Answer Key

NOTE: In this answer key, where the contracted form is given, the full form is also correct, and where the full form is given, the contracted form is also correct.

 Present Progressive

CHECK POINT

It's happening now!

CHART CHECK 1

be + base form of verb + *-ing*
be

CHART CHECK 2

F

EXPRESS CHECK

are . . . leaving
are . . . performing OR 're . . . performing

1 I'm working very hard these days, but I have some good news. Right now, I'm sitting at a desk in the Entertainment Section of the *Tribune*! Of course I'm still taking journalism classes at night as well. The job is temporary—Joe Sims, the regular reporter, is taking this month off to write a book. This week we're preparing to interview your favorite group, the Airheads. In fact, at this very moment they're flying into town by helicopter. They're performing at the King Theater all week. How are you doing? Are you still writing music? Oops! The crew is calling me. They're leaving for the theater now. Write soon!

2 2. are . . . going
3. is waiting OR 's waiting
4. 'm working
5. 're not doing OR aren't doing
6. 're . . . sitting
7. 'm sitting
8. 'm . . . thinking
9. are staying

3 3. Why are you touring again?
4. What are you working on these days?
5. Who's singing with you now?
6. Is she replacing Toti?
7. No, she isn't. OR No, she's not.

4 I ~~write~~ **'m writing** to you from my hotel room. Everyone else is ~~sleep~~ **sleeping**, but I ~~sitting~~ **'m sitting** here and watching the ocean. We're staying at the Plaza in Atlantic Beach, and the view is beautiful. The tour is ~~goes~~ **going** well. The audience is crazy about the new songs, but the fans ~~is~~ **are** always asking for you. How is the baby? She has a great voice. ~~Do~~ **Are** you teaching her to sing yet? Maybe both of you will come along for the next tour!

 Simple Present Tense

CHECK POINT

Hank's Working Habits

CHART CHECK

T, T, F

EXPRESS CHECK

Why does he rush

1 In today's fast-paced world, we never escape stress. Stress always affects us psychologically, but according to Dr. Roads, author of the new bestseller, *Calm Down!*, it also affects us physically. For example, stress causes high blood pressure. Doctors often prescribe medication for stress-related illnesses. Medicine usually lowers a patient's blood

(continued on next page)

pressure. But, Dr. Roads <u>claims</u>, "You <u>don't</u> (always) need pills. Relaxation exercises <u>are</u> (sometimes) as effective as pills. For example, breathing exercises both <u>relax</u> you and <u>lower</u> your blood pressure. It only <u>takes</u> a few minutes!"

3. take
4. rushes
5. isn't
6. is
7. doesn't finish
8. worries
9. doesn't have
10. doesn't have

3. Does he work on reports in the afternoon? No, he doesn't.
4. When does he see clients? He sees clients from 9:00 to 12:00.
5. Does he take a lunch break? Yes, he does.
6. What does he do from 12:30 to 5:00? He returns phone calls.
7. Where does he go at 5:30? He attends OR goes to night school.

I'm so tired. I ~~have never~~ ^{never have} time to relax. I work all day and ~~studies~~ ^{study} all night. My boss ~~tell~~ ^{tells} me that I need a vacation. I agree, but ~~I~~ ^{I'm} afraid to take one. Does my boss ~~thinks~~ ^{think} that the office can function without me? I ~~dont~~ ^{don't} want them to think I'm not necessary. But my wife is unhappy too. She ~~complain~~ ^{complains} that she never sees me anymore. My schedule ~~are~~ ^{is} crazy. I don't think I can keep this up much longer. I don't ~~wants~~ ^{want} to quit night school, though. I think ~~often~~ ^{often} that there has to be a better way.

U N I T 3 Non-Action Verbs

has the flavor of chicken

CHART CHECK
T, T

'm tasting, tastes

ALINE: This steak <u>tastes</u> delicious. Your salmon <u>looks</u> good too.
BEN: Here, I'm putting some on your plate. I <u>think</u> you'll like it.
ALINE: Mmm. I <u>like</u> it. Funny, I usually (don't like) fish.
BEN: Red (has) that effect on people.
ALINE: I <u>have</u> no idea what you're talking about. What <u>do</u> you <u>mean</u>?
BEN: Well, colors can change the way we (feel). For example, people often (feel) hungrier in a red room. I <u>notice</u> that you're looking right at the red wallpaper.
ALINE: And I certainly <u>feel</u> hungry right now. I'm eating half your salmon.
BEN: That's OK. I'm tasting your steak.

2. is looking
3. cost
4. wants
5. hates
6. seems
7. likes
8. doesn't suspect
9. know
10. is thinking
11. doesn't have
12. hears

2. 'm tasting
3. needs
4. Do . . . want
5. tastes
6. think
7. 'm thinking
8. isn't
9. sounds
10. 'm looking
11. don't know
12. is
13. 'm smelling
14. 'm not
15. love
16. smells
17. know
18. mean
19. feel

Not a good day! I feel kind of depressed and I'm ~~having~~ ^{have} a headache. I'm ~~needing~~ ^{need} to do something right away to change my mood and get rid of this pain. Last week, I read an article about how smells can affect mood and even health, so right now I ~~smell~~ ^{'m smelling} an

orange (for the depression) and a green

apple (for the headache). They smell nice,

but I'm not thinking that I notice a difference
don't think

in how I feel! I think I'm preferring to eat
prefer

something when I feel down. But I worry

that I'm weighing too much. So, at the
weigh

moment I have a cup of peppermint tea with
'm having

lemon. The article says that the peppermint

smell helps you eat less. Well, I don't know

about that! A chocolate ice cream sundae

sounds pretty good right about now!

It's seeming that there are no easy solutions.
seems

 Present Progressive and **Simple Present Tense**

CHECK POINT

F, T

CHART CHECK

two parts
two forms

EXPRESS CHECK

PRESENT PROGRESSIVE			
SUBJECT	**BE**	**BASE FORM + -ING**	
I	am	buying	
You	are	buying	flowers now.
He	is	buying	

SIMPLE PRESENT TENSE		
SUBJECT		**VERB**	
I		buy	
You	usually	buy	chocolates.
He		buys	

1

June 28: I'm sitting in a seat 30,000 feet above the earth en route to Argentina! I usually have dinner at this time, but right now I have a headache from the excitement. My seatmate is eating my food. She looks happy.

June 30: It's 7:30. My host parents are still working. Carlos, my father, works at home. My little brother Ricardo is cute. He looks (and acts) a lot like Bobby. Right now, he's looking over my shoulder and trying to read my journal.

July 4: The weather is cold now. I usually spend the first weekend of July at the beach. Today I'm walking around in a heavy sweater.

August 6: I feel so tired tonight. Everyone else feels great in the evening because they take long naps in the afternoon.

2

1. b. 'm waiting
    c. look
    d. 'm working
    e. 's talking
    f. isn't looking OR 's not looking
    g. looks
    h. doesn't mean
2. a. 's talking
    b. 're taking
    c. 're standing
    d. Do . . . think
    e. 're dating
    f. don't think
    g. means
    h. come
    i. stand
3. a. is . . . walking
    b. starts
    c. has
    d. walks
    e. appear
4. a. are . . . shaking
    b. know
    c. shake
    d. meet

3 It's 12:30 and I ~~sit~~ *'m sitting* in the library right now. My classmates are eating lunch together, but I'm not hungry yet. At home, we ~~eat never~~ *never eat* this early. Today our journal topic is culture shock. It's a good topic for me right now because I'm ~~being~~ pretty homesick. I miss my old routine. At home we always ~~are eating~~ *eat* a big meal at 2:00 in the afternoon. Then we rest. But here in Toronto ~~I'm having~~ *I have* a 3:00 conversation class. Every day, I almost fall asleep in class, and my teacher ~~ask~~ *asks* me, "Are you bored?" Of course I'm not bored. I just need my afternoon nap! This class ~~always is~~ *is always* fun. This semester, we ~~work~~ *'re working* on a project with video cameras. My team is filming groups of people in different cultures. We are ~~analyze~~ *analyzing* "social distance." That means how close to each other these people stand. According to my new watch, it's 12:55, so I ~~leave~~ *'m leaving* now for my 1:00 class. Teachers here really ~~aren't liking~~ *don't like* when you come late!

UNIT 5 Imperative

CHECK POINT

giving instructions on how to do the Jab

CHART CHECK

don't include a subject

EXPRESS CHECK

AFFIRMATIVE

BASE FORM OF VERB	
Listen	to the music.
Touch	your toes.
Stand	straight.

NEGATIVE

DON'T	BASE FORM OF VERB	
Don't	listen	to the music.
Don't	touch	your toes.
Don't	stand	straight.

1
2. c	4. e	6. a
3. b	5. d	7. f

2
2. Wash six strawberries.
3. Cut the strawberries in half.
4. Pour orange juice into the blender.
5. Add the fruit to the orange juice.
6. Blend the ingredients until smooth.

3
2. Learn	7. Take
3. Decrease	8. Choose
4. Increase	9. Don't wait
5. Become	10. Register
6. Don't miss	

4 For the Black Belt essay, Master Gibbons gave us this assignment: ~~You write~~ *Write* about something important to you. My topic is *The Right Way*, the rules of life for the martial arts. First, ~~respects~~ *respect* other people—treat them the way you want them to treat you. Second, ~~helped~~ *help* people in need. In other words, use your strength for others, ~~not to~~ *don't* use it just for your own good. Third, ~~no~~ *don't* lie or steal. These are the most important rules to me.

SelfTest

(Total = 100 points. Each item = 4 points.)

SECTION ONE

1. **B**	5. **D**	9. **C**	13. **D**
2. **D**	6. **A**	10. **B**	14. **D**
3. **A**	7. **B**	11. **A**	15. **B**
4. **A**	8. **B**	12. **A**	

SECTION TWO

(Correct answers are in parentheses.)

16. **A** (swims)
17. **C** (is raining)
18. **B** (are you)
19. **C** (don't)
20. **B** (seems)

21. **C** (hate)
22. **A** (usually arrives)
23. **B** (aren't OR are not)
24. **D** ('m always losing)
25. **B** (*delete* you)

UNIT 6 Simple Past Tense: Affirmative Statements

CHECK POINT

1989
1999

CHART CHECK

two
–*d* or –*ed*

EXPRESS CHECK

was, were
came
saved

 1 Matsuo Basho (wrote) more than 1,000 three-line poems, or "haiku." He (chose) topics from nature, daily life, and human emotions. He (became) one of Japan's most famous poets, and his work <u>established</u> haiku as an important art form.

Matsuo Basho (was) born near Kyoto in 1644. His father <u>wanted</u> him to become a samurai (warrior). Instead, Matsuo <u>moved</u> to Edo (present-day Tokyo) and <u>studied</u> poetry. By 1681, he (had) many students and admirers.

Basho's home <u>burned</u> down in 1682. Then, in 1683, his mother <u>died</u>. After these events, Basho (felt) restless. Starting in 1684, he <u>traveled</u> on foot and on horseback all over Japan. Sometimes his friends <u>joined</u> him, and they (wrote) poetry together. Travel (was) difficult in the seventeenth century, and Basho often (got) sick. He <u>died</u> in 1694, during a journey to Osaka. At that time he (had) 2,000 students.

 2

2. wrote
3. were
4. led
5. became
6. left
7. saw
8. wore
9. wrote

10. addressed
11. appeared
12. happened
14. saw
15. bit
16. ate
17. drank
18. hopped

 3 Today in class we read a poem by Robert
          enjoyed
Frost. I really ~~enjoy~~ it. It was about a person
   chose
who ~~choosed~~ between two roads in a forest.
          spent
Before he made his decision, he ~~spents~~ a lot

of time trying to decide which road to follow.
             was
Many people thought the person ~~were~~ Frost.
      took
In the end, he ~~take~~ the road that was less

traveled on. He decided to be a poet. That
        changed
decision ~~change~~ his life a lot.

Sometimes I feel a little like Frost.
         decided
Two years ago I ~~decide~~ to come to this
        was
country. That ~~were~~ the biggest decision of

my life.

 # UNIT 7 Simple Past Tense: Negative Statements and Questions

CHECK POINT

?, F, T

CHART CHECK 1

not
did not

CHART CHECK 2

was, were
did

EXPRESS CHECK

Did she have a navigator?
She didn't fly alone.

 1

2. No
3. Yes

4. No
5. Yes

6. Yes
7. No

2. Where did she study? (At) Columbia University.

3. How long was she a social worker? (For) two years.

4. Where did her last flight leave from? (From) New Guinea.

5. How many books did she write? Three.

6. What was her nationality? American.

7. When did she disappear? (In) 1937.

 3. Were   **9.** Did . . . dream

4. No . . . weren't   **10.** didn't think

5. didn't want   **11.** Were

6. Did . . . feel   **12.** No . . . wasn't

7. Yes . . . did   **13.** Was

8. didn't keep   **14.** No . . . wasn't

 Hi! Did you ~~received~~ *receive* my last letter? I didn't ~~knew~~ *know* your new address so I sent it to your old one. When ~~you moved~~ *did you move*? Did your roommate move with you? Right now I'm on board a plane flying to El Paso to visit Ana. Did you ~~met~~ *meet* her at the conference last year? I wanted to visit her in June, but I ~~no had~~ *didn't have* the time. At first I was going to drive from Los Angeles, but I decided to fly instead.

This is only my third flight, but I love flying! I ~~didnt~~ *didn't* know flying could be so much fun!

Hope to hear from you.

 UNIT 8 *Used to*

a habit he had in the past

CHART CHECK 1

T

CHART CHECK 2

did . . . use to

used to
use to
say

 In many ways, fashion <u>used to be</u> much simpler. Women <u>didn't use to wear</u> pants to the office, and men's clothes never <u>used to come</u> in bright colors. People also <u>used to dress</u> in special ways for different situations. They didn't use blue jeans as business clothes or wear jogging suits when they traveled. Today you can go to the opera and find some women in evening gowns while others are in blue jeans. Even buying jeans <u>used to be</u> easier—they only came in blue denim. I'm still not used to buying green jeans and wearing them to work!

 2. used to have   **5.** used to wear

3. used to dress   **6.** used to carry

4. used to dance

3. *(Answers may vary slightly.)*

2. They (only) used to come in two styles. (high-top and low-top)

3. How much did a pair of men's high-tops use to cost?
(They used to cost) 98¢.

4. No. Women's sneakers didn't use to cost the same as men's sneakers. Women's sneakers used to cost less than men's sneakers.

5. They (only) used to wear low-top sneakers.

6. There used to be (only) two sizes. (small and large)

 When I was younger, clothing didn't ~~used~~ *use* to be a problem. All the girls at my school used to ~~wore~~ *wear* the same uniform. I used to think that it took away from my freedom of choice. Now I can wear what I want, but clothes cost so much! Even blue jeans, today's "uniform," used to be cheaper. My mom ~~uses~~ *used* to pay less than $20 for hers. I guess they didn't ~~used~~ *use* to sell designer jeans back then. You know, I ~~was~~ used to be against school uniforms, but now I'm not so sure!

Past Progressive

CHECK POINT

what she was doing at the time of her accident

CHART CHECK 1

F

CHART CHECK 2

before the subject

EXPRESS CHECK

A: were . . . staying
B: was staying

2. F
3. T
4. ?
5. T
6. F

3. were sitting outside.
4. wasn't snowing.
5. were wearing sunglasses.
6. weren't wearing gloves.
7. was serving drinks.
8. wasn't serving lunch.
9. wasn't smiling.
10. was holding a cell phone.

3. was recovering
4. wasn't performing
5. were . . . thinking
6. were waiting
7. wasn't thinking
8. were watching
9. were . . . snowboarding
10. was watching
11. (was) dreaming
12. Was . . . practicing
13. was

4 Tonight, Sheila and I ~~was~~ *were* looking at some photographs from my snowboarding trip with Fritz's family last year. By the end of the evening, we *were* laughing like crazy. That was my first experience on a snowboard, so the pictures were pretty embarrassing. In one shot, I was ~~came~~ *coming* down the slope on my back. In another one, my board ~~were~~ *was* falling out of the ski lift while I was riding up the slope. Fritz ~~was taking~~ *took* that picture from the lift entrance. Good thing he ~~not~~ *wasn't* standing right under me! Where was I when Fritz was falling down the slope? I guess I wasn't ~~carry~~ *carrying* my camera. It was amazing how fast Fritz's girlfriend, Karyn, learned that weekend. She was doing jumps by the second day. By that time, I ~~spent~~ *was spending* a lot of time at the ski café.

Past Progressive and Simple Past Tense

CHECK POINT

2, 1

CHART CHECK

F, T

EXPRESS CHECK

When
was he driving

2. F
3. T
4. F
5. T

4. were waiting
5. noticed
6. Was . . . speeding
7. got
8. was
9. was going
10. reached
11. wasn't
12. were crossing
13. hit

14. Did . . . stop
15. saw
16. didn't
17. was talking
18. was driving
19. didn't stop
20. weren't paying

21. were walking
22. Was . . . snowing
23. happened
24. was
25. wasn't
26. started
27. arrived

2. she was driving home, she listened to her car radio.
3. She pulled over to the side of the road . . . the visibility got very bad.
4. She heard about the accident . . . she was listening to the news.
5. She drove to the police station . . . it stopped snowing.
6. she was talking to the police, she was thinking about her editorial for the morning paper.

Yesterday, a man was talking on his cell
              driving
phone while he was ~~drive~~ his car. Maybe
 was
he ^ checking his daily planner while he

was making his next appointment. He was

certainly not concentrating on the road
                 turned
when the light suddenly ~~was turning~~ red.
              tried
The two men in the street ~~were trying~~ to

jump out of the way when they saw him, but

it was too late. No one was badly hurt, but

that was just luck. Last year, the City Council
     didn't pass
~~weren't passing~~ the "talking and driving

law." We need that law!

SelfTest

(Total = 100 points. Each item = 4 points.)

SECTION ONE

1. **A**	4. **B**	7. **A**	10. **C**
2. **D**	5. **A**	8. **B**	11. **C**
3. **D**	6. **B**	9. **D**	12. **B**

SECTION TWO

(Correct answers are in parentheses.)

13. **C** (call)	20. **A** (did)
14. **C** (was)	21. **D** (got)
15. **A** (were)	22. **C** (got)
16. **D** (were sleeping)	23. **B** (was driving)
17. **B** (not)	24. **B** (*delete comma*)
18. **D** (dropped)	25. **D** (saw)
19. **A** (was)	

UNIT 11 — Present Perfect: *Since* and *For*

CHECK POINT

T

CHART CHECK 1

have + past participle
base form of verb + –*d* or –*ed*

CHART CHECK 2

a length of time

EXPRESS CHECK

driven: irregular
competed: regular
won: irregular
tried: regular

Martina Hingis picked up her first tennis racket at the age of two. Since then, she has become one of the greatest tennis players in the world. Born in Slovakia, she has lived in Switzerland for many years. She became the outdoor Swiss champion at age nine. Since then she has won many international competitions including Wimbledon, the U.S. Open, and the Australian Open.

For young stars like Martina, life has its difficulties. They are under constant pressure to win, and they don't have time to just hang out with classmates. In fact, Martina hasn't attended school since 1994, and she has been in the public spotlight for years. But she seems to be handling her success well. Since she turned professional, she <u>has played</u> tennis all over the world and <u>has earned</u> millions of dollars. She sees her life as normal because tennis <u>has been</u> the most important thing to her (since she was a little girl).

 3. 've been
4. for
5. For
6. has attended
7. hasn't done
8. Since
9. has taken
10. hasn't gotten
11. Since
12. has met
13. hasn't thought
14. 's known
15. since

 2. How long has she lived in Switzerland? (She has lived in Switzerland) for many years.
3. Has she won any competitions since the outdoor Swiss championship? Yes, she has.
4. Has she attended school since 1994? No, she hasn't.
5. How much money has she earned since she began her career? (She has earned) millions of dollars.
6. How long has tennis been important to her? (Tennis has been important to her) since she was a little girl.

 have been
I ~~am~~ in Ms. Rodriguez's physical education
     for
class ~~since~~ two months. I enjoy it a lot and
      missed
have only ~~miss~~ two classes since the

beginning of the semester. I especially like
         haven't played
tennis, but since September we ~~don't play~~
     has
because the weather ~~have~~ been too cold. I
       won
also like volleyball, and my team has ~~win~~

two games since we ~~have~~ started to compete

with Lincoln High School. I'm looking

forward to the next game.

Present Perfect:
Already and *Yet*

CHECK POINT
F

CHART CHECK 1
use *already*
use *not . . . yet*

CHART CHECK 2
T

EXPRESS CHECK
Have you had lunch yet?
Yes, I/we have. OR No, I/we haven't.

 2. c
3. a
4. b
5. d

 3. Has . . . disappeared already OR yet
4. Yes . . . has
5. have already developed
6. haven't been able . . . yet
7. Has . . . made . . . yet
8. No . . . haven't

 3. Helmut has already baked the cake.
4. Gisela has already bought flowers.
5. Helmut hasn't put the turkey in the oven yet.
6. Gisela has already washed the windows.
7. Helmut has already mopped the floor.
8. Gisela has already hung the balloons.
9. Helmut hasn't washed the dishes yet.
10. Gisela hasn't wrapped the gifts yet.

            gone
I'm in a hurry. I haven't ~~went~~ shopping
  yet
~~already~~, but I'll do it on the way home. Rita
 has
~~have~~ already had dinner and she's already
          called
had her bath. Have you ~~call~~ Mr. Jacobson
      already called
yet? He's ~~called already~~ three times today.
    hasn't
His daughter ~~has~~ gotten her flu shot yet.

Is it too late? See you later.

UNIT 13 Present Perfect:
Indefinite Past

CHECK POINT

now

CHART CHECK 1

T

CHART CHECK 2

before the past participle

EXPRESS CHECK

Have you ever watched "The Simpsons"?
Yes, I/we have. OR No, I/we haven't.

2. F   **4.** F   **6.** F
3. T   **5.** F   **7.** T

2

2. 've had   **6.** 've . . . wanted
3. 've stopped   **7.** have . . . traveled
4. Have . . . talked   **8.** 've traveled
5. have . . . wanted   **9.** have . . . made

3

2. I've never even been in a chat room.
3. How have you changed as an actor?
4. I've become a better team player lately.
5. who has been your role model?
6. Charlie Chaplin has had great influence on me.
7. What has been your best moment on this show?
8. Jimmy has just won the Emmy.
9. what have you found most rewarding about this experience?
10. I've met some fantastic people on this show.

4   watched
I've just ~~watch~~ the Blind Date episode on
          ever
Feldstein! Have you ~~never~~ seen anything so

funny? I LOVE this show! It's the best show
      seen   've
I have ever ~~saw~~ in my life. I really enjoyed
                noticed
it lately. By the way, have you ~~notice~~ that

Jimmy and Arlene are beginning to get
               has
along? I think Jimmy ~~have~~ started to really

like her. Last night Arlene ~~has~~ moved right

next door to Jimmy, but he doesn't know it
yet! I can't wait to see what happens on the
next episode. Does anyone know when
Jimmy's book is coming out?

UNIT 14 Present Perfect and
Simple Past Tense

CHECK POINT

T

CHART CHECK 1

the present perfect

CHART CHECK 2

have + past participle

EXPRESS CHECK

met, have been

1

Many modern marriages are finding
interesting solutions to difficult problems.
Joe and Maria, for example, (have been)
married since 1995. After their wedding, the
couple <u>settled</u> down in Boston, where Maria
<u>opened</u> an accounting business. Then in 1997
Joe <u>lost</u> his job. By that time, Maria's new
business was booming, so they <u>didn't consider</u>
moving. Joe never <u>found</u> a new job in Boston,
but in 1998, he <u>got</u> a great offer on the other
side of the country—in Los Angeles. The
couple (has lived) apart ever since. How
(have) they (handled) this "commuter marriage"
up to now? Joe notes, "It certainly
(hasn't been) easy. We've been) geographically
separated, but we've grown) a lot closer
emotionally. For that reason, it's been)
worth it."

2. T   **4.** F
3. F   **5.** T

2
3. haven't stopped
4. has . . . been
5. slept
6. haven't gotten
7. 've seen OR have seen
8. didn't do
9. didn't bother
10. Have . . . tried OR Did . . . try
11. Yes, I have. OR Yes, I did.
12. 've drunk
13. drank

3
5. Did you start your business before your marriage?
6. No, I didn't.
7. How long have you owned your own business?
8. (I've owned my own business) since 1995/for *six* years.
9. When did you find your job in Los Angeles?
10. (I found my job in Los Angeles) in 1998/*three* years ago.
11. Has your commuter marriage been very difficult?
12. Yes, it has!

4
It's 8:00 P.M. It ~~was~~ *'s been* a hard week, and it's not

over yet! I still have to finish that report.
started
I've ~~started~~ it last Monday, but so far, I've
written
~~wrote~~ only five pages. And it's due next
has been
week! Work ~~was~~ so difficult lately. I've

worked late every night this week. I'm tired,
didn't get
and I ~~haven't gotten~~ much sleep last night.
saw
I miss Joe. I've ~~seen~~ him last weekend, but

it seems like a long time ago.

Present Perfect Progressive

 **POINT**
People are still collecting Beanie Babies.

CHART CHECK 1
T

CHART CHECK 2
been + base form + *-ing*

EXPRESS CHECK
A: has
B: For
A: been
B: collecting

1
2. b   4. b   6. b
3. a   5. a

2
3. have been flying
4. has been living
5. has been sending
6. have been appearing
7. has . . . been attracting
8. has been choosing
9. Have . . . been standing
10. No, they haven't.
11. haven't been asking

3
2. He hasn't been testing the inline skates.
3. He hasn't been shooting baskets.
4. He's been eating pizza.
5. He hasn't been drinking soda.
6. He's been building a racing car.
7. He's been playing video games.
8. He hasn't been sending e-mail messages.

4
Thank you very much for the Pokémon
playing
cards. My friend and I have been ~~play~~ with
've
them all day. So far, I ~~am~~ been winning.
has
I really love Pokémon. My Mom ˄ been buying

the toys for us because she thinks they're
have been
cute too. All my friends ~~were~~ collecting the

cards for months now. Tonya loves the
She's
computer game you sent too. ~~She've~~ been

asking me to play with her, but I've been

having too much fun with my cards. How
thinking
have you been? I've been ~~thought~~ about you

a lot. I hope you can come and visit us soon.

UNIT 16 Present Perfect and Present Perfect Progressive

CHECK POINT

F, T

CHART CHECK

T

EXPRESS CHECK

A: eating
B: has . . . been
A: has OR 's
B: Has
A: No . . . hasn't

2. T   **4.** F   **6.** T
3. T   **5.** T

2. has published
3. have already died
4. has given
5. has spoken
6. have been waiting
7. has lived OR has been living
8. has worked OR has been working
9. has created

2. 've . . . seen
3. has been living OR has lived
4. has experienced
5. has survived
6. have tested
7. have hunted
8. have saved
9. has been moving
10. has been eating
11. (has been) resting
12. has been raining OR has rained
13. have found OR have been finding

Elephants and their ancestors have been
living
~~live~~ on this planet for 5 million years.

Scientists have found their bones in many

places, from Asia to North America. Present-
have
day elephants ~~has~~ also survived in different

kinds of environments, including very dry

areas in Niger, grasslands in East Africa,

and forests in West Africa.

Because of their great size and strength,
fascinated
elephants have always ~~fascinating~~ humans.

Our fascination has almost caused African

elephants to become extinct. Poachers
killed
(illegal hunters) have already ~~been killing~~

hundreds of thousands of elephants for the

ivory of their tusks. After 1989 it became

illegal to sell ivory. Since then, the elephant
grown OR been growing
population has ~~been grown~~ steadily.

Recently several countries have been

protecting elephants in national parks, and
become
herds have ~~became~~ larger and healthier.

UNIT 17 Past Perfect

CHECK POINT

Oprah decided on a career.

CHART CHECK 1

T

CHART CHECK 2

before the subject

EXPRESS CHECK

A: arrived
B: hadn't

2. T   **4.** F   **6.** T
3. T   **5.** F

2. hadn't yet gotten
3. had already gotten
4. hadn't yet been
5. hadn't yet gotten
6. had already been
7. hadn't yet built
8. had already starred

3
2. Had he reviewed . . .   No, he hadn't.
3. Had he reviewed . . .   Yes, he had.
4. Had he met . . .   No, he hadn't.
5. Had he taped . . .   Yes, he had.
6. Had he worked out . . .   Yes, he had.

**4**
Oprah Winfrey is an amazing person! By the
                         had
time she was twelve, she ~~has~~ already decided
on a career. Not long afterward, she got her
                                    had
first radio job. Although she hadn't ~~have~~ any
experience, she became a news reporter.
                                      had
When she got her own TV talk show, she ~~has~~
already acted in a major Hollywood movie.
By the late 1980s "Oprah Winfrey" had
become
~~became~~ a household word. Then in 1994 she
decided to improve the quality of talk-show
themes. She also made a personal change.
She had always had a weight problem, but
in 1995 TV viewers saw a new Winfrey.
                lost
She had ~~losed~~ almost ninety pounds as a
result of dieting and working out. She had
                competed
also ~~compete~~ in a marathon. She has really
been an inspiration to many people.

**UNIT 18** **Past Perfect Progressive**

CHECK POINT
   T

CHART CHECK
   been

EXPRESS CHECK
   A: had . . . been practicing
   B: had been practicing
   A: Had . . . been practicing
   B: hadn't, had been practicing

1
2. e   4. a   6. c
3. d   5. f

2
2. had been planning
3. had been joking and laughing
4. had been practicing
5. had been running
6. had been looking forward
7. had been waiting

3
3. had you been running
4. had you been dating
5. Had you been living
6. No, I OR we hadn't
7. Had you been expecting
8. No, I hadn't

4
I just got back from the marathon! I'm tired
but very happy. When I crossed the finish
                      had
line, I ~~have~~ been running for four hours and
twenty-five minutes. Jeremy was standing
                              waiting
there. He had been ~~waited~~ for me the whole
time. We were both soaking wet—I, because
                                     had
I had been sweating; he, because it ~~has~~ been
raining just a little while before. I was so
                              looking
glad to see him. I had been ~~look~~ forward to
this day for so long and hoping that I could
finish the race in less than four and a half
hours. When I got home, I called my parents.
           been
They had ∧ watching the marathon on TV and
had actually seen me cross the finish line!

SelfTest

(Total = 100 points. Each item = 4 points.)

SECTION ONE

1. **C**	5. **B**	9. **C**	12. **A**
2. **D**	6. **C**	10. **A**	13. **D**
3. **C**	7. **B**	11. **B**	14. **B**
4. **A**	8. **B**		

SECTION TWO

(Correct answers are in parentheses.)

15. **C** (*delete* has)
16. **D** (yet)
17. **C** (seemed)
18. **A** ('ve been reading)
19. **A** (Have)
20. **D** (for)
21. **D** (taken)
22. **B** (has already been in business OR for fifty years already)
23. **C** (drink)
24. **C** (*delete* 've)
25. **C** (had)

UNIT 19

Future: *Be going to* and *Will*

CHECK POINT

The man is going to fall into the hole.

CHART CHECK 1

three

CHART CHECK 2

F

CHART CHECK 3

T

EXPRESS CHECK

It's going to rain.
I'll get an umbrella.

1 **Items checked:** 2, 4, 5

2
2. He's going to take a trip.
3. He's not going to drive. OR He isn't going to drive.
4. He's going to give a speech.
5. He's going to answer the phone.
6. He's not going to watch TV. OR He isn't going to watch TV.

3
3. 'll . . . use
4. Will . . . get
5. won't
6. will have
7. 'll repair

8. will . . . be
9. will have
10. will look
11. 'll open
12. 'll adjust

13. 'll . . . control
14. Will . . . prevent
15. will

16. will . . . cost
17. won't be

4 I'm sorry that we ~~will no~~ **won't** be able to get together in Madison. Martha, too, will ~~misses~~ **miss** you. Perhaps we can get together sometime next month. Martha and I ~~am~~ **are** going to be in Minneapolis until July 15. After that, we are going ᵥ visit our son in **to** Phoenix. His wife is pregnant and ~~will~~ **is going to** have a baby the first week in July. It's hard to believe that we're ~~gonna~~ **going to** be grandparents! How exciting that you ᵥ going to talk at **are OR 're** the conference! I'm sure it ~~wills~~ **will** be great.

I've got to run now. The sky is getting really dark and ~~it'll~~ **it's going to** storm. I want to get out of this office before then. More later.

UNIT 20

Future: Contrast

CHECK POINT

T, F

CHART CHECK

T, F

EXPRESS CHECK

I'm leaving in five minutes.
Are you going to the conference in May?

1
RUSS: Ellen! It's nice to see you. <u>Are</u> you <u>presenting</u> a paper this week?
GREEN: Hi, Rick. Yes. In fact, my talk <u>starts</u> at two o'clock.
RUSS: Oh, maybe <u>I'll go</u>. What <u>are</u> you <u>going to talk</u> about? Robots?
GREEN: Yes. <u>I'm focusing</u> on personal robots for household work.

RUSS: I'd like one of those! Where's your son, by the way? Is he here with you?

GREEN: No. Tony stays in Denver with his grandparents in the summer. I'<u>m going to visit</u> him after the conference. So, what are you working on these days?

RUSS: I'm still with the Mars Association. In fact, we'<u>re going to be holding</u> a news conference next month about the Mars shuttle launch.

GREEN: That's exciting. Maybe I'<u>ll see</u> you there.

RUSS: Great. The conference <u>begins</u> at noon on the tenth.

2. it's going to rain
3. I'll see
4. I'll call
5. I'm going
6. I'm mailing
7. I'm giving
8. will you be, lands, I'll see

1. 'll wait
2. 's going to rain, 'll check OR 'm going to check
3. do . . . board OR will . . . board OR are . . . going to board, 're flying
4. 'll carry
5. do . . . land OR are . . . going to land OR will . . . land OR are . . . landing, 're going to be OR 'll be
6. 're going to get OR get OR 're getting OR 'll get, 'm having OR 'm going to have
7. 're going to start OR 'll start OR start

"Good evening, ladies and gentlemen. This
~~will be~~ *is* your captain speaking. We ~~be~~ *are* going to leave the Earth's gravity field in about fifteen minutes. At that time, you ~~are~~ *will be* able to unbuckle your seat belts and float around the cabin. Host robots ^*are going to* OR *will* take orders for dinner soon. After these storm clouds, we ~~are having~~ *'re going to have* OR *'ll have* a smooth trip. The shuttle arrives on Mars tomorrow at 9:00. Tonight's

temperature on the planet is a mild minus 20 degrees Celsius. By tomorrow morning the temperature ~~is~~ *will be* 18 degrees, but it ~~is feeling~~ *'s going to feel* OR *'ll feel* more like 28 degrees. Enjoy your flight."

UNIT 21 Future Time Clauses

CHECK POINT

The child is planning her future.

CHART CHECK

T, F

EXPRESS CHECK

What will she be when she grows up?
She's going to be a scientist.

2. T **4.** T **6.** T
3. F **5.** F

2. They are going to move to a larger apartment . . . Jeff gets a raise.
3. . . . they move to a larger apartment, they're going to have a baby.
4. Sandy will get a part-time job . . . they have their first child.
5. . . . Sandy goes back to work full-time, their child will be two.
6. Sandy will work full-time . . . Jeff goes to school OR Jeff will go to school . . . Sandy works full-time.
7. Jeff will find another job . . . he graduates.

I.
graduate
II.
1. get, 'll have OR 'm going to have
2. save, 'll buy OR 'm going to buy
3. 'll feel OR 'm going to feel, am
III.
1. get up, 'll buy OR 'm going to buy
2. speak, 'll ask OR 'm going to ask
3. 'll look OR 'm going to look, go
4. go, 'll improve OR 'm going to improve

4 Tomorrow is my first dance recital! By the time I ~~will~~ write my next journal entry, it will already be over! As soon as we finish the performance**,** there ^{is} ~~are~~ going to be a big party for us. Reporters will be there when we enter the room. While we ~~will~~ celebrate, the press will interview members of the dance group. As soon as I get up Sunday morning**,** I'll buy the paper and read the interviews. We're going to perform this show for

two weeks. As soon as it's finished,
we ^{'re going to learn OR 'll learn} ~~learned~~ a new program. I'm so excited.

Ever since I was little, I've wanted to be a ballet dancer.

UNIT 22 Future Progressive

CHECK POINT
Before 12:00

CHART CHECK
T

EXPRESS CHECK
Will you be working tomorrow?
Yes, I will. OR No, I won't.
What are you going to be doing?
(Answers will vary.)

1 Today we find most robots working in factories around the world. But what <u>will</u> robots of the future <u>be doing</u>? One Massachusetts Institute of Technology designer predicts that in just a few years, small, intelligent robots <u>are going to be taking</u> care of all the household chores. This is going to make life a lot easier. While one robot is cooking dinner, another one

will be vacuuming the floor. But what about outside the home? <u>Will</u> robots <u>be playing</u> <u>football</u> or <u>fighting</u> wars? Scientists aren't sure. What is certain, however, is that robots <u>will be playing</u> a more and more significant role in our lives.

 2
1. **c.** 'll be going
2. **a.** are . . . going to be leaving
   b. won't be getting
3. **a.** are . . . going to be coming
   b. 'll be taking
   c. Are . . . going to be having
   d. No, we aren't. OR No, we're not.
4. **a.** 'm going to be visiting
   b. won't be buying

 3
2. will be dusting OR is going to be dusting . . . is vacuuming OR vacuums the living room.
3. will be repainting OR is going to be repainting the kitchen . . . is doing OR does the laundry.
4. is making OR makes . . . will be recycling OR is going to be recycling the garbage.
5. will be giving OR is going to be giving Mr. Gee . . . is shopping OR shops for food.
6. will be making OR is going to be making . . . is helping OR helps Tony with homework.
7. is playing OR plays . . . will be walking OR is going to be walking the dog.

 4 In the future, robots will be ^{performing} ~~perform~~ more and more tasks for humans. This will ^{have} ~~be having~~ both positive and negative effects. On the one hand, while robots ^{are doing OR do} ~~will be doing~~ the boring and dangerous jobs, humans will be devoting more time to interesting pursuits. In this way robots ^{are} ~~is~~ going to be making life a lot easier for humans. On the other hand, the widespread use of robots is going _^^{to} create a lot of future unemployment. People will _^^{be} losing their jobs as robots fill their positions. And some

robots could even become dangerous.
I'm afraid that in the not-too-distant future,
robots will be operating nuclear power
stations! And before too long, robots are
going to be ~~fight~~ *fighting* in wars. Although, on
second thought, that will be better than
humans killing each other!

Future Perfect and Future Perfect Progressive

CHECK POINT

He hasn't been saving for three years yet.

CHART CHECK 1

F

CHART CHECK 2

T

EXPRESS CHECK

driving, driven

1

2. F   4. F   6. T
3. T   5. F

2

3. won't have graduated
4. will have attended OR will have been attending
5. won't have bought
6. 'll have been driving
7. won't have opened
8. 'll have been saving
9. will have accomplished

3

3. graduate
4. 'll have already been thinking
5. is born
6. won't have graduated . . . yet
7. will have already finished
8. celebrate
9. won't have started . . . yet
10. 'll have already been getting
11. open
12. 'll have already become

4

By August I'll ~~be~~ *have been* a word processor for
ten years. And I'll ~~earn~~ *have earned* OR *have been earning* almost the same
salary for three years! That's why I've made
a New Year's resolution to go back to school
this year. First I'm going to write for school
catalogs and start saving for tuition. By March,
I'll have ~~figure~~ *figured* out how much tuition will
cost. Then I'll start applying. By summer,
I ~~had~~ *'ll have* received acceptance letters. In August,
I'll talk to my boss about working part-time
and going to school part-time. By that time,
I'll have ~~saved already~~ *already saved* enough to pay for a
semester's tuition. By next New Year's Day,
I'll have been ~~study~~ *studying* for one whole semester!

SelfTest

(Total = 100 points. Each item = 4 points.)

SECTION ONE

1. C   5. B   9. C   13. C
2. A   6. B   10. A   14. B
3. A   7. A   11. B
4. B   8. B   12. C

SECTION TWO

(Correct answers are in parentheses.)

15. B (be)
16. D (will go)
17. D (finish)
18. C (driving)
19. A (be traveling)
20. A (will finish OR is going to finish)
21. B (work OR be working)
22. C (already OR *delete* yet)
23. A (will you)
24. D (is)
25. B (have)

UNIT 24 Wh- Questions: Subject and Predicate

CHECK POINT

the events on the night of May 12th
the names of people who saw the witness

CHART CHECK 1

T

CHART CHECK 2

F, T

EXPRESS CHECK

What happened last night?
What did you do next?

1

2. a	**4.** b	**6.** e
3. d	**5.** c	

2

2. How did you get home?
3. Who gave you a ride?
4. What happened next?
5. Who(m) did you see?
6. Who is Deborah Collins?
7. What did you do?
8. How many people called you?

3

3. What time (OR When) does court begin?
4. How many witnesses testified?
5. Why did the jury find Adams guilty?
6. What happened?
7. How long (OR How many weeks) did the trial last?
8. Who spoke to the jury?
9. How much did Adams pay his lawyer?
10. Who(m) did the district attorney question?

4

       did
What time ^ the suspect return home?
    saw
Who ~~did see~~ him? Were there any witnesses?
Who
~~Whom~~ was at home?

Why did he call A. Smith?
      happened
What ~~did happen~~ next?
    did he
Where ~~he did~~ go?
       did he take
How much money ~~he took~~ with him?

UNIT 25 Tag Questions

CHECK POINT

The man is commenting on the weather.

CHART CHECK

F, T, T

EXPRESS CHECK

You're an actor, aren't you?

1

KAY: Hi, Tom. It's a nice day, <u>isn't it?</u>

TOM: Sure is. Not a cloud in the sky. How are you doing?

KAY: Good, thanks. You don't know of any vacant apartments, <u>do you?</u> My son is looking for one.

TOM: He is? I thought he was staying with you.

KAY: Well, he really wants a place of his own. Do you know of anything?

TOM: As a matter of fact, I do. You know the Sobotas, <u>don't you?</u> Well, I just found out that they're moving to New York next month.

KAY: They are? What kind of apartment do they have?

TOM: A one-bedroom.

KAY: It's not furnished, <u>is it?</u>

TOM: No. Why? He doesn't need a furnished apartment, <u>does he?</u>

KAY: Well, he doesn't have furniture. But I guess he can always rent some, <u>can't he?</u>

TOM: Why don't you give your son my number, and I'll give him some more information?

KAY: Will you? Thanks, Tom.

2

2. j	**5.** b	**8.** c
3. h	**6.** g	**9.** e
4. f	**7.** a	**10.** d

3

2. did you	**5.** aren't you
3. doesn't it	**6.** don't you
4. haven't they	**7.** isn't it

4

              hasn't
BEN: It's been a long time, Joe, ~~haven't~~ it?

JOE: That depends on what you mean by a
           it
long time, doesn't ~~that?~~

BEN: What are you doing around here, anyway? It's dangerous.

JOE: I can take care of myself. I'm still alive, ~~amn't~~ *aren't* I?

BEN: Yes, but you're still wanted by the police, ~~are~~ *aren't* you?

JOE: Look, I need a place to stay. You have a place, don't you? Just for one night.

BEN: I have to think of my wife and kids. You can find someplace else, ~~can~~ *can't* you?

JOE: No. You've got to help me!

BEN:: I've already helped you plenty. I went to jail for you, ~~haven't~~ *didn't* I?

JOE: Yeah, OK, Ben. You remember what happened in Vegas, ~~do~~ *don't** you?

BEN: OK, OK. I can make a call.

OR: You don't remember what happened in Vegas, do you?

Additions with *So, Too, Neither,* and *Not either*

CHECK *POINT*

The men like the same things.

CHART CHECK

T, F, T

EXPRESS CHECK

and neither is Mark
and so does Gerald

1
2. F	4. T	6. T	8. T
3. T	5. F	7. F	9. T

2
2. too	4. did	6. So
3. neither	5. either	7. So

3
2. did I	4. do too	6. do I	8. too
3. can I	5. do I	7. do I	

4 My brother is just a year older than I am. We have a lot of things in common.

First of all, we look alike. I am 5'10", and so ~~he is~~ *is he*. I have straight black hair and dark brown eyes, and so does he. We share many of the same interests too. I love to play soccer, and he *does* too. Both of us swim every day, but I can't dive, and ~~either~~ *neither* can he.

Sometimes, being so similar has its problems. For example, last night I wanted the last piece of chocolate cake, and so ~~does~~ *did* he. Often I won't feel like doing the dishes, and neither ~~won't~~ *will* he. Worst of all, sometimes I'm interested in dating a certain schoolmate, and so ~~he is~~ *is he*. However, most of the time I feel our similarities are really nice. So does my brother.

SelfTest Ⅴ

(Total = 100 points. Each item = 4 points.)

SECTION ONE

1. A	4. A	7. D	10. A
2. C	5. D	8. D	11. B
3. A	6. D	9. B	12. C

SECTION TWO

(Correct answers are in parentheses.)

13. **C** (isn't)
14. **C** (didn't)
15. **D** (has his brother)
16. **D** (have)
17. **A** (did you work OR were you working)
18. **D** (it)
19. **D** (?)
20. **D** (I am too OR so am I)
21. **D** (they)
22. **C** (aren't)
23. **D** (he)
24. **C** (go)
25. **A** (Why did you)

UNIT 27 Ability:
Can, Could, Be able to

CHECK POINT

F

CHART CHECK 1

T

CHART CHECK 2

be

CHART CHECK 3

a form of *be*

EXPRESS CHECK

A: Is . . . to
B: is . . . can

A surprising number of young people <u>have been able to create</u> successful Web-based businesses. One young entrepreneur is Sam Roberts. Sam <u>could design</u> Web pages when he was eight, but he got his break at twelve when a writer hired him to design a Web site. Sam's first business failed because he and his partner <u>weren't able to get along</u>. However, his new business, Webman, is up and running. Another young businessman, Jay Leibowitz, <u>was able to sell</u> two software programs when he was fourteen. He made $30,000 on the deal and now Jay runs his own Web site. Dan Finley writes reviews of new software. He started his business at sixteen. A full-time college student, Dan <u>can pay</u> a staff of writers and still earn $500 a month. Although they all make money, all three started out to have fun at their hobby, not to make a profit.

2. Sam
3. Dan
4. Sam

1. can, 'll be able to
2. hasn't been able to, can
3. can't, 'll be able to
4. haven't been able to, can't, can't, 'll be able to

2. Were . . . able to communicate
3. can help
4. couldn't follow

5. couldn't decide
6. can manage
7. 'll be able to organize
8. be able to speak

Today in my Will B. Happy Teamwork course, I learned about work styles—"Drivers" and "Enthusiasts." I'm a Driver, so I can make decisions, but I'm not able ^to^ listen to other people's ideas. The Enthusiast in our group can ~~communicates~~ ^communicate^ well, but you can't depend on her. Now I understand what was happening in my business class last year, when I couldn't ~~felt~~ ^feel^ comfortable with my team. I thought that they all talked too much and ~~didn't~~ ^weren't^ able to work efficiently. I ~~could~~ ^was able to^ get an A for the course, but it was hard. I can do a lot more alone, but some jobs are too big for that. Our instructor says that soon the Drivers will ^be^ able to listen and the Enthusiast ~~could~~ ^will be able to^ be more dependable.

UNIT 28 Permission:
May, Can, Could, Do you mind if . . .?

CHECK POINT

The student is asking the teacher to allow him to take the test tomorrow.

CHART CHECK 1

could

CHART CHECK 2

F, T

EXPRESS CHECK

A: helps
B: Not at all, help

2. f   **4.** c   **6.** b
3. e   **5.** a

2

3. Do you mind if he stays
4. I do
5. May I use
6. you may not OR you can't
7. you can't start
8. do you mind if I borrow
9. Not at all OR No, I don't OR Go right ahead
10. you may open
11. Can I come
12. you can't

3

(Answers may vary slightly.)

2. Could I use your phone?
3. May I (OR we) park here?
4. Could we move up a few rows?
5. Can we (OR he) tape the concert?
6. Do you mind if I (OR we) leave?

4

2. B (can't)
3. B (change)
4. B (can)
5. C (have)
6. A (may not OR can't)
7. D (plays)
8. A (No, I don't OR Not at all)
9. C (we)
10. A (Yes, we can OR Sure OR Certainly)

UNIT 29

Requests:
Will, Can, Would, Could, Would you mind . . .?

 **POINT**

asking someone to do something

CHART CHECK 1

T

CHART CHECK 2

OK

EXPRESS CHECK

A: Would
B: No, not
A: will OR can OR would OR could
B: can't

1

1. MARCIA: Hi. You must be the new office assistant. I'm Marcia Jones. Let me know if you need anything.
   LORNA: Thanks, Marcia. <u>Could you show me the coat closet?</u>
   MARCIA: Certainly. It's right over here.
2. LORNA: Marcia, <u>would you explain these instructions for the fax machine?</u>
   MARCIA: Sure. Just put your letter in here and dial the number.
3. MARCIA: I'm leaving for lunch. Would you like to come?
   LORNA: Thanks, but I can't right now. I'm really busy.
   MARCIA: Do you want a sandwich from the coffee shop?
   LORNA: That would be great. <u>Can you get me a tuna sandwich and a soda?</u>
   MARCIA: Sure. <u>Will you answer my phone until I get back?</u>
   LORNA: Certainly.
4. MARCIA: Lorna, <u>would you mind making some coffee?</u>
   LORNA: I'm sorry, but I can't do it now. I've got to finish this letter before 2:00.

2

2. a	4. b	6. b
3. a	5. a	

3

2. you file these reports?
3. turning on the lights?
4. you buy some cereal?
5. you call back later?
6. you shut the door OR you mind shutting the door?

4

The meetings are going well but they have been extended a day. Could you please call ~~call please~~ Doug Rogers to try to reschedule our sales meeting?
Certainly OR Of course OR Sure
~~Not at all.~~ I'll do it right away.

We'll need three extra copies of the monthly sales report. Would you ask Ann to take care of that?
Certainly OR Of course OR Sure
~~Yes, I would.~~ (Ann—Could you do this?)

(continued on next page)

I hate to ask, but would you mind ~~to work~~ *working*
on Saturday? We'll need the extra time to go

over the new information I've gotten.

Sorry, but I ~~couldn't~~ *can't*. My in-laws are

coming for a visit. But Rob Lin says he

can come in to the office to help out.

One last thing. I was going to pick up those

new business cards, but I won't be back in

time. Would you mind doing that for me?

Not at all OR *I'd be glad to*
~~Yes, I would.~~ I'll stop at the printer's

during my lunch break.

 UNIT 30

Advice:
*Should, Ought to,
Had better*

 CHECK **POINT**

The interviewer is suggesting a type of job for
the applicant.

CHART CHECK 1

T

CHART CHECK 2

should

EXPRESS **CHECK**

A: Should
B: No . . . shouldn't

 1 **Items checked:** 1, 5, 6

 2
2. shouldn't	**5.** should
3. should	**6.** 'd better not
4. shouldn't	**7.** 'd better

3
2. You should (OR You ought to) look neat
3. What time should I arrive?
4. you shouldn't (OR you'd better not) arrive
   after 7:15
5. Should I bring a gift?
6. You shouldn't (OR You'd better not) buy an
   expensive gift

7. What should I buy?
8. you should (OR ought to) get some flowers

 4 We are so happy to hear about your new job.

Congratulations! Just remember—you

shouldn't ~~to~~ work too hard. The most

important thing right now is your schoolwork.
ought to
Maybe you only ~~oughta~~ work two days a

week instead of three. Also, we think you'd

better ask your boss for time off during

exams. That way you'll have plenty of time
'd
to study. You ~~would~~ better give this a lot of

careful thought, OK? Please take good care
better not
of yourself. You'd ~~not better~~ start skipping
work
meals, and you definitely shouldn't ~~worked~~
'd
at night. At your age, you ~~will~~ better get a

good night's sleep. Do you need anything

from home? Should we send any of your

books? Let us know.

 UNIT 31

Suggestions:
*Could, Why don't . . . ?,
Why not . . . ?, Let's,
How about . . . ?*

 **CHECK** **POINT**

F

CHART CHECK 1

does not change for different subjects

CHART CHECK 2

F

EXPRESS **CHECK**

Let's take the train.
Maybe we could take the train.
Why not take the train?
How about the train?

1

EMILY: Why don't we go to the races?
I hear they're really exciting.

MEGAN: I'd like to, but I need to go shopping.

EMILY: Then let's go to the Temple Street
Market tonight. We might even see
some Chinese opera in the street
while we're there.

MEGAN: That sounds like fun. If we do
that, why not go to the races this
afternoon?

EMILY: OK, but let's get something to
eat first in one of those floating
restaurants.

MEGAN: I don't think we'll have time.
Maybe we could do that tomorrow.
Right now, how about getting *dim
sum* at the Kau Kee Restaurant
next door? Then we could take the
Star Ferry to Hong Kong Island
and the racecourse.

EMILY: Sounds good. Here's an idea for
tomorrow. Why not take one of
those small boats—*kaido*—to
Lantau Island? When we come
back, we could have dinner at the
Jumbo Palace.

MEGAN: Let's do that. It's a little expensive,
but at least it floats!

2

2. How about   5. Let's
3. Why don't we   6. Let's not
4. Maybe we could

3

2. going to the beach?
3. buy another one.
4. we take a trip together?
5. try that new seafood place.

4

Emily   3:00

I'm going shopping. I'll be

back at 5:00. Let's ~~eating~~ ^{eat}

at 7:00. OK?

Megan

Megan   4:00

7:00 for dinner is fine.
                 going
How about ~~go~~ to a movie afterward_×?

See you later.

E.

Emily   5:00

I'm going to be too tired

for a movie. Maybe we could
             hang
just ~~hanging~~ around the hostel after

dinner. Let's talk about it later.

I'm taking a nap.

M.

M—   6:00

Let's not eat at the same restaurant tonight_×.
         try
Why don't we ~~trying~~ a new place?

How about Broadway Seafood_×?

I'll meet you downstairs at 7:00.

E.

UNIT 32
Preferences:
*Prefer, Would prefer,
Would rather*

CHECK *POINT*

Teenagers like to watch TV better than they
like to do other things.

CHART CHECK 1

would prefer ('d prefer)

CHART CHECK 2

the gerund or the infinitive

EXPRESS CHECK

read, than, shopping

1

2. F   4. F   6. T
3. F   5. F   7. T

2. I'd rather not cook   **5.** I'd rather have
3. Would . . . rather go   **6.** I'd rather not
4. I'd rather not   **7.** I'd rather see

1. prefer . . . to
2. 'd rather . . . than, prefer OR 'd prefer
3. 'd prefer
4. prefer . . . to
5. 'd rather . . . than
6. do . . . prefer . . . , prefer . . . to

For my study, I interviewed fifty men and

women. There was no difference in men's

and women's preferences for TV. I found that

everyone prefers watching TV ~~than~~ ^{to} going to

movies. Men and women both enjoy news

programs and entertainment specials.

^{watch}
However, men would rather ~~watching~~

adventure programs and science fiction,

while women prefer soap operas. Men also

like to watch all kinds of sports, but women

^{than}
would rather see game shows ~~to~~ sports.

Reading preferences differ too. Men prefer
^{to read OR reading}
~~to reading~~ newspapers, while women would

rather read magazines and books. When men
^{to read OR reading}
read books, they prefer ~~read~~ nonfiction and

^{prefer}
adventure stories. Women ~~are preferring~~ novels.

SelfTest

(Total = 100 points. Each item = 4 points.)

SECTION ONE

1. A	**5. C**	**9. A**	**12. A**
2. B	**6. C**	**10. C**	**13. B**
3. D	**7. B**	**11. D**	**14. D**
4. D	**8. B**		

SECTION TWO

(Correct answers are in parentheses.)

15. D (able to dive)	**21. D** (give)
16. D (?)	**22. C** (to)
17. C (better not)	**23. C** (was able to)
18. A (Would)	**24. C** (*delete* we)
19. B (borrow)	**25. D** (than)
20. D (ask)	

UNIT 33 Necessity: Have (got) to and Must

CHECK POINT

a requirement

CHART CHECK 1

F

CHART CHECK 2

a form of *do*

EXPRESS CHECK

A: does . . . have to
B: must

DMV: Department of Motor Vehicles. May
I help you?
BEN: I'm moving to California soon. <u>Will I
have to get</u> a California license when
I move?
DMV: Yes, you <u>will</u>. California residents
<u>must have</u> a California driver's license.
BEN: When <u>will I have to get</u> my California
license?
DMV: You <u>have to replace</u> your old license
ten days after you become a resident.
So come in and apply for your California
license right after you get there.
BEN: <u>Do I have to take</u> any tests to
exchange my Illinois license for a
California license?
DMV: Since you already have an Illinois
license, you <u>won't have to take</u> the
road test. But you <u>will have to take</u>
the written test.
BEN: How about the eye test?
DMV: Oh, everyone <u>has got to take</u> the
eye test.
BEN: OK. Thanks a lot. You've been very
helpful.

2. 've to (OR 've got to) pick up
3. Do . . . have to change
4. I don't
5. didn't have to do
6. 've to (OR 've got to) take
7. Does . . . have to pack
8. he doesn't
9. 's got to (OR has to) help
10. 've had to call

2. must turn	**5.** must ride
3. must drive	**6.** must not walk
4. must not drive	

How are you doing? We've been here about
six weeks. It's strange living in the suburbs.

There's no public transportation, so you've
got
~~get~~ to drive everywhere. I had to ~~signs~~ *sign* up

for driver's ed this semester so I can get my

license by summertime. It's the law here that
must
everyone ~~musts~~ wear a seat belt. I used to

hate to buckle up, but with the traffic here,

I have changed my mind. There are a lot of
got to
freeways, and you've ~~gotta~~ know how to

change lanes with a lot of fast traffic. Even my
has
Mom ~~have~~ had to get used to it. Dad works at
had
home, so he hasn't ~~has~~ to do a lot of driving.

Have you beaten those computer games

yet? I'm having a lot of trouble with "Doom."
've
You⌃got to write to me and tell me how to

get past the fifth level!

Choice: *Don't have to*
No Choice: *Must not*
and *Can't*

 **POINT**
stop to ask for directions

CHART CHECK 1
do

CHART CHECK 2
F

EXPRESS CHECK
He doesn't have to stop here.
You must not drive too fast.

New drivers are usually excited about their
new freedom: "My mom <u>doesn't have to drive</u>
me everywhere anymore! I <u>don't have to ask</u>
my friends for rides to school!" When you
don't have your own car yet, any price seems
worth paying. But once you buy a car, you
(can't forget) your car payments and insurance
premiums, or you won't be a driver for very
long. You (can't leave) gas and maintenance
out of the budget either. Car sharing offers
an alternative to these problems, however.
Members of car-sharing groups have a car
when they need one for either short trips
or vacations, but they don't have the high
expenses of ownership. They pay very little
to use a shared car, and they <u>don't have to</u>
<u>worry</u> about maintaining the car or paying
the insurance. Fees for short trips are only
about $3.00 an hour plus $0.50 per mile.
Groups do not have strict requirements
either. Members (must not have) bad
driving records or poor credit, and they
(must not return) the cars in poor shape or
they will pay extra.

2. can't yell	**6.** don't have to get
3. can't turn	**7.** haven't had to buy
4. can't park	**8.** can't bring
5. don't have to worry	**9.** don't have to listen

2. don't have to bring	**5.** don't have to be
3. must not play	**6.** don't have to leave
4. must not dive	

We got to the motel late this evening because
we got lost. But we were lucky—they kept
didn't have to
our room so we ~~must not~~ find another motel.

(continued on next page)

Jimmy is really happy because he ~~don't~~ *doesn't* have to go to bed until after 10:00, when the swimming pool closes. We ~~mustn't~~ *don't have to* leave until 11:00 tomorrow (checkout time), so we can stay up later. Yosemite is only four hours away, so we won't ~~had~~ *have* to drive the whole day tomorrow. It's going to be exciting. My parents say we absolutely must not ~~to~~ go out by ourselves because there are bears there. I'd love to see a bear (from the inside of the car). I'll send a postcard of one.

Expectations:
Be supposed to

CHECK POINT

the usual way something is done at a wedding

CHART CHECK

T

EXPRESS CHECK

A: were
B: was

It <u>Wasn't Supposed to Be</u> a Big Wedding

Providence, July 19—The Stricklands wanted a quiet wedding—that's why they eloped to Block Island, off the Atlantic Coast of the United States. The island is quite small, so the Stricklands packed their bikes for the ferry trip. The weather <u>was supposed to be</u> lovely, and they had asked the mayor to marry them on a hill overlooking the ocean.

"When we got there, we found a crowd of cyclists admiring the view," laughed Beth.

When Bill kissed his bride, the audience burst into loud applause and rang their bicycle bells. "We <u>weren't supposed to have</u>

fifty wedding guests, but we love cycling, and we're not sorry," Bill said.

While packing the next day, Beth left her wedding bouquet at the hotel. Minutes before the ferry <u>was supposed to leave</u>, Bill jumped on his bike, got the flowers, and made it back to the ferry on time. "Cyclists <u>are supposed to stay</u> fast and fit," he said.

2. F   **3.** F   **4.** T   **5.** T

2. a. Were . . . supposed to do
 b. No, they weren't
 c. were supposed to deliver
3. a. is supposed to start
 b. are . . . supposed to stand
4. a. aren't (OR 're not) supposed to be
 b. aren't (OR 're not) supposed to see
5. a. 'm supposed to wear
 b. 's supposed to rain
6. a. 's supposed to be

I'm so sorry—I know I ~~am~~ *was* supposed to write to you last week about my plans to visit. I've been awfully busy. My friend Netta is getting married soon, and she's asked me to be her maid of honor. She and Gary want a big wedding. They're supposed to have about two hundred guests. I have a lot of responsibilities. I ~~will be~~ *am* supposed to give Netta a shower before the wedding (that's a party where everyone brings presents for the bride). I am also ~~suppose~~ *supposed* to help her choose the bridesmaids' dresses. The best man's name is Jim. He'll help Gary get ready. I haven't met him yet, but he's ~~supposes~~ *supposed* to be very nice.

I'd better say goodbye now. I *was* supposed to leave for rehearsal five minutes ago.

P.S. About my visit—I'm ~~supposing~~ *supposed* to get some time off in July. Would that be convenient?

Future Possibility:
May, Might, Could

CHECK POINT

F

CHART CHECK 1

T

CHART CHECK 2

in answers

EXPRESS CHECK

B: might
A: might
B: might not

ALICE: I just heard that it <u>may snow</u> today. Are you going to drive to work?

BILL: No. I'll take the 7:30 train instead.

ALICE: I'll take the train with you. I have some work to do in the library.

BILL: Great. Why don't you cut your afternoon class and have lunch with me too?

ALICE: Oh, I <u>couldn't do</u> that. But let's meet at the train station at 6:00, OK?

BILL: I <u>might have to work</u> until 8:00 tonight. I'll call you and let you know.

1. Certain
2. Impossible
3. Possible

2. could   4. may not   6. may
3. might   5. 'm going to   7. might

3. She's going to a meeting with Mrs. Humphrey at 11:00.
4. She may (OR might) have coffee with Sue after class.
5. She's going to go to work at 1:00.
6. She may (OR might) go shopping after work.
7. She may (OR might) take the 7:00 train.
8. She's going to pick up pizza.

Every few years, the ocean near Peru becomes warmer. Called El Niño, this variation in temperature ~~maybe~~ *may* cause

weather changes all over the world. The west coasts of North and South America might ~~to~~ have heavy rains. On the other side of the Pacific, New Guinea might ~~becomes~~ *become* very dry. Northern areas could have **warmer,** wetter winters, and southern areas could become much colder. These weather changes affect plants and animals. Some fish ~~mayn't~~ *may not* survive in warmer waters. Droughts could ~~causing~~ *cause* crops to die, and food may get very expensive. El Niño may happen every two years, or it ~~could~~ *may OR might* not come for seven years.

Will El Niños get worse in the future? They could ~~be~~. Pollution holds heat in the air, and it ~~will~~ *may OR might OR could* increase the effects of El Niño, but no one is sure yet.

Assumptions:
May, Might, Could, Must, Have (got) to, Can't

CHECK POINT

making a guess

CHART CHECK 1

T

CHART CHECK 2

F

EXPRESS CHECK

A: could
B: might, can't

2. d   4. b   6. a
3. e   5. g   7. c

2. must   6. might be
3. 's got to   7. couldn't
4. could   8. might not
5. Could   9. may

3 **2.** I might (OR could) be
3. It could (OR might OR may) be the cat
4. You must eat a lot
5. Could it be
6. it can't (OR couldn't) be
7. It must come from your own pipe.
8. There can't (OR couldn't) be any other explanation.
9. there could (OR might OR may) be

4 The main character, Molly Smith, is a college ESL teacher. She is trying to find her dead grandparents' first home in the United States. It may ~~being~~ ^{be} in a nearby town. The townspeople there seem scared. They could ~~be~~ ^{might OR may OR could} have a secret, or they ~~must~~ just hate strangers. Molly has some old letters that might lead her to the place. They are in Armenian, but one of her students ~~mights~~ ^{might} translate them for her. They ~~hafta~~ ^{have to} be important because the author mentions them right away. The letter must contain family secrets. Who is the bad guy? It couldn't be the student because he wants to help. It might ~~to~~ be the newspaper editor in the town.

UNIT 38 **Advisability** in the Past

CHECK POINT
regrets things in his past

CHART CHECK 1
F

CHART CHECK 2
T

CHART CHECK 3
ought to have

EXPRESS CHECK
A: have
B: should have

1 **2.** T   **4.** F   **6.** T
3. T   **5.** T

2 **2.** shouldn't have done
3. should have studied
4. could have done
5. ought to have gone
6. shouldn't have stayed
7. could have prevented
8. might . . . have called
9. Should . . . have contacted
10. shouldn't have
11. could have saved

3 **2.** I shouldn't have eaten all the chocolate.
3. She might have called.
4. He could have offered to lend me some (money).
5. I shouldn't have jogged five miles yesterday.
6. They shouldn't have charged me (for the plastic bags).
7. I ought to have invited Cynthia (to the party).
8. He might have sent me a card.

4 About a week ago, Jennifer was late for work again, and Doug, our boss, told me he wanted to get rid of her. I was really upset. Of course, Jennifer shouldn't ~~had~~ ^{have} been late so often, but he might ~~has~~ ^{have} talked to her about the problem before he decided to let her go. Then he told me to make her job difficult for her so that she would quit. I just pretended I didn't hear him. What a mistake! I ~~oughta~~ ^{ought to} have confronted him right away. Or I could at least have warned Jennifer. Anyway, Jennifer is still here, but now I'm worried about my own job. Should I ~~of~~ ^{have} told Doug's boss? I wonder.

have handled

Maybe I should ~~handle~~ things differently

have

last week. The company should never ~~has~~

hired this guy.

39 Speculations about the Past

CHECK POINT

if it was possible that something happened

CHART CHECK 1

T

CHART CHECK 2

could

EXPRESS CHECK

have carved, might have

 2. a **4.** c **6.** b
3. f **5.** d

 2. They must have been
3. They may have
4. He might not have been
5. He must have

 2. could not have built
3. had to have gotten
4. must not have known
5. could have carved
6. (could have) transported
7. might have been
8. may have lived
9. must have had

4 In 1927, Toribio Mexta Xesspe of Peru

have been

must ~~be~~ very surprised to see lines in the

shapes of huge animals on the ground below

his airplane. Created by the ancient Nazca

culture, these forms are too big to recognize

from the ground. However, from about

600 feet in the air the giant forms take

shape. Without airplanes, how could an

have

ancient culture ~~had~~ made them? What

purpose could they have had? Author Erich

von Däniken believes that the drawings

marked

might have ~~mark~~ a landing strip for the

spacecraft of astronauts from another

planet. Archaeologists, however, now believe

that the ancient Nazcan civilization might

have developed *have*

~~develop~~ flight. They could ~~of~~ built hot-air

designed

balloons and ~~design~~ the pictures from the air.

SelfTest

(Total = 100 points. Each item = 4 points.)

SECTION ONE

1. C **5. A** **8. B** **11. B**
2. B **6. B** **9. D** **12. A**
3. B **7. D** **10. A** **13. C**
4. B

SECTION TWO

(Correct answers are in parentheses.)

14. C (must not have known)
15. D (leave)
16. C (have)
17. B (looked)
18. A (have got to)
19. C (can't)
20. A (must not)
21. B (have)
22. A (may OR might OR could)
23. A (was OR is)
24. C (have to)
25. A (should have)

40 Adjectives and Adverbs

CHECK POINT

warm and cozy

CHART CHECK

F, F, T

EXPRESS CHECK

A: slow, slowly
B: slow, slow

 1 Students! Are you looking for a <u>special</u> place to live? Come to 140 Grant street, Apt. 4B. This apartment is (absolutely) <u>perfect</u> for two <u>serious</u> students who are looking for a <u>quiet</u> neighborhood, just 15 minutes from campus. This <u>lovely</u> apartment is in a <u>new</u> building. It is a <u>short</u> walk to the bus stop. The <u>express</u> bus goes (directly) into town. At night the bus (hardly) makes any stops at all. You can walk (safely) through the <u>wonderful</u> parks on your way home. The rent is (very) <u>affordable</u>. Call for an appointment: 555-5050. This apartment will rent (fast).

 2 2. terribly disappointed
3. surprisingly easy
4. extremely safe
5. incredibly fast
6. awfully slowly
7. very clearly
8. unusually loud
9. exceptionally pleasant

 3

2. large	7. quiet
3. beautifully	8. hardly
4. happily	9. nice
5. busy	10. shy
6. nice	11. good

4 Some apartment ads are so ~~funnily~~! One ad
described a place as "~~warmly~~ and cozy." It was
really hot and crowded, but the owner insisted
that it suited me ~~perfect~~. I was trying very
~~hardly~~ not to laugh while he was describing
it, so I had to leave quickly. Another place
I saw was supposed to be "nice and ~~cutely~~."

Above funny / *warm* / *perfectly* / *hard* / *cute*

What a mess!! I left that place very ~~fastly~~
too. I'm not asking for the moon! I only want
a small place in a clean building with
friendly neighbors. I'm looking at another
place tomorrow. The ad says, "Clean and
bright. Small but convenient apartment on
lovely, ~~quietly~~ block." I wonder what that
really means!

Above: fast / *quiet*

Participial Adjectives

CHECK POINT

F

CHART CHECK

T

EXPRESS CHECK

exciting	excited
interesting	interested
frightening	frightened
amusing	amused
tiring	tired

 1 In some countries, people who are <u>interested</u> in meeting others turn for help to personal ads in newspapers and magazines, and online. A (surprising) number of busy people view these ads as a practical way of increasing their social circle. "I've tried hard to meet people on my own," said one <u>satisfied</u> customer. "I was new in town and wanted to make friends fast. The personals provided me with a quick way of meeting many (interesting) people in a short period of time." Others are not so <u>impressed</u>. "I think it's kind of (depressing) when people need to resort to placing ads to make friends," observed one man. "A friend of mine tried the ads several times and was really <u>disappointed</u> with the results. It's just not personal enough."

2. puzzled
3. puzzling
4. interesting
5. interested
6. fascinating
7. fascinated
8. disappointed
9. surprising
10. surprised

 2. boring
3. interested
4. fascinating
5. amused
6. horrifying
7. confusing
8. depressed
9. amazed
10. amusing
11. exhausted

 Just got home. I'm ~~disappointing~~ *disappointed* with the evening. At first I thought Jake was an ~~interested~~ *interesting* guy, but tonight I felt somewhat bored with his company. We saw a very ~~entertained~~ *entertaining* movie, but Jake didn't like it. In fact, it seems like we have completely different tastes in things. After the movie, I tried to make conversation, but all I really wanted was to go home. So, I told him I was ~~exhausting~~ *exhausted* and didn't want to get home late. If he asks me out again—I'm not ~~interesting~~ *interested*. Trying to meet people can be very ~~frustrated~~ *frustrating*.

Adjectives and Adverbs: Equatives

 **POINT**

riding speed, control of bike

CHART CHECK

as, an adjective or an adverb

EXPRESS CHECK

A: as expensive as, as well as   **B:** as good as

 So you were riding the trails this weekend, and you hit the dirt. Now your clothes look <u>as bad as</u> your bike. Never mind. They'll look <u>as good as</u> new next weekend. We checked out three major brands of detergent,

and we can tell you which ones clean best and which ones don't remove trail stains (<u>as effectively as</u>) others.

Overall, Brite and Kleen aren't <u>as expensive as</u> Trend, but they didn't perform (<u>as well</u>) either. However, they were almost <u>as good</u> in particular categories. Trend removed both mud and grass stains effectively. Brite removed mud just (<u>as effectively as</u>) Trend, but it didn't remove grass stains (<u>as well</u>). Kleen was effective on grass stains, but not on mud. Brite cleaned clothes (<u>as thoroughly as</u>) Kleen, but again, Brite and Kleen weren't <u>as good as</u> Trend in this category. On the other hand, Brite came out on top in brightening. Colors washed in Kleen and Trend just didn't look <u>as bright as</u> the ones washed in Brite.

 1. b. aren't as wide
  c. aren't as hard
2. a. cleans as effectively as
  b. isn't as unfriendly
  c. sounds as exciting as
  d. expresses . . . as clearly as
3. a. was as noisy as
  b. (will) pedal as quietly as

 2. doesn't stop as slowly as
3. isn't as expensive as
4. doesn't feel as comfortable as
5. isn't as cheap
6. rides as comfortably as
7. handles as well as
8. don't handle as well as
9. shifts as easily as

 RE: Not as many bruises!

Inexperienced riders should try the South Trail at Bearpaw Park. The scenery is just as ~~beautifully~~ *beautiful*, but its riding track isn't as unfriendly ~~than~~ *as* the North Trail's. The slopes aren't as steep, and you won't fall as ~~frequent~~ *frequently* because there aren't as many

(continued on next page)

rocks. It isn't as short ~~like~~ ^{as} the North, so you'll still get a good ride, and you won't feel as discouraged at the end of the day.

RE: the (expensive) new Trax

Does anyone have any experience with this bike? I test-drove it around the store parking lot, and I'm not impressed. My old Trax shifts ~~as just~~ ^{just as} easily, and it handles as smoothly too. Of course it's not as ~~lightly~~ ^{light}, but then it doesn't cost $999 either.

UNIT 43 Adjectives: Comparatives

CHECK POINT

different from the old restaurant

CHART CHECK

F, T

EXPRESS CHECK

more . . . than

 1 **2.** T   **3.** T   **4.** F   **5.** F

 2
2. less expensive than OR isn't more expensive than
3. hotter . . . spicier than
4. more fattening than
5. healthier OR more healthy than

 3
2. better . . . better,
the better . . . the more expensive
3. the more popular . . . the slower
4. worse . . . worse, the smokier . . . the worse
5. The more crowded . . . the noisier
6. The bigger . . . the harder
7. more . . . more delicious, heavier . . . heavier

 4 Pete's Place has just reopened under new management. The dining room looks bigger, ~~more bright~~ ^{brighter}, and prettier ~~as~~ ^{than} the old one.

Although the food isn't better, it *is* just as good. The menu is more varied and less ~~expensiver~~ ^{expensive}. Try one of their pasta dishes. You won't find a ~~more~~ fresher tomato sauce in town. And leave room for dessert. They just keep getting ~~good~~ ^{better} and better.

The wait staff is friendly but not able to handle large numbers of people—the_^^{more} crowded the restaurant, the slower the service. At dinnertime the lines outside this popular eatery are getting longer and ~~more long~~ ^{longer}. Try lunchtime for a quieter and ~~relaxeder~~ ^{more relaxed} meal.

UNIT 44 Adjectives: Superlatives

CHECK POINT

special

CHART CHECK

the, –est, most or least

EXPRESS CHECK

(the) nicest
(the) most beautiful
(the) warmest
(the) happiest

 1 You are the best mother in the whole wide world. You are the smartest, the brightest, and the funniest of all moms I've ever known. You are the nicest mom I've ever had. You are the most wonderful and definitely the least mean. No mom in the whole wide world is better than you. You are the greatest mother of all. I love you very, very much! Happy Mother's Day!

2
2. the happiest . . . of my life
3. the best . . . in the school
4. the coldest . . . of the year
5. the nicest . . . in our family OR of all
6. the wisest . . . of all OR in our family

3 2. is the most unusual gift.
3. is the least practical gift.
4. is the smallest gift.
5. is the biggest gift.
6. is the most expensive gift.
7. is the funniest gift.

4 Ramadan is the ~~seriousest~~ *most serious* time in Muslim culture. During Ramadan, we do not eat from sunup to sunset. This is difficult for everyone, but teenagers have the hardest time. Right after Ramadan is the Eid al-Fitr. This holiday lasts three days, and it's the ~~most~~ happiest time of the year. The morning of Eid, my family gets up early and goes to the mosque. After we greet our neighbors by saying "Eid Mubarek" (Happy Eid), we go home. We eat the *biggest* ~~big~~ breakfast you have ever seen. Our parents give us gifts, usually new clothes and money. One year, Eid came around the time I graduated from high school. That year, I got the most beautiful clothes and the *fattest* ~~fatter~~ envelope of money of all the children in my family. Eid Mela is part of Eid al-Fitr. On that day, we all go to a big park. Last year at Eid Mela, I had the *best* ~~better~~ time of my life. I met my old high school friends, and we all ate junk food and showed off our new clothes.

 **UNIT 45 Adverbs:** Comparatives and Superlatives

CHECK POINT
T

more or *less*, *the*

EXPRESS CHECK
than, *the best*

1 In the first soccer game of the season, the Golds beat the Silvers, 6 to 3. The Silver team played a truly fantastic game, but its defense is still weak. The Golds defended the ball much <u>more aggressively than</u> the Silver team did. Of course, Ace Jackson certainly helped win the game for the Golds. The Golds' star player was back on the field today to the delight of his many fans. He was hurt badly at the end of last season, but he has recovered quickly. Although he didn't play as well as people expected, he still handled the ball like the old Ace. He certainly handled it <u>the most skillfully</u> of anyone on the team. He controlled the ball <u>the best</u>, kicked the ball <u>the farthest</u>, and ran <u>the fastest</u> of any of the players on either team. He played hard and helped the Golds look good. In fact, <u>the harder</u> he played, <u>the better</u> the Golds performed. Watch Ace this season.

And watch the Silvers. They have a new coach, and they're training <u>more seriously</u> this year. I think we'll see them play <u>better and better</u> as the season progresses.

2 2. better
3. faster
4. less
5. more rapidly
6. harder
7. the most slowly OR the slowest
8. the most clearly
9. the longest
10. more quickly than
11. more completely than

3 3. the most slowly OR the slowest
4. more slowly than OR slower than
5. the farthest
6. faster than
7. higher than
8. the best
9. the worst

4 Last night I watched the Lakers and the

Bulls. Both teams played more aggressively
than
∧I've ever seen them. In fact, they played the
best
~~better~~ of any game I've watched this season.

In the first half, Michael Jordan sprained his

left ankle, and Shaquille O'Neal was out of

the game because of fouls. But they still didn't
than
start the second half any slower ~~that~~ the first.

With Jordan out, Kukoc scored the most
frequently
~~frequenter~~ of any player. He's been playing
better and
~~more and more~~ better as the season goes on.
the
In fact, ∧more he plays, the better he looks.

The Bulls won 97 to 88. The Lakers seemed
less
to get tired at the end. They played ~~little~~

and less consistently as the game went on.

SelfTest

(Total = 100 points. Each item = 4 points.)

SECTION ONE

1. **C**	5. **C**	9. **D**	12. **C**
2. **A**	6. **A**	10. **B**	13. **D**
3. **A**	7. **B**	11. **A**	14. **B**
4. **B**	8. **C**		

SECTION TWO

(Correct answers are in parentheses.)

15. **C** (the less)	21. **B** (*delete* more)
16. **C** (of)	22. **B** (most)
17. **B** (amazed)	23. **C** (more)
18. **C** (cute)	24. **C** (disgusting)
19. **B** (harder)	25. **B** (hot)
20. **A** (run as quickly)	

Gerunds:
Subject and Object

CHECK POINT

exercise

CHART CHECK

–ing, not

EXPRESS CHECK

A: Drinking
B: drinking
A: not drinking

1 Swimming is great exercise. It's healthy,
fun, and relaxing. Because swimming is a
"low-impact" sport, most people enjoy
participating in this activity without fear of
injury to their bones or muscles. Jogging,
which is a "high-impact" activity, can at
times be harmful. I know this from personal
experience. Last year while I was jogging,
I injured my right knee. I don't go jogging
anymore. After a painful month of recovery,
I stopped running and switched to water
sports. I'm now considering joining a
swimming team and competing in races.

2
2. Eating	6. swimming
3. Not drinking	7. walking, running
4. increasing	8. not going
5. doing	

3 2. quit smoking
3. go swimming
4. denied OR denies smoking
5. acknowledges being
6. is avoiding eating
7. is considering taking

4
Smoking
Ways I Can Quit ~~Smoke~~ Cigarettes
smoking
Pick an exact date to quit ~~smoke~~.
Cutting
Stop smoking completely. (~~Cut~~ down is

harder than stopping all at once.)
being
Avoid ~~to be~~ around other smokers

(at least at the beginning).

Exercising
Start exercising daily. ~~To exercise~~ can

reduce stress.
Not
~~No~~ drinking coffee may help too.
being
Imagine ~~been~~ a non-smoker. Positive mental

images can help.
joining
Consider ~~to join~~ a support group.
asking
Don't delay ~~to ask~~ for help. Call Dr. Burns

right away!

Keep trying and don't give up!

 Gerunds after Prepositions

 **POINT**

F, T, F

CHART CHECK

a preposition, the gerund

EXPRESS CHECK

A: joining
B: joining

 We, the members of the Student Council, would like to share with you the thoughts and concerns of the general student body. As you probably know, many students are complaining about life on campus. We are interested <u>in meeting</u> with you to discuss our ideas <u>for dealing</u> with these complaints.

We know that you are tired <u>of hearing</u> students complain and that you are not used <u>to working</u> with the Student Council. However, if you really believe <u>in giving</u> new ideas a try, we hope you will think <u>about speaking</u> with our representatives soon. We look forward <u>to hearing</u> from you soon.

 2. in listening
3. about going, about driving
4. to staying, relaxing
5. for having
6. at learning
7. on coming
8. on reading, (on) going

 2. We can make changes by telling the administration about our concerns.
3. The administration can help by listening to our concerns.
4. In some cases, students just complain instead of making suggestions for improvements.
5. Students get annoyed with some teachers for coming late to class.
6. You can improve your grades by studying regularly.

 I have been attending Longtree College for
studying
a year. I'm very happy about ~~study~~ here.

At first, it was a little hard getting used to
speaking
~~speak~~ English all the time, but now I feel
communicating
very comfortable about ~~communicate~~ in my

second language.

I just joined an international student
about
group, and I'm excited ~~with~~ meeting new

people. Summer break is coming, and a few
doing
of us are planning on ~~do~~ some traveling
joining
together. Before ~~to join~~ this group, I used to

spend holidays alone.
hearing
Please write. I look forward to ~~hear~~

from you!

Infinitives after Certain Verbs

CHECK **POINT**

Megan thinks "Impatient" should consider his proposal more.

CHART CHECK

F, T, F

EXPRESS **CHECK**

I want to write to Annie.

1 Slow down! You <u>appear to be</u> in too much of a hurry. You've only known this person for a month and yet you <u>asked her to marry</u> you! What's the big rush? *Why* can't you <u>afford to wait</u>? Are you afraid that if she <u>gets to know</u> you better, she may <u>decide not to tie</u> the knot? I agree with your girlfriend. You <u>need to consider</u> things more carefully. You can't <u>expect her (or yourself) to make</u> such an important decision so quickly. If you don't <u>want to regret</u> a hasty decision, I <u>advise you both to get to know</u> each other better before you hurry to the altar.

2
2. attempt to find
3. warns single people not to leave
4. urges them to use
5. fail to plan
6. plan to fail
7. wish to meet
8. Ask two friends to read
9. Choose to participate
10. advises people not to feel
11. wants to be

3 *(Answers may vary slightly.)*
2. would like Tom to call her at 10:00.
3. reminded Emily to buy gas (today).
4. invited Marta to join them for coffee.
5. agreed to be home by 10:30.
6. forgot to go to the 2:00 staff meeting.
7. encouraged her to try again.
8. needs to use the car (tonight).

4 Annie advised me ~~joining~~ ^{to join} a club or take a class, and I finally did it! I decided ~~become~~ ^{to} a member of the school's Outdoor Adventure Club, and I went to my first meeting last night. I'm really excited about this. The club is planning a hiking trip next weekend. I definitely want to go rafting in the spring. At first I didn't want ~~signing~~ ^{to sign} up, but the leader was so nice. He urged me ~~to not~~ ^{not to} miss this trip, so I put my name on the list. After the meeting, a group of people asked me to

go out with them. We went to a coffee shop and talked for hours. Well, I hoped ^{to} make some friends when I joined this club, but I didn't expect everyone ~~being~~ ^{to be} so friendly. I'm glad Annie persuaded me ~~no~~ ^{not} to give up.

UNIT 49 Infinitives after Certain Adjectives and Certain Nouns

CHECK POINT
Finding good fries is difficult.

CHART CHECK
to + base form of verb
certain nouns and adjectives

EXPRESS CHECK
It's convenient to eat fast food.
That's a low price to pay.

1 Please take a few <u>minutes to complete</u>^N this questionnaire about fast-food restaurants. Check (✓) all the answers that are appropriate for you.

1. How often are you <u>likely to eat</u>^A at a fast-food restaurant?
   ❏ 1–3 times a week
   ❏ 4–6 times a week
   ❏ more than 6 times a week
   ❏ never

2. In your opinion, fast food is:
   ❏ <u>good to eat</u>^A
   ❏ a <u>way to save</u>^N time
   ❏ <u>fun to order</u>^A occasionally
   ❏ <u>unhealthy to have</u>^A every day

3. Which statement best describes your feelings about the cost of fast food?
   ❏ It's a high <u>price to pay</u>^N for convenience.
   ❏ You get a lot for just a little money.

4. Is it a good <u>idea to include</u>^N healthy choices in fast-food menus?
   ❏ Yes   ❏ No

2. delighted to find
3. way to go
4. fun to eat
5. pleasure to eat
6. mistake to bring

7. outrageous to see
8. good to eat
9. essential to have
10. difficult to go

2. ready to cry
3. willing to work
4. hard to wake up
5. surprised to hear
6. eager to get

7. important to keep
8. time to decide
9. chance to show
10. easy to find

Tonight I made the decision ~~asked~~ *to ask* Chris

to take the night shift. I really thought she

was going to be glad ~~for getting~~ *to get* the offer.

She has her own rent *to* ⋀ pay, and I know it's

hard for ~~she~~ *her* to meet all her expenses. Looks

like she was the wrong person ~~I asked~~ *to ask*! The

problem was, she wasn't willing to ~~said~~ *say* Yes

or No, and I'm afraid I got a little impatient.

It was wrong of me to threaten to ask Steve.

I could tell that she was pretty upset to hear

that. I'll think about giving her the promotion

anyway. She deserves ~~getting~~ *to get* a break.

Infinitives
with Too and Enough

CHECK POINT
F, T

CHART CHECK
too

EXPRESS CHECK
She's too young to vote.
We're old enough to work.

2. b   **4.** b   **6.** b
3. a   **5.** a

2
2. It's too far for us to get home by ten. **G**
3. I'm mature enough to take care of myself. **G**
4. It's too dangerous to drive at night. **M**
5. I worry too much to give you permission. **M**
6. You aren't experienced enough to drive that far. **M**

3
2. cheap enough for us to afford
3. large enough to hold
4. too good for me to miss
5. big enough to share
6. too late to stop
7. old enough to stay
8. early enough to come
9. too slow to beat
10. safe enough to drive

4
The Phish concert was awesome! Now I'm

too excited ~~for sleeping~~ *to sleep*. That Mike Gordon

can really sing. My voice isn't ~~enough good~~ *good enough*

to sing in the shower! After the concert we

were really hungry, but it was ~~to~~ *too* late to go

for pizza. I HATE this stupid curfew! It's too

weird ⋀ *to* understand. My friend Todd works

and has to pay taxes, but the law says he's

too young ~~for staying~~ *to stay* out past 10:00! That's

crazy enough to make me want to scream.

That reminds me. I sure hope my mother

changes her mind soon enough for ~~I~~ *me* to buy

a ticket to the Hampton concert. They sell

out very quickly. Why doesn't she think

I'm mature ⋀ *enough* to drive fifty miles? I'll have to

do it sometime! Well, I'd better try to get

some sleep or I'll be too tired ~~too~~ *to* get up in

the morning.

UNIT 51 Infinitives of Purpose

CHECK POINT

an address book, a dictionary, a note pad

CHART CHECK

T, F

EXPRESS CHECK

I use an organizer to store addresses.
I set my alarm clock in order not to oversleep.

1

YOKO: It's 5:00. Aren't you going home?

LEE: No. I'm staying late to finish this report. What about you? Are you going straight home?

YOKO: No. I'm going to stop at the bank to get some cash. Then I'm going to Lacy's Department Store to take advantage of the sale they're having.

LEE: Oh, what are you going to get?

YOKO: One of those new electronic organizers they're advertising. I've been looking for something to help me with my work.

LEE: What's wrong with just a regular calculator?

YOKO: Nothing. But sometimes I have to convert other currencies to dollars.

LEE: What else are you going to use it for?

YOKO: Oh, to store important names and phone numbers and to balance my checkbook.

LEE: What did we do before they invented all these electronic gadgets?

YOKO: We made a lot of mistakes!

2

2. To withdraw $100.
3. To invite Rika and Taro to dinner.
4. To buy milk and eggs.
5. To buy batteries.
6. To get gas.

3 **First Part:**

3. f   **4.** a   **5.** d   **6.** e   **7.** c

Second Part:

3. She went to the store (in order) to buy some dishes.
4. We disconnected our phone in order not to get any phone calls.

5. He turned on the radio (in order) to listen to the news.
6. He didn't tell me he was sick in order not to worry me.
7. She bought a Datalator (in order) to store information.

4 I went to Dr. Towbin ~~for getting~~ *to get* my teeth cleaned today. While I was waiting, I used my Datalator to study for the TOEFL. Then I used it to ~~helps~~ *help* me pronounce "novocaine" and "dental floss" for my appointment. After the dentist, I checked my schedule and saw "Rika and Taro, dinner, 7:30." I should use it in order ~~to not~~ *not to* forget appointments! Luckily, my recipes are already on the Datalator, so I used them ~~for making~~ *to make* a quick shopping list. When I got home, there was a note on my door—"Call bldg. super." I checked the Datalator dictionary to find "bldg. super." The "building superintendent" wanted to come up in order *to* fix the doorbell! Rika, Taro, and I played with the Datalator all evening. You can program it ~~for~~ to play computer games too. I don't know how I lived without it!

UNIT 52 Gerunds and Infinitives

CHECK POINT

F, T

CHART CHECK

T, F, T

EXPRESS CHECK

to go, Going, talking, to talk OR talking

1

2. T   **4.** T   **6.** T   **8.** T
3. F   **5.** F   **7.** T

2. to trust
3. to forget, to remember
4. going
5. to remember
6. to turn off
7. Playing, improving

 (Answers may vary slightly.)
2. meeting Natalya last year (at Richard's party).
3. spilling grape juice (on the couch).
4. listening to jazz OR listening to Richard play jazz (at his parties).
5. going dancing (some time), to go (dancing some time).
6. to give Marta a ride home, to stay a little longer.

 What a great party! I usually avoid ~~to go~~ *going* to parties because it's such a problem for me to remember people's names. I'm so glad I read that book about ~~improve~~ *improving* your memory. The author suggested ~~to do~~ *doing* exercises, and they really helped. I stopped ~~to worry~~ *worrying* about what people would think of me, and I tried to pay attention to what people were saying. As a result, I had a great time! I'm even planning ~~going~~ *to go OR on going* dancing with this guy Lev.

I have an English test tomorrow, so I should stop writing now and start studying. The book even had some good tips about ~~study~~ *studying* for an exam. I hope I remember ~~using~~ *to use* some of them tonight!

Make, Have, Let, Help, and *Get*

CHECK POINT
T

CHART CHECK
T, F, T

EXPRESS CHECK
A: to correct
B: correct
A: stay
B: stay

1
2. F **4.** F **6.** F
3. T **5.** T

2
2. let   **5.** got   **8.** had
3. made **6.** made **9.** had
4. had   **7.** let   **10.** made

3
2. made her work
3. didn't let them use (their) dictionaries
4. had him clean
5. got him to pronounce
6. didn't let her speak
7. didn't make her leave

4 When I was a teenager, my parents never let me ~~to~~ play until I had finished all my homework. They even made me ~~helping~~ *help* my brothers with their homework before I could have any fun. On the one hand, they certainly got me ^*to* learn a lot. On the other hand, they made me ~~became~~ *become* too serious. I wish they had let me ~~to~~ have a little more fun. When I become a parent, I want to have my child ~~learns~~ *learn* responsibility, but also I would want to let ~~he or she~~ *him or her* have fun. As Ben Franklin said, "All work and no play makes Jack become a dull boy." I want to avoid that mistake.

SelfTest

(Total = 100 points. Each item = 4 points.)

SECTION ONE

1. C **3. A** **5. D** **7. A**
2. A **4. B** **6. C** **8. C**

9. **A**	11. **B**	13. **B**
10. **D**	12. **C**	14. **A**

SECTION TWO

(Correct answers are in parentheses.)

15. **B** (to change)	21. **D** (to seeing)
16. **C** (trying)	22. **A** (to buy)
17. **B** (finding)	23. **D** (not to fall)
18. **A** (Getting)	24. **B** (watching)
19. **B** (not to)	25. **D** (to do)
20. **C** (old enough)	

UNIT 54 Phrasal Verbs: Inseparable

CHECK POINT

in a restaurant

CHART CHECK

before the direct object

EXPRESS CHECK

We ran into Bob.
He was eating out.

1 Ho Da-ming's new restaurant was failing. His customers rarely (came back). Why? Mr. Ho contacted a feng shui consultant to (find out). Feng shui (meaning "wind and water") is the ancient Chinese art of placing things in the environment. According to this art, the arrangement of furniture, doors, and windows affects our health, wealth, and happiness. Mr. Ho was concerned about his business, but he didn't (give up). Following the consultant's advice, he remodeled and redecorated his restaurant. His actions (paid off.) Soon business (picked up) and Mr. Ho became rich. "It was the best decision I ever made," he glows. And he isn't alone in his

enthusiasm. Feng shui (has caught on) with modern architects and homeowners everywhere.

1. has caught on	4. find out
2. came back	5. give up
3. paid off	6. picked up

2
2. back	6. out
3. up	7. up
4. up	8. out
5. up	

3
2. turned out	6. give up
3. come up with	7. paid off
4. went up	8. go back
5. kept on	

4 Sorry the apartment is such a mess. I got ~~down~~ *up* late this morning and didn't have time to straighten ~~out~~ *up*. I'm going to the gym now to work ~~off~~ *out* for an hour. I should get ~~across~~ *back* before you, and I'll clean up then. How about eating ~~tonight out~~ *out tonight*? Afterward, we can get together with some of the guys and maybe see a movie. Or maybe we'll come ~~over~~ *up* with a better idea.

Oh—I ran ~~Tom into~~ *into Tom* at school. He'll drop ~~off~~ *by* to see you later.

UNIT 55 Phrasal Verbs: Separable

CHECK POINT

George is getting an idea for an invention.

CHART CHECK

Direct objects that are nouns can go before or after the particle.

EXPRESS CHECK

dreamed up that idea OR dreamed that idea up, dream it up

1 Did you know that two college dropouts <u>thought up</u> (the idea) of the first personal computer? What's more, they <u>put</u> (it) together in a garage. Inventions don't have to come out of fancy laboratories. Average people in classrooms, kitchens, and home workshops often <u>dream up</u> (new and useful ideas).

The ability to think of something new seems like magic to many people, but in fact anyone can develop the qualities of an inventor. First, inventors follow their curiosity. The Swiss inventor George de Mestral wanted to <u>find out</u> (the reason) it was so hard to remove burrs from his dog's coat. His answer led to the idea for Velcro®, now used to fasten everything from sneakers to space suits. Second, inventors use imagination to <u>put</u> (things) together in new ways. Walter Morrison watched two men tossing a pie pan to each other and <u>thought up</u> (the Frisbee®), one of the most popular toys in the world. Perhaps most important, successful inventors don't quit. They continuously <u>look up</u> (information) about their ideas and <u>try</u> (new designs) <u>out</u> until they succeed.

2
2. set up
3. filled . . . up
4. keep . . . away
5. picked up

6. paid . . . back
7. carry out
8. brought about

3
2. figure it out
3. fill them out
4. handed it out

5. do it over
6. turn them in

4 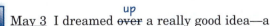 May 3 I dreamed ~~over~~ *up* a really good idea—a jar of paint with an applicator like the kind used for shoe polish. It can be used to touch *up* ~~on~~ spots on a wall, when people don't want to paint a whole room. I know a manufacturer. I'll call ~~up him~~ *him up* and order several types, so I can try them ~~in~~ *out*.

July 3 I filled ~~down~~ *out* an application for a patent and mailed it yesterday. I'll be able to set *up* a strong and convincing demonstration of the product ~~up~~ soon.

August 30 I demonstrated the product at an exhibition for decorators. I wanted to point out that it's very neat to use, so I put *on* white gloves for the demonstration. It went over very well.

SelfTest

(Total = 100 points. Each item = 4 points.)

SECTION ONE

1. A	**5. D**	**8. D**	**11. A**
2. C	**6. C**	**9. D**	**12. C**
3. A	**7. D**	**10. A**	**13. B**
4. B			

SECTION TWO

(Correct answers are in parentheses.)

14. A (it over)
15. D (up)
16. D (off the bus)
17. D (back)
18. B (get on the bus)
19. D (off)
20. A (up)
21. B (her up)
22. D (wake you up)
23. D (pick some stamps up for him . . . OR pick up some stamps for him . . .)
24. D (Meg into)
25. B (along)

UNIT 56 Nouns

CHECK POINT
Ra II

CHART CHECK 1

F

CHART CHECK 2

T, F

EXPRESS CHECK

were, was

Was (Columbus) really the first explorer to discover the (Americas)? (Thor Heyerdahl) didn't think so. He believed that ancient people were able to build boats that could cross oceans. To test his ideas, he decided to build a copy of the reed boats that were pictured in ancient paintings and sail across the (Atlantic) from (North Africa) to (Barbados). (Heyerdahl)'s team also copied ancient Middle Eastern pots and filled them with food for their journey—dried fish, honey, oil, eggs, nuts, and fresh fruit. (Ra), the expedition's boat, carried an international group including a (Norwegian), an (Egyptian), an (Italian), a (Mexican), and a (Chadian).

The first trip failed, but everyone survived and wanted to try again. Departing on (May) 17, 1970, under the flag of the (United Nations), (Ra II) crossed the (Atlantic) in 57 days. The expedition proved that ancient civilizations had the skill to reach the (Americas) long before (Columbus).

3. Food	**13.** are
4. is	**14.** Is
5. are	**15.** equipment
6. ideas	**16.** batteries
7. beans	**17.** news
8. rice	**18.** stops
9. Potatoes	**19.** clothing
10. are	**20.** cold
11. trips	**21.** bothers
12. vegetables	**22.** bags

October 27. I've been on the ~~canary~~ Islands [*Canary*] for three days now. I'll start home when the ~~weathers are~~ better. [*weather is*] I was so surprised

when I picked up my ~~mails~~ today. [*mail*] My family sent me some birthday presents. My ~~Birthday~~ is the 31st. [*birthday*] I won't open the gifts until then.

~~october~~ 29. [*October*] I think the weather is getting worse. I heard ~~thunders~~ today, [*thunder*] but there wasn't any rain. I stayed in bed with my cat, Typhoon. Every time it thundered, ~~typhoon~~ and I snuggled up closer under [*Typhoon*] the covers. I started reading a ~~Novel~~, [*novel*] *Brave New World.*

October 30. I left the Canary Islands today—just like ~~columbus~~. [*Columbus*] There's a strong wind and plenty of sunshine now. I went 250 ~~Miles~~. [*miles*]

October 31. I'm 21 today! To celebrate, I drank some ~~coffees~~ for breakfast [*coffee*] and I opened my presents. I got some perfume and pretty silver ~~jewelries~~. [*jewelry*]

November 1. The ~~electricities are~~ very low. [*electricity is*] I'd better not use much until I get near ~~new~~ York. [*New*] I'll need the radio then. It rained today, so I collected ~~waters~~ for cooking. [*water*]

UNIT 57 Quantifiers

CHECK **POINT**

a good supply of chocolate

CHART CHECK

T, F, T, T

EXPRESS CHECK

A: many   **B:** much   **A:** many

Are you ready? Many people don't realize that some natural disasters such as

earthquakes can strike with (little warning). It may take <u>several days</u> for assistance to reach you. Prepare your disaster kit in advance! Here are <u>a few tips.</u>

- Water may be unsafe to drink. Store (enough water) for <u>several days.</u> Each person needs a gallon per day for cooking and washing.
- You will also need food for <u>several days.</u> It's a good idea to store (a lot of canned meat, fruit), <u>vegetables</u>, and (milk). However, also include <u>several kinds</u> of high-energy food, such as peanut butter and jelly. And don't forget (some "comfort food") like cookies and chocolate!
- If you don't have (any electricity), you might not have (any heat) either. Keep <u>some blankets, sleeping bags,</u> and extra <u>clothes</u> for everyone.
- Prepare a first aid kit with <u>some pain relievers, several sizes</u> of bandages, and an antiseptic.
- The ATM's might not be working. Do you have (any cash)? You shouldn't keep (much money) in the house, but you should have <u>a lot of small bills</u>, and <u>a few larger bills</u> too.

2.
2. any
3. Several
4. a great deal of
5. a lot of
6. Many
7. a few
8. much
9. few
10. Some
11. a little
12. a few

3.
1. b. a few
   c. many
   d. much
   e. a few
   f. a little
2. a. a little
   b. few
   c. a few
   d. little
   e. a few

4.
We had a big storm last week, and we lost the electricity for ˄*a* few days. Once I got over being scared, it was a lot of fun—a little like

camping out. We have an electric furnace, so we didn't have ~~some~~ *any* heat. We slept in our sleeping bags around the fireplace. We sure used up ~~many~~ *a lot of* wood! Mom baked some bread in an iron pan in the fireplace. She had to try several times, but it was really good when it worked. We ate it with ˄*a* little peanut butter. The first night we had ~~much~~ *a lot of* problems figuring out what to do. It got dark early, and we only had a ~~little~~ *few* candles—and no TV! Cindy is five, and she was really freaked out until we made hot chocolate over the fire. Finally, everybody took turns telling stories. I found out that Dad knows a lot ˄*of* good stories.

UNIT 58 Articles: Indefinite and Definite

CHECK *POINT*
There is only one Earth.

CHART CHECK
F, T, T

EXPRESS CHECK
a, The

1.
2. a
3. b
4. b
5. b
6. a

2.
2. an
3. a
4. an
5. an
6. the
7. a
8. the
9. the
10. the
11. a
12. the
13. the

3.
2. the
3. the
4. a
5. a
6. the
7. The
8. an, the
9. the

4 Once there was a plumber named Mario.
The plumber   *a*
~~Plumber~~ had ‸beautiful girlfriend. One day,
an
a̶ ape fell in love with the girlfriend and
the
kidnapped her. The plumber chased ‸ape to
rescue his girlfriend.

This simple tale became *Donkey Kong*,
the
a̶ first video game with a story. It was
an
invented by Sigeru Matsimoto, a̶ artist with
Nintendo, Inc. Matsimoto loved ~~the~~ video
games, but he wanted to make them more
interesting. He liked fairy tales, so he
a
invented ‸story similar to a famous fairy tale.
The story
~~Story~~ was an immediate success, and
Nintendo followed it with *The Mario Brothers*.
The rest is video game history.

 Ø (No Article) and *The*

CHECK POINT
the little girl

CHART CHECK
indefinite
plural

EXPRESS CHECK
 A: the   **B:** Ø   **A:** the   **B:** Ø

 1 Do you enjoy amusement parks? Tomorrow,
Blare Gardens will open to the public for
the first time. The park features a wide
variety of rides and games that will appeal
to both adults and children. And of course
an amusement park would not be complete
without cotton candy and hot dogs. The food
at Blare Gardens promises to be very good.
Come early, bring the whole family, and be
sure to stay for the fireworks display that

takes place right after the sun sets. So,
check it out! You won't be disappointed.

2

2. Ø	10. Ø	18. the
3. Ø	11. Ø	19. Ø
4. Ø	12. Ø	20. the
5. the	13. the	21. Ø
6. Ø	14. the	22. Ø
7. Ø	15. the	23. Ø
8. Ø	16. Ø	24. the
9. Ø	17. the	25. the

3

2. the	7. Ø	11. The
3. the	8. Ø	12. the
4. Ø	9. Ø	13. the
5. the	10. Ø	14. the
6. Ø		

4 Hi! Blare Gardens is awesome! This is ‸best
the
vacation we've ever gone on! I love the rides
here. I mean, I've been on ~~the~~ roller coasters
before, but nothing is like the one they've
the
got here! And ‸food is great too. I usually
the
don't eat ~~the~~ hot dogs, but ‸hot dogs here are
the
great. So is ‸pizza. Do you like ~~the~~ amusement
parks? If so, you've got to get your family
the
to come. The only problem is ‸crowds here.
People have to wait to get into *everything*—
even the restrooms! See you soon.

 Reflexive Pronouns and Reciprocal Pronouns

CHECK POINT
F

CHART CHECK
F, T

EXPRESS CHECK
 A: yourself
 B: myself

1 Self-talk is the way we explain a problem to ourselves. It can affect the way we feel and how we act. Tom and Sara, for example, both lost their jobs when their company laid off a lot of people. Sara kept herself fit and spent time with friends. Tom gained ten pounds and spent all his time by himself. They were both unemployed, so the situation itself can't explain why they acted so differently from each other. The main difference was the way Tom and Sara explained the problem to themselves. Sara believed that she herself could change her situation. Tom saw himself as helpless. Later, everyone got their jobs back. When they all talked to one another back at the office, Tom grumbled, "They must have been desperate." Sara replied, "They finally realized they need us!"

insulting—like the way our high school math teacher used to talk to us. I thought, Jan and I treat each other well. He forgave
me
~~myself~~ for my mistake right away, and I forgave him for forgetting our dinner date two weeks ago. Jan and I could forgive
each other
~~themselves~~, so I guess I can forgive myself.

SelfTest

(Total = 100 points. Each item = 4 points.)

SECTION ONE

1. **C**	4. **C**	7. **C**	10. **C**
2. **B**	5. **A**	8. **C**	11. **C**
3. **D**	6. **A**	9. **C**	12. **A**

SECTION TWO

(Correct answers are in parentheses.)

13. **A** (is)	19. **D** (*delete* the)
14. **C** (Thanksgiving)	20. **B** (much time)
15. **B** (is starting)	21. **C** (few)
16. **B** (May)	22. **B** (a little)
17. **D** (the)	23. **B** (one another's)
18. **A** (*delete* A *and capitalize* Money)	24. **B** (a little)
	25. **D** (the accountant)

2
1. yourselves
2. herself, ourselves
3. myself, yourself
4. each other, yourself
5. itself, ourselves
6. yourselves, one another

3
2. yourselves	7. myself
3. themselves	8. myself
4. himself	9. yourselves
5. yourselves	10. myself
6. each other OR one another	

4 I forgot to call Jan on his birthday.
myself
I reminded ~~me~~ all day, and then I forgot anyway! I felt terrible. My sister Anna said,
yourself
"Don't be so hard on ~~yourselves~~," but I didn't
herself
believe her. She prides ~~her~~ on remembering everything. Then I read an article on self-talk. It said that people can change the
themselves
way they explain problems to ~~theirselves~~.
myself
I realized that the way I talk to ~~me~~ is

UNIT 61 The Passive: Overview

CHECK POINT
the number of years the magazine has existed

CHART CHECK
T, T, F

EXPRESS CHECK
were printed

1
2. A	7. A
3. P	8. P
4. A	9. A
5. P	10. P
6. P	

2
3. Tagalog is spoken
4. is spoken by 417 million people
5. Seventy-one million people speak
6. Arabic is spoken by
7. speak English
8. Swahili is spoken OR
People speak Swahili

 3
3. is published (~~the publisher~~)
4. is read (~~readers~~)
5. have been hired by our
international offices
6. were purchased (~~the company~~)
7. are used (~~our writers~~)
8. is advertised (~~advertisers~~)
9. was interviewed by *Live at Ten TV*
10. was seen by millions of viewers

 4
Two-thirds of Bolivia's five million people
are located
~~locate~~ in the cool western highlands known

as the Altiplano. For centuries, the grain
grown
quinoa has been ~~grew~~ in the mountains.
are
Llamas ᴧraised for fur, meat, and

transportation. And tin, Bolivia's richest
mined
natural resource, is ~~mining~~ ~~by miners~~ in

the high Andes.

The Oriente, another name for the

eastern lowlands, is mostly tropical. Rice is

the major food crop, and cows are raised for
found
milk. Oil is also ~~find~~ there.

Although Spanish is the official language,

Native American languages are still spoken

~~by people~~. Traditional textiles are woven by
is
hand, and music ᴧplayed on reed pipes whose

tone resembles the sound of the wind

blowing over high plains in the Andes.

UNIT 62 **The Passive** with Modals

CHECK POINT
somebody has to do something about
Ed's snoring

CHART CHECK 1
T, F

CHART CHECK 2
a modal or an auxiliary verb

EXPRESS CHECK
A: Will . . . be prepared
B: it won't, will be prepared

 1
Space Station *Unity* <u>will be completed</u>
within the next decade, and international
teams of astronauts will then be sharing
close quarters for long periods of time. What
<u>can be done</u> to improve living conditions in
space? Here's what former astronauts
suggest:
• **FOOD** It doesn't taste as good in zero
gravity. Food <u>should be made</u> spicier to
overcome those effects. International
tastes <u>must</u> also <u>be considered</u>.
• **CLOTHING** Layered clothing could help
astronauts stay comfortable. The top
layer <u>could be removed</u> or <u>added</u> as
temperatures vary.
• **SLEEPING** Because of weightlessness,
sleep is often interrupted in space.
Comfortable restraints <u>must be provided</u>
to give a sense of stability.
• **EMOTIONAL NEEDS** People need "down
time" in space just as they do on Earth.
Time <u>ought to be provided</u> for relaxation
and privacy.

 2
2. Is . . . going to be prepared
3. (is going to be) squeezed
4. will be prepackaged
5. can be warmed up

6. should . . . be chosen
7. has to be offered
8. could be selected
9. Will . . . be used
10. had better be attached
11. ought to be made

2. should be kept
3. ought to be improved
4. could be designed
5. can be removed
6. ought to be given
7. are going to be delivered
8. will be done
9. will be stored

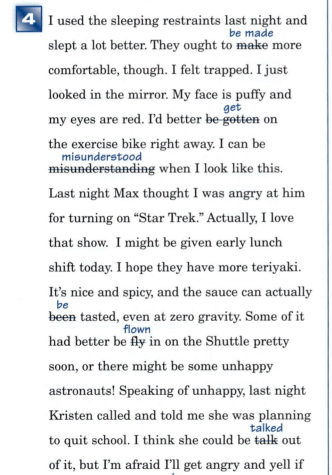

I used the sleeping restraints last night and
slept a lot better. They ought to ~~make~~ more
      be made
comfortable, though. I felt trapped. I just
looked in the mirror. My face is puffy and
        get
my eyes are red. I'd better ~~be gotten~~ on
the exercise bike right away. I can be
misunderstood
~~misunderstanding~~ when I look like this.
Last night Max thought I was angry at him
for turning on "Star Trek." Actually, I love
that show. I might be given early lunch
shift today. I hope they have more teriyaki.
It's nice and spicy, and the sauce can actually
 be
~~been~~ tasted, even at zero gravity. Some of it
    flown
had better be ~~fly~~ in on the Shuttle pretty
soon, or there might be some unhappy
astronauts! Speaking of unhappy, last night
Kristen called and told me she was planning
      talked
to quit school. I think she could be ~~talk~~ out
of it, but I'm afraid I'll get angry and yell if
    be
we discuss it. I might‸overheard by others.
We need some privacy here!

The Passive Causative

CHECK **POINT**
went to a hair salon

CHART CHECK
F, T, F

EXPRESS **CHECK**
A: done
B: done, do

2. T   4. T   6. T
3. T   5. F

3. Amber had the dog groomed.
4. They are going to get the windows washed.
5. They had the carpets cleaned.
6. Amber is going to have her ears pierced.
7. Jake got his hair cut.
8. They are going to have food and
drinks delivered.

1. OR have it shortened
2. get (OR have) it dry cleaned
3. 're getting (OR having) them washed OR
're going to get (OR have) them washed
4. 'm getting (OR having) it cut OR 'm going
to get (OR have) it cut
5. get (OR have) it colored
6. Did . . . get (OR have) it painted

The party was tonight. It went really well!
The house looked great. Mom and Dad had
          cleaned
the floors waxed and all the windows ~~clean~~
professionally so everything sparkled. And
    painted the whole house
of course we ~~had the whole house painted~~
ourselves last summer. (I'll never forget
that. It took us two weeks!) I wore my new
         had
black dress that I ~~have~~ shortened by Bo, and
    got my hair cut
I ~~got cut my hair~~ by André. He did a great
job. There were a lot of guests at the party.
had invited OR *invited almost fifty people*
We ~~had almost fifty people invited~~, and they

(continued on next page)

almost all showed up! The food was great too. Mom made most of the main dishes herself, but she had the rest of the food *prepared* ~~prepare~~ by a caterer. Mom and Dad hired a professional photographer, so at the end of the party we all ~~took our pictures~~ *had our pictures taken*. Dad's getting them back next week. I can't wait to see them!

SelfTest XII

(Total = 100 points. Each item = 4 points.)

SECTION ONE

1. C	**4.** B	**7.** C	**9.** D
2. D	**5.** C	**8.** B	**10.** B
3. A	**6.** B		

SECTION TWO

(Correct answers are in parentheses.)
- **11. C** (by)
- **12. A** *(delete* were*)*
- **13. C** (be corrected)
- **14. D** *(delete* by the printer*)*
- **15. A** *(delete* was*)*
- **16. D** (return)
- **17. C** (them done)
- **18. C** (be discussed)
- **19. A** (was painted)
- **20. C** (couldn't OR wasn't able to)
- **21. B** (grown)
- **22. D** (was working)
- **23. B** (have to be replaced)
- **24. C** (cleaned)
- **25. A** (be made)

UNIT 64 Factual Conditionals: Present

CHECK POINT
T

CHART CHECK
T, F, F

1. b   **2.** c   **3.** a

 1
If you run into problems on your journey, know your rights as a passenger. Often the airline company is required to compensate you for delays or damages. For example, the airline provides meals and hotel rooms if a flight is unduly delayed. However, the airline owes you a lot more if it caused the delay by overbooking. This can occur especially during holidays if airlines sell more tickets than there are seats. If all the passengers actually show up, then the flight is overbooked. Airlines usually award upgrades or additional free travel to passengers who volunteer to take a later flight. However, if no one volunteers, your flight may be delayed. In that case, the airline must repay you 100 percent of the cost of your ticket for a delay of up to four hours on an international flight. If the delay is more than four hours, you receive 200 percent of the cost of your ticket.

2
1. OR The best time to go to Hong Kong is November or December if you hate hot weather.
2. If you're traveling with your children, take them to Lai Chi Kok Amusement Park in Kowloon. OR Take your children to Lai Chi Kok Amusement Park in Kowloon if you're traveling with them.
3. If you need a moderately priced hotel, I suggest the Harbour View International House. OR I suggest the Harbour View International House if you need a moderately priced hotel.
4. If you like seafood, there are wonderful seafood restaurants on Lamma Island. OR There are wonderful seafood restaurants on Lamma Island if you like seafood.
5. If you're fascinated by Chinese opera, you might like the street opera in the Shanghai Street Night Market. OR You might like the street opera in the

Shanghai Street Night Market if you're fascinated by Chinese opera.

6. If you'd like to get a good view of Hong Kong, you should take the funicular to the Peak. OR You should take the funicular to the Peak if you'd like to get a good view of Hong Kong.

3

2. I spend a lot of time at the pool if I stay at a hotel.
3. If I stay with friends, I spend time with them.
4. It's not so nice if I get a "Dracula."
5. It's very rewarding if you don't mind hard work.
6. If you have three roommates, you don't have trouble finding dogwalkers.
7. If a flight has an empty seat, I ride for free.

4

What a great weekend! If Lou and Teri aren't the best hosts in the world, I ~~won't~~ *don't* know who is. I've invited them to New York, but if you live in the Bahamas, you rarely want to leave. Tomorrow at midnight I fly roundtrip from New York to Pittsburgh. There's always a price to pay. If I get a free weekend in the islands, I always get a "Dracula" afterwards. Oh, well. If I ~~won't~~ *don't* fall asleep, I can usually get a lot of reading done. Pat and Kim both flew to London yesterday. I hope someone can walk Frisky for me. Usually, if ~~I'll be~~ *I'm* working, one of them is off. If Frisky is alone for a long time, he ~~barked~~ *barks* a lot. That disturbs the neighbors. Maybe I should just leave the TV on for him. He's always very calm if the TV is on. Or maybe I'd better call Pat and ask her about her schedule. If it ~~was~~ *'s* 6:00 P.M. here in New York, it's 11:00 P.M. in London. That's not too late to call.

CHECK POINT

F, F

CHART CHECK

the *if* clause
when the *if* clause comes first

EXPRESS CHECK

If she wins, she'll fight crime.

1

| 2. e | 4. a | 6. d |
| 3. c | 5. g | 7. b |

2

3. get
4. If
5. win
6. 'll take OR 'm going to take
7. If
8. become
9. 'll try OR 'm going to try
10. will . . . do OR are . . . going to do
11. if
12. lose
13. If
14. lose
15. 'll continue OR 'm going to continue
16. Unless
17. cooperate
18. won't be OR isn't going to be
19. if
20. don't elect
21. 'll be OR 'm going to be

3

(possible answers)

3. If I take out student loans, I won't have to depend on my family, OR I won't have to depend on my family if I take out student loans.
4. If I go to law school, I'll earn more money. OR I'll earn more money if I go to law school.
5. If I earn more money, I'll be able to pay back my (student) loans quickly. OR I'll be able to pay back my (student) loans quickly if I earn more money.
6. If I pay back my loans quickly, I'll put my sister through college. OR I'll put my sister through college if I pay back my loans quickly.

7. If I go to law school, I'll go into politics.
OR I'll go into politics if I go to law school.

8. If I go into politics, I'll be able to improve
life for others. OR I'll be able to improve
life for others if go into politics.

9. If I go into politics, I'll get elected to the
city council. OR I'll get elected to the city
council if I go into politics.

10. If I get elected to the city council, I'll run
for mayor. OR I'll run for mayor if I get
elected to the city council.

4 Should I campaign for student council
president? I'll have to decide soon if I ~~wanted~~ *want*
to run. If ~~I'll be~~ *I'm* busy campaigning, I won't
have much time to study. That's a problem,
because I'm not going to get into a good
college ~~if~~ *unless** I get good grades this year. On the
other hand, there's so much to do in this
school, and nothing ~~is getting~~ *will get* OR *is going to get* done if Todd
Laker becomes president again. A lot of
people know that. But will I know what to
do if ~~I'll~~ *I* get the job? Never mind. I'll deal
with that problem~~,~~ if I win.

*OR if I don't get

 66 **Unreal Conditionals:**
Present

CHECK POINT
F

CHART CHECK
F, T, F

EXPRESS CHECK
would, if, were

1 **2.** T   **4.** F   **6.** F
3. T   **5.** F

2 **2.** wouldn't like
3. weren't

4. couldn't identify
5. were
6. loved
7. 'd hate OR would hate
8. drove
9. 'd hate OR would hate
10. were
11. 'd hate OR would hate
12. weren't
13. might be

3 **2.** If Schroeder didn't love Beethoven, he
wouldn't play his sonatas all the time.
3. If Charlie Brown had enough friends, he
wouldn't feel lonely.
4. If Sally knew her teacher's name, she
could send her a card.
5. If Linus weren't smart, he wouldn't find
clever solutions to life's problems.
6. If Woodstock and Snoopy didn't have a
close relationship, Woodstock wouldn't
confide in Snoopy.
7. If Rerun's parents didn't refuse to let
him have a dog, he wouldn't try to
borrow Charlie's dog.
8. If Pigpen took enough baths, he wouldn't
be filthy.

4 I've got to stop staying up late reading
"Peanuts"! If I weren't always so tired, I ~~will~~ *would*
be able to stay awake in class. Whenever the
teacher calls on me, I don't know what to say.
Then I get really embarrassed because of that
cute red-haired girl that I like. I would talk
to her if I ~~wouldn't be~~ *weren't* so shy. My friend Jason
says, "If I ~~was~~ *were* you, I'd ask her to a party," but
I'm too afraid that if I asked her, she would
~~have said~~ *say* no. After class, I played baseball.
Nobody wanted me on their team. If I ~~play~~ *played*
better, I would get chosen sometimes. Life is
hard! I can really understand that Charlie
Brown character in "Peanuts." In fact, if I didn't
laugh so hard while reading "Peanuts,"
I would ~~cried~~ *cry*!

UNIT 67 — Unreal Conditionals: Past

CHECK POINT

F

CHART CHECK

the *if* clause

the *if* clause comes first

EXPRESS CHECK

would have studied

1.

2. F	**4.** F	**6.** T
3. T	**5.** F	

2.

2. could (OR would) have gone OR would have been able to go, hadn't lost
3. could have gone, hadn't gotten
4. wouldn't have known, hadn't shown
5. hadn't helped, could have gone
6. might not have led, hadn't married
7. would have been, hadn't lived

3. *(Answers may vary slightly)*

1. OR Clarence would have had more self-confidence if he had been a first-class angel.
2. If George hadn't been unhappy about his business, he wouldn't have yelled at his daughter on Christmas Eve. OR George wouldn't have yelled at his daughter on Christmas Eve if he hadn't been unhappy about his business.
3. Poor people couldn't have bought (OR wouldn't have been able to buy) houses if George's business hadn't loaned them money. OR If George's business hadn't loaned them money, poor people couldn't have bought (OR wouldn't have been able to buy) houses.
4. If Mr. Potter had been able to trick George, George would have sold Potter the business. OR George would have sold Mr. Potter the business if Potter had been able to trick George.
5. If George's Uncle Billy hadn't lost $8,000, George wouldn't have gotten into trouble with the law. OR George wouldn't have gotten into trouble with the law if his Uncle Billy hadn't lost $8,000.

6. If George's friends had known about his troubles, they would have helped him right away. OR George's friends would have helped him right away if they had known about his troubles.
7. If George's friends hadn't collected money for him, he would have gone to jail. OR George would have gone to jail if his friends hadn't collected money for him.

4.

It's funny how things work out sometimes.
If George ~~hasn't~~ *hadn't* wanted to jump off that bridge on Christmas Eve, I might never have ~~getting~~ *gotten* an important job like saving him. And if he hadn't been so stubborn, I would never ~~had~~ *have* thought of the idea of showing him life in Bedford Falls without him. One of the saddest things was seeing all those people who didn't have homes. If George ~~gave up~~ *had given up* and sold his business to Mr. Potter, then Potter would have rented run-down apartments to all those people. But because of George, they now have good homes. By the time we were finished, George realized he really had a wonderful life. In fact, he ~~will~~ *would* have gone to jail happily x if his friends hadn't given him the money he needed. Well, luckily they helped him out, and he didn't go to jail. And I got my wings and became a first-class angel!

UNIT 68 — Wish: Present and Past

CHECK POINT

that day

CHART CHECK 1

the simple past

CHART CHECK 2

the past perfect

EXPRESS CHECK

knew, had known

1
2. T   4. F   6. T
3. F   5. T

2
2. would go away
3. had
4. didn't have to deal
5. could entertain
6. could have invited OR
   had been able to invite
7. had known

3
2. I wish my husband would ask for a raise.
3. I wish my wife had been able to balance (OR could have balanced) the check book last month.
4. I wish my boyfriend weren't out of shape OR were in shape.
5. I wish I weren't too old to go back to school.
6. I wish I could stop (OR were able to stop) smoking
7. I wish my son called (OR would call) me.
8. I wish my parents had understood me.

4
Today I told Dr. Grimes, "I wish there ~~was~~ *were* a way to spend more time with my boyfriend, but we're both too busy." He just said, "If wishes were horses, beggars would ride." That's cute, but I wish I ~~understand~~ *understood* its meaning. Maybe it means that wishing won't solve problems. Well, that's why I went to see him!!! I wish he ~~will tell~~ *had told* me what to do right then and there, but he refused. Speaking of wishful thinking, I wish Todd and I could ~~have spent~~ *spend* the weekend together next week. My exams are over, but he has to fly to Denver to his job.

If wishes were horses, I'd ride one to Denver. Hey! Todd is always saying, "I wish you would come with me sometimes." I guess I *can* go with him to Denver. Dr. Grimes must have meant that I can solve my own problems. Now I wish I ~~haven't~~ *hadn't* been so rude to him.

SelfTest

(Total = 100 points. Each item = 4 points.)

SECTION ONE

1. **C**   4. **A**   7. **B**   10. **D**
2. **B**   5. **D**   8. **C**   11. **A**
3. **A**   6. **C**   9. **C**   12. **D**

SECTION TWO

(Correct answers are in parentheses.)

13. **D** (seen)   20. **D** (were)
14. **B** (could have)   21. **C** *(delete* will*)*
15. **B** (won't)   22. **C** *(delete comma)*
16. **B** (have)   23. **C** (would have)
17. **B** (were)   24. **C** (get)
18. **A** (could have)   25. **C** (could)
19. **A** ('ll eat OR
    are going to eat)

UNIT 69 Adjective Clauses with Subject Relative Pronouns

CHECK POINT

F

CHART CHECK

nouns
in the middle of the main clause, after the main clause

EXPRESS CHECK

That's the man who works in the cafeteria.

1 Almost everyone has friends, but ideas about friendship vary from person to person. For some, a friend is someone <u>who chats with you on the Internet</u>. For others, a friend is a person <u>who has known you all your life</u>—someone <u>whose family knows you, too</u>. Others only use the term for someone <u>who knows your innermost secrets</u>. Although different people emphasize different aspects of friendship, there is one element <u>which is always present</u>, and that is the element of choice. We may not be able to select our families, our co-workers, or even the people <u>that ride the bus with us</u>, but we *can* pick our friends. As anthropologist Margaret Mead once said, "A friend is someone <u>who chooses and is chosen</u>." It is this freedom of choice <u>that makes friendship such a special relationship</u>.

2
1. OR that have
2. who (OR that) have
3. that (OR which) are
4. who (OR that) faces
5. that (OR which) is
6. whose . . . are
7. whose . . . include
8. that (OR which) appears OR appeared OR has appeared
9. who (OR that) doesn't read OR hasn't read

3
2. Mexico City is an exciting city that (OR which) attracts a lot of tourists.
3. Marta has a brother whose name is Manuel.
4. He works for a magazine that (OR which) is very popular in Mexico.
5. Manuel writes a column that (OR which) deals with relationships.
6. An article that (OR which) discussed friendships won a prize.
7. A person who (OR that) has a lot of friends is lucky.

4 A writer once said that friends are born, not made. This means that we automatically become friends with people who ~~they~~ are compatible with us. I don't agree with this writer. Last summer, I made friends with some
were OR are
people who's̷ completely different from me.

In July, I went to Mexico City to study Spanish for a month. In our group, there
who OR that
was a teacher ~~which~~ was much older than I am. We became really good friends. In my first week, I had a problem which was getting me down. Mexico City is a city
that OR which
~~who~~ has a lot of distractions. As a result, I went out all the time, and I stopped going to my classes. Bob helped me get back into my studies. After the trip, I kept writing
are
to Bob. He always writes stories that ~~is~~ interesting and encouraging. Next summer,
that OR which
he's leading another trip ~~what~~ sounds interesting. I hope I can go.

UNIT 70 **Adjective Clauses** with Object Relative Pronouns or *When* and *Where*

CHECK POINT
T

CHART CHECK
the subject of the adjective clause
F

EXPRESS CHECK
I see all the movies that he directs.

1 At the age of nine, Eva Hoffman left Poland with her family. She was old enough to know what she was losing: Cracow, a city ⟨that⟩ she loved as one loves a person, the sun-baked villages ⟨where⟩ they had taken summer vacations, and the conversations and escapades with her friends. Disconnected from a city ⟨where⟩ life was lived intensely, her father would become overwhelmed by the transition to Canada. Eva would lose the parent ⟨whom⟩ she had watched in lively conversation with friends in Cracow cafés. And nothing could replace her friendship with the boy ⟨whose⟩ home she visited daily, and ⟨whom⟩ she assumed she would someday marry. Worst of all, however, she would miss her language. For years, she would feel no connection to the English name of anything ⟨that⟩ she felt was important. *Lost in Translation: A Life in a New Language* (New York: Penguin, 1989) tells how Eva came to terms with her new identity and language. It's a story ⟨that⟩ readers will find fascinating and moving.

2
1. OR that
3. who OR whom OR that
4. stayed OR were staying
5. which
6. had
7. that OR which
8. wanted
9. that OR which
10. have experienced
11. where OR in which
12. were
13. who OR whom OR that
14. take care of

3
1. OR . . . in which I grew up . . .
2. The house that (OR which) we lived in was beautiful. OR The house in which we lived . . .
3. Emilia and I shared a room where (OR in which) we spent nights talking.

4. Across the hall I had a good friend who (OR whom OR that) I went to school with. OR . . . with whom I went to school.
5. I took piano lessons from a woman who (OR whom OR that) I met in the bakery.
6. I remember one summer when (OR that) the whole family went to the lake.
7. Those are good times that (OR which) I'll always miss.

4 Tai Dong is the small city in southeastern
    where OR *in which* OR *that . . . in*
Taiwan ~~which~~ I grew up. My family moved there from Taipei the summer when I was born. The house in which I grew up ~~in~~* is on a main street in Tai Dong. My father sold tea, and my mother had a food stand in our front courtyard where she sold omelets early in the morning. A customer who I always chatted with ~~him~~ had a son my age. We were
    whose
best friends. A cousin ~~who his~~ family I visited every summer lived with us. He was
    who OR *whom* OR *that*
an apprentice ~~which~~ my father was teaching the tea business to. On the first floor of our
    in which OR *where*
house we had a huge kitchen ~~in where~~ we all gathered for dinner. It was a fun and noisy place. The bedrooms where the family
    were
slept ~~was~~ upstairs. My two brothers slept in
    that OR *which*
one bedroom. I slept in one ~~what~~ I shared with my older sister. My younger sister shared a bedroom with another cousin
who OR *whom* OR *that*
~~which~~ my family had adopted.

*OR the house which (OR that) I grew up in

Adjective Clauses:
Identifying and
Non-Identifying

 **POINT**

F

CHART CHECK

non-identifying
T

EXPRESS CHECK

It was the computer ~~which~~ we saw at
E-Lectronics.

2. T	**4.** F
3. T	**5.** F

6. F

 ˌtech • no • ˈpho • bia *(noun)* a fear ~~that~~
some people have about using technology

If you have it, you're one of the 85 percent
of people ~~that~~ this new "disease" has struck.
Maybe you bought a phone on which you
can program 25 numbers—then couldn't
turn it on. Or perhaps you have just read
that your new CD player**,** which you have
finally learned how to use**,** will soon be
replaced by DVD**,** which you had never even
heard of.

Some experts say that things have just
gotten too complex. William Staples**,** who
authored a book on the electronic age**,** tried
to help a friend who had just bought a new
stereo. The stereo**,** which worked before**,**
wasn't working anymore. "On the front of
the stereo receiver it literally had a couple
of dozen buttons," says Staples. Donald
Norman**,** who has written about the effects
of technology on people**,** blames the
designers of these devices, not the people

who use them. "The best way to cure
technophobia is to cure the reasons that
cause it—that is, to design things ~~that~~
people can use and design things that won't
break," claims Norman. Michael Dyrenfurth**,**
who teaches at the University of
Missouri–Columbia**,** believes we cause our
own problems by buying technology ~~that~~ we
just don't need. "Do we really need an
electric toothbrush?" he asks. According to
Dyrenfurth, important technology ~~that~~ we
can't afford to run away from actually exists.
To prosper, we have to overcome our
technophobia and learn to use it.

2. My new cell phone, which I bought a
month ago, has become a necessary part
of life.
3. I remember the day when I was afraid to
use my new computer.
4. Now, there are psychologists who (OR that)
help technophobes use technology.
5. Dr. Michelle Weil, who is a psychologist,
wrote a book about "technostress."
6. I work in an office where (OR in which)
the software changes frequently.
7. A lot of people who work in my office
suffer from technostress.
8. Some people dream of a job they can do
without technology.

 I just read a book called *Technostress***,** which
was written by Dr. Michelle Weil. Her
co-author was Dr. Larry Rosen, ~~that~~^{who} is her
husband and also a psychologist. According
to the authors, everybody feels stress about
technology. Our cell phones and beepers,
~~that~~^{which} we buy for emergencies, soon invade
our privacy. Just because they can, people

(continued on next page)

contact us at places where we are relaxing. Another problem is having to learn too much too fast. Technological changes, ^which^ used to come one at a time, now overwhelm us. Dr. Weil suggests dealing with technostress using tips from her latest book**,** which can be purchased from her web site.

SelfTest XIV

(Total = 100 points. Each item = 4 points.)

SECTION ONE

1. **B**	4. **C**	7. **B**	10. **C**
2. **A**	5. **B**	8. **C**	11. **B**
3. **D**	6. **B**	9. **B**	12. **C**

SECTION TWO

(Correct answers are in parentheses.)

13. **C** (where)
14. **A** (who)
15. **C** (*delete* he)
16. **B** (whose)
17. **B** (that OR which OR *delete* what)
18. **D** (*delete* it)
19. **C** (discuss)
20. **B** (which)
21. **A** (who)
22. **C** (in which OR where)
23. **B** (with whom)
24. **C** (when OR that OR *delete* which)
25. **A** (whose)

UNIT 72 Direct and Indirect Speech: Imperatives

CHECK *POINT*

"Don't eat a heavy meal before bed."

CHART CHECK

direct speech
T

EXPRESS **CHECK**

to go, Don't work

 1 Can't sleep? You're not alone. Millions of people are up tossing and turning instead of getting their zzzz's. Dr. Ray Thorpe, Director of the Sleep Disorders Clinic, (says), "Don't think that loss of sleep is just a minor inconvenience." During an interview he (told) me to think about what can happen if people drive when they're tired. Every year up to 200,000 car accidents are caused by drowsy drivers. Then he (asked) me to think about a recent industrial disaster. Chances are that it was caused at least in part by sleep deprivation.

Being an insomniac myself, I asked Dr. Thorpe for some suggestions. He (told) me to stop drinking coffee. He (said) to have a warm glass of milk instead. "A lot of old-fashioned remedies work. Have a high-carbohydrate snack like a banana before you go to bed," he (said). But he (advises) patients not to eat a heavy meal before turning in for the night. What about exercise? "Regular exercise helps, but don't exercise too close to bedtime," he (suggested). Finally, he (told) me not to despair. "Don't worry about not sleeping. It's the worst thing to do," he (said). I don't know. After thinking about those industrial accidents, I doubt I'll be able to sleep at all!

 2

2. that night	7. there
3. told	8. explain
4. my	9. not to
5. to watch	10. the next
6. said	11. to get

 3

1. OR He said to pull over and take a brief nap.
2. OR He told them not to take a long nap.
3. He told them (OR He said) to sing to themselves.
4. He told them (OR He said) to turn their radios to an annoying station.
5. He told them (OR He said) not to drink coffee.

6. He told them (OR He said) to open their windows.
7. He told them (OR He said) to let cold air in.
8. He told them (OR He said) to be careful when they stop their cars.
9. He told them (OR He said) not to stop on a deserted roadside.
10. He told them (OR He said) not to drink and drive.

 4 In writing class today, Juan read one of his stories. It was wonderful. After class, the teacher invited me ‸*to* read a story in class next week. However, I asked her ~~no~~ *not* to call on me next week because I'm having trouble getting ideas. She ~~said~~ *told* me not to worry, and she said to wait for two weeks. Then I talked to Juan, and I asked him ‸*to* tell me the source for ~~your~~ *his* ideas. He said that they came from his dreams, and he told me ‸*to* keep a dream journal for ideas. He invited me ×*to* read some of his journal.× It was very interesting, so I asked him to give me some tips on remembering dreams. He said ~~getting~~ *to get* a good night's sleep because the longer dreams come after a long period of sleep. He also ~~tell~~ *told* me to keep my journal by the bed and to write as soon as I wake up. He said ~~to no~~ *not to* move from the sleeping position. He also told me ~~to don't~~ *not to* think about the day at first. (If you think about your day, you might forget your dreams.) Most important—every night he tells himself ~~that~~ to remember his dreams ~~tomorrow~~ *the next* morning.

 **UNIT 73** **Indirect Speech:** Statements (1)

 **POINT**

"It looks great on you!"

CHART CHECK

the punctuation
the verb tense in the statement
pronouns in the statement

EXPRESS

told, was

1 At 9:00 Rick Spivak's bank phoned and (said) that his credit card payment was late. "The check is in the mail," Rick (replied) quickly. At 11:45 Rick left for a 12:00 meeting across town. Arriving late, Rick (told) his client that traffic had been bad. That evening, Rick's fiancée wore a new dress. Rick hated it. "It looks just great on you," he (said).

Three lies in one day! Yet Rick is just an ordinary guy. Each time, he (told) himself that sometimes the truth causes too many problems. He (told) himself that his fiancée was feeling good about her purchase. Why should he hurt her feelings?

Is telling lies a new trend? The majority of people in a recent survey (said) that people were more honest ten years ago. Nevertheless, lying wasn't really born yesterday. In the eighteenth century, the French philosopher Vauvenargues told the truth about lying when he (wrote), "All men are born truthful and die liars."

 2
2. has
3. told
4. that
5. had
6. she
7. had made
8. had lied
9. was quitting
10. had fired

3 2. Lisa said (that) she had just heard about a job at a scientific research company.
3. Ben said (that) he had majored in science at Florida State.
4. Lisa told him (that) they wanted someone with some experience as a programmer.
5. Ben told her (that) he worked as a programmer for Data Systems.
6. Lisa said (that) they didn't want a recent college graduate.
7. Ben told her (that) he had gotten his degree four years ago OR before.
8. Lisa said (that) it sounded like the right job for him.

4 Once when I was a teenager, I went to my Aunt Leah's house. Aunt Leah collected pottery, and when I got there, she ~~said~~ **told** me that she ~~wants~~ **wanted** to show me her new bowl. She told ^**me** she ~~has~~ **had** just bought it. It was beautiful. When Aunt Leah went to answer the door, I picked up the bowl. It slipped from my hands and smashed to pieces on the floor. When Aunt Leah came back, I screamed and said ~~what~~ **that** the cat had just broken ~~your~~ **her** new bowl. Aunt Leah got this funny look on her face and told me that it ~~isn't~~ **wasn't** important. I didn't sleep at all that night, and the next morning, I called my aunt and confessed that I ~~have~~ **had** broken her bowl. She said ~~I~~ **she** had known that all along. I promised that I ~~am~~ **was** going to buy her a new one someday. We still laugh about the story today.

*OR *She said she . . .*

UNIT 74 Indirect Speech: Statements (2)

CHECK POINT
"It will be windy."

CHART CHECK
ought to, might, should have

EXPRESS CHECK
Jim said that he might move soon.

1 2. "The winds may reach 170 miles per hour."
3. "There will be more rain tomorrow."
4. "You should try to leave the area."
5. "We can expect a lot of damage."

2 2. They said (that) it was going to pass north of there.
3. They said (that) it might become a tropical storm when it landed there.
4. They said (that) they had had to close some bridges the day before because of high tides.
5. They said (that) they wouldn't restore electricity until today.
6. They said (that) the schools there might be closed for a while.
7. They said (that) they ought to use bottled water for a few days.

3 2. He said (that) it was true, and (that) they would probably become more frequent.
3. He said (that) the planet might be getting warmer, and (that) that could cause more severe storms.
4. He said (that) emergency workers should have arrived much more quickly.
5. He said (that) the new satellites would help. He said (that) if they didn't have them, they wouldn't be able to warn people.

4 We had some excitement here because of the hurricane last week. Jim's mother called just before the storm. She said she ~~is~~ **was** listening to the weather report and that she was worried about us. She told Jim that if

we
~~you~~ two weren't so stubborn, we ~~will~~ *would* pack

up and leave immediately. Jim's father told

us how to get ready for the storm. He said

we should ~~have~~ put tape on our windows
then
right ~~now~~ and that we ought to fill the

bathtub with water. He also told Jim that

we should buy a lot of batteries before the
that night
storm hit ~~tonight~~. Sue called. She said that

her place was too close to the coast and that
there *she*
she couldn't stay ~~here~~. She told me ~~I~~ wanted

to stay with me and Jim. She said she should
have
‸called us sooner. I told her she should come
then
right ~~now~~. Then we listened to the weather

advisory, and the forecaster said that the
was
storm ~~is~~ going to go out to sea. She said it
wouldn't
~~won't~~ hit this area at all!

UNIT 75 Indirect Questions

CHECK *POINT*
"Why are you still single?"

CHART CHECK 1
F, T

CHART CHECK 2
F, T

EXPRESS CHECK
why he had quit his job.

 A few weeks ago, Melissa Morrow had a
stress interview, one which featured tough,
tricky questions and negative evaluations.
First, the interviewer asked <u>why she couldn't
work under pressure</u>. Before she could answer,
he asked <u>who had written her application
letter for her</u>. Melissa was shocked, but she

handled herself very well. She asked the
interviewer <u>whether he was going to ask
her any serious questions</u>. Then she left.

Companies give stress interviews in
order to watch how candidates handle
pressure. Suppose, for example, that there
is an accident in a nuclear power plant. The
plant's public relations officer must remain
calm when reporters ask <u>how the accident
could have happened</u>. Be aware, however,
that in some countries, like the United States,
certain questions are not allowed unless
they are directly related to the job. If your
interviewer asks <u>how old you are</u>, you can
refuse to answer. The interviewer also should
not ask <u>whether you are married</u> or <u>how much
money you owe</u>. If you think a question is
improper, ask <u>how the question relates to the
job</u>. If it doesn't, you don't have to answer.

Items Checked: 2, 3, 5

2. He asked when the interview was.
3. He asked where the company was.
4. He asked if (OR whether) she needed
   directions.
5. He asked how long it took to get there.
6. He asked if (OR whether) she was going
   to drive.
7. He asked who was going to interview her.
8. He asked when they would let her know.

3. Pete asked if (OR whether) she was
   interviewing with other companies.
4. Claire asked what her responsibilities
   would be.
5. Claire asked how job performance was
   rewarded.
6. Pete asked what her starting salary at
   her last job had been OR had been at her
   last job.
7. Pete asked if (OR whether) she had gotten
   along well with her last employer.
8. Claire asked if (OR whether) they hired
   many women.

4 I did some stress questioning in my interview
with Carl Treng this morning. I asked
Mr. Treng why ~~couldn't he~~ *he couldn't* work under
pressure. I also asked him why ~~did~~ his
~~dislike~~ *disliked* supervisor dislike him. Finally, I inquired
when he would quit the job with our
company. Mr. Treng answered my questions
calmly, and he had some excellent questions
of his own. He asked ✗ if we expected changes
on the job. ✗ He also wanted to know how
often ~~do~~* we evaluate employees. I was
impressed when he asked why ~~did I decide~~
I had decided
to join this company. I think we should
hire him.

*OR *how often we evaluated*

 Embedded Questions

CHECK **POINT**
  Should we leave a tip?
  Is the service included?

CHART CHECK
  F, T

EXPRESS CHECK
  A: ?   B: .

1 **This book is for you if . . .**

• you've ever avoided a situation just
  because you didn't know <u>how much to tip</u>.

• you've ever realized (too late) that you
  were supposed to offer a tip.

• you've ever given a huge tip and then
  wondered <u>if a tip was necessary at all</u>.

• you've ever needed to know <u>how to
  calculate the right tip instantly</u>.

• you're new to the United States and you're
  not sure <u>who you should tip here</u>.

• you'd like to learn <u>how tipping properly
  can get you the best service for your money</u>.

What readers are saying . . .
"I can't imagine <u>how I got along without it</u>."

"Take *Tips* along if you want a stress-free
vacation."

 2 2. how to tell if the tip is included in the bill.
  3. why service people in Iceland refused
     my tips?
  4. how much to tip airport porters.
  5. who expects a tip and who doesn't.
  6. I should tip my ski instructor.
  7. tipping is still illegal there.
  8. to tip anyway.

3 2. how much to tip (OR how much we should
     tip) the taxi driver?
  3. where the Smithsonian Museum is?
  4. where we can buy (OR where to buy)
     metro tickets.
  5. we could rent a car and drive?
  6. what they put in the sauce.

 4 When you live in a foreign country even a
small occasion can be an adventure! Before
my date with Janek tonight, I didn't even
know what ~~should I~~ wear! Jeans? A dress?
I should OR to
John's Grill isn't a fancy restaurant, but it
was Janek's birthday and I wanted to make
it a big occasion. Miuki was very helpful, as
always. I knew how to get to John's Grill,
but I didn't know how long it was going to
take to get there. ✗ I left at 6:00, which
should have given me plenty of time, but

when I got off the bus, I wasn't sure ~~if~~ to *whether*

turn left or right. I asked a police officer

where ~~was John's~~, and I was only a few *John's was*

minutes late. I had planned to take Janek

out for a special dessert afterward, but

I couldn't remember how ~~X~~ to find the place

Miuki had suggested, and Janek has been

here even less time than me. (Anyway, the

desserts at John's turned out to be very

good.) Then, when we got the bill, I was

wondering whether to tip or ~~no~~. I had to ask *not*

Janek ~~did he know~~. Fortunately, he had read *if he knew*

Tips on Tipping, so he told me to leave

about 15%.

SelfTest

(Total = 100 points. Each item = 4 points.)

SECTION ONE

1. **D**	4. **C**	7. **C**	9. **C**
2. **A**	5. **A**	8. **A**	10. **D**
3. **B**	6. **C**		

SECTION TWO

(Correct answers are in parentheses.)

11. **A** (told OR said to)	19. **D** (it costs)
12. **D** (.)	20. **C** (runs)
13. **D** (then)	21. **D** (?)
14. **D** (was coming)	22. **D** (, ")
15. **D** (there)	23. **B** (if you could)
16. **B** (whether or not OR if)	24. **C** (not to)
17. **A** (whether)	25. **B** (I could)
18. **D** (might have stopped)	